C000010559

CHILDREN IN EXILE

CHILDREN IN EXILE
Thekla Clark

Chatto & Windus
LONDON

Published by Chatto & Windus 1998

2 4 6 8 10 9 7 5 3 1

Copyright © Thekla Clark 1998

Thekla Clark has asserted her right under the Copyright, Designs and Patents Act
1988 to be identified as the author of this work

First published in Great Britain in 1998 by
Chatto & Windus
Random House, 20 Vauxhall Bridge Road,
London SW1V 2SA

Random House Australia (Pty) Limited
20 Alfred Street, Milsons Point, Sydney,
New South Wales 2061, Australia

Random House New Zealand Limited
18 Poland Road, Glenfield,
Auckland 10, New Zealand

Random House South Africa (Pty) Limited
Endulini, 5A Jubilee Road, Parktown 2193, South Africa
Random House UK Limited Reg. No.954009

A CIP catalogue record for this book is available from the British Library

ISBN 0 7011 6590 1

Papers used by Random House UK Limited are natural,
recyclable products made from wood grown in sustainable forests.
The manufacturing processes conform to the environmental
regulations of the country of origin.

Typeset by SX Composing DTP, Rayleigh, Essex
Printed and bound in Great Britain by Mackays of Chatham PLC

Dedicated to Sarin Khul
and all the other victims of the Khmer Rouge madness

Grateful thanks to
James Fenton, Darryl Pinckney and Lorna Sage (yet again) for
everything, Lisa Darnell for invaluable suggestions, corrections
and assistance, J.B. the brightest, boldest, most beautiful of
publishers, for taking a chance.

Grateful acknowledgements are made by the publisher and the
author to James Fenton and Penguin Books Ltd for the use of
quotations from his poem 'Children in Exile'.

CONTENTS

PREFACE

My husband John and I are Americans who have lived in Italy for most of our lives. We met in Florence where we had both come to live, he from Georgia, I from Oklahoma. John arrived in 1949 to study Renaissance Philosophy and Art History at the University. He had previously attended an American College whose curriculum consisted of reading 'The Hundred Great Books'. All studies were from original sources, history directly from Herodotus, geometry from Euclid, philosophy from Socrates. When studies leapt from Dante to Machiavelli in one fell swoop John felt he had missed something. He determined to seek out that missing two hundred year gap in Italy.

During our adolescence, war-torn Europe was terra incognita, forbidden, isolated. The opening up of Europe after 1945 was a moment of great exhilaration for all of our generation. Armed with what he called 'The Family Fulbright' of one hundred dollars a month John set out for Florence. With this money he rented a decent flat, ate well in carefully chosen trattorias and was even able to buy books. Most of his fellow students lived on less. The arrangement was clearly temporary and John, never short on ideas, cast about for a more permanent solution to ensure his stay in Italy. His Art History professor (the brilliant and eccentric Roberto Longhi) was enthusiastic about John's plan to create a photographic colour archive of works of art: so enthusiastic he financed the project. This grew into the *Società Scala* and an extensive archive of European works of

ix

art. John retired in 1989 because of ill health but *Scala* still flourishes.

I came to Florence in 1953 as a tourist, lost my head over the place, and in 1954 moved here with my daughter Lisa for what was to be a three month visit. I stayed and stayed and stayed. John and I married here in 1961 and our son Simon was born here in 1965. Our work is here, our home is here. We are, however, still bound to America by citizenship, blood ties, tradition and a strong love.

Throughout the sixties we watched with mounting concern as American involvement in Southeast Asia increased. We longed to do something, we didn't know exactly what. We had signed countless petitions, we'd written to a congressman. We'd felt outraged and diminished by American foreign policy. We'd also felt helpless and eventually cobbled together a sort of policy of our own.

We had already tried to make a home for a refugee. Our close friend – a friend so close he is family – the poet James Fenton, was at one time a correspondent in Southeast Asia. In 1973 I asked his help in finding a Vietnamese child we might bring to the West to live with us. He suggested a teenage boy who had acted as an ad hoc interpreter for him. The boy, who was fifteen at the time, was named Lam Xuan Binh. We began to correspond with Binh and even exchanged photographs. However, getting him out of South Vietnam at the time presented a problem. He was almost old enough for military service and the government was desperate for soldiers. The American Consul in Florence did his best and Italian immigration papers were not difficult but the South Vietnamese refused to let him go. His letters were charming and in his photograph he is leaning on a hideous, modern statue of the Virgin Mary in front of the convent where he had gone to school and learned his English. He was a lean, smiling youth carefully dressed in jeans purchased, he wrote us, with one of the cheques we sent him. He also used some of the money to buy English books and wrote, 'I am still your rich boy'. Our correspondence continued for over a year but as he reached his sixteenth birthday our hopes for getting him out diminished. Then the letters stopped and the last cheque was never cashed. James learned later that he had joined the Viet Cong. Still later we heard from Binh's sister that 'our rich boy' had been killed. I cursed the bureaucrats who had kept him back.

In 1975 Saigon fell. We saw photographs of Vietnamese clinging to the helicopters taking Americans to safety and we realized we had lost more than a war. When the opportunity came through the Italian charity *Caritas* to help Vietnamese 'boat people', we felt there was finally something we could do. In 1979 we offered a home to a Vietnamese family and a little over a year later, to the remains of a Cambodian one. We live in a rambling, battered house in the Tuscan countryside. My daughter Lisa was then grown up and Simon was in school in London, so space was no problem. Or perhaps empty space *was* a problem. We'd always had a house full; full of children, full of our friends, Lisa's friends, Simon's friends. We acted on impulse, impulse born of the chagrin we felt at American policies coupled with the human impulse of wanting to help the helpless. In any case the whole thing crept up on us bit by bit. The moment was right, the action now seems inevitable. What it seemed at the time, I, honestly, no longer remember. I suppose we wanted to be good.

We were concerned about what we were taking on, but not really worried. After all we had adapted, painlessly, to another culture. (Florence is quite a distance from Albany, Georgia or Oklahoma City.) But our moves had been simple, from one Indo-European language to another; one form of Christianity to another; a similar climate; a landscape and an architecture we were familiar with from books. And above all there were no closed frontiers, no barbed-wire, no blockades: if we ever wished for another change all we had to do was pack our bags. How could our experience possibly be of use to these people whose main concern was to remain alive, whose knowledge of another world, another culture, another language was almost nil?

There was a great deal we didn't know. We didn't know that hills are frightening, we didn't know that Vietnamese and Cambodians are historic enemies, that most Orientals find milk products nauseating. We had to learn how to provide the right kind of home, a place they could grow into easily and, just as easily, out of. We had to show them that moving held no further terrors and that they were safe at last. We had to learn that our curiosity and their memories weren't always compatible. That it helped to talk but that talk and memory must come when and how it suited them. John and I realized we would have to learn to understand customs, traditions and lives completely different from our own. Even if we were able to take all this in, could we, without personal and emotional knowledge, make use of what we were learning? If we couldn't, how could we possibly be of any real help in the fiendishly difficult business of their adjustment?

This story deals with our education as well as theirs. Similarities in ideas and morality helped us understand each other. Differences, from taste to manners, helped us define each other. For the most part it was good will, on both sides, and what grew into an affection so strong I do not hesitate to call it love. Our horizons and our hearts were enlarged.

PART I

In dangerous camps between facing armies,
   The prey of pirates, raped, plundered or drowned,
In treacherous waters, in single file through the minefields,
   Praying to stave off death till they are found,

Begging for sponsors, begging for a Third Country,
   Begging America to take them in –
It is they, it is they who put everything in hazard.
   What we do decides whether they sink or swim.

IT BEGAN IN 1975 after the fall of Saigon and the end of a war we had opposed from the beginning. The well-publicized plight of the 'boat people' was a further link in a chain of shame and helplessness. My husband, John, and I talked and talked about it, we moaned and commiserated with like-minded friends but we did nothing.

One day John saw a notice in our local Florentine newspaper that the Italian charity *Caritas* was to hold a public meeting to explain what could be done to help the 'boat people'. John went alone to the meeting because we had quarreled, violently, about something that must have seemed important at the time. After the last word is screeched and the final door is slammed, I usually go to bed with a novel. John 'does' something. This time he did indeed do something. The meeting was an avalanche of rhetoric, accusations, counter-claims and *aria fritta* (fried air) from citizens seeking a public forum. Finally John stood up and said that all this talk of political and social position was simply fascinating but what could he personally do to help. The question was asked in all sincerity and it was answered in all practicality. A well-fed, balding priest sitting on the platform said 'See me on your way out'. As he was leaving, John felt a firm hand on his shoulder. It was the chubby determined priest who shoved a piece of paper at him and said 'Just sign here. How many do you want?' Startled, but pleased by something concrete at last, John signed up to offer housing, sustenance and employment to a family of not more than four.

We began to look forward eagerly to the arrival of the refugees. We even practiced – I would be the Vietnamese and John would, by gesture and simple speech make me feel at home. Then we would reverse the roles. We waited and waited but there was only silence. We tried to trace Don Fabrizio (the chubby priest) of *Caritas*, the only name we had, but failed. We waited and in time almost forgot. Months later – John says it was three but I remember it being even longer – we got a card in the mail. It was a printed form that I thought was someone's dental appointment until I noticed that John Clark had been assigned blank blank blank which consisted of blank blank. The spaces had been filled in by hand to tell us that the 'Du Cau family' of 'three units' was now ours. There was no more information.

Again we rang *Caritas*, and this time we were put through to Don Luigi Bartoletti. Don Luigi had become the 'responsabile' (man in charge) of all the Asian refugees in Tuscany. 'Our' family, he told us, was being brought, with a group of other refugees, to a monastery quite near our house and we could go to meet them the day after tomorrow. What, we wondered, did these units consist of – two grandparents and a maiden aunt? Don Luigi assured us that we would be pleased and kept what information he had to himself. A Florentine with a pronounced local accent, Don Luigi had a 'no nonsense' approach that coupled with a salty Tuscan humour left him marginally short of rudeness. It was, we learned, his answer to the chronic disorganization of the volunteers, the charity and Italians in general. It was his method of controlling the love of rhetoric and the unbridled individualism, bordering on anarchy, that surrounded him. Italian benevolence, operatic style and natural wit limit frustration when things don't get done, or at least make the messes more attractive.

It was the middle of a stormy November in 1979 when we

drove the few miles from our house along the deserted, twisting road to *L'Incontro* – a sixteenth-century monastery whose name means 'The Meeting'. Legend has it that Saint Domenic met and lovingly embraced Saint Francis here, a popular subject for Renaissance painters. On a clear day there is a splendid view of the valley of the Arno with the city like a Renaissance painting in the background. A row of cypresses, black against a tempestuous sky, marked the beginning of the monastery. We parked the car and walked towards the only light in view which came from a square, newish building attached to the renovated church. There was no answer to our knock but the door was unlocked so we stepped into an icy corridor, dimly lit but freshly painted. As we walked along we heard noises, noises like spring rain that grew louder, but never loud. Following our ears we came to a large dining room and identified the sound. It was the sound of Asian laughter, which I would come to recognize as a leaven to almost any conversation: embarrassment, doubt, complication, difficulty, bewilderment, mortification and of course, joy were all expressed in that gentle laughter. There were, I learned through the Orientals, moments in which laughter is less callous or heartless than tears.

In the refectory were about twenty Vietnamese of all ages in the middle of an Italian lesson. The teacher, a pretty girl in blue jeans, was as amused and delighted as her pupils. A substantial man who looked, except for his soutane, like my local butcher came over to us. It was Don Luigi. After the ritual exchange of compliments (considerably briefer than usual) he introduced us to 'our family'. Tuyen, the father, was fairly tall, incredibly thin with lank pitch-black hair and the dirty-beige pallor that comes from lack of food. His wife, Trinh, who seemed little more than a child, looked even thinner and her delicate face was tense and strained. Tuyen threw his arms around John in an awkward but deeply moving gesture and buried his head on John's shoulder. We were all surprised, including Tuyen himself. All except Don Luigi who had, he rather condescendingly told us later, the 'advantage of The Faith.' Everyone in the room joined with the general delight and the room itself seemed to rock with Asian laughter. I had felt like a spectator looking through the keyhole but suddenly the doors were flung wide open and Trinh and I kissed unselfconsciously. Trinh knew a few words of English, enough to say 'Thank you for life'. What one answers to that I still don't know. Their smiles and laughter made an answer unnecessary.

We went upstairs to a tiny cell-like room where our third unit, a baby as pale and fragile as a piece of old porcelain, slept with his hands above his head in what I knew from my own children to be the ideal position for tranquil rest. A born baby-snatcher, I left the room with a reluctance that Trinh understood immediately. Our expressions of genuine delight were cut short by Don Luigi who took John aside and said, 'Now what about this job?' I began to feel as though we were trying to join an exclusive club whose membership was already oversubscribed. I found myself apologizing for our simple arrangements but was interrupted by John who is not an easy man to rattle. In his flawless Italian, he convinced Don Luigi of our good intentions. Don Luigi was too much of a Tuscan to express approval and certainly not optimism – a proper Tuscan when asked 'How are you' answers 'Non c'e male' (not too bad) or if he is feeling exceptionally well, 'Bene per ora' meaning alright for now. Whether it was the general atmosphere or John's impeccable accent, I don't know but Don Luigi seemed satisfied enough. After expressions of affection all round and one more look at the baby we left, promising to return in a week (health controls were necessary) to collect 'our' new family and take them home. On the way back John and I kept laughing and congratulating each other, passing our euphoria back and forth as though it were some delectable dish or precious wine. When we got home we each took a stiff drink to sober up.

The move itself was simple as their possessions were few. *Caritas* had explained to us that their eleven-month stay on the infamous Malaysian island of Pulan Bidong had meant that what few valuables they brought with them had disappeared. Ostensibly a haven for refugees, by all accounts Pulan Bidong was more like a concentration camp: the refugees were confined, half-starved and brutalized by Malaysian guards. Tuyen's watch and Trinh's wedding ring had been traded for food and enough plastic to cover the shelter Tuyen had built out of driftwood. Fortunately Trinh had been able to nurse the baby who was only four months old when they left Vietnam. The baby's two cousins who were older (two and four) lost all their teeth and quite a bit of hair from malnutrition.

There are those who believe – like my mother – that sleep is the great healer; I hold with those who favour proper food. We were able to provide both. Recovery came remarkably quickly, and as they began to relax and gain weight it became clear how pretty Trinh was and how attractive Tuyen. The baby was enchanting. When he first came to us he was fifteen months old and not only could he not walk he didn't even have strength enough to sit up. His fontanelle was not closed, and he had no muscular control over his eyes. This was due to malnutrition. A friend who is a doctor later told me that had the baby remained on the island in those conditions that within another three or four months he could have been permanently brain damaged. Instead, within three months he was everywhere, a golden, dimpled delight with even one eye straightened out.

We had, in those days, an Italian couple, Bruno and

Bruna, working for us and living in the house. Their peasant sense of practicality was jolted by our decision to take in the Du Caus but there were never any signs of resentment or jealousy on either part. While continuing to think us quite mad they learned to love the Vietnamese. There were clashes of culture. Both Bruno and Bruna were scandalized by the Oriental method of toilet training. Bo (whose name means precious) ran about with holes in his clothes at the appropriate places, followed closely by his mother with a damp cloth. When Bo caught a cold John and I were amazed to see Trinh scraping an object that looked menacingly like a dragon's tooth. After she had shaved off a number of grains she put them in a brew and fed this to the baby. I do not recommend either practice but must admit that Bo's cold cleared up and that he was toilet trained in record time.

The first winter was harsh and they all suffered. Shots against whooping cough came too late and all three caught it. Trinh had chilblains and Bo had two permanent red circles on his cheeks, like those painted Russian dolls. I realized for the first time just how levelling winter is – how unreliable the sun, how unpredictable the winds, how upsetting the early darkness – especially so for anyone born into a tropical climate. The bareness, the stripping down of colour, the cruel wind, the bitter, bitter cold, surprised and frightened Trinh. 'Will it ever end?' she asked. Then, almost suddenly, the cold ceased, the wind became a breeze, the sun shone through a rip in the sky that widened until it became a dazzling blue with soft white clouds designed to hold the wind in place. I couldn't help feeling that it was our reward. The Vietnamese seemed to draw a deep, inaudible sigh of relief, as though they were finally safe.

Tuyen started work in the laboratory at *Scala* a few weeks after his arrival. At first I drove him to work but at Christmas we gave him a motorbike so that he could feel more independent. I learned later that in those first months his hands were always icy, almost frozen. He knew nothing about gloves; in South Vietnam even coats were a status symbol and not a necessity.

A new language is difficult for almost anyone, for Tuyen it was traumatic. Even after all these years his spoken Italian is atrocious and although he knows and understands the language well he is not easily understood. He had a terrible time that first year. Tuscan humour was a mystery to him, a troublesome one. What was in reality normal banter, heavy-handed but not ill-intentioned, offended his Oriental male pride and he tried to strike back with his limited understanding and even more limited Italian. I was called in to *Scala* to arbitrate. When he tried to plead his own case to me, words failed him and he laid his head down on the table and cried, oh, how he cried! He wept with the abandonment of a child, with a sorrow born of ignorance and loneliness. It was harrowing for us both. Through Don Luigi we found a priest a few hours' drive away who had lived in China and Vietnam and spoke both languages. We took Tuyen to see him in his remote and beautiful country parish. With him was a Chinese nun, elderly and battle scarred. My heart sank as she greeted Tuyen with a barrage of sounds, aggressive even to my unknowing ears. The priest, an elderly, white-haired, soft spoken man in carpet slippers and a shawl around his shoulders, raised a delicate, blue-veined hand and turned her off like a tap. He then talked to Tuyen, softly and soberly. Soberly, until he brought out a bottle of fiery liquor that he had distilled himself, an Italian adaptation of the Chinese Mai Tai. I forced down a small part of my glass. Tuyen and the priest each had two and we left after almost an hour, reeling and smiling. Whether it was the priest's encouragement, time and knowledge or basic Italian humanity I don't know, but within a few months it all straightened out. Even today Tuyen is still friends with some of his ex-colleagues, all differences long forgotten.

It was easier for Trinh who spoke a few words of English and did well in her Italian lessons. She and I would meet everyday for an hour's talk and language practice and within a short time we were able to have a proper conversation. It was in this way that Trinh was able to tell me the story of her family.

Trinh's family name was Van: her father, Xiem Thang Van had fled to Vietnam in the face of the Japanese invasion of China in the thirties, the first in a long line of family refugees. He lived through the Japanese conquest of Indochina and the French occupation that followed. The French rulers created the State of Vietnam with the former Emperor Bao Dai as head of state. The defeat of the French by Vietnamese forces at the battle of Dien Bien Phu on May 7, 1954, ended French domination. An international peace conference was immediately called in Geneva. The treaty signed there called for temporary partition of the country, to be followed by elections in 1956, when the Vietnamese would decide their own government.

The 1954 Geneva Peace Accord seemed to presage a better future for the country, and for Xiem as well, who was working as a baker in the southern town of Chau-Doc, almost at the Cambodian border. In 1955 he met his future wife and his fortunes changed definitively. Because he had been born in China he was accepted as a son-in-law by a rich Chinese/Vietnamese family. (Those Chinese coming directly from the Middle Kingdom were considered superior to those born locally.) Xiem's father-in-law controlled a large portion of river traffic and owned a fleet of small boats. The young family (Trinh as the eldest was born in Chau-Doc in 1956) moved to a village on the Xa No River, a tributary of the Mekong, shortly after the birth of the second child in 1957.

Meanwhile in Saigon, Ngo Dinh Diem, the Prime Minister under the sybaritic Bao Dai, was busy consolidating his personal power and doing his best to thwart the Geneva Peace Accord. The United States supported Diem in blocking the implementation of the elections – elections that seemed certain to be won by the Communists. An experienced anti-French and anti-Communist politician, Diem seemed to be the man who could best advance America's interests in the region. The magnitude of Washington's mistaken judgment is now easily apparent. That the direction of an important phase in American History could be shaped by the strength and weakness of this one man seemed impossible but as American involvement in Vietnam increased this became more and more evident.

The father-in-law had left the river traffic in Xiem's hands and moved to Saigon as an adviser to the last of the Nguyen rulers, Bao Dai. He had long been an important member of the Hoa Hao sect. Ostensibly a religious offshoot of Buddhism, the sect, like the larger Cao Dai Catholic movement, became in effect a private army at the service of the highest bidder. The sect had collaborated with the Japanese and received French funding and support. The founder of the Hoa Hao, a faith-healer named Huynh Phu So, was murdered by the Communists in 1947. From then on the Hoa Hao army of an estimated 15,000 men retaliated by killing Communists in the western Mekong Delta. Instead of forging an alliance, Diem set out to destroy them, convinced that, at the time, pro-French forces were more of a menace to his power than the Communists. Sustained by American military and economic aid he reigned in the Cao Dai, the Binh Xuyen (an organized criminal society) and Hoa Hao armies. One of the Hoa Hao leaders was caught and guillotined publicly in Can Tho. Diem then dethroned Bao Dai. Now firmly in power Diem proclaimed the Republic of Vietnam (RVN) at the end of 1955. In the name of the Republic he passed laws ordering arrest and detention of any person he deemed a menace to security. Later the laws were enlarged to permit execution as well, even on suspicion. Diem had devised an exotic philosophy of his own: a mixture of Catholic, Confucian and Indian concepts cemented by his admiration of the Nazis and their methods. What emerged was a philosophy so confused and incoherent that it would never have been taken seriously had it not become the official policy of a government with American support. Diem's absolute authority brought him adherents of a sort, cronies and family members whose corruption knew no limit.

In January 1963 at Ap Bac (the hamlet of Bac) on the Delta, ill-equipped guerrilla forces of the Viet Cong defeated a modern army four times its size in the first battle of the American War in Vietnam. In retrospect it is easy to call it a 'turning point', at the time it must have appeared more as a thunderbolt, hardly possible to believe. In fact it was not believed and the Americans and the South Vietnamese refused to recognize the defeat. Trinh and Tuyen were only children when this battle took place but Tuyen remembers the celebration that followed the news. They grew up to radio reports that were, of course, heavily censored. Not until they were in their teens did they begin to wonder how it happened that, in spite of great 'triumphs' on the battle-field and government declarations that the war was over, it still dragged on. The unrest in the country grew under Diem's abuse of power until it led to a series of Buddhist riots. The world was shocked by pictures of Buddhist monks burning themselves to death in protest. International disgust increased. America withdrew aid to Diem early in 1963. In

November of that year there was a military coup and Diem and his brother were assassinated. America resumed aid to the Republic and by December of 1963 there was a considerable military presence of around 16,000 troops in the country.

The Republic (RVN) that Diem created lasted for over twenty years: he ruled for nearly half that time. When Diem fell from power he left behind a state that was completely dependent on foreign (American) aid. His systematic destruction of all opposition meant that the only intact power able to succeed him was the military. Intense rivalry broke out among senior officers in the RVN jockeying for high command. High command meant power, careers and money. By far the most politically able of all the generals was Nguyen Van Thieu. He managed to survive the chaos, create his own political machine and was elected President of the RVN in 1967. Unhampered by ideology, as Diem had been, Thieu was able to integrate the political, military and economic powers. Getting rich was their common goal.

Trinh's grandfather had been ruined by Bao Dai's overthrow and her family was left with only a small piece of land in the isolated village of Mot Ngan along the Xa No River. Trinh's parents lived there with their rapidly expanding family. The marriage was a happy one and certainly fruitful – twelve children, all of whom survived childhood and, except for Trinh and her youngest sister, are still living in Vietnam. The village was one kilometer away from the provincial centre. It was not a favourable location as in between was a fairly large military installation which meant that the village was sometimes shelled, either by the Viet Cong or by incompetent RSVN soldiers. Trinh grew up to the sounds of war and intermittent shelling. Her first experience of death was when she was eight. The small school Trinh and her younger brother attended suffered a direct hit and fifteen children were killed or severely wounded. Mines strewn along the riverbank designed to keep the enemy at bay also maimed two local residents. Three times Trinh's family had to escape the advancing Viet Cong. They were fortunate enough to be able to hide on their grandfather's cargo boat and sail to Cai Rang. Cai Rang was a primarily Chinese settlement on the outskirts of Can Tho, the largest city on the southern Mekong Delta. They had a house there whereas most refugees lived on boats until the danger passed.

The Van family resources were few but Trinh's father, in proper Chinese fashion, insisted that the children be educated. When they finished the local school Trinh and her brother were sent to school in Can Tho. Although the distance was not great the only method of travel was by an ancient, primitive ferry boat. As the voyage of eighteen kilometers took over two hours, Trinh and her brother lived in Can Tho and came home only on weekends. One terrible day when she was seventeen and on her way home from school her boat was stopped. The river was blocked because of a battle somewhere near the camp. She saw smoke rising from her village and heard the familiar sounds of gunfire. Defying her elders on the boat, she jumped off and walked towards the noise. It was about three or four kilometers' distance and she went slowly, always on the lookout for mines. By the time she reached the camp the fighting was over and the dead were lying on the ground in neat rows. She began to count them, then stopped, shocked at her behaviour. A small distance away were bodies of the Viet Cong scattered as they had fallen, untouched and unclaimed. Trinh made it home in a daze broken only when her father began to scold her for taking such risks. The scolding kept the hysterics at bay, at least for a while.

It was at the school in Can Tho that Trinh and Tuyen met.

Trinh was eleven and her brother ten when they started the new school. They spent mornings at the Vietnamese school and afternoons at a Chinese one, following a curriculum set up by the Taiwan schoolboard that included studies in Vietnamese. Trinh was the better student but Tuyen was the school hero, good at sports, handsome and the proud owner of a Honda motorcycle. When they were eighteen Trinh 'compromised' herself: she was seen riding on the back of the Honda. When the news of her indiscretion reached Mot Ngan, Trinh's mother wept: no one would marry her now, least of all Tuyen.

They were never hungry. With time the sharpness of fear dulled and sometimes years passed without trouble. Then an outburst of fighting or bombing would break the lull. From 1968 to 1971 a series of Viet Cong victories forced Trinh's family to flee once more and they spent nearly three years in Cai Rang. After 1971 they were able to move back to Mot Ngan and Trinh's two youngest siblings (numbers eleven and twelve) were born at home. Tuyen's brother, Hue, was able to buy his way out of the military. His father bribed government officials to issue new documents stating that Hue was under age for service: these made Tuyen younger still and neither of them ever served. Tuyen's brother-in-law was less fortunate. He served several years as a soldier for the South until he could stand it no longer. Then he went to a doctor who told him that with an injection he could impair the vision in one eye. The doctor swore that the damage would be temporary: it wasn't and he now has an artificial right eye. Most of his unit was wiped out in a disastrous attempt to disrupt the Ho Chi Minh trail so perhaps the bargain he made was not a bad one.

They no longer believed radio reports about the war so that when it actually ended they were all taken by surprise. Can Tho prepared itself as best it could for the conquering soldiers. Sympathisers lined the streets for hours waiting for the soldiers to arrive. Some shops were closed and some houses tightly shuttered. Their owners still believed what they read in the censored press and heard on the radio. Slowly the victors came into town: there was no triumphal parade, just groups of soldiers from the country, some from across the river, some who had been underground. When it became clear that there was nothing to fear from these joyous, exhausted men and women the whole city turned out to meet them. However, with time they began to behave like conquerors. At first their demands were simple: no long hair on young men, no tight trousers on the girls, no publicly displayed affection in couples.

The Du Cau family was a prosperous one living in Cai Rang near the South Vietnamese city of Can Tho on the fertile Mekong Delta. They had a small 'wok' factory in which both sons worked after school. Tuyen's father, who was, like most Chinese, non-political was allowed to keep the factory running. He made 'things' and 'things' were necessary to the population. At first they noticed little difference until raw material became harder and harder to come by as local resources were drained to help other, poorer, parts of the country. Trinh's family's commercial activities were outlawed although impossible to suppress. As people began to grumble about the lowered standard of living anti-Chinese feeling grew, encouraged by new restrictions. Tuyen's father was canny and had amassed enough gold to buy passage for his wife, daughter, son-in-law, and their three sons, as well as Tuyen and his older brother Hue, with their wives and children (thirteen people in all). He stayed behind for reasons that we only discovered later. John and I speculated as to why and romanticized what turned out to be un-heroic behaviour and a banal situation.

At the end of the war Vietnam experienced a form of what

is now called ethnic cleansing. The victims were the many Chinese who lived and worked there. By 1976 it had reached the very southern tip of the country where the Du Caus lived. It was a time of terrible insecurity and things seemed certain to get worse. A relative was executed for having served as an officer in the South Vietnamese army, Trinh's brother was refused entry into university and Tuyen's cousin lost his job because, although born in Vietnam, he was ethnic Chinese. The Du Caus decided it was time to leave. Their departure was semi-official as bribes had to be paid. The trick was in finding the right officials to bribe. Buses were organized (exactly by whom they never found out) and passed along the towns and villages on the Delta collecting those who had paid and whose names were on a mysterious list. Their bus contained for the most part people they knew at least by sight so they were filled with the sadness of parting, unaware of the dismay and terror that they were to know later.

When they arrived at the strip of land called Mo-O (bird's beak) on the Mekong and saw the rusty old boat twenty metres long and barely three and a half metres wide together with the crowd of terrified people waiting, they were shocked. There was, however, much worse to come. Each person was allowed to take only two changes of clothing and anything else was confiscated. They were searched for hidden gold or valuables. Once again, bribes worked and Tuyen was able by sacrificing half his money to bring part of his savings with him. Then they were herded into the hold, all 280 of them huddled together within a space that allowed practically no movement at all. For four days and nights they had no sanitation whatsoever and the fear, the swaying of the ancient boat for people who had never been to sea and the stifling heat made most of them violently sick. On the second day out a small child died and her body, wrapped in her two changes of clothing, was handed from one to another so that one of the crew could drop it overboard. Tuyen wondered that such a small package could be so heavy. Lam Ba, who was married to Tuyen's brother, Hue, was delirious to the point of not recognizing her younger son who was little more than a year old, so he was passed over to Trinh who already had four-month-old Bo. Lam Ba was so weak that she had to be carried off the boat when they finally landed. There was no food but Tuyen says that didn't matter as everyone was so sick and the surroundings so filthy that no one could eat anyway. Buckets of drinking water were sent down by one of the crew. However, the water had been collected from the Mekong before they put out to sea and it caused diarrhea and more nausea although some relief for those who could keep it down. Horrible as it was, Trinh's brother had a worse time. When he tried to leave a storm forced the boat to land on an island that belonged to Vietnam. There he was picked up by the police, taken back and thrown into prison and later sent to a re-education centre. He was kept there for over six months before he was released.

Trinh and Tuyen's skipper was so inexperienced that he landed them at first on the wrong island where armed Malaysian guards turned them away. Then they were dumped on a deserted island where they stayed for three days. What little food they had, mostly rice, came from the boat. Fortunately there were coconut palms and the shells were used as cups and plates for the rice which they boiled in sea water. Trinh said the mixture was so bitter that it took her several tries each time before she could keep it down. After three days representatives of the UN and the Red Cross came to the island and took them to the official refugee camp at Pulan Bidong where they were delivered into the hands of hostile Malaysians. The price for all this (including the necessary bribes) was approximately five thousand U.S. dollars per person, in gold, with a discount for children under ten. At Pulan Bidong they found hundreds of other refugees in varying stages of despair. The relief agencies allotted five dollars a day per person for food, which should have been sufficient. The money was, however, paid to the camp's local directors and from this the refugees received a small sack of rice, one tin of peas, one tin of sardines and one of meat each week. Each family was given a pot for cooking but nothing else. Everything, says Tuyen, was for sale. When they first arrived Trinh wanted to change her filthy clothes and was shy about changing in the open. They asked a fellow refugee if she might go into his straw shelter to change. Certainly, he said, for two dollars. Trinh changed behind a tree.

The refugees' section of Pulan Bidong was covered with makeshift shelters surrounding three semi-permanent buildings. The first two large ones housed the camp's Malaysian administrators and guards. The third was an office where forms could be filled out requesting asylum. At one time there were as many as forty thousand refugees and the one office must have seemed pitifully small to them. A representative from the American and other Consulates came once a month to sift through the papers and decide who the fortunate ones would be. Tuyen's brother-in-law had family already established in the States so they, with their three sons, were able to leave for America within a few months. For the rest of the family – 'our' three, Tuyen's brother, wife and two sons and his mother – there seemed to be nothing but extended misery. Bit by bit their material and physical reserves shrank. Trinh says they were saved because they were by the water and could at least keep clean. Tuyen tried to dig a well and, on the fifth try, luckily found drinking water.

One morning Trinh woke up to find five-month-old Bo's face was red, swollen and almost unrecognizable. It was covered with insect bites. They acted immediately. Tuyen learned that on the other side of the island Malaysian boats passed near to the shore and sold goods. His mother gave him a small piece of gold she had managed to hide. He exchanged this with the camp's guards for Malaysian money – at a wickedly fraudulent rate. He found a piece of a barrel, put it under his arm and walked over the mountain to the other side of the island. When the boat came in sight he swam out to meet it. With his Malaysian money he bought some food and a piece of nylon from the sailors. He swam and walked back with his newly acquired prize. He sold the nylon for a profit of nearly eight Malaysian dollars. With this he bought a mosquito net for Bo. The price was outrageous but Bo was safe. This became Tuyen's regular routine: walking and swimming and trading. Sometimes it was food, sometimes plastic, but without it Trinh says they wouldn't have survived. The Malaysian guards learned about this and collected their toll. Sometimes as many as five or six would waylay Tuyen, each demanding his tax: there was nothing to do but pay. Despite huge weight loss the muscles in Tuyen's legs became so developed he could no longer wear the trousers he had brought from Vietnam.

When other refugees left – for a 'third country' – they sold the thatched shelters they had been living in, but Trinh told me with justifiable pride that when they left they gave their shelter to a family with no money and four children. They were confined behind barbed wire and without the sea would have been even more desperate. Members of the Chinese colony on the island came to the edge of the fence and threw food and clothes to the refugees. Little got through this way but at least they were not totally forgotten. Trinh brought to Italy a sleazy, Susie-Wong red dress with huge yellow flowers that had been tossed over the wire by a toothless old lady who no longer had any use for it.

They had been there for over ten months when one glorious day Don Della Perugia of *Caritas* arrived on the island. A loudspeaker broadcast to the refugees that Italy had several hundred places and he would talk to anyone who wanted to go there. Many of the Vietnamese had never heard of Italy and most of the others had got their knowledge from the cinema; 'Mafia and Pizzas'. The more well-off (at this time there were still a few who hadn't been resettled) objected to the good Don, 'In Italy too many Communique'. Don della Perugia, who is a man of presence and authority, assured them that was no problem. 'We take care of that,' he promised. All the Du Caus (eight of them) were accepted. Trinh says she looked at her frail baby and burst into tears, tears of relief. It was, Trinh says, like a Vietnamese folk tale of lost children faced with the choice of two paths through the woods. They knew nothing of Europe, only that it would be different and at that stage in their lives it was certain to be better. How could she worry about the future when day to day improvisation occupied her completely? The fact that she would have to face new situations she was not prepared for by tradition or culture never entered her mind. *Caritas* obtained an attractive apartment for Tuyen's brother, Hue and his family, including his mother, in the village next to ours, so no one felt abandoned. 'Were you frightened?' I asked Trinh. Nothing frightened her, she told me, but waking every morning to see her baby getting weaker and weaker.

The Du Caus are ethnic Chinese although all, except Tuyen's mother, had been born in Vietnam. Tuyen's mother had chosen, or been chosen, to come to Vietnam. Seeking a wife, Tuyen's father went to China, found Mai, married her (she was eighteen) and brought her back to Can Tho, where she produced a daughter and two sons as well as demonstrating a remarkable head for numbers. (To see her at her abacus was a privilege.) She was a handsome woman, her looks marred only by a huge gold tooth flashing in what seemed a permanent smile. It was with considerable surprise that I learned the story of her marriage. Her husband took up with a Vietnamese woman younger than Mai by whom he had two more children. A not unfamiliar story, but with an Oriental twist. When the children (a boy and a girl) were old enough to be educated, their father took them from their Vietnamese mother and delivered them to his Chinese wife so that they could grow up as proper Chinese. I was flabbergasted at the system and even more so at the acceptance by both wives. When I met Mai I was prepared to find her meek and obedient. Obedient she had certainly shown herself to be and she seemed as passive as an unconcerned cat, but when I saw her on two different occasions defending her sons from their father I realized how foreign I was and how superficial my judgment.

The Italian experiment had proved a success for both brothers and their families. Letters went back to Vietnam regularly – slowly as the post was still primitive – filled with the wonders of The West. Tuyen's father, who I always referred to as 'The Father', decided after a year or so to come to Italy. We learned later he had been having trouble with his Vietnamese wife, which probably had something to do with his decision to come over. Perhaps it was the desire to see the rest of his family or the glorious tales of Italy that changed his mind. I'll never know exactly why – but arrive he did. When he stepped off the plane at Rome airport, all two hundred pounds, six foot two of Chinese manhood, he was greeted ecstatically by both his sons, their wives and the three grandsons. Equally enthusiastic was Mai who was more than willing to resume her duties.

Shortly after his arrival we had the entire family to dinner.

Our dining room was formerly the stables and is long and narrow, so by necessity as well as preference, we have a 'fratino' table named for those used in monastery refectories. John always sits at one end, and when we have guests, I sit at the other. That night I gave my place to The Father, partly because of language problems but mostly because I could see him only at the head of the table, any table, a position he accepted naturally. He was the kind of man who automatically became the host at whatever gathering he attended, knowing full well it was the most important position. What a handsome man he was and how unwavering were his opinions relayed to us through his family's translations. He looked like any romantic's idea of a Chinese emperor and accepted homage with practiced grace.

We had renovated the stone barn near our house for Trinh, Tuyen and Bo. The house was small but charming. Trinh sewed beautifully and Tuyen was a first-rate carpenter so they managed the lack of space with ingenuity and Oriental colour. The Father chose to move there although a room had been set aside for him at the house of Hue, the elder son. Trinh and Tuyen gave up their room to him and moved in with Bo. Soon Mai moved in, too. That was just as well as The Father required and received an enormous amount of attention. That Mai bathed him I put down to a quaint old Oriental custom but when I saw her putting on his shoes I thought it a bit much. Difficult, dictatorial, dreadful, indeed he was and I, for one, wished that he had stayed in Vietnam. And yet, one day when I saw him alone in the garden (he never did any work) looking at nothing, into nothing, I felt a terrible sorrow, stronger than I had ever felt for the others. It was, I think, being in the presence of so much loss. When it became clear just how much trouble he caused I was free to return to the enjoyment of my original dislike without a qualm. Sooner than anticipated, tensions began to rise. Trinh's face looked stretched; Tuyen was silent; I saw less and less of Mai's gold tooth. Only The Father and Bo were unaffected. We now discovered why he had stayed in Vietnam. It seems that The Father had quarrelled with his Vietnamese wife, left her and their children and taken up with yet another woman. He spoke openly about his new liaison and failed to notice, or disregarded, the family's indignation. Mai said nothing but Trinh took issue and dared to criticize The Father, a position she admits she would never have taken in Vietnam. Here she was living her new life to the full. The Father was appalled and took every opportunity to challenge Trinh.

Trinh had her own (Oriental) way of disciplining Bo. He would kneel in front of her and at her commands either pull his own hair or slap his own face. Auto-criticism begins early. I never said a word against this although it was quite an effort not to. (It was an even greater effort not to enjoy the spectacle, it was so beguiling.) The Father felt this system satisfactory only for women and took to beating Bo with a strap. Trinh, who prides herself on her modernity, was outraged and sounds of discord grew louder in a strange counterpoint like Chinese Opera without the gongs. The Father felt cheated because he hadn't gone to America and because Trinh stood up to him and was sustained by Tuyen (with what effort on his part I can only imagine). Things worsened with Trinh often in tears. Her family had been insulted, she had been called a 'horse' (the Oriental equivalent of bitch) and The Father persisted in trying Tuyen's filial loyalty. There was no back-tracking and to continue like this was intolerable. Tuyen's sister in America had opened a Chinese take-away and was doing well. She offered to take the parents but there were further problems. They were safe in Italy so refugee status papers were unattainable. A whiteish lie wouldn't hurt, I thought and it might work. So I sent them to the American Consulate here in Florence to ask for a tourist visa knowing that once in the States their daughter could apply for papers there. The consular staff had been faced with situations such as these before and the visa was denied. Virtue battled with necessity, briefly. The Father had to go. I went the very next day to the Consulate to see an acquaintance who was Vice Consul, looked her straight in the eye and lied and lied and lied. A tourist visa was arranged.

Fortunately there is a frequent turnover of Consulate personnel in Florence and my former friend was already on her way to London when the Consul General called me in a bit of a rage. I protested my innocence (lying once more) and would do it again, scolding and all.

After Mai and The Father left everyone's life changed. Bo was put in nursery school and Trinh went to work. The depth of Trinh's happiness irradiated her whole body. She had a wonderful laugh that seemed to come from deep in her lungs. She almost seemed a lung herself – so full of breath, so full of happiness. Tuyen still worked for John but when Trinh went to work they were able to save more money. They first sent Trinh's family enough to rebuild their house and set up some of her sisters in business. Later they even sent the money to build a bridge across the tributary of the Mekong where Trinh's family lived.

By 1984 the political climate in Vietnam had changed considerably and Trinh and Tuyen decided that it was safe for Trinh to go to see her family and to take six-year-old Bo with her. Although the war had been over for several years and the south had not been damaged to the extent that the north of the country had, people were still incredibly poor and living conditions primitive. Bo was frightened and too young to hide his anxiety. Nevertheless, after the first week or so the huge, loving family overcame his fears and all he missed were his tortellini and spaghetti and a proper bathroom. They were visitors from another planet in this small hamlet several hours' boat trip from the metropolis of Can Tho. People came long distances just to look at them, to gaze at their clothes, to admire Bo's toys and bombard them with questions about the outside world. The whole family became celebrities, and they seemed to spend their entire time taking photographs of each other. Trinh felt like a princess and asked if it was wrong to enjoy that. I assured her it wasn't. Since then all three have made several trips and the only limits to their travels are time and expense. By their second visit the atmosphere in Vietnam had undergone even more notable changes. The new freedom and the beginning of a modest economic recovery made life far more pleasant for them all. No need to feel guilty about our good fortune, Trinh assured me, as all my married sisters now have television.

They were blissfully young. When they came to Italy the combined ages of the three of them totalled 45. They were together, too, so adjustment came fairly quickly. When I think what they had to cope with I am filled with admiration: new traditions, usage, conventions, habits, religion, fashion, a completely different conception of time, new foods and above all that beastly language. Trinh was fascinated when I told her the story of the Tower of Babel. Oh, glorious day when the whole earth was of one language! Trinh said Jehovah was unnecessarily cruel and I agreed with her.

Although neither Trinh nor Tuyen ever left their history behind, they were soon able to add on to it their new experiences and to accept the habits, thoughts and behaviour of others. Trinh had always been interested and informed about the outside world when they were in Vietnam.

26

Although she always addressed her father in Chinese and would never have been allowed to marry a Vietnamese, most of her close friends were Vietnamese. Perhaps because his father's hold was stronger, Tuyen was more Chinese orientated – all through the war his mother had said neither she nor her sons could die as she had to go back once more to China. Both sets of parents have indeed gone to China within the last few years, but none of the younger generations feel this pull. The idea of finding themselves in a position they considered temporary soon diminished and first Trinh and not too much later, Tuyen, realized that exile was a permanent state, not just a transitory one, and as such required new definition. Soon they were able to speak of the past with neither nostalgia nor resentment. Having a very young child growing up as an Italian and a mixture of Vietnamese, Chinese and Italian friends helped. They became Italian citizens after five years in the country and we all celebrated. We are residents of a small town outside Florence called Bagno a Ripoli and it was in the *Municipio* (City Hall) there that the ceremony of citizenship took place. The first such occasion in Bagno and of great importance to everyone, curiosity mixed with tenderness. The law required four witnesses (John and I were not eligible as we are not Italian citizens) but there was no shortage. Between friends and colleagues there were twelve. The ceremony was simple and happily brief, the spumante flowed and the Mayor gave Trinh her first congratulatory kiss.

PART II

'What I am is not important, whether I live or die –
   It is the same for me, the same for you.
What we do is important. This is what I have learnt.
   It is not what we are but what we do,'

Says a child in exile, one of a family
   Once happy in its size. Now there are four
Students of calamity, graduates of famine,
   Those whom geography condemns to war,

Who have settled here perforce in a strange country,
   Who are not even certain where they are.
They have learnt much. There is much more to learn.
   Each heart bears a diploma like a scar –

Phnom Penh had fallen to the Khmer Rouge before Saigon but there was little or no news from there. When the news did come out it was so horrific, so devastating it was difficult at first to believe. We felt more helpless than ever.

Once again we turned to James for counsel and assistance. He had spent a great deal of time in Cambodia, especially during the 'Decent Interval' between the Paris Agreement of 1973, which ended direct American participation in the war, and the final victory of the Khmer Rouge in 1975. He had made many friends there and it was through one of them that we, in a roundabout way, made contact with our Cambodian family.

After the Du Caus had been with us for almost a year James came to visit. He had just returned from a trip to a Thai/Cambodian frontier refugee camp to find a friend who had worked for him in Phnom Penh. His experience was similar though less dramatic than that of Sidney Schanberg, the journalist whose story was filmed in *The Killing Fields*. In the camp he was besieged by refugees begging his help in getting them to a 'third country'. Among them was a twelve- or thirteen-year-old Cambodian orphan boy who made a great impression on him. This boy was teaching himself English and his cleverness and charm delighted James. James sent him some English text books and promised to do what he could for him. Because of the experience with Binh, and seeing how well the Du Caus had adapted to Tuscan life, he thought of us. James felt that here was a boy capable of learning another language and absorbing another culture, someone who would profit from exposure to the West.

As he talked John and I kept looking at each other and long before James had finished his story John was nodding his head. We were sitting around the swimming pool where two-year-old Bo and his four- and six-year-old cousins, Peng and Ang, were splashing. The deliciousness of those babies made me happy and, in a strange way, eager to take on more responsibility, and more love. We talked it over and decided that we could probably afford to take on another child. It was a big step, and we spent many hours discussing it with James.

But what were we going to do? There was no Don Luigi, no *Caritas*. I remembered that the Italian Ambassador to Thailand was a friend of friends so I wrote asking his advice and if possible his help. He was, as to be expected, extremely polite. Repeated letters and telexes to the Embassy in Bangkok brought an invitation to dinner but not much in the way of information. There seemed little that they could do as all I had was the boy's name (Samreth Soarith Khul) and a tracing number at the Children's Center 8, Khao-I-Dang Refugee Camp. With only this information they were unable to contact the lad. A profound contempt for bureaucracy and considerable arrogance led me to believe I could do better on the spot, so I decided to fly to Thailand and 'fight City Hall' from there. I was determined to do everything possible to keep bureaucracy from destroying another child. I first stopped in London, to consult with James.

Over a sumptuous tea at Brown's Hotel in London I received instructions and information from James together with bookings he had arranged for me. His advice was complicated but invaluable. It included a list of offices where permission to visit the camp could be obtained and various instructions: 'Go to Joint Operation Centre; Supreme

Command; Ministry of Defense' and a mysterious note in James's handwriting: 'Task Force 80' (neither of us remember what it or he meant). I needed to obtain, according to James, a pink card to enter the camp. I ended up, after three irritating days in Bangkok, with a white printed form from the Ministry of Defense written in Thai. I took this document to the Supreme Command. The official there, in impeccably starched khakis, asked me if I remembered Deanna Durbin and wrote four short lines in graceful Thai script at the bottom. He then took it into his superior for signature (in pencil) and a stamp that didn't want to stick. Strange how comforting a cyclostyled piece of paper can be. I felt armed, protected, invulnerable and went away hoping to be challenged so that I might wave my miraculous paper in the air. Still following James's instructions, I went to the Trocadero Hotel to look up the concierge, Rocky (not his real name he told me) who, according to James, knew everyone and arranged everything. The Trocadero looked wicked in a Hollywood way – not old or attractive enough for Graham Greene decadence – and was where most of the visiting journalists stayed.

James had made reservations for me at the Inter-Continental hotel for what he said was my comfort and I was grateful. Rocky engaged a Thai taxi, and negotiated what seemed to me a very reasonable price, for the fourth day of my stay (Friday) when I planned to go to the camps. I slept little Thursday night and was up shortly before five in the morning for my six o'clock appointment in front of the Siam Inter Continental. The driver was also eager and I found him waiting for me at twenty to six with the car's air conditioning already functioning. It was November and very hot. Bangkok at that hour of the morning was happily free of traffic jams but not a bit more attractive. Water was still standing in spots where the drains had backed up, garbage had not been collected for days, the fetid air was heavy with the smell of spoiled fruit and flowers, corpses of mongrel dogs were left alongside the road (I counted three that day).

It was, the Thai taxi driver assured me, a pleasant four-hour drive from Bangkok to the Refugee Camp at the Cambodian border. Except for a stop for petrol and a cool drink (beer for me and an orange drink of dubious colour for him) we had been on the road for nearly six hours before we sighted anything. More than once I thought myself mad to have made the trip at all but never once during that long dreary day did I think of turning back. Driving out of Bangkok into the countryside calmed me down. The paddy fields glowed with a green I had never seen before, ever changing yet repeating itself. The driver's card, which he showed but didn't give me (I suspect he only had one), advertised him as 'a English speeker'. He seemed pleased to have someone to practice on and chattered away, which was comforting, like rather discreet movie music. Fields and villages disappeared; a reddish-grey dust was everywhere and the newly laid asphalt was covered with it. I had been on the lookout for the hills that marked the Cambodian border and the end of the camp but the dust and the heat-haze hid them until we had almost arrived. I was thinking vertically, of hills, but what struck me was surrealy horizontal. If it is true (as I read somewhere) that the imagination pictures objects vertically and reality pictures them horizontally, this was 'reality' to drown in. The buildings (low thatched huts) seemed to cover the land without end. There were, I learned from one of the aid workers, 120,000 people housed there, down from a previous high of 150,000.

The pass that I had spent three days obtaining from the Thai authorities did not include the driver so I left him at the camp's entrance. He locked himself in the car, stretched out and waved me off happily.

I wonder if the aid worker was as sublimely wonderful as he remains in my memory. An Italian-American named Tom Generico, he had been working at the camp for more than two years. His rapport with the Cambodian refugees seemed to me just right: a humorous, concerned authority. He teased and was teased by the young and was fatherly to the tiny peasant woman who came into his office in tears; he was as proud of his halting Cambodian as his interpreters were of their English. Once arrived at Khao-I-Dang I willingly put myself in Tom's hands. He showed me around the office and then took me to the Children's Center 8 with its rows of bunk beds and photographs covering all available wall space. When a refugee arrived in camp his photograph was taken and circulated in the hope that the new arrival would be recognized, if not by family members or friends, at least by someone from his village. Families were often reunited that way. He found Samreth's picture for me and the sight of a bewildered young boy holding tightly on to a placard with his name (incorrectly spelled) written in large block letters made me more determined than ever to find him. There was nothing of childish sadness in that face, only the gloom of adult grief: grave and mute. The sight of all those photos, and an occasional blank space to denote success, filled me with an almost personal grievance.

Samreth had been helping some of the volunteer doctors and had gone with them to another, smaller camp fairly nearby. So, after thanking Tom and his Cambodian assistants, the driver and I took off for the second camp, Panat Nikhom Holding Centre, Chonburi. It was run by a young woman, Churu Naktipwan. She was pretty in that small-boned Thai way and spoke French and passable English. She told me that Samreth's photograph had been recognized by his mother and he had been sent to a third camp to meet her. I got back into the taxi for the third camp, which was smaller still, but full of activity. We arrived just as huge sacks of rice were being distributed. I found this suffocatingly depressing. Perhaps it was the permanence that those huge sacks implied. Perhaps, coming from the world of the rich, it was seeing the desires and needs of the destitute. Worse still was the news that Samreth and his mother were on their way back to Khao-I-Dang. It was then almost dark so a further trip would have been dangerous and we wouldn't have been admitted. There was nothing for it but to return to Bangkok.

Back in the car I began to cry. I felt a fool crying in the back of a Thai taxi. I cried as softly as possible trying not to disturb my friend, the driver. He offered to do anything, drive through the night, break down the gates, anything: but we went back.

I somehow managed to get through the visits and calls to various Embassies, Relief Agencies and Government Offices in Bangkok that followed, though I remember little about the remaining days. People were generally pleasant and promises were made but at that stage I felt little hope. The day before my flight home I collapsed at a shopping centre near my hotel. The souvenir-shop owner seeing my distress brought out a chair and a glass of water and after sitting with my head down and being cooed over by some children, I made it back to my room. I called the hotel doctor. I was in a fog, confused and anything but pleased when he congratulated me on my new president – until then I had satisfactorily avoided thinking about the American election and the victory of Ronald Reagan. When the doctor could find nothing wrong and learned that I had been to the camps he prescribed Valium, and it worked like a charm. Still in a daze from all the wretchedness I had seen, as well as the Valium, I flew back home.

All the written messages to Samreth had gone through, thanks to Tom. A letter arrived in Florence shortly after my

36

return. It was written in the name of Samreth's mother, Sou Sary, and said: 'I thank your letter sent to me on Nov 20, 1980 and said that you will help me and my family for living in Italian in the future. Myself and my family are very happy to wait for that.' Then she, or the person who wrote the letter for her went on to say, 'I am informing you that since my arrival in Khao-I-Dang I have quiet often got the sadest news on Kampuchea and about the Khmer people in general who have been suffered from the Vietnames.' I learned later that Sary considered the Vietnamese her saviours and had not understood the words of her scribe. The arrival of the Vietnamese had made escape possible (nor would she have said 'Kampuchea', a Khmer Rouge name). Ironically many of those who escaped with her were from the ranks of her tormentors. The letter continued, 'It is quite obvious to me that the separation of relatives and blooded people as well as the lose of all properties and previous belonging make the whole Khmer meet with their endless sorrows. I am earnestly hopeful, I shall be receipt of your reply in the short time.' Then she told us that her family consisted of herself, Samreth and his younger sister, Kilen. John and I were surprised but pleased. I rang Don Luigi with the news. He asked if I thought the girl really was a sister: I answered 'Chi se ne frega' (politely translated as 'Who gives a damn?') 'Ben detto' said Don Luigi, emphatically.

At that stage matters seemed more urgent than ever so I, having lived in Italy for more than twenty years, resorted to a local custom called *raccomandazione* (literally the word means recommended, actually it means pulling strings). I rang a friend in Milan, a Socialist Senator, and explained the problem. He 'recommended' me to ring the private telephone number of a functionary he knew at the *Ministero degli Estero* (Foreign Ministry). Within a week we received telex confirmation from the Italian Embassy in Bangkok. Approval had been granted for Samreth, mother and sister to come to Italy and as soon as the necessary medical examinations had been done, they would be on their way.

'Abbia pazienza' (Be patient, a necessary and useful Italian phrase) said the functionary when I rang his secret number after a two-month silence. I tried. Then, three days later on Monday 16 February, John received a phone call in his office; it was the efficient functionary. His message: Thursday 19 February, 1981, at six o'clock in the morning the Khul family arrives at the Roman airport of Fiumicino. He went further: the family consisted of Sou Sary (the mother), Samreth, the sister Kilen and the *piccolo bambino*. John was no longer surprised – he was in shock! 'Where did he come from?' he wanted to know. 'That is what we were wondering, too' was the answer. 'How old is the *piccolo bambino*?' John asked thinking he might be an indiscretion of the camp. He was, as near as could be figured out, eight years old. John and I speculated: was he really a brother? Did it matter if he wasn't? How was he found? None of our speculations came anywhere near the actual facts as we were later to learn them.

On the Wednesday we drove to Rome and spent the night in a hotel near the airport. Neither of us slept. I had a noisy, churning stomach and John couldn't stop talking. We rose early and rushed through an icy rain to the airport. The Air Thai plane had come in seventy minutes ahead of schedule, and the Roman officials were still shaking their heads in wonder when we arrived. There was no one left in the arrival lounge but two Carabinieri and the Khuls. The first thing that struck me was their beauty; Sary, Samreth and Kilen; the delicacy and the beauty. Hiding behind Samreth's back was the '*piccolo bambino*' but when I put out my hand he came forward and took it trustingly. Kilen and her mother were wearing cotton sarongs and T-shirts, the boys shorts and T-shirts. All wore plastic flip-flops without socks. Samreth was carrying a minute duffel bag that seemed to hold the family's entire possessions. They came towards me with the Buddhist gesture of clasped hands and bowed head but when I kissed each one they seemed neither frightened nor dismayed. Samreth spoke some English and Sary some French so welcome was made clear.

In Italy jokes – the Irish or Polish variety – are made about the Carabinieri and the two that morning might well have qualified. They were, luckily for us, wonderfully humane. They saw my anxiety, the shivering Cambodians and the deserted lounge. Taking it all in, especially the latter, they let us leave without any of the dreaded formalities, which included, we had been told, the possibility of a temporary quarantine. I signed a large register and took consignment of the family, as though it was a cumbersome but possibly valuable package. Never had I so blessed an organizational muddle. We rushed out of the airport (I didn't want to risk seeing any other officials) to find John waiting at the exit with the motor running and the car heater blazing.

Houssara, the *piccolo bambino*, sat in front with John and myself, the others in the back. I mostly noticed how softly they chattered, how beautifully they smiled. Most of the conversation was carried on through Samreth, the English speaker of the family, although it was clear that he deferred to his mother. John had said to me before they arrived, 'Would it be too much to ask if the girl was pretty?' He was dazzled by Kilen's loveliness, Sary's dignified beauty and Samreth's romantic head. Houssara was an instantly lovable, agile, grinning imp. The three-hour drive to Florence seemed interminable, it was as though the world had stopped. It reminded me of my first transatlantic flight. I now felt that the entire world was encapsulated in our old Alfa

Romeo. Children are naturally more aware of the future than adults. We are forever worrying about the present or regretting the past. That day I felt positively childlike. Never have I felt so willing to be defined, influenced or even determined by what was to happen next.

John had thought that music would ease the tension and put *The Nutcracker* on the car tape recorder. It was an astute idea, lifting the atmosphere and distracting us all. The Goldberg Variations would have been an even better choice but how were we to know that this soon. We stopped at one of the Autostrada restaurants but no one had any appetite. On our way out we passed a glass case inside which was a gimcrack toy automobile. Houssara stopped and put his hand, palm up, on the glass to get as close as possible to the wondrous object. John bought the car for him and he squealed with surprise. His expectancy level was very low. Even after he had been with us for a while he was always amazed by any gift no matter how small. The anticipation of pleasure was missing to such a degree that he never seemed unhappy when he didn't get a gift, unusual in any child, incredibly rare in an eight-year-old. On the other hand a gift, no matter how welcome, was never thought of as a bribe as it often is with young children. Pleasure was so unexpected it was greeted with wonder and unequivocal delight. Houssara had never had the chance to learn the rights and wishes of a child. Samreth tried to tell John it hadn't been necessary to buy the car but Sary, who was wiser, hushed him. Back in the car Houssara fell asleep clutching his car. He slept until John stopped the car by the roadside, needing a pee. By then it had begun to snow. None of the Cambodians had ever seen snow but at least the older ones had heard or read about it. To Houssara it was a complete revelation and he scrambled out of the car, lifted his face to the sky and laughed and laughed.

We left the Autostrada at Firenze Sud and took the back road for home. As we neared our house on the steep, winding road with its terraced olive groves which to us is so beautiful, conversation ceased and smiles became forced and infrequent. Only Houssara seemed unaffected. Something was obviously wrong but we didn't find out until later that 'hills' meant danger: bandits, tigers, unmentionable terror. We had much to learn. Nor had we thought about the age-old enmity between the Vietnamese and the Cambodians. I thought shyness was the reason for the rather cool reception given and received by the two families when we introduced them. That first night when Tuyen picked up a sleeping Houssara and carried him to bed I was startled to see Sary stiffen. Wrapped in our own familiar neuroses and prejudices, we are apt to dismiss those of others without proper consideration. There is an old Cambodian proverb the children loved to repeat that translates roughly: The Chinese will never lose his shrewdness; the Vietnamese will never lose his wickedness and the Cambodian will never lose his sexiness.

That first night after everyone was in bed and the house was quiet, John and I opened a bottle of cold Vernaccia and took it into our bedroom. We were so tired, too tired even to drink the wine in our glasses. We lay in bed scarcely able to move, with nothing fitting to say to one another, only a numb happiness. To try and talk about it would have seemed wrong: we lay back and shared the sudden sense of quiet and rest and relief.

The first days passed rapidly, as excitement quickly gave way to exhaustion. We were in the middle of a fierce winter: any winter would have been fierce for the Cambodians, but 1981 was record-breaking. Sleep and warm clothing were the priorities for everyone. A look into Samreth's duffel bag revealed two extra sarongs, two pairs of shorts and three T-shirts, plus a Bible translated into Cambodian (a gift of the Camp's Missionaries), a pestle with a crudely hollowed-out wooden mortar and a string of garlic. Telephone calls to friends brought an avalanche of warm clothing, most of it very chic. My bedroom became a cross between a bazaar and a boutique, and there was great giggling as clothes were tried on and accepted or discarded. Everyone except Houssara had very definite ideas as to what suited. Style gave way to comfort for Kilen who put on two skirts, two sweaters and four pairs of socks before she snuggled into a lined wind-breaker. Sary managed to look elegant in an oversized woolen dress that she draped like a sarong and Samreth rigged himself up as a stylish cross country skier. Only Houssara didn't seem to feel the cold or care what was put on him.

To begin with only Samreth went out of the house. No one else wanted to leave. Sary was too depressed; Kilen too obsessed with food, spending most of her time in the kitchen, cooking, eating or looking lovingly at the pantry shelves, arranging and re-arranging fruits and vegetables until she created a still life worthy of a Dutch painting. They had all been adequately fed in the camp although the diet seemed to consist of rice, beans, tinned sardines and Spam. The tins were wonderful they said, their only objection was to the over-abundance of beans. Kilen soon became plump, too plump for her tiny frame. I could not, and would not, dis-courage her from eating – it was so important to her. Many years later she told me that her mother kept saying she must save food for her older brother, she must eat less as there were four of them and she feared we would not keep them if they ate too much. I will never know if this was meant seriously or was a mother's strategy to make Kilen lose weight. Kilen still believes it was the former and Sary no longer remembers. At the time Kilen was convinced that in a former life she had been ungenerous with a Buddhist monk's begging bowl and this was her punishment. She seemed resigned to put on weight until she burst.

Each boy had a room to himself and Sary and Kilen shared a twin bedroom (I always found them in the same small bed those first days). Samreth had Lisa's old room (she had moved into her own house a few years before) and Houssara had the room at the very top of what was once a watchtower. We reckoned that the extra flight of stairs wouldn't bother him. What we hadn't reckoned with was the terror of finding himself alone. The youngest of a large family, from a society where generations still live together, herded by the Khmer Rouge into a camp at five, he had never spent a night alone. He stood at the foot of each flight of stairs leading to his room (there were four), paused, looked around carefully and muttered incantations before ascending. With each flight of steps the pauses grew longer, the incantations louder until at the foot of the final stairs his voice could be heard distinctly rooms away. The words themselves made no sense even to Samreth who, seeing his fear, offered to accompany him. The offer was firmly, heroically, refused.

Music was a big help. John had ordered two series of records made by UNESCO, one of Cambodian and one of Vietnamese traditional music. We were very proud of ourselves when we presented these. Everyone listened politely, probably trying as hard as I was to find them fascinating, and then Trinh asked if we had *West Side Story* and Kilen and Samreth began singing Khmer Rouge songs. The greatest success was a record known as 'Bo's music' – a recording of medieval music from the court at, of all places, Prague. For some reason, perhaps the drum and cymbals and simple rhythms of these brief, lively pieces caught everyone's fancy

43

and soon we were all dancing with the indefatigable Bo.

As every foreign resident in Italy knows an office of fundamental importance is *L'Ufficio per Stranieri* at the *Questura* (the office for foreigners of the civilian police). It is here that all foreigners wanting to live in Italy must register, within ten days of arrival. If accepted the newcomer is issued with a *Permesso di Soggiorno* valid from one to four years depending on official assessment of the applicant's potential. Until recently many people, including myself, ignored the law but the document has now become a necessity. No bank account can be opened, no automobile purchased, no work permit obtained, no official document signed without exhibiting a *Permesso di Soggiorno*. Armed with as many documents as possible I took Samreth and Sary with me to fill out the forms for the *Soggiorno* and to request the Geneva Convention passports to which they were entitled as stateless persons and political refugees. The Florentine *Questura* in February 1981 was chaotic, but I was perfectly at home there as I had done the paperwork for Trinh and Tuyen, and after several fruitless visits, in true Italian style, I had made a friend. The Dottoressa Giovanna Nocera was slight, very southern, and so nearsighted she held all papers within inches of her pebble-thick lenses, tilting her head in her effort to sneak up on the words. She was intelligent, determined and wished us all well. She ran her department with iron-handed efficiency. I wonder how many frightened refugees (political and economic) owe their relative well-being to the Dottoressa Giovanna. I happened into the *Questura* the day before she retired and there was gloom and confusion everywhere. Her particular responsibilities had been divided into three sections, each section with its own head. The new Dottoresse were all younger, better dressed and in full possession of their faculties, yet they inspired little confidence either in me or in their fellow workers.

When Giovanna had finished the mound of documents for Sary and Samreth, we were ushered into the office of the *Maresciallo*, head of the local police, to be signed up once more. Large, greying and rather handsome, the *Maresciallo* wore his authority with a certain ease. He sat me down in a fake-leather chair in front of his large, empty desk and motioned to Sary and Samreth to take straight-back chairs slightly behind me. Since we had little to say to one another, Dottoressa Giovanna having done all the work, he struck up a conversation about world affairs. His knowledge was limited but not his indignation which was wide and fierce. I am a past master at the exchange of banalities and since the *Maresciallo* needed to pass a certain amount of time before lunch we went at it seriously. At one moment he railed against the Khmer Rouge with such vehemence I turned around to take in Sary and Samreth and let them enjoy his condemnation. I was stunned to see them clutching each other in abject terror. They hadn't understood a word of the conversation and the violence of this powerful man plus the mere mention of the Khmer Rouge had terrified them both. I apologized profusely and the *Maresciallo* patted their hands and hugged Samreth for reassurance. I cursed myself for my insensitivity and ignorance.

Looking at Sary it was difficult to believe what had happened to her. Physically she seemed unmarred: she had the slimness of a girl as well as clear eyes and glowing, golden skin. She walked with out-turned feet in the manner of Oriental women, her back was straight but not stiff and she had the diplomat's gift of well timed silences. She was a beautiful woman which made the sorrow in her eyes more poignant still. She did her best to be jolly but sometimes, when the children were at school, I would find her sitting in the corner of the kitchen in a straight-back chair (she always did this when she was particularly depressed). She seemed to welcome company, so that when I could I sat with her, speaking little. The air was thick with despair, mottled with grief. When she did speak it was always the same: she would look around her in disbelief, shake her head and say, 'Where are they, where are my tall brothers?'

Of the three children, Samreth looked the most like his mother. In a strange way, Samreth's head seemed too substantial and important for his body. It was a wonderful head, the skin pulled tautly over high cheekbones, a nose that was almost aquiline, large sensuous lips and a dreamy far away look in his eyes as though he was searching for a setting star. He had a long, deep dimple on his left cheek and, thank heavens, crooked teeth that marred the perfection. He had enormous, immediate and continuous success with girls – and with their mothers, too.

Kilen was lovely although she did her best to disguise it. She could not hide her smile, her grace and when she spoke, her voice. One always felt she pulled back even when standing still and it took several months before she could accept a compliment without running from the room. She was neat, almost prim, and her clothes were always a size too large. She admired her friends, the girls in her class at school but she never dared to imitate their style. Her timidity slowly lessened, she once embraced me out of genuine feeling and then seeing what she had done pretended to give me a massage to conceal her impulsiveness. After about a year the embraces were no longer tentative and embarrassing to her and she began to hug John with almost the same force. We had always held large, boisterous birthday parties for Simon and Lisa and it was a tradition I wanted to continue with the children. Houssara was delighted with the idea, Samreth accepted graciously but sceptically, Kilen refused. She was still not comfortable being the centre of attention.

Houssara was an immediate success with everyone who

came to the house and at school as well. There were no outward signs of suffering on this sturdy, well-built eight-year-old with the mischievous, practically permanent grin. There is an Italian word *birichino* that describes him well: lively, shrewd, slightly naughty and irresistible. One friend suggested a great future for him organizing the Cambodian Mafia – how very little she understood! His mind never stopped turning over ideas, even at eight or nine. He was unstinting with his affections which he gave with a spontaneity that not everyone understood. Those that did (and still do), treasure the affection, those that misread him have wounded him, sometimes severely. For a child so young he had quite an accurate picture of the strength and weakness of others but not always of his own. His sense of humour was sometimes over-charged. He knew when to stop, instinctively, but was tempted at times to keep on going. He often played practical jokes: the pleasure of deception without serious intent or malice delighted him. He did, however, save his harshest jokes for those in whom he felt a lack of authentic feeling. He once told me that since he knew who he was and what he wanted, he found it odd that this wasn't easily recognizable to others. His ideas and feelings were subject to change but never ungenuine at the time.

One of his earliest attachments (a friendship so deep that most adults preferred to ignore it) was with a girl his age who lived near us. They were in the same class at school and inseparable after school. For two years they saw one another daily, automatically. Then the girl moved away with her parents and went to another school. She cried for weeks before the move and his face was grey with disappointment. They exchanged visits, sometimes sleeping over at each other's house until she suddenly began to bloom as young girls do and outgrew him. Now they are once again friends. I have realized, only recently, that he never considered himself a child, even as an eight-year-old. A friend's four-year-old daughter came to visit last year when Houssara was twenty-one. Her mother had supplied her with distractions to relieve the boredom of adult company. She took out her large colouring book and Houssara was fascinated as he had never seen one before – he had skipped that part of his life.

He was unbelievably generous with his new possessions. We had bought him an electric train, at first just a modest few cars and tracks, then a great friend added on to it a splendid series of bridges, towns, tracks and cars until the set was extraordinary. The whole set was so large we built a waist-high wooden platform with a hole in the middle for Houssara to stand in and control the lot. Another friend bought him a railroad worker's cap for authenticity: Houssara thanked him but refused to wear it – he told me later that it made the whole thing look like a game. It was most impressive. His school friends came to admire it and Houssara demonstrated with great dignity but always gave way to the others and allowed them to become chief engineers. We often went, in those days, to a small, Italian speaking town near the Istrian coast, and we usually took the children with us. Houssara made a friend at once, a boy a year younger named Samuele. They became such friends that Houssara asked if he might give Samuele his train set as Samuele's family now had electricity in their house and they were far too poor ever to buy him such a magnificent gift. On the following trip we arrived with the entire set boxed carefully by Houssara and Samreth (who thought his brother mad). The excitement and pleasure when we drove to Samuele's house was intense – both theirs and ours.

Shortly after their arrival we had a visit from James who wanted to see how Samreth was settling in and to meet the rest of the family. We were joined by James's sister, Elizabeth, a great favourite with them all, especially

Houssara, who admitted, years later, that she had been his first love. James took Samreth to Pisa for the day. They climbed the Leaning Tower, which frightened Samreth – he saw it as the work of a malign force. The trip was, however, a success as it emphasized Samreth's special position as first born and allowed him to feel he had a 'home' to return to after an exciting day out. Then Elizabeth had an inspired idea. She and James took the entire family on the train to Pistoia (a half-hour train ride, but their first) and a visit to the zoo with lunch, Houssara told me, at the 'best' restaurant he had ever been to. (It was also his first!)

Not all 'treats' were so successful. Lisa, who lives close by, and a friend, decided to take all three children camping at the sea. Elaborate preparations were made, a luxurious tent was bought together with the latest cooking equipment, a new roof-rack was put on the car with a great deal of difficulty. Everyone but Houssara hated the trip. The idea that sleeping in a tent could be fun never entered their minds. Kilen refused to go into the sun as she didn't want to get darker and sat huddled in the tent the entire time while Samreth built complicated figures in the sand. Houssara and Lisa were the only ones in the water. The new cooking equipment was not even unwrapped: the only thing they enjoyed was the pizzeria and trattoria food at night – the picnic during the day was too reminiscent of past meals in the paddy. They cut the 'vacation' short and Lisa said they only began to laugh and chatter as they neared home. 'I loved camping at their age' said Lisa, forgetting that she had always lived in a comfortable house. She and her friend said they felt rather like a divorced couple who had undertaken a holiday together for the children's sake – everyone trying to put a brave face on what was obviously not a success. Even pizzas and ice cream and forced jollity could not mask the fact that the whole thing had been a dreary mistake.

I remarked to James, who had spent quite a bit of time in Cambodia and who knew the language, on what seemed to me a lack of maternal attention in Sary, especially towards Houssara, the youngest. He explained that it was the responsibility of the older children in a family to care for and discipline their younger siblings. Having been brought up in a large family herself, Sary realized the importance of each child having a distinct place within the family group. Both Kilen and Samreth were zealous in doing their duty when it came to discipline. Sary told me years later that when a child was born it was handed straight over to the nurse. She had done her part; she had produced the child and its daily care would now be the duty of others. It was clearly tradition and custom, not lack of love. Sary would sometimes gaze at them all with such amazement and scared, swift love that it was painful to watch and I would be forced to look away.

I believe that parents should, whenever possible, explain things to a child – it was something I had always tried to do with my own children. How was I to manage now? The children had to learn, but their mother was present as part of our 'family'. It was a difficult path to tread for everybody, requiring more tact than I would normally use. For the first weeks at least language would be an insurmountable obstacle, and then there were cultural differences to tackle as well. And yet there had to be some rules. Kilen gave me an early opportunity to explain, wordlessly and, I hope, painlessly. The issue was unimportant, a can of dogfood that she felt was too good for an animal and which she proceeded to eat to show me. There were lessons to be had for both of us. I learned that children can be satisfied with an explanation that they can't possibly understand and that a firm 'no' means just that, even though it seems to make no sense at all. At the very least the child learns that what he wants to know is difficult to understand, which is in itself a kind of self-knowledge. She learned, I found out later, that I could be humoured without enormous effort on her part. I liked being humoured by Kilen and her rare compliments grew to mean a great deal to me. She and I had the most turbulent relationship of all. Only after a while could we pass time together without serious misunderstanding which usually ended in rows or, if we were lucky, laughter. One day there was a confusion about collecting her from a friend's house. I made two trips of several kilometres each as she wasn't at the spot where she was supposed to meet me. When I finally collected her I was cross, very, and gave her a severe talking-to. She put her head down and her shoulders began to shake. 'Now, don't cry,' I said, afraid I had gone too far. 'I'm not, I'm not,' she said and I could see then that she was doubled up with laughter, I looked so funny when I was furious. We were both laughing so hard I had to stop the car. 'You see,' she told me, 'you have become much more mature.' I thanked her and we both agreed that maturity was something hilarious.

On the language front, we arranged for a local secondary school teacher named Roberta to come to the house daily to give Italian lessons to all four. We also tried to teach them as much as we could ourselves. It was an unusual situation as we were teaching them to speak Italian which was not our own first language. Each had his own method of dealing with the new knowledge. An old friend of ours, Luigino Franchetti, himself an accomplished linguist, said Italian was the simplest language to 'speak at', in other words, it is relatively easy to make oneself understood in Italian but it is one of the most difficult languages to speak perfectly. My knowledge of other languages is limited but I do not doubt him. Both of our children speak Italian as a first language and John is almost as perfect. I, alas, have little ear and although fluent, my Italian is far, far from correct. I warned Kilen not to use me as an example but she had already worked out that for herself.

Sary, I was to learn, had lived in government circles and accepted instruction graciously and smiled a great deal. Samreth charmed Roberta and soon became 'teacher's pet'. He was the first to try speaking Italian. Strangely for someone so musical he had little 'ear' for language. Perhaps saying he had little interest is more accurate. For such an emotional boy he was extremely practical about words: he quickly learned the necessary ones and their basic application. Using these, with little concern for sequence and none for grammar, he soon made himself understood. After an impressive start his spoken or written Italian scarcely improved. Within a year or so he began to write poetry in Italian, some of which I still have. His poems consist of unconnected, disturbing images and intensely personal moments that would fascinate any analyst. What got him through school was his extraordinary visual memory as he was able to memorize whole pages from his text books.

Kilen, the only one who had an interest, even a passion, for language, listened intently and her lips moved as she followed everything Roberta said. I heard her afterwards repeating the day's lesson, chirping away in a near perfect imitation of Roberta. Kilen was, like the birds, never off-key, her voice was unmusical only when she was frightened. She was a fantastic mimic, curing me of two behavioural 'tics' of which I had been unaware until I recognized them in her imitations.

Houssara was completely indifferent to the lessons although he sat quietly at Samreth's orders, like a well-behaved puppy. He showed no noticeable progress until John made him a series of cards with Italian words printed on them, which he used to construct airplanes or houses.

When he made an airplane out of a full sentence John felt rewarded. Since he was so young John and I thought he would have very little trouble with the language. We were wrong but for unusual and very personal reasons. From the time he could speak at all he wanted to have what he later called philosophical discussions. Even at ten 'The Meaning of Life' interested him more than soccer. He wanted to talk about those things inside himself, his thoughts and feelings, long before he had a suitable vocabulary. His mind was quick and genuinely curious, his conversations often difficult, if not impossible, to follow. I once asked him the name of a familiar object, I don't remember exactly what but it was something as simple as 'chair' and he didn't know the word for it. When I asked why he said, 'If it's outside of me I can show it to you, can't I?' He nurtured his ideas, clung to them and fought for them the way most children fight for toys. The ideas themselves were often extravagant, even absurd – something he never admitted but must have sensed as he began to discard the more exotic ones.

Our knowledge about Cambodia came from news reports, a book by Norman Lewis, *A Dragon Apparent*, and conversations with James. We were, quite naturally, curious and eager for more information, especially about the children. Samreth would shake his head and mutter 'terrible, terrible' and not much more. I could not bring myself to question Sary. Kilen was silent, too, until the feast of San Giovanni. John the Baptist is the patron saint of Florence and his feast day on 24 June calls for a large and noisy celebration. Although we live in the country it is only thirteen kilometres to the Duomo and sound travels, especially the sound of an elaborate firework display. John was away on business and Lisa and I were sipping wine and chatting in my bedroom at the head of the first flight of stairs when we heard a bloodcurdling shriek. We rushed upstairs to find Kilen in near hysterics and Sary and Samreth sitting on the stairs clutching each other. From this distance the fireworks sounded for all the world like a serious bombardment. Houssara did not wake up at all. When we had explained and calmed everyone down, Kilen began to talk. All the words that had been dammed up inside her came rushing out. It was like Phnom Penh she said. The beginning of all the years of horror were the bombardments. For a few moments she felt she was no longer safe, would never be safe, that the terror was starting all over again. She talked and talked until her tears choked her. She told us of her older sister, Poutherein, who they had lost contact with but hoped was still alive. Samreth folded himself into himself like a lotus blossom at sundown and Sary sat pale and silent throughout. This was somehow the beginning of our sharing, in a very limited way, their experiences.

Samreth, too, began to open up and talk about his past. One day he came home from school in dismay. Some of his friends had asked him about Cambodia and he had told them a few stories. After a bit it was clear to him that, although no one said so, they did not believe him. 'And I did not even tell them the really terrible things,' he said.

Even Sary began to talk about the past. For the most part about her losses, her husband, her children, her parents and her brothers. Sary was the eldest of seven, after her were three beloved brothers. They all perished. The oldest was an engineer and was forced by the Khmer Rouge to supervise the digging of an irrigation canal and was then killed in the wholesale slaughter of the 'intellectuals' that followed. The second had been a supporter of Pol Pot and had secretly supplied him and his troops with money and ammunition. When he learned the truth about Khmer Rouge brutality he starved himself to death. She never learned how the third – she assured me the most beautiful of all – died. In Khao-I-Dang she met his wife's parents who had somehow survived. They told her what little they knew. His name had been called by the Khmer Rouge, together with their daughter and the couple's child. They all three disappeared. A week or so later they saw one of the Khmer Rouge cadres distributing their clothes to some of the workers. They could only assume the worst.

Houssara mentioned only one recurring memory, a ghastly one. He was not quite four years old when a Khmer Rouge soldier held a knife to his throat and demanded to know who his father was. Naturally he was frightened and admitted that his father was a Senator. 'How many wives does your father have?' they asked. 'Only my mother,' said Houssara. 'How many houses?' 'Only one.' The child's 'confession' had led to the harsh treatment their father received at the hands of the Khmer Rouge and, indirectly, to his death. Houssara cut himself off from his past completely, so completely that he could not recall it even when he tried. He was, of course, very young but somehow I don't think that was the only reason. When questioned, he would invent wild, cinematic stories of Marines and helicopters with himself wounded and cared for by beautiful blondes. We soon learned not to question him at all. Strangely he is renowned among his friends in Italy for his extraordinary memory. Whenever these aging twenty-three-year-olds want to remember something from their collective past, they call on Houssara. His memory for things since his arrival here is phenomenal.

As for Cambodia, he could understand the anger and the fear of the others but had no thought of revenge or retribution. He was, in fact, the only one of the children who ever talked about going back to Cambodia. The past was too present and too painful for the others to even think of a return. I found it a blessing that Houssara's mind was free to know or not know. What others knew or thought about him never bothered him as it did the older two. He seemed instinctively to understand that there were certain things that he couldn't help people knowing and as for the rest, he didn't care. Young as he was he had made his choice, probably unconscious at first but later a willed, conscious one.

Kilen tried to show a spirit of forgiveness. 'I know Pol Pot doesn't care if I forgive him but I don't care if he doesn't care,' she said. She seemed to feel that forgiveness would put all the horror behind her. Perhaps in the long run it did help but the nightmares continued with the same intensity. Scarcely a night passed without hearing her screams or moans. Is there a point, I wondered, where forgiveness is of no use? She came to me in tears once saying, 'My heart is closed and I'm still bitter.' Kilen had a larger vocabulary than the boys or her mother but many words and expressions came directly from the dictionary. The move to Italy had jolted Kilen: Sary was too depressed to notice; Samreth too busy; Houssara too young for it to be more than a pleasant surprise. But for Kilen it was traumatic. She would wake up in the morning not realizing where she was, a common occurrence to any new arrival, but not knowing if she herself was real. Was this a dream or was the past horror only a nightmare? The change was so rapid, the difference so enormous that she was bewildered and frightened. The absolute newness of it all seemed to strip her of herself. She would walk through the fields near our house and ask aloud, 'Is this freedom? Is this me?' The more her imagination soared the more she craved reality. In those first months she was enormously attached to food and continually overate: as though the fullness of her stomach, even the belly-aches, gave her concrete proof of her existence.

Samreth, on the other hand, longed for revenge, and the bloodier the better. He and Tuyen became friends, after circling around each other for the first few weeks. Their initial distrust was talked away during long night sessions around the dinner table led by our daughter Lisa who explained things in a vaguely dialectical way – she was a Marxist then, although a wildly unorthodox one. For whatever reasons, and I vote for proximity and general goodness, the barriers came down entirely for both families. Tuyen and Samreth had the most bizarre conversations in a mixture of Chinese, Vietnamese and Italian. Each was an expert in the martial arts and they practised Kung Fu among the olive trees. Samreth, suspended in the air, hands splayed and hair flying was amazing and beautiful in his own way, and to see him climb a gigantic live oak as though it were a coconut palm was a treat. I was less charmed by the dexterity with which Tuyen and Samreth handled the Con, two metal bars joined by a chain used in Asian martial arts. It whistled menacingly in the air as they twirled it around with amazing speed. (Houssara had none of these talents and seemed not at all interested.) This martial phase, intense as it was at first, faded and they no longer seemed to need hatred and dreams of vengeance as a shelter and a bond. I was also pleased to note that Samreth and Tuyen no longer talked, with relish it seemed to me, about all the refinements of torture used on the Vietnamese by the Cambodians and vice versa. These two, the gentlest and most sensitive lads, must have felt a certain cruelty was expected of them, at least in talk. Just when I congratulated myself on beginning to understand their culture I heard them launch into a discussion of something they called 'head tea', one of the most complicated and terrifying forms of torture I had ever heard of. I begged them to stop and of course they did, laughing, and clearly thinking me most peculiar.

We put the children in our local schools as soon as possible.

We knew the system well – Simon, after all, had been through it – and we trusted that it would accommodate the Cambodians without any serious problem. The elementary and middle schools of Bagno a Ripoli have such an excellent reputation that couples with young children settle here just for that reason. Houssara was first, entering the third grade with children of his own age. One of the children's mothers said, as she asked if he could come to play at their house, 'He is much in demand.' Even today, at twenty-three, four of his closest friends are boys he first met in the third grade. He is also very much at home with the parents and families of his friends. The elementary school teachers often found him more of a challenge than they were prepared for. He took his shoes and socks off in class, found it impossible to sit still and once lovingly squeezed the breast of a pretty teacher. Instead of becoming a pariah he became a hero, which says something for the imaginations of eight-year-old schoolboys with an Italian Catholic education. His peers actually understood him and his problems better than the elementary school teachers did. One teacher complained to me that she found it difficult to discipline him because his friends would object whenever she tried. Only in Middle School did he find the kind of teacher who really helped him: the Professoressa Scatena. She was a strict disciplinarian, but a just one, and he loved her. Like most children, he loved justice. He never asked for favours, even as a small child: justice was what he craved, without indulgence or apology. John and I liked to watch him, unobserved, when he was hatching an idea. He had a concentration that astounded us. His forehead narrowed with curiosity or widened with joy when he found the answer. Later, as he grew older, conversations on the telephone with his mates were often conducted in mathematical equations as he tried to help them with their homework.

When Kilen and Samreth entered Middle School they

were placed in classes with children younger than themselves. They were both small and delicately built so that there was none of that hulking, overgrown feeling that older children get with their younger peers. That they were both beautiful helped, especially in Italy where physical beauty is valued highly, even demanded. When I registered them with the police I took a year off Kilen's age as I didn't want her to feel too far behind the others. I didn't have the heart, or the courage, to change Samreth's birth date as we found that he was born on the same day as Simon. That seemed a bond not to be tampered with. I didn't realize at the time that I was doing Kilen a disservice. At Khao-I-Dang the officials had already done the same thing in what they considered her best interests. Instead of twelve, she was fourteen when she came to us. This 'lie' preyed on her mind and she finally confessed her true age in tears years later. I blamed myself, yet again, for ignorance and arrogant meddling in the lives of others.

Samreth was instinctively good with numbers and resolved complicated mathematical problems long before he could understand what the teacher was saying. Shortly after he started school he volunteered to go to the blackboard and when he solved a difficult problem the class broke into wild applause. He possessed both charm and intuition and he never lost either. More important still he never overworked the former or depended entirely on the latter. A rich and elderly homosexual friend of ours took a great fancy to Samreth. He was not frightened by homosexuality itself, as he enjoyed the attentions of other gay friends of ours. The courtly exchange of compliments around our dinner table delighted him and he did his share of playful flirting. But this one friend was different. I took all three children to visit his grand home and gardens, and they were enthralled. However, when Samreth saw the magnificent, though gloomy, dining room with the table set for two and realized he was the only one expected to stay to lunch, he was terri-fied and refused the invitation. He told me later that he was scared of not knowing what to talk about, but I think he was disturbed by the weakness he sensed in the older man.

Samreth had the most extraordinary rapport with animals. It wasn't just that he was born a Buddhist: it was Kilen who, in Cambodia, had been the religious one. Samreth once found a baby owl fallen from its nest. He adopted him and the bird adored him. They became insepa-rable and Samreth wore the owl on his shoulder like a fluffy garment, hand-fed him raw meat, and slept with him until the bird was old enough to fly away. Only then did he admit, rather like a new father, that the bird's nocturnal habits had destroyed his sleep night after night. He managed to bathe our cat, male and half-wild though he was, in the tub and then to dry his fur with a hair dryer; the cat followed him about adoringly even after such a humiliation. He had much the same effect on teenage girls. We live three kilometers up a very steep road and more than one pretty girl bicycled or walked the distance just to see him.

At school Kilen initially had more trouble with her studies than either of the boys. She worked longer hours than her brothers and made considerable progress at home with John and myself. With others she was so terribly shy that when-ever a teacher asked her a question, even her name, she gig-gled uncontrollably and was unable to speak. Her first scholastic year was a disaster and she had to repeat it. I learned later that she was thought to be 'wanting' by one teacher who asked in a faculty meeting that something be done about her. Fortunately, this teacher found herself vehe-mently opposed by all the others. This particular teacher retired after Kilen's first year. The second year she had a teacher, Professoressa Zanobini, who had an adopted Filipino nephew. With patience and understanding she was able to reach Kilen who flowered. Even her dress-sense improved. It was Samreth who understood Italian fashion and style long before Kilen did and some of her earlier 'get-ups' could have caused ridicule from less sensitive peers.

Kilen and Samreth both drew and painted extremely well and their pictures were soon on display at school: that helped, too. Kilen chose French as her foreign language and did well. The students all started out at the same level and her natural ability plus hard work soon took her to the top of the class. Her confidence in her 'public' self grew and at home she terrified Houssara and bossed both her mother and me. In proper Oriental fashion she deferred to Samreth and John. In Cambodia she had been a 'Daddy's girl' and John happily did his best to take Daddy's place. He was delighted with her as a pupil. Once while he was giving her a geography lesson he explained *dolce pendenza* (gentle slope) to her. 'Do you understand?' he asked. She reached over and stroked his expanding tummy and said '*dolce pendenza*'. That became one of our first family jokes: useful and unifying. John only drew the line when she offered to pluck out his beard as she had done for her father. I could not remember when it happened, but soon I could no longer imagine our lives without the Du Caus and the Khuls.

John and I wanted to introduce the children to our own culture as painlessly as possible. The first Easter we concentrated on chocolate eggs and let the rest of the rituals go. Samreth and Kilen decorated lovely hollowed out real eggs the following Easter, some of which I still have. By Christmas we felt that there was enough language and familiarity to do a bit more. The children learned a certain amount about Western culture at school but when Samreth came home one day and wanted to know why everyone laughed when he asked, 'What is a Madonna?' we felt the time had arrived for further instruction. Putting up the creche that first Christmas was a simple beginning. Sary followed the story in her Cambodian translation of the Bible. Moss was gathered, artificial lakes were made, animals were arranged and rearranged, candles were placed in strategic spots. It was a triumph. Then came the tree under the supervision of Simon, home for his school holidays and pleased to share the artistic responsibility. Christmas morning routine is unoriginal and unvarying in our house and I love it. The presents are placed under the tree; John lights a fire in the fireplace; we put carols on the record player; the children pretend to sleep until they are called; Lisa and the Du Caus arrive and then the day begins. Our Christmas is much more about eating, drinking and present-giving than religion but something came across. There had been quite a bit of religious instruction for the residents of the camps as there were missionaries everywhere and everyone had a great deal of time to kill. The missionaries at Khao-I-Dang must have been a sadistic lot though as all Samreth and Houssara could remember from hours of teaching was the Crown of Thorns and the Crucifixion.

John and I have, like most parents, tried to do what we consider the right thing by and for Simon and Lisa. We spent countless hours – John is a theorizer and I am a babbler – discussing how best to help them become independent and responsible. Those hours were as nothing compared to the length of our discussions about the Cambodians. We were frightened, terrified, of not doing the 'right' thing, a fear we hadn't felt before, at least not so strongly.

Love and understanding are seldom, if ever, on the same level, but some recognizable, instinctive reaction to and from one's biological children (I suppose it is DNA or something scientific) makes life less complicated. We did our best to make up for this with the Cambodians with good will on both sides. All three children, in varying degrees, became willing to recognize that there were things they couldn't understand. This, in a strange way, made life not more but less mysterious. Unquestioning acceptance, credulity if you like, can be a terrible weakness in adults but for these children it was an added strength. John and I were aware of their faith in us, and found it unsettling and pleasurable at the same time.

All three had a fierce need for physical contact. I woke up one morning to find Samreth gently stroking my face. Kilen was delighted with the Italian custom of kissing on both cheeks which she practised with the zeal of a convert, shy as she was. And Houssara as a small child was on my lap or John's almost before we sat down. Tradition and culture kept Sary from cuddling her children so they made the most of the strange but comforting Western ways. Having been surrounded and subjected to capricious, unyielding, dangerous behaviour sharpened the children's sensitivity. Such terrifying circumstances made them both more wary, and more foresighted but fortunately for us, not less trusting, when trust was once given. Trust like affection was offered spontaneously and somehow always at the right moment, like a master chef opening the oven door when the soufflé was at its peak.

Each was capable of fierce anger, even rage. Kilen's was directed at herself for what she felt were unpardonable short-comings. Once she forgot a book at school that she needed in order to prepare the following day's lesson and I came upon her sobbing, pulling her own hair and cursing herself in Cambodian. Samreth's rages, which were terrifying but fortunately brief, were against any possible offense or imagined threat to himself or his family. I soon learned to wait until the rage wore itself out. I could no more have stopped it than I could have frozen a waterfall. Houssara grew angry with anyone he suspected of not loving him enough. His flare-ups were often followed by distant and prolonged silences, that dissolved as abruptly as they arrived. As they began to feel safer, all three became more and more in control of their emotions. I remembered all my own irrational and very ordinary childhood fears, but horrifying all the same: the sounds of night, the dark itself, driving past the cemetery, snakes and creeping things of the imagination. If fears independent of experience are real enough to a child, what must the terror born of experience be like? Those stored deep in the memory must surely be the strongest. Houssara still today has a terror of flies anywhere near meat. Not just a normal repulsion but an irrational horror. After my assurances and persuasion Kilen agreed to go for Italian lessons from a sixty-year-old priest in a nearby parish, who had offered to tutor her. She insisted, however, on wearing trousers because of her fear of men. Her sister Poutherein (we had discovered through the Red Cross that she was alive and settled in California), couldn't stop washing her hands she was so worried about germs and for over a year she scrubbed the telephone after each use. It took years of safety to overcome their immediate fears and to allow for a bit of reflection. In some cases they never succeeded.

Our first serious cultural difference came early and unexpectedly. The four Khuls were in the kitchen, John was away and I was in my bedroom at the top of the stairs when I heard a great commotion. I rushed down to find Samreth beating Houssara with the dog's leash and the other two watching passively. Houssara's 'crime', I found out later was that he hadn't been studying enough. I stopped Samreth and did my best to explain that we did things differently. I learned that in Cambodia older children had a 'right', even a duty to beat the younger ones. Samreth never hit his brother again although he was sometimes sorely tempted. Houssara told me years later that he was never afraid of Samreth, but that Kilen terrified him when he was small. I tried to teach them the idea of right and wrong as opposed to good and evil, but for children who had lived under the sign of evil it was not a simple concept. Good, they understood as Buddhists, and God knows they had experience enough of evil. But it was not easy for them to grasp the distinction between these absolutes and an everyday sense of good and bad behaviour, or the fact that a simple, human transgression need not be exorcized or beaten out of the culprit like an act of evil. I don't know if I ever got this concept across completely. I do think I convinced them that the aberration of the Khmer Rouge was an evil of the past and no longer the fourth dimension in their lives. If I could make no promises about life or the future, at least I could promise they were safe from that particular horror.

Kilen was the most articulate, and told me stories of her life in Cambodia that usually ended with us both in tears. She also had the worst, or at least the most discernible, nightmares: I often heard her screams during the night. Houssara never cried. He was seldom distressed but if he was he would curl up on the floor like a wounded animal and sleep, sometimes for hours and hours. Sary hadn't cried, she said, since her little girl of nine died. She had black depressions and told me she longed to cry but couldn't. The strangest thing finally unblocked her. There was a programme on Italian television that the children loved, a rather dreadful adventure series based on a book by Salgari (a turn-of-the-century hack) called 'Sandokan'. It was shot in Malaysia, and like most Italian films, was lovely to look at. The children adored the indomitable hero played by an incredibly handsome Indian actor and persuaded Sary to watch it with them. The setting was so reminiscent of Cambodia – the clothes, the rivers, the trees, and the different plants, all of which she kept pointing out to them with sighs of pleasure – that she began to cry. We all cheered and cheered.

I found myself telling moralising stories to engage the children's imagination. They recognized the underlying truths even without completely understanding the stories. Once after such a tale I said to Kilen 'You see, how things change, you won't always be in this position.' She said, 'I won't be anywhere always.' What the past had done to their imaginations I never really found out. To me it was remarkable that none of them brought away anything of those terrible times except the suffering. What I mean is that since children, all children, learn by imitation, and since language itself, behaviour and habits are all acquired that way, they might easily have picked up something of the viciousness or falseness that surrounded them. Evil is so much easier to imitate than good: war can be imitated easily, peace less so. But despite everything they had seen or known they somehow still hoped, even expected, that good would be done to them. They had an uncritical and touching faith in 'America', the America of their dreams, the America of their father's promises. Their father had spent some time in California as a student and year by year the family myth grew until America became another name for the Great Good Place. When our politically minded daughter, Lisa, finally got Samreth and Kilen to 'boo' an appearance of Kissinger on the television she felt she had really accomplished something. It was not until they actually went to America that their attitudes changed and became more realistic.

Sary had grown up in a static society in which most people lived and died where they were born and where her sense of her own value was determined by birth. She was less disturbed by what the children perceived as social injustice. It was easier for her to accept things as they were, not for any rational or moral reason, but just because they were. I know little about Buddhism but I suspect its teachings had something to do with her resignation and acceptance. Cambodian beliefs seemed to me unique: a mixture of Buddhism, old Hindu rites and folklore. Added to this was the combination of magic and black arts practised by the Chams, the largest indigenous minority in the country. Many Cambodians from Phnom Penh visited the Cham community on the peninsula where the Mekong River meets the inland sea, Tonle Sap. They went to seek predictions for the future, to obtain love-potions or help in eliminating rivals. Even the educated and the most sophisticated Cambodians had a respect for, if not a complete belief in, magic. Even among the Buddhist monks there were fortune-tellers and astrologers. Each regiment of soldiers had its own *Lok Kru* or magician whose spells and potions were supposed to make them invulnerable in battle. Lon Nol's more bizarre actions must have resulted from a magician's prompting: he was a firm believer and there is certainly no rational explanation for some of his behaviour. Sary herself was adept at telling the future (the children consulted her before exams) and interpreting dreams. Sary said that in Buddhist reincarnation the highest stage one could reach, before sainthood, was to become 'an Englishman'.

Each in his own way had been saddened, stunned or strengthened by survival. Sary had lost the most. When she came to Italy she was forty-three and within the last five years most of her family had been destroyed. She repeated this litany of her terrible losses with the constancy and devotion of a woman telling the beads in her Rosary. Sary had been born, privileged, into a world without change and had assumed that the world would continue to hold still so that her children could grow up in it, too. The abrupt, convulsive,

67

upheaval in Cambodia, unforeseen by many people, was yet another incomprehensible burden for her to bear.

Towards the end of April the weather improved and with it Sary's spirits. The children's enthusiasm and obvious happiness was infectious and Sary began to smile more and more often. Not those forced smiles that make the lips look thin and the eyes disappear, but real, relaxed, joyful smiles. She was a beautiful woman and Tuyen, who had become the unofficial head of all Asian refugees in our part of Tuscany, was asked by a fellow Cambodian to arrange an introduction. After the first meeting he made her an offer of marriage. The refugee was a widower and she was not surprised, just not at all interested. She was not ready to re-marry she told me. Furthermore, from his use of language she knew him to be a former member of the Khmer Rouge. The offer was politely but decisively refused.

At first I drove everyone to school but soon the children were ready for the adventure of the school bus. The bright yellow *Scuolabus*, driven by alternating bearded youths, both named Roberto, was a constant in our valley: clocks were set when the high-pitched horn announced its arrival. Since we live far out in the country the children were collected early and had one of the longest bus rides. They made friends easily and were soon familiar with the expressions, phrases, including some stunning swear words, that children everywhere pick up from their peers. They also learned local customs, fads and taste. Some fads they refused: none of them liked Italian pop music or mini-skirts. Samreth disliked the noise in discotheques although he was a Michael Jackson fan early on. His friends accepted these heresies and in many cases followed Samreth's lead.

Preparing for the eight o'clock school bus was no longer the panic it was at first. Routine was a great help in allaying anxiety. I watched with fascination as each child patched together structures that would help meet all these new challenges. Consciously or not, each built a separate identity complete with his own idiosyncrasies. Family jokes are, I realized, very helpful in such situations. The beginning of the day was important. I had tried, and failed, to teach them about the Western idea of breakfast. As a child I had hated breakfast and even now I take only caffe latte, so perhaps I wasn't the best teacher but I don't think the lesson would have worked even with a British cooked breakfast enthusiast. They preferred to eat meat or fish with rice or noodles together with the ubiquitous *Nuc Mam* fish sauce. I stayed out of the kitchen as they ate their morning meal and opened all the windows when they left. Each child had distinct food preferences: Kilen ate everything except strawberries which gave her hives; Samreth loved raw vegetables and steak; Houssara would eat any variety of fish at any time of day. There was never any danger of addiction to cokes or junk food, thank God, and Samreth and Kilen were excellent cooks.

Kilen always sat at the very back of the bus, at first out of shyness and later because it had become her place. The second year she had a group of girls who vied for the seat next to her. We bought Samreth a motorbike for his birthday so he felt independent and much more mature. This was never resented by the other two, after all he was 'first born'. Italian law allows a 50cc motorbike at fourteen, so Houssara knew all he had to do was wait. Not so Kilen who, after a disastrous experiment with a bicycle, had decided against anything with two wheels. Samreth was a natural trendsetter although he could not be called a leader: he was too suspicious of any organization, even his own. His successes with girls continued until he found real love with a fellow student at art school. Then neither he nor she had eyes or time for anyone else. Their romance was well known at school and applauded and encouraged by their fellow students. Also, to my surprise, by the girl's mother.

All three children were generous with their affections and straightforward with their emotions (sometimes too much so). Each child had a willingness to part with anything he was fond of that I found unusual. They grew naturally, never taking more than they needed – like young trees that grow taller and thinner for their share of sunlight.

PART III

From five years of punishment for an offence
    It took America five years to commit
These victim-children have been released on parole.
    They will remember all of it.

Fɪʀsт самЕ тне musicians – eight because the Sous were an important family – then Sary's brothers and her father, then her mother walking alone followed by Sary herself with her four attendants supporting an embroidered canopy over her head, all walking slowly to her new home, the home of her husband. An old Cambodian custom decreed that the bride be secluded for fifteen days before her marriage. The first week she was completely covered with a paste whose basic ingredient was turmeric, to make her skin paler and more beautiful.

Sary's wedding took place when she was eighteen. Her mother, who had married at fifteen, had supervised the match, although the choice was Sary's. Her family was prominent – her father ran the Cambodian postal system, and they were well-off. As Sary was lovely it was not surprising that there were several suitors. She told me, proudly, that she had chosen Sarin Khul (or Khul Sarin as she called him in the Cambodian fashion) for his intelligence and his gentleness. She had never been alone with him before they were married and had only seen him a few times.

The marriage was a success not only for the six children it produced. They had a real companionship, unusual in an Oriental marriage. Sarin was a teacher, journalist and senator. Sary spent a great deal of time with her husband and was interested and well informed about politics, meeting many of the local leaders and foreign diplomats. Sarin taught her how to smoke cigarettes so that she would feel more at ease, he said, with foreign wives. Her political views may have been simplistic – she found it hard to believe that their old friend, Khieu Sampan, who gave his money to the poor and lived a simple austere life, could sanction Khmer Rouge brutality. Sarin had no such illusions: 'You must realize,' he said, 'that Khieu has begun to dress like a cowboy.' Everything was symbolic in Cambodia, then as in the past, and Khieu Sampan's new dress code revealed the shift in his politics.

By all accounts Sarin was a remarkable man: intelligent, honourable and, under the circumstances, patriotic to the point of folly. Many times he could have escaped Cambodia but he felt it his duty to stay in his country and fight the regime in power – first Sihanouk and then the Khmer Rouge. Sarin sought unselfish and impartial justice: he was vehemently and outspokenly opposed to the prevalent corruption. As a journalist he spared no one in his condemnation and as a senator, he spoke out whenever possible. Appalled when he learned that food the Red Cross intended for refugees from the countryside was stolen and sold on the black market, he mobilized family and friends. Even the children were enrolled. When a group of lorries carrying rice, sugar, salt and dried fish arrived, Sarin rode 'shotgun' on the lead lorry and placed friends or relatives on the others to ensure their safe arrival at the destined government enclaves. The children remember one particular day when they were allowed to help in the distribution of food. Sarin and the other men rode up front in the cabs with the drivers while the women and children were bundled in the back with the supplies. No one wanted to ride in the lorry carrying the dried fish but all the others were full. The caravan was noisy and joyous. They went far from Phnom Penh near to an old temple. Journalists and colleagues Sarin had asked to be present gave the day an air of importance as well as festivity.

The children were so proud of the way their father took charge. Young as they were they could not help noticing the respect and admiration of the refugees – this was obviously not his first trip. The women measured out the food and the men distributed it from the back of the lorries. Poutherein, the eldest daughter, even today remembers her feelings of pride mixed with jealousy. Strangers seemed to be witnessing her father's love in a stronger form than she had ever experienced.

She and Samreth, who were less than a year apart in age, had planned on selling the empty food sacks and asked their father's permission. Sarin, the untainted, refused them saying that the sacks must go back to the Red Cross. The children argued that surely an organization as huge and important as the Red Cross had no need for empty sacks while they could sell them for quite a bit of money. Busy as he was, Sarin stopped everything and gave them a lecture on the beginning of corruption. Their anger and disappointment at the time was acute. Now the story is told with pride, an important part of the family legend. Sarin, with his fearless integrity, was the kind of man who might well begin a reform movement or even a revolution and yet be one of its first victims. The impartial, the humane and the unselfish cannot for long be leaders of a violent movement.

Much contemporary Cambodian history is bound up in the person of Norodom Sihanouk, who was crowned king in 1941 and remained in power in one form or another until 1970. In 1955, in an astute political move, he abdicated the throne in favour of his father. That way he could stand for the elections due to take place by the terms of the Geneva Peace Accord. No longer a monarch he now referred to himself as a politician of the people and he scored an overwhelming victory at that year's polls. He then ruled as Prince through his father. He also ruled as Prime Minister and

Chief of State. Not content with that he was also a film director, magazine editor, saxophone-playing jazz-band leader and ran the country's lucrative gambling concession. After his electoral victory Sihanouk became more and more autocratic but he never succeeded in uniting his country. In his memoirs, *My War with the CIA*, he says that he did not think it necessary for Cambodia to imitate Western-style democracy with its multi-party system. He reserved his strongest criticism for the educated middle class, describing them as 'Neither Prince nor People'. Understandably the intellectuals drifted away from Phnom Penh, the more conservative members to join Son Ngoc Than's Khmer Serei, those of the left to join the Communist underground.

Sihanouk encouraged American aid to his country in the late fifties and early sixties. However, when he began to suspect that many of his ministers and generals were becoming dependent on American help and, even worse, absorbing American ideas, he began to reconsider his position. He was undoubtedly angered at the South Vietnamese raids into Cambodian territory that began in 1958 and enraged when he learned that weapons supplied by American aid could not be used to oppose the invaders. American aid, he was told, was for the purpose of repelling Communist aggression only. Meanwhile border disputes continued with the United States supporting its clients, Saigon and Bangkok. A South Vietnamese incursion into Stung Treng Province (in the Northeast near both Laos and Vietnam) in 1958 brought a vigorous protest from Cambodia to the International Control Commission but nothing was done and border violations continued. It was not until 1965 that the ICC published a report accusing South Vietnam of hundreds of violations of Cambodian territory in 1964 and 1965. The Commission concluded that not a single raid was provoked by Cambodia.

As well as his desire to maintain Cambodian neutrality, Sihanouk had a respect and admiration for the Vietnamese who were fighting 'American aggression'. He was the only head of state to attend Ho Chi Minh's funeral in Hanoi in 1969. Sihanouk had reason to suspect that American policy was to encourage raids by both Thais and South Vietnamese, thus putting pressure on him to request American intervention in Cambodia. He reacted, totally in character, in quite the opposite way: he began to forge ties with Peking. The assassination of President Diem of South Vietnam in 1963 must have come as a shock to Sihanouk. Shortly afterwards he began an uncharacteristic program of nationalisation and economic reform, swinging sharply to the left. He became convinced that Hanoi was winning the war in Vietnam and moved in accordance. Then in 1963 he took a dramatic and daring step by rejecting the American Aid program that had been in effect since 1955 and demanding that all aid missions be closed and all Embassy personnel sent home. He gave as his official reason the United States' support of his old enemy Son Ngoc Than. His rejection of American aid was not universally approved in Phnom Penh. Some American officials sensed this and made contact with the then Minister of Defense and Chief of Police, Lon Nol. When the head of the American military mission paid his farewell visit to the ministry, he was assured by Lon Nol of his friendship, and the support of the troops under his direct command. This information was relayed to Washington. The White House did not ignore Lon Nol's offer: it was accepted, and eventually acted upon with dire results.

The definitive break between Cambodia, in the person of Sihanouk, and the United States did not come until May of 1965, following closely upon the landing of the American Marines in South Vietnam. Even before this Sihanouk had allowed the North Vietnamese forces to use the bordering zones between Cambodia and South Vietnam as military bases. This, in turn, led to more extensive border raids carried out by South Vietnamese and Americans into Cambodian territory. Shortly after the inauguration of Richard Nixon as president secret bombing missions were begun by the United States. The targets were the North Vietnamese bases within Cambodian territory but it was inevitable that Cambodian civilians, mostly peasants, were also killed. Cambodian peasants, unlike their Vietnamese neighbours, were not accustomed to bombing. To isolated, semi-literate, superstitious people these raids must have seemed like works of black magic; nothing human could possibly effect such destruction.

Imperious as only an hereditary Southeast Asian king could be, Sihanouk was a brilliant, if unscrupulous, politician. He shrewdly played Chinese, American and Soviet interests against each other. In public statements he maintained that he never wanted Cambodia to become a Communist country and sent his troops against the Khmer Rouge even as he was moving closer and closer to Hanoi. He had in the past, when expedient, worked with French colonial rulers and with Japanese conquerors. He was surrounded by sycophants whom he lavishly rewarded when he was pleased. He accepted little advice, absolutely no criticism and often indulged in temper tantrums. His face was round, boyish and unlined; his voice squeaky and excited; his charm, like his volatility, undeniable (he was known to the popular American press as 'Snooky'). To his credit he tried to maintain Cambodia's neutrality and to oppose, by any means, the extension of war in Southeast Asia. American concern with Sihanouk's neutrality grew as American involvement in Vietnam increased. His largely successful policy of 'extreme neutrality' was never accepted in powerful circles within Cambodia and Washington. Opposition to this policy eventually brought about his downfall.

Sarin Khul was opposed to the corruption of Sihanouk's court. He was a follower of Son Ngoc Than and very pro-American. Relatively little has been written about Son Ngoc Than, but he was an important figure in Cambodia during the struggle against French colonialism in the thirties and forties. He was the first modern intellectual proponent of Khmer nationalism, began the first Khmer language newspaper and was a leader in the effort to modernize Cambodia and turn it into a democracy. Than was called 'the father of the Cambodian independence movement' by many. Sihanouk however always referred to him as a 'traitor'. It is true that he collaborated with the Japanese during World War II (he was Prime Minister under a Japanese-sponsored government in 1945) and is reported to have collaborated with the CIA from 1958 to 1970. The former in the hopes of freeing Cambodia from French domination, the latter in ridding the country of the Monarchy's absolute rule. Than's movement attracted many of the educated middle-class who were inspired by his opposition to corruption, colonialism and absolute monarchy.

Sihanouk considered Son Ngoc Than a Communist and sneered at his followers as 'intellectuals'. Son Ngoc Than's movement was undercut when Cambodia obtained its independence from France in 1953. The fledgling Cambodian Communist Party was also decimated. At the Geneva Peace Conference in 1954 Cambodia's neutrality was recognized and both Hanoi and Peking agreed that the minuscule force of Cambodian Communists (later to be called the Khmer Rouge) be disbanded and its members sent to Hanoi. 'Proletarian solidarity' was not a serious concern to the negotiators of the treaty. A few Cambodian Communists remained in the jungle where they had been operating but several thousand were sent to Hanoi. Those who remained in the jungle, and those who came to join them later, considered this a betrayal, a betrayal that was neither forgotten nor forgiven. Even the official date of the founding of the Party was changed. Formerly the date had been 1951 when the Lao Dong (Workers') Party was formed in Vietnam, now it was decreed that 1960 was the actual date of the birth of the Khmer Rouge. The Party's leaders and their followers sought to distance themselves from any Vietnamese influence. In 1963 a small group, led by Saloth Sar, as Pol Pot was still called then, went underground in the jungle and there they lived until their final victory. They left behind them a reputation for honesty and anti-corruption. It was they who formed the leadership of the Khmer Rouge, bound together by blood and marital ties and the French education that most of them had received. In 1967 Sihanouk's forces crushed a left-wing revolt in the province of Battambang. Some of the surviving leaders fled to the bush to join those already there, among them Khieu Sampan, Hu Nim and Hou Youn, all of whom had held important positions in Sihanouk's government. Power remained in the hands of Pol Pot and the men and women of 1963 and with the exception of Khieu Sampan, the others had little influence or were eliminated.

Sihanouk, denouncing the super-powers America and the Soviet Union as 'depraved', collaborated with the North Vietnamese. In 1963 he allowed them to establish base camps along Cambodia's border with South Vietnam and to ship supplies through the port of Sihanoukville. It was Sihanouk's policy to play off the rival factions within the country in the same way that he encouraged foreign influences to compete for his favour. However, his sagacity and maneuvering were not enough to protect his country. Opposing forces were too strong and he failed. His power was based upon an almost mystical communion with the Cambodian peasants to whom he was a semi-divinity, and whose support and affection he never lost. Typically, he used this attachment to his own advantage. When making an unpopular decision he placed the blame on the indignation of the peasants whose wishes, he claimed, were sacred. Because Cambodia remained essentially a feudal kingdom he was, however, unable to subdue the warlords, local chiefs and rich landowners who held power in various parts of the land.

In spite of his capricious and erratic behaviour Sihanouk was constant on one important issue: opposition to America's attempt to bring Cambodia further into the war in Southeast Asia. In spite of outside pressure he refused (in 1956) to join the American-sponsored Southeast Asia Treaty Organization (SEATO). This brought him into conflict with Lon Nol and Prince Sirik Matak, as representatives of the officer corps and the political and business elite. The White House backed Lon Nol, and the coup which deposed Sihanouk took place in 1970 while Sihanouk himself was out of the country. He learned of the coup as he was being taken to the airport in Moscow for a flight to Peking. On arrival in China he was met by Chou En-lai and accorded the honours of a head of state. Within a few days Sihanouk announced that he had formed a National Front of Kampuchea together with the Khmer Rouge to fight Lon Nol. He received pledges of support from the Viet Cong, the North Vietnamese, the Pathet Lao and eventually, the Chinese. Sihanouk did not return to his country for three years.

In April that year the border raids gave way to a full-scale invasion by South Vietnamese and American forces – an invasion not sanctioned by the United States Congress, unknown to most Americans and disastrous for all concerned. The struggle between President Nixon and Congress increased. The American Congress had a proviso in every military appropriation bill that prohibited bombing Cambodia except to protect Americans in Vietnam. By 1973 there were no longer any Americans left there but the bombing did not stop. The White House continued to abuse its power and gave as justification the need to eliminate North Vietnamese troops who were poised to conquer South Vietnam. Not until late in 1973 was Congress able to withhold funds and stop the bombing of Cambodia.

The coup that brought Lon Nol to power vastly increased corruption. Graft was nothing new in Cambodia but with the advent of American military aid it became monumental. Some Embassy officials in Phnom Penh urged America to pressure Lon Nol to end, or at least, curb the corruption but the White House paid no attention. Lon Nol became more and more dictatorial, taking counsel only from the White House or his 'spiritual advisers'. At one point he arrested his closest and most important collaborator, Prince Sirik Matak, who had dared criticize the government. In an interview to the *New York Times* Sirik Matak warned America that the Lon Nol regime could not last and that if nothing was done Cambodia would fall to the Communists. He, too, was ignored. One American Embassy official said Lon Nol seemed to have been chosen only for his incompetence. All through 1974, the American Ambassador, John Gunther Dean, urged Kissinger to negotiate a 'controlled solution'. This would mean removing Lon Nol from power, requesting the return of Sihanouk, and arranging a truce with the Khmer Rouge. The White House, once again, refused to listen until it was too late. Sihanouk's insistence on Cambodian neutrality was one of the excuses given for his overthrow and replacement by Lon Nol. That and what was known as 'The Nixon Doctrine in its purest form.' Senator George McGovern, an outspoken critic of the war in Indo-China, put it bluntly when he was quoted by U.P.I. in 1971 – the

Nixon Doctrine meant 'We pay them for killing each other.'

Before the Khmer Rouge victory Cambodia became a dangerous place for Sarin. He made enemies among important members of Sihanouk's government. Sarin's good friend, the Japanese Ambassador, offered to take the two older girls (Kilen and Poutherein) to Tokyo for safety but he refused to separate the family. It was a decision he came to regret and later when the misery was greater, he admitted that separation would have been a better choice. I thought about Anne Frank and how the desire for unity destroyed that family, too. Sarin determined to teach his family how to survive in the country. He had been born in Kompong Thom in the centre of Cambodia, north of the great inland sea, Tonle Sap. Kompong Thom was also the birthplace of Pol Pot and Deuch, the head of the notorious death camp, Tuol Sleng. Sarin understood the 'other' Cambodia, the land that was not part of the fertile, rice-growing, Buddhist-loving section along the Mekong River and Tonle Sap. One of the most primitive 'other' regions, the land of the Kuy, a wild and forested area, lay merely a few kilometers north of Kompong Thom. He insisted on lessons in survival: what edible foods could be found in the woods; the use of natural herbal remedies, the boiling of certain flowers as a cure for sunstroke, grasses that could be used as poultices to draw out infection, the bark of a tree that when boiled produced a liquid that could reduce swelling. He taught Samreth how to fish and Samreth's fondest and deepest memories of his father are the days they spent together on the river. This was the first theme Samreth wrote about in Italian and he was furious when the teacher considered it not a serious subject for an essay. Kilen loved quoting her father, her first efforts in Italian were towards interpreting his words. She kept repeating one of his favorite phrases, 'If you die today, you don't have to die tomorrow.' This seemed to her a great comfort.

Samreth had a more complex memory of his father. The mixture of pride and anger with which Samreth spoke of him was in marked contrast with Kilen's worship or Houssara's ignorance (he scarcely knew his father). Sary's first pregnancy had ended in miscarriage and Samreth (her second) was born at seven months, shortly after the death of Sarin's father. The night of Sarin's father's death Sary had dreamed of seven stars and seven bolts of golden cloth. According to Buddhist belief Samreth was the reincarnation of his paternal grandfather and there was no question in Sary's mind that this was the case.

Houssara was born in July of 1972 when the American bombardment of Cambodia had been in operation for over two years. Fortunately for Sary it was an uncomplicated birth. The North Vietnamese bases had been damaged but not destroyed and they were moved farther and farther into the interior of Cambodia. As a result the range of the bombing was notably increased, resulting in more and more civilian casualties. Refugees from the countryside were streaming into the bloated, decaying city of Phnom Penh. They were trying to escape death from the blanket bombings which were destroying large sections of rural Cambodia. The wounded staggered into the city, often dragging the broken bodies of their comrades, in the vain hope of help. The hospitals were no better than medieval pesthouses with three or four patients to a bed or lying, with their wounds untreated, on the filthy floor. Treatment, when available, was rudimentary and often brutal: there was no anaesthetic left in any hospital, and the few available medicines were to be found only on the black market at highly inflated prices, where gold was the only accepted exchange.

Conditions in the Khul household were less horrifying but life must have been incredibly difficult for them all, especially Sary. Sarin was busy helping the refugees and she was left in charge of the household consisting of her parents, her two younger sisters and six children, aged from a recently born infant to a boy of eleven. Sarin would drive every day to the edge of town where broken down buses brought a pitiful tide of refugees from the countryside. There he would collect families laden with what possessions they were able to salvage and drive them to the city, several miles away. If they were fortunate and had relatives he would see them settled. In most cases the new arrivals had no place to go and Sarin took them to the overcrowded government enclaves and found them a place there. On an average day he would settle seven or eight families that way. It was, he said, only a gesture, a sign that these wretched people were not totally forgotten: to the refugees it must certainly have seemed much more. Sarin's integrity (or foolhardiness) was severely tested by circumstances. One refugee family, hearing of his efforts, came to the house in tears. They had, they told him, lost everything in the bombing and were now living in a government enclave. There they had planted vegetables and built a shack to make a temporary home for their seven children. They had just learned that they were to be turned out as the land was being leased to the Americans: once again they had nowhere to go. The profit, and it would surely be enormous, from the lease was going directly to the Commander in Chief of the Cambodian army. Since the country was under martial law there seemed no recourse. Sarin's sense of justice and duty obliged him to act no matter what dangers were involved. He took his camera and with Sary driving the car, circled about the land carefully photographing the plight of the refugees with a special emphasis on the food plots. Then, bolder and more imprudent than ever, he went to the American Embassy. There he found a sympathetic and evidently important member of staff. 'You are here to help Cambodia, are you not?' asked Sarin. The Embassy official assured him that was certainly his personal intention as well as government policy. Sarin told him the story of the refugees and showed the photographs he had taken. The official was surprised – by his ignorance or his innocence – he had believed the land to be often flooded and unused swamp land. The result was that the deal was called off and the refugees were no longer forced to move. Sarin had requested that his name not be mentioned, but that was evidently asking too much. The story was all over Phnom Penh within a few days and Sarin had made another powerful enemy.

The years that followed 1972 were even more destructive. The massive American–South Vietnamese bombardment intended to destroy the Khmer Rouge only strengthened their resolve and made them more unyielding, more extreme. Peasant boys and girls, slimy and cold and huddled in hastily dug, muddy trenches were pounded day and night by the most powerful and sophisticated weapons. Fatal casualties in some units were as high as fifty per cent. Almost miraculously they edged forward: an under-equipped, brutalized force many of whom were still in their teens. They somehow pushed on to the capital commanded, urged and driven by a handful of jungle-hardened leaders. They laid siege to Phnom Penh itself, first blocking the Mekong so that no supplies could get through. Food became scarce, medical supplies exhausted, but the city was saved from famine by an American airlift of food. The city avoided capitulation in 1973 and 1974 only thanks to the arrival of the rainy season, and possibly the Khmer Rouge's lack of ammunition.

The final assault of the Khmer Rouge began on January 1, 1975, the onset of the dry season. The circle around the city tightened and by March they were within one mile of the Pochentong airport. The airlift of food and ammunition was suspended. On 12 April John Gunther Dean, the American Ambassador, announced the evacuation of all American officials. He offered places on the waiting helicopters to members of the Cambodian government or politicians who wished to join him. Unlike Vietnam the retreat was orderly, 82 Americans, 159 Cambodians and 35 other nationals left without incident. Astonishingly few Cambodians accepted his offer. Matak (Sihanouk's cousin and one-time ally of Lon Nol) decided to stay behind although his name was high on the Khmer Rouge's death list. He made his way, together with about eight hundred foreigners and over six hundred Cambodians, to the French embassy which was the only Embassy still open. The conquerors refused to recognize extra-territorial status or diplomatic privilege and demanded that all Cambodians within the Embassy be surrendered immediately. Failure to do so would ensure that all foreigners would be subject to summary 'justice'. The French officials had no choice. Khmer Rouge vengeance when it came was swift and terrible.

Despite the blow of American abandonment, the government soldiers kept on fighting. They fought without their officers, without ammunition, without food and without hope. The government finally surrendered on 15 April and 17 April saw the triumphal entry of the Khmer Rouge into Phnom Penh. Most people thought the war was over. That first day there was dancing and celebration.

Early on the morning of 15 April during the Cambodian New Year the Khul family heard shouting in the streets. Samreth went out on his bicycle and came home to report a white flag flying over the barracks nearby. 'Turn on the radio,' said Sary. There they heard that the government of Lon Nol (who was himself safely out of the country) was to surrender and people were told to hang out white flags. Then there was a call for all military and civilian physicians and surgeons as well as all medical students to report at once to the medical reception centre at Borei Keila (Olympic) Stadium. The family had two close friends who were doctors. They learned later that one reported, one did not. Neither survived. This announcement was followed by the regular Buddhist prayers – that day they lasted longer than usual – and then by martial music. Afterwards the radio went dead. Soon the house was filled with aunts, uncles, cousins and close friends. The children were surprised when they were sent away so that there could be a meeting of the adults and some of the excitement began to wear off. Sary's uncle, Khy Tang Lim, an important minister, was troubled; no one knew what to expect.

When the Khmer Rouge marched into Phnom Penh on the morning of April 17, 1975, people lined the streets to welcome them. They were so young, these soldiers, so ragged, so gaunt, not at all Samreth's idea of conquerors. The cheers were genuine, people believed the war was over at last. Sary and her family were no exception. Only Sarin was apprehensive when he heard of the approaching army. He left home at four in the morning to help some friends from parliament (whose names were on the Khmer Rouge death list) make their way to a safe hiding place. Because of his liberal record and published opposition to Sihanouk and Lon Nol, he believed that neither he nor his family would be in any immediate danger. Agents of Sihanouk had tried to kill him after he had written a scathing attack in the *Courier Phnompenois* against government corruption. He accused, with proof, some of Lon Nol's officers of stealing the pay of the soldiers under their command. The article had caused a sensation and surely made its way to the Khmer Rouge hideaway in the jungle. His instructions to Sary, however, showed a lingering doubt. He told her that at the first signs of trouble she was to take her parents and the children to

Kompong Thom and he would rejoin them there. 'What signs, what trouble?' she wanted to know.

'If they have been too long in the bush, you'll know,' he said. He took off his eyeglasses, buried his books and papers, put on short trousers and left before dawn promising to be back in a few hours.

The family had no chance to act on Sarin's instructions. Almost at once the young, unsmiling victors put into practice their own fearful plan. First they ordered the evacuation of the hospitals. Shivering with fever, bloated by disease, maimed by bombardments, patients were forced out of hospitals all over the city. Cripples led the blind, parents carried their children in plastic bags, those who had strength pushed the beds of the dying. Then attention was turned to the Hotel Phnom where the Red Cross had tried to establish a neutral zone. It too was emptied of workers and wounded alike. The next day Khmer Rouge soldiers went from house to house to evacuate the residents and to send them, if possible, back to the towns of their birth. Khmer Rouge troops converged on the city from different sections of the country and there seemed to be no clear chain of command. The soldiers who controlled the centre section of the city where the Khul family lived came from the Southwest part of the country. These troops were the most disciplined but also the most radical and fierce. The Khul family was told that the move was necessary to save their lives since the Americans were preparing a mammoth bombardment. The Khmer Rouge soldiers posed as saviours in this part of the city. They also said that the move was for only three days or at most a week until all dangers had passed.

Sary, her parents, children and sisters were sent to the village where Sary's mother had been born. Sary's mother at first refused to leave but was finally persuaded to do so. Her eventual death from malnutrition and overwork weighed heavily on Sary's conscience. There was, however, no alternative but to insist that she accompany them. The old and the sick who were left behind perished without exception, and perished alone. Samreth brought out his bicycle and loaded it with food. He was teased by the others for always thinking of his stomach but when they found there was no food along the road they were all grateful to him. Sary, her two younger sisters and the older children loaded her brother's car with valuables, clothes and three fifty-pound sacks of rice – Sarin had taken the family car the morning before. Then they all pushed the car. The car was full of petrol – Sarin had prepared for the worst – but it was impossible to drive. Over a million (some estimates claim that there were as many as two-and-a-half million people involved), inhabitants of Phnom Penh swarmed out of their homes, their hospitals, huts and enclaves at the same time. The Khmer Rouge allowed only one exit from the city. The streets were clogged with people, many of whom had brought their animals with them, all struggling hopelessly to move forward – a stampede in slow motion. It was easy to get lost, some children were tied to their parents. People who fell or staggered were left where they fell and even trampled on. When the evacuees asked where they were to find food and medicine they heard the *Angka* would provide.

The *Angka* (Organization) or *Angka Loeu* (Supreme Organization) had taken over their lives. Orders from the *Angka* conveyed through the fierce young soldiers must be obeyed immediately and without complaint. The old Cambodia was finished. Year zero of Democratic Kampuchea had begun. Although it was only a short distance conditions on the road were so chaotic it took them weeks to arrive. They crept along always guarded and commanded by boys and girls dressed in black with red scarves, carrying Kalashnikovs. Shots were fired from time to time to keep the crowd moving or just to frighten them. They were driven like cattle. Samreth who, like most boys of his age, was fond of Westerns thought that the guards modeled themselves on cowboys. People and animals dragged along, slept, ate and relieved themselves on the road. The elderly, the sick and the very young died there, too, and the bodies were left by the roadside for the Khmer Rouge to collect. The city was divided and some evacuations were harsher than others; often people had only ten minutes to collect their possessions and move out. The real purpose (there were no American bombs) was twofold; to empty the hated city of those who had prospered while they, the new rulers, lived like animals in the jungle; and to make it easier to check on people's backgrounds in the towns where they, or their parents, were born. Another factor was the small number of Khmer Rouge forces. The estimated size in the entire country was sixty to seventy thousand men and women, many untrained and still in their teens. A force that small would have great difficulty controlling a city of well over one million inhabitants, which together with the government enclaves brought the total population to around three million. The family was told that they were to be sent to the village where Sarin's great-grandmother was born. The Khmer Rouge program was to eliminate or make agricultural labourers of all the 'soft city folk', as they were called. Only that way could the perfect new society begin in earnest.

When the evacuees arrived in their designated part of the country they were called 'New People' to distinguish them from the peasants or 'Old People' who had always lived in the zone. During the evacuation Samreth was a great help: he was small and agile, swift and unafraid. Once, when the grandmother complained of thirst he waited until their guards weren't looking, jumped over a fence and shinned up a coconut palm. From that vantage point he saw a terrible sight not visible from the road. There were two old men, one lying, one barely sitting by another tree: they had obviously been abandoned. The stronger of the two lifted a hand to signal to Samreth, the second was too far gone even to do that. The family couldn't understand why Samreth was crying as he brought them the precious coconuts.

After two days on the road Sary realized that they were not going to be given any food at all. They were unable to cook their rice as there was neither space nor firewood. They had only gone a short distance so she decided to make her way back to the house and collect some foodstuffs. She saw smoke coming from fires in the city, she heard cries and whimpers from the innocent victims and thought she detected menacing shouts from the conquerors. On her way back to her family Sary learned far worse. As she was struggling along the road she heard an infant's cry coming from an abandoned house. Pushing and shoving her way through the crowd she finally reached the house, which had been a day care centre. The adults in the house had been forcibly evacuated and the babies under their care deserted. No one was allowed to move independently in the city so the mothers of these infants could not come to collect them. It was mercilessly hot, the infants had probably not been fed since the evacuation two days before and those left with any strength were wailing. The babies were naked and piled together in the centre of a large room. Sary said that they looked like so many fish squirming in the heat. She picked up one under each arm hoping to save at least these two. When she got to the road a boy in black threatened her with his AK-47 and made her take them back. She never learned what happened to those babies. There seemed to have been hundreds of them at the time but in thinking it over she says it was more likely ten, or maybe twenty. Whatever the number, their cries, and her helplessness haunted her, haunts her still.

They finally arrived at the town where Sary's mother had been born. Instead of the usual friendly respect, they were greeted by hostile villagers. The Khmer Rouge were very much in charge and the inhabitants were silent and subdued. All the houses in the village were closed to them, so they built themselves a temporary shelter under a tree. Sary's parents were so shattered by the forced move that they were unable to do more than sit speechless by the roadside, each being brave for the other. To them it must have seemed as though the Buddhist prophecy that darkness would descend and evil rule the world had come terrifyingly true. The grandfather's head and hands shook visibly. The grandmother never left his side, although she was never seen to touch him. Sary was now head of the family which at that point consisted of eleven people (her parents, sisters, six children and herself). Upon arrival they were immediately sent to register for work and from there directly to the paddy, even the bewildered grandparents and three-year-old Houssara. The cadres realized there was little to gain from the presence of the grandparents and they were set to carrying water instead of planting or digging ditches. Houssara was presented with a tiny hoe and encouraged to use it. This, they told him, is your proud new life, the future is yours. American oppression is over.

It was here that the now useless car and Samreth's bicycle were taken from them. It was here also that Sarin found them about a month or so later. Sarin's relief and joy at finding the family still alive can be imagined. The family who had almost given up hope of ever seeing him again greeted him with an enthusiasm that belied their dazed and weakened state. They all felt stronger in his presence. Sarin had taken some friends into South Vietnam thinking they would be safe where Son Ngoc Than was. He refused to stay with them. Sary was aghast; 'Why didn't you stay where you were safe?' she wanted to know. He told her he didn't want to live without her and the children.

Conversation was difficult, even the simplest kind. Khmer Rouge spies were everywhere and even the children were monitored. Children were used as informers, encouraged to report any incorrect remarks even from their own parents. Sary impressed on them all the need for secrecy, silence and discretion. When Sarin arrived in the village he was interrogated by the cadres now in charge. The family blessed his foresight in changing his clothes and burying his glasses which were a sure sign of a hated intellectual, but were terrified that one of the villagers would identify him. Either out of fear or gratitude for past kindnesses, no one came forward. During the interrogation Sary fainted, struck her head, and began bleeding. Instead of stopping the proceedings this only intensified the interrogation. No one offered to help her. When one of the cadres asked Sarin why a man in his position wasn't safely out of the country, Sarin answered, 'Since when was a farmer a man of position under Sihanouk?' Sarin seemed completely without fear and soon had his interrogators laughing. He was far too clever for these unschooled soldiers scarcely out of adolescence. It also taught Sary a lesson she was never to forget. No matter how terrified she was, she never again allowed her fear to show in front of any member of the Khmer Rouge.

Sary's mother was the first to die, which was unexpected. She was a vigorous woman, proud and erect and much younger than her husband. The Cambodian equivalent of a tomboy, she had married at fifteen. Her husband and her mother had to forbid her climbing trees during her first pregnancy. She, the ruling matriarch, terrified her sons, Sary's 'tall brothers' and intimidated even her husband. During her middle years the mother became very religious and spent a great deal of time in the Pagoda. She ate sparingly and often fasted as Buddhist ritual required. Sary felt that the scarcity of food would bother her less than the others. Perhaps it did. It was the indignity, I think, more than anything else. The Khmer Rouge soon learned that there was little work to get out of her. They put it down to her age and her white hair. She and her whole generation were expendable and the sooner the better. She did what was required of her, slowly and silently, never raising her eyes to the guards. She never spoke. She used her silence as a weapon rather than a shield. She put aside some of her minuscule portion of rice for her husband who ate it as though under orders. The first satisfaction she showed was at Sarin's arrival. She had been waiting and praying for his return. She made the Buddhist gesture of bowed head and clasped hands and he knelt before her in tears. After a few weeks the grandmother died in her sleep. Sarin went to the 'leader' to report the death and was told that he could bury her after the day's work was over. Little did they know that this was a privilege. A privilege they would long for in the future and one that would not be repeated.

After a few months Sarin, Sary, her father and her two younger sisters as well as the six children were force-marched to a spot between Maung and Battambang in what became the Northwest Zone, fairly close to the border with Thailand. They were finally allowed to stop after what Kilen remembers as at least two months of walking and sleeping by the roadside. Along the way were derelict houses, empty and still, eerily quiet. Occasionally they saw some elderly people too weak or too ill to move who waved to them sadly. Only the very young cried, the others were stunned into silence. No one knew how long they walked: they walked until they were commanded to stop. No one knew which day it was. Each day was like the last, the commands were the same, the rations were the same, the misery was the same. When they finally stopped it was on a piece of land that was little more than a clearing in the jungle. There seemed to be hundreds of people already there living in makeshift shelters. Together with their group they were told they must build themselves a place to live. They arrived after dark and in the rain, only the cadres had shelter, they had none. Sary had wisely brought with her a mat made of plastic instead of the traditional straw. This kept the rain out. That night she and Sarin sat up holding the mat over the heads of the sleeping children. The next day Sarin felled some trees, stripped them for supports and collected palm leaves which Sary and the girls sewed together to make a roof. Sary found a piece of a wall from an abandoned bamboo shelter and dragged it back for their use. Despite all of Sarin's efforts the roof leaked and the wall of palm leaves shook in the wind. When the night rains were strong, they woke up drenched, the dirt floor turned into mud.

By this time their food supplies were exhausted and they were very hungry indeed. Samreth cut his leg which became swollen and badly infected and left him unable to walk. One morning he woke up to find the wound crawling with maggots: he screamed. The maggots, however, in eating away the putrefied flesh may well have prevented gangrene. Sarin went into the woods, found some leaves which he pounded into a thick paste and placed on the wound: it eventually healed. Poutherein had jaundice and was too weak to move. Kilen was the strongest of the children, and was able to help her parents. She went out every day with her father to look for roots or anything edible and she begged rice from the cadres. The place was vile as there was no sanitation, and the rains had churned the earth into a mass of mud and excrement. Diarrhea had afflicted almost everyone and many people were too weak to dig holes for their needs. Hunger drove people to desperate measures. Two young girls in a nearby shelter sat with their mother as she gave birth. When the baby was born they seized the placenta which they roasted and ate. The guards were shocked when they heard this and the two girls were taken away. The guards could afford to be 'shocked', their stomachs were full. The death rate rose alarmingly, and within about six or seven months the settlement had turned into a ghost town. The shelter closest to the Khuls had been filled with a large noisy family but it slowly became quieter and quieter until there was no one left. They never found out what happened to the bodies.

As she saw her siblings starving, Kilen became bold. Aged nine she went far afield to beg. This was against orders as any unauthorized movement was strictly forbidden. She even went as far as the town of Maung where the Khmer Rouge had their headquarters. Sometimes she was lucky and was given some rice and a few half-rotten vegetables from friendly soldiers. 'Please, sir, uncle,' she would say, 'can you give me some rice or some old vegetables?' Often she was chased away with nothing and once was given some roots but threatened with death if she returned. Once when questioned about her father, she lied and said he was a *cyclopousse* (a cycle-taxi driver). 'Your skin is too light' the soldiers said, 'your father must have been more important than a taxi-driver.' They laughed at her, gave her some rice and let her go. It was the small-grained variety that before the war was fed only to the pigs. But they gave her half a sackful and Kilen was grateful. She had to pass near a river that often had corpses in it floating downstream and one day she counted nine. She waded across this river almost every day. The most dangerous spot of all was the train station at Maung as it was always heavily guarded and no one was allowed near it. Kilen often had to pass it and she did so full of fear, looking both ways and praying hard.

The family's need was so great and the excitement when she was successful so joyous that she kept going back for yet one more time. Until one dramatic day. She had asked some soldiers for permission to pick up wild fruit that had fallen from the trees. The permission had been granted but there was no fruit left. She was so worried that she failed to notice that a Khmer Rouge soldier had followed her on his bicycle. He stopped her as she neared a wood. She was with her younger brother, Noi, known in the family as Anut. The soldier promised to show Kilen where oranges grew wild in the woods. Noi was told to keep watch and warn them if anyone approached. She followed the soldier deeper and deeper into the woods. Finally he stopped but she saw no oranges. When he told her to lie down she knew she was in trouble and that something terrible could happen to her. She kicked him hard, screamed and ran away crying. As she reached Noi she called to him to start running, but Noi was so frightened that he was unable to move. Then another soldier who had heard her screams saw her and came over to ask what had happened. After she had sobbed out her story he shook her silent, made her promise not to tell anyone and gave her two Cambodian grapefruit. He grabbed hold of the soldier as he was coming out of the woods and began to beat him around the head. At the first sight of blood, Kilen and Noi began to run and ran all the way back to the family, carefully hugging the precious grapefruit (which Kilen assures me are much larger and sweeter than the Western kind). She told her parents what had happened. She had never seen her father cry before.

Noi became ill. He could no longer eat even the meagre rations that were available and then he was afflicted with diarrhea. The diarrhea increased in force accompanied by severe retching. The others worked all day and into the night while he lay alone in the shelter, sipping the herbal brew his father made for him that in spite of its increased bitterness did not stop the diarrhea. He grew thinner and thinner and his eight-year-old face became that of an old man. He asked to be taken to the hospital. Sary did her best to dissuade him. When he turned to her with bowed head, hands in the attitude of prayer, and said, 'Please, please, I don't want to die, I want to live,' she gave in. For three days they visited him in the hospital after working hours. On the fourth day Kilen was told that he had been transferred to Maung. They were not allowed to go to Maung, and never saw him again. They went on hoping that some news would come through, but after a few months they gave up hope and realized that he must be dead. Like other hospital dead he had probably been buried in a mass grave. They never learned where.

Sarin was ordered to leave the others and go to work on a construction site. He was forbidden to see his family or have any contact with them. He sometimes had news of them from friends or even more occasionally caught sight of one of them working in the fields. By 1975 American bombardments had almost completely destroyed Cambodian agriculture. This in a country where before the war almost ninety per cent of the population was dependent on agriculture. The Khmer Rouge set out to restore it, together with the canals and irrigation system vital to its development. In Cambodia control of the waters was essential as the monsoon, when it arrived, was very strong and lasted for only a short period. The new government demanded that over a million hectares of new fields be irrigated. That meant the construction of canals, dikes and dams. There were few tools and practically no technicians but there was an enormous supply of manpower. The Khmer Rouge took as its model the slave society of ancient Angkor. Under this system agriculture supported the cities and the Temples. The 1959

99

doctoral thesis of Khieu Sampan, one of their leaders, served as the Khmer Rouge Manifesto. In his thesis Khieu argued that the cities were parasitical and that Cambodia's strength and future lay in the development of the countryside. Cambodia, he wrote, should become industrialized but this could only happen if agriculture was developed first. An expanded and enlarged agriculture could in turn support industrialization and make Cambodia completely self-sufficient. This required almost complete mobilization of the country as a labour force. There were no arguments against this policy, no questions and no delay in its enforcement. Work on irrigation projects took place during the winter dry season, between the harvest and the early planting. For the remaining part of the year people worked in the fields and the countryside was covered with labourers – men, women and children. Currency was abolished together with the telephone and the postal system. The temple complex of Angkor Wat became the symbol of the revolution. Pictures of Pol Pot or Communist heroes were not displayed, only photographs or crude drawings of the temples.

Sarin was set to work constructing a dam. Sary volunteered to go into the fields for longer hours than required, hoping to spare her father labour she feared, rightly, would be too much for him. It was the beginning of the rainy season and by sheer good fortune she found a piece of nylon that protected her head as she worked. She was allowed to take her elder daughter, Poutherein, with her. Samreth had been sent to work in another paddy with boys his own age. When Sary first began to work the nylon proved invaluable but when the rains grew stronger and the mud became gummy it was of less use. Walking, even lifting one's foot was a problem, but they kept at it doggedly. Sary was ingenious when the break for midday rice came. She built a small mud fort around herself, put Poutherein on her lap, covered her head with the precious nylon and, miraculously, they slept.

As soon as a child was six family life completely ceased and he was taken to a work camp where he lived with other children his age. There were to be no blood ties in the New World, family names and terms of endearment were outlawed, too. Everyone was addressed as *Mit bong* (comrade), literally comrade older brother. Samreth as the eldest was taken away first. Then Poutherein. She went with her aunts – Sary's sisters – to a women's camp. She was tall for her age and hoped to be allowed to stay as she had heard the food was better and more plentiful than in the children's camps. It was – but the work, digging canals out of land as hard as rock, was backbreaking. Her aunts were strong young women in their twenties, she was not yet twelve. Desperate, she ran away to join her father on the dam construction site. She was caught and sent back to her camp. By this time she was so weak that the only job the 'leader' felt she was capable of was watching and feeding the chickens and ducks (supplying food for the cadres). She lived in the chicken coop and thought herself very fortunate. The only drawback was the chicken fleas: she scratched and scratched knowing she must pay something for this cushy job. She could also eat some of the ducks' food, another bonus. She drew what water there was from a stagnant puddle at the back of the chicken coop, which was also the watering place of the cows who slopped in the mud there. At first she was afraid to drink the water, it was so dirty, but then she realized she would soon die of thirst without it. Once a week they were allowed to go to the river. It took most of the day as it was miles away down a steep canyon. It was a beautiful walk down through fields of wild flowers and lush undergrowth: the walk back was hellish.

Sary had been left behind with the two youngest children and her dying father. One day she almost lost her youngest daughter, Puit. The child saw a small sack of salt lying, unclaimed, on the path near their shelter. It had undoubtedly been dropped by accident and it seemed to belong to no one so the five-year-old girl picked it up to take to her mother. A Khmer Rouge guard saw her, grabbed her by the hair and dragged her into Sary's shelter as the evening meal was being prepared. The soldier announced that this pale, trembling child was a thief: A thief! The grandfather staggered to his feet to protect the girl and screamed abuse at the soldier but Sary was too quick-witted for them all. She pushed her father aside and slapped the little girl's face. 'How dare you?' she said, 'After all the *Angka* has done for you? How could you become a thief when the *Angka* loves you, protects you from the Americans, shame, shame!' She promised she would deal with the child and deal harshly. The soldier went away satisfied. Only then did the shaking child and the grandfather began to sob. Sary comforted them as best she could.

Both Sary and Sarin believed that the grandfather would not last long after his wife's death. They were wrong. Some of the grandmother's strength seemed to pass on to him. This spare, elegant man continued to carry water and do the most humble tasks assigned to him, solemn and dignified as though he was still running the National Post Office. His tremors persisted but did not noticeably increase and he was even able to make the long, painful forced march to the new settlement. When they finally arrived, in the rain, they found one of his old friends who had a small place in his shelter. The friend took him in until Sarin was able to complete the family 'home'. The grandfather was invaluable when Poutherein contracted jaundice and Samreth hurt his leg: telling stories, cheering the children, singing songs and changing dressings on Samreth's wound. Since his work kept him nearer to the shelter than the others, he was Noi's closest companion during his fatal illness. He began to decline when Sarin was sent away, but he kept to his assigned tasks. As each child was taken away he became more and more childlike himself. After the episode with Puit and the salt he was lucid as he told Sary that her quick thinking had saved the child, but he never spoke intelligibly after that. Then Puit was sent to a children's camp and he was alone with Sary and Houssara. One day he collapsed while he was carrying water to the workers in the paddy fields. No one picked up the body (which may or may not have had life left in it) until the day's work was over. By that time he was certainly dead. When Sary heard about it, the body had been taken away with two others, who had died the day before in the neighbouring paddy. Sary heard no more.

A new 'leader' was appointed to Sary's section. She had seen him before and knew immediately she had somehow offended him. She trembled for them all. His name was Chac and he was a square-faced, shrill-voiced man of indeterminate age. He was, however, a firm believer in Khmer Rouge doctrine, which he followed assiduously. He singled Sary out but in order to punish her he must first catch her in error. The easiest way to catch a woman, Sary said, was to appoint her to be a cook for the cadres. Hunger was such that nearly all the cooks at one time or another took a piece of food from the cooking pot: a serious crime. Sary was aware of this and aware of the constant spying. She never took so much as a spoonful of soup, she did no 'wrong doing' and Chac's plan failed. She was soon sent back to the fields.

Later, after the grandfather's death, she heard through friends that a guard had tried to poison Sarin. Sarin suspected what had happened and knew the antidote. He was very ill, so ill that he was allowed to send for Sary. She asked Chac for permission to see her husband one more time. Fortunately, the rules allowed this and after a full day's work she walked the several hours to Sarin's camp arriving just before dawn. She shook the dust from her clothes, smoothed her hair and hid her fears as best she could. Then she went directly to the 'leader'. 'Why?' she demanded, 'do you want to kill my husband? Tell me, comrade, has he done anything wrong, was he not good?' The 'leader' denied all knowledge of the attempt and promised to help them. He did. He allowed Sary and Houssara to come to live in Sarin's camp. It was a brave and generous act. The Khmer Rouge had divided the country into geographical zones, then into regions (*dambans*), then into districts (*srok*) and finally into sub-districts (*khum*). Fortunately Sarin's 'leader' had a *srok* and Chac merely a *khum* so he was overruled.

At that time things had eased a bit and they were given a small piece of land (about ten square metres) that could be cultivated for their own use. They grew some corn. Sarin insisted that they share their produce with the others. When Sary objected that they were too hungry to be so generous, he told her that others were just as hungry and that if they did not help they would soon have no neighbours. After a few months a new 'leader' was appointed and Sary and Houssara were sent away. A year or so later Sary learned that the first (kindly) 'leader' had been executed together with his entire family. They never learned the reason. Within their communes the power of the 'leaders' was absolute – while it lasted. They, too, were subject to the abrupt changes and power struggles within the *Angka*.

Rumours of political upheavals circulated throughout the camps. The only reliable proof of any rumour was the easing, or increasing, of the work load, or a change in the food supply. In August 1975 it was announced that currency was going to be re-introduced. There were continual rumours regarding the struggles within the Khmer Rouge between the so-called moderates from the zone east of the

Mekong against the more radicalized Chinese-orientated cadres from the Southwest. The North and Northwest zones seemed to be in conflict with the rulers in Phnom Penh over the suppression of all personal freedom. A slight improvement in late 1975 and early 1976 was quickly and completely reversed with the ascendancy of Pol Pot over his rivals and the elimination of anyone who questioned his authority. Chances for whatever freedom of choice that might have come with the re-introduction of money vanished. The food supply around Maung, where the family was, grew especially scarce in late 1976 and 1977. Sarin was still working at the dam site. Kilen, 'Daddy's girl' once caught sight of him as she was being marched to her own place of labour. Seeing her father with a beard, a headscarf and a loin cloth was a shock. The girls were singing as they marched (Kilen says they always had to sing when there was anyone around) and she sang extra loud hoping he would recognize her voice. He did not look up and she was afraid to call out to him. Mercifully, she did not know that this was to be her last glimpse of him.

Houssara was only three when the Khmer Rouge came to power so his recollections were far more limited than those of the older children. Khmer Rouge policy was to place children in camps for what was called political education, and was in reality brainwashing, indoctrination and hard labour in the rice paddy or on construction sites. One by one Sary's remaining children were taken away. Houssara, being the youngest (his family name is Pul which means 'the last') was the only child left with her in 1977. They were both starving. Houssara said to his mother, she tells me: 'Ma, the next time the soldiers come around tell them I am six. That way they will take me away and we'll both have more to eat.' He was five. He was taken to the children's camp and Sary found herself alone for the first time in her life. Houssara's bravery and generosity were conquered by loneliness and fright and he came running back to Sary. She was terrified, fully aware of the penalty for breaking 'the rules'. She immediately took him back to 'the leader', emphasizing the child's desire to go to the camp sooner than his actual age permitted, and promising it would not happen again. A few weeks later she found him once again curled up on her floor. This time she was even more frightened. 'He'll kill you' she said and when this seemed to make little difference to an exhausted, battered five-year-old she tried, 'He'll kill me, too'. This had more effect and they managed to sneak him back into camp before he was missed. When he made his third escape, she completely lost control. She began shaking violently, her eyes rolled back in her head until only the whites showed and the terrorized child realized for the first time the enormity of what he had done. Sary fed him her week's supply of rice and the two of them made their way back to the children's camp. The path led along a deep canal and at one point Sary said, 'If you ever run away again they will kill not just you and me but Samreth, Poutherein, Kilen and Puit as well. I don't want to live without my children so I'll throw myself in the canal now. It is far better than seeing my children die.' Houssara fell on his knees in front of her, begged for forgiveness and swore never to run away again. He never did.

By this time a new ruling had set up communal kitchens and no 'private' food was allowed. Anything that could be scavenged or found in the woods had to be carefully hidden. In many camps the punishment for hiding food was stoning, usually to death. This ruling with its baleful punishment intimidated most people but not Samreth. He and one of his friends managed to catch two fish when they were bathing in the river, somehow catching them in their hands. Samreth wanted to keep them alive as long as possible but the danger of discovery was too great. The boys hid their catch in their shirts and the fish stayed cool for the long walk back to camp. Once there the problem was how to hide the precious catch and what to do with it. The traditional methods of preserving fish were out of the question – there was no salt and drying in the sun took too long and was too smelly. They tried edging up to the camp fire and thrust one fish into the embers but it had to be retrieved before it was anywhere near cooked. If the Japanese eat raw fish, why can't we, they decided. Where and how they were to be eaten was the next and perhaps most serious of all their problems. In the camp Samreth was known for his prowess in climbing trees so no one thought it strange when he tried the tallest one around (till then unclimbed) and with a certain effort made it to the very top. He was cheered by some of his fellows who had no idea that he was there to hide his raw and half-cooked fish. The catch was safe and for the next two nights Samreth and his friend (who was on a lower branch) had a tree feast. Never had anything tasted so wonderful! Not everyone in the family however was so fortunate or so enterprising. Poutherein was once reduced to eating raw snails and Sarin to eating raw worms retrieved from a cow pat.

Sarin became ill from overwork and harsh treatment. He was taunted at the site as the 'American' or the 'Great Senator' and given the most arduous and humiliating jobs. He was kicked and beaten if he staggered or fell. He grew weaker and weaker and finally succumbed to high fever and delirium. Eventually he became so ill that he was sent back to Sary. He was ordered to go to the hospital. At first he refused. Despite his pleas, or perhaps because of them, he was taken forcibly to the local hospital. There was no medicine available so Sary boiled a root to make a brew capable, she believed, of bringing down even the highest fever. She took it to the hospital hoping to give it to him. Both she and

Sarin were convinced, and, tragically, they were right, that this hospital was a sort of clearing house where the unwanted died without too much fuss or outside knowledge. She was not permitted entry but an old friend whose services as a doctor were still needed by the Khmer Rouge saw her, took the brew and pleaded with her to leave at once and not come back. The visit did not go unobserved and the next day Sary was sent to work far away, too far to walk to the hospital. She learned through the doctor how Sarin died; his guard had injected air into his veins to economize on bullets. 'He knew his end was near,' said the doctor and sent loving messages to them all. As soon as she heard the news Sary went back to the hospital and asked the 'leader' if she might have his body for proper burial. 'No need' she was told, the *Angka* had taken care of everything for her.

At Khao-I-Dang she met the doctor's daughter who confirmed the story and added that her own father had survived for only a short time afterwards. When Sarin died Sary was surprised at the extent of genuine mourning. Where so many died daily mourning had become a luxury, grief an extra burden. Sarin's kindness had not gone unnoticed. He had drained himself in the service of his fellow victims. Often he had stayed awake at night when it rained filling the earthen water jugs for his neighbours to spare them a trip to the river. Exhausted by a long day's labour most people slept through the night rains and failed to fill their water pots. Sarin did it for them, saving them a long and difficult walk. When he had food he shared it, when children were ill he found herbal medicines for them, when the elderly grew weak he sat with them and cheered them as best he could. His teaching skills were helpful, too. There were several ethnic Chinese who scarcely knew how to speak Khmer. Under the zenophobic Khmer Rouge regime it was a serious offense to utter any words that were not Khmer. Sarin held secret classes for them at night. Several old people came to Sary surreptitiously in tears: weeping for the dead was not permitted in the new order. These elderly people bewailed their lost 'son' as they called Sarin, lamenting that it was he and not they who had died.

Although she was unable to save her parents or her husband, Sary did manage to rescue some of her children. Her courage and quick thinking saved Samreth's life. He had been caught by a Khmer Rouge soldier stealing a piece of fruit. He had been condemned. First of all he was forced to dig his own grave as per the *Angka* custom, then tied to a tree with a bunch of mangoes just out of reach and left to sit in the sun. He was very, very hungry. The soldiers brought his mother to see his disgrace. Instead of weeping and begging to have him released, she sized up the situation at a glance and began to scream: 'If my son is a traitor to the people and steals their food, he should be punished, punish him as you like, I want to see his evil blood flow.' The soldiers were so impressed that after a severe warning to Samreth they let him go. He had been tied up without food or water for over ten hours. Samreth was terrified by his mother's performance believing it to be her true feeling. Their camps were close enough for him to visit her occasionally. After this he did not come near her for over three months. One day Sary saw Samreth running past her shelter and she ran after him and grabbed him. Samreth was terrified, fell to his knees and begged his mother not to hurt him. He was too young to understand what had happened. The loss of his mother was to him more dreadful than any threat of the Khmer Rouge. Sary held the shaking boy tightly as she explained. To ask for kindness or sympathy from the Khmer Rouge, she told him, only made them more brutal, she knew it was useless to plead with them. Samreth understood that she had been pretending in order to save his life and thanked her. They both hugged and cried. Samreth, afterwards, visited his mother whenever it was permitted.

Months later Houssara became very ill. He was taken from his camp to the hospital where Sary went to visit him. He had been placed in the ward with the dying. He was hemorrhaging internally and blood dripped continually from his rectum. Knowing hospital conditions and seeing that Houssara had already been placed with the dying, Sary went to her group 'leader'. She told him her youngest son was dying and asked that she be allowed to take him into her shelter. She explained calmly that no extra ration of rice would be necessary and that she would gather leaves and roots in the woods to make medicines for the child. The 'leader' looked at her carefully and asked, 'Are you a doctor?' 'I am not a doctor,' she told him, 'I am a mother and I know that my son's case is hopeless.' She went on to say 'If the *Angka* does not want me to bring my son back to die, well that is alright, too, but I feel I must try.' She asked him if he would be willing to let his own child die in the hands of the *Angka*, and that if he could, so could she. He said certainly he would be willing. The reply unnerved her, but not for long. She rose to her feet and burst into laughter that gradually became hysterical. When the 'leader' wanted to know why she was laughing she told him she was content, even happy, as she had done all she could for her son and she need feel no guilt. The *Angka* had decreed that her son should be left to die in the hospital, so be it. She never found out exactly what it was that made the 'leader' change his mind, but she was given the permission she craved. She went to the hospital, put the emaciated, bleeding body of Houssara in a piece of cloth and carried him 'home'. Every day from then on, before she left for the fields, she filled an iron cooking pot with sand covered with water and placed this on the child's stomach to cool it. After about five days the bleeding stopped. Houssara was a survivor by vocation. After the bleeding stopped, little by little Houssara began to grow stronger. Soon he was strong enough to be taken back to his camp where he stayed until the Vietnamese arrived some six or seven months later.

Khmer Rouge policy to separate families and place all children in camps according to their age and sex was to create the new people, the pure, the perfect people, the true sons and daughters of the Khmer Rouge, free from any outside influence. There was an almost mystical belief in the possibility of perfection, with an elaborate set of rules to be followed. These rules seemed to possess a horrible clarity unhampered by judgment or experience. When the regime's unrealizable economic goals failed to materialize its leaders claimed the rules had not been observed and enemies within were blamed. Violence and terror were institutionalized to protect the revolution and to lead the way to perfection. Absolute loyalty to the new government was demanded. Most revolutions recruit among the young: there is a strong appeal, the promise of the future, the excitement. The Khmer Rouge went further, they used the young as a basis for their revolution. Children were encouraged to spy on one another and on their parents. Some soldiers had run away from home at twelve years old: the Party became their family. No one received a formal education, they were indoctrinated, trained to obey rather like a prized animal. On command they ran, clear-eyed, into battle. Complete domination over the country gave the Khmer Rouge the opportunity to put their wild, pseudo-scientific theories into practice. The seemingly endless supply of guinea pigs kept the practice going as they continued to try out their ideas.

When Kilen was taken off to the children's work camp she was wise enough, even at ten, to hide her beauty. Her memory of the attempted rape was vivid. She smeared mud on her face, never tidied her hair and mumbled disjointed sentences when spoken to. All this primarily to escape the unwanted attentions of the camp guards. 'I didn't want to be where I was or who I was,' she said. She created a strange other child, like the imaginary friend of a lonely childhood. This was originally for her own safety but later became something more. Slowly this creature developed a life of her own and Kilen found herself being the protector for this poor 'wanting' girl no older than herself and the roles were reversed. The camps were, from Kilen's description, a combination of daily drudgery and distrust: cruel and terribly isolating. I have often wondered how this collective madness affected them. After all, it lasted for over four years. Within such a system it was impossible for a child to feel the uniqueness, importance and individuality so necessary for his development. How could any child trust or believe in anyone or anything that made him feel so unimportant?

On arrival the children's clothes were taken from them and they were dressed in black: there was a choice between trousers or a skirt. Kilen chose a skirt because she felt holes wouldn't show up so clearly and in the vain hope that she might hide some food under it. Each child was issued with a spoon, a hoe and a sickle and told that they must be carefully guarded as they could not be replaced and if lost or broken the child must hoe, cut and eat with her hands. Kilen hid her spoon and slept with her feet on her sickle and her arms around her hoe. They were also given a rag (like the traditional *kromah*) that was to serve as headgear, towel, handkerchief or anything else. These were their possessions; they never saw their shoes again. The boys and girls were separated as were any family members. At one point Kilen and Poutherein found themselves in the same camp: a comfort to them both. No one knew that they were sisters. They developed a language and a series of signs that the others could not understand, an essential precaution because the rules forbade certain conversations and any show of emotion or affection was severely punished. Their 'language' consisted mostly of signs and sounds of sorrow – they developed an algebra of their own against the arithmetic of others.

Poutherein was so weak from continual illness that she could hardly work but Kilen was able to help her fill her work quotas. This did not escape the notice of the spies. Poutherein was subjected to criticism and the sisters were terrified. Twice she was singled out by one of the other girls and reported to the leaders. With the cruelty of the miserable the other girls chose to torment Poutherein sensing her weakness. One night in the shelter she completely lost control and screamed at the other girls calling them animals. She still remembers the relief she felt after her outburst, all possible danger forgotten. At least she was still a person with feelings, a person who could make her presence felt to others, even if in a negative, painful way. Kilen begged her to stop, telling her she would get the whole family killed. Neither of them slept that night, certain it would be their last. They hugged each other, they cried silently, they sat together and waited for daybreak. Strangely, nothing was reported: they never understood why but were thankful. Not long afterwards Poutherein was sent to another camp, a camp for older children. They were almost relieved when she was transferred. It was hard not to say a proper farewell to each other, tears were forbidden and it would be as dangerous as talking about the good food they had eaten in the past. Their 'language' helped.

In Kilen's camp the children slept on the ground on thin mats, their only shelter a thatched roof supported by four tree trunks stripped clean in spots. Amazingly the roof let in practically no rain but during a storm all the children had to sleep in the very middle as the sides were open. Kilen talked little to her fellow victims, even at that age there were spies among them, making friends could be dangerous. The work load was so heavy that the girls, aged between ten and twelve, had little strength left for chat. The silence in the shelter was broken only by the sounds of weeping children or the shrieks of nightmares. Awakened at dawn, given a bowl of watery rice, the children were taken to the rice paddy for a day's work that lasted until nightfall. There was a break in the middle of the day with more soup eaten in the paddy where they tried to catch a bit of rest. The food was sparse but enough to sustain life. What was torture was the lack of sufficient water. Kilen said she often squeezed what she could from the mud in the rice paddy, or if possible drank the water remaining in a footprint or better still, hoof print where the ground had been pressed down. A meager supper at night and then, what they dreaded most, political indoctrination. For Kilen the most miserable part of a miserable day. The children, some sixty or seventy in each camp with guards and bosses, or as Kilen called them, 'Pol Pots', bringing the total to almost a hundred, sat cross-legged on the ground forming a circle, the camp's bosses in the center close to the fire. The children huddled together for warmth and to support the bodies of the most exhausted. They were congratulated on their great good fortune as chosen daughters of the Khmer Rouge and they cheered and sang in their poor cracked voices. The compliments did not apply to them all: the guards would often single out a child who would be made to stand and bear criticism. Usually the charge was lingering at her work. The child was made to apologize and all the others clapped and chanted a number. The numbers were terrifying because three complaints signified disappearance and no one was naïve enough not to realize what that meant. Kilen was forced to clap but only mouthed the number. When it was 'three' the guilty child took her place on the ground in silence and even the guards were still for a while. One dreadful night a child was singled out for stealing an orange. 'What shall we do to her?' screamed the guards. The children screamed, 'Orange soil, orange soil . . .' This time Kilen screamed with them as the guards were especially menacing. The child's death was inevitable so what could they do but play to their tormentors? The killings took place out of eyesight but not out of hearing and the sounds haunt Kilen still: 'That sound weighs on my heart,' she says.

Fragile and delicate as she looked Kilen was a strong and productive worker. She was 'promoted' to a First Line camp after about a year. The routine was the same only the food was better and a bit more plentiful. This unfortunately did not last long and Kilen was sent to Bung Trou Yun in the mountains where conditions were harsher than ever, so harsh that she became very ill. She was sent back and then to the hospital. In the hospital she was surrounded by death – very few patients survived their stay. There were no medicines and coconut juice was used to cure everything. Most of the 'doctors' and 'nurses' could barely read or write. The only advantage was that one was not forced to work. This, for someone as weak and ill as Kilen, was blessing enough. There was an old woman in the bed next to hers who was dying of dysentery. 'Just like my little brother,' thought Kilen. No one had come near the old woman except to cut a hole in the bed for the continual flux. Her uneaten food was not taken away and it attracted flies and ants. The stench was unbearable. Weak as she was herself Kilen tried to keep the flies away and to keep from retching as she washed the old lady every day. She crawled to the river nearby to wash her filthy clothes and she changed the old lady as if she were her infant. She held her hand as she died.

Kilen grew stronger and was discharged from the hospital and sent back to the 'First Line'. On her way there she ran into Poutherein who was being sent, together with her entire camp, to Bung Trou Yun, the fearsome camp in the mountains. Kilen was aghast as Poutherein was still very weak. She warned her sister of the dreadful conditions of the place and so frightened her that Poutherein determined not to go. Together with several others she hid when the members of the camp were rounded up for transfer. They could not escape notice for long and one by one they were all caught. They were herded together and closed in a sealed compound all day. When night came they were taken outside to a clearing among banana trees and seated in a circle around three heavily armed 'leaders'. The slight moon had just begun to rise, the sky was dark and immense. The shadows of the trees made a confining wall that seemed to move closer and closer. Although the night air was warm Poutherein shivered, her body covered with the sweat of fear. One of the 'leaders' had a flashlight – a wonder in itself. He flashed the light on their faces one at a time. Each thought it a signal of death to come. There were three men among the dozen or so women. Each man was called to the center and beaten badly with rifle butts. Two of the men were stoic and only grunted under the blows. The third begged his tormentors to stop, promising to do anything they wanted. It was this luckless third who was taken into the banana grove by one of the armed men. The terrified group heard pleas, screams and then silence. The cadre emerged, his bayonet still bloody. The rest were told that their lives would be spared but that they must leave for Bung Trou Yun the next morning. They all agreed as though it were a treat: at least they were alive.

They were on their way at dawn as it was a six-day walk. They never arrived. The Vietnamese had invaded and all order broke down. Kilen was vague about time, understand-

116

ably so. No one had a watch, even the guards had little artificial light and only the sun could be relied upon. When the day was sunny, four large steps from one's shadow signified nine o'clock but often they forgot to measure. Time was reckoned by the cultivation of rice: the planting, weeding and harvesting delineated the year more clearly than any calendar. The routine was dreary and exhausting but in a way, welcomed: she felt safer in the paddy, Kilen said. There was neither time nor wish for the new and exciting experiences that most children love, expectations were few and pleasure completely absent. Four and a half years taken from a childhood is an eternity.

PART IV

They have found out: it is hard to escape from Cambodia,
  Hard to escape the justice of Pol Pot,
When they are called to report in dreams to their tormentors.
  One night is merciful, the next is not.

I hear a child moan in the next room and I see
  The nightmare spread like rain across his face
And his limbs twitch in some vestigial combat
  In some remembered place.

I WANTED TO HEAR their stories in a more complete form than the bits and pieces that popped out from time to time. For example, when we bought Houssara a bicycle Samreth was reminded of how he had loaded his own with food when he was forced out of Phnom Penh, but here he stopped.

What follows is what I have managed to piece together. Getting complete stories was not easy. Sary is confused and the language presents a problem with her, although she is a wonderful actress and has shown me a great deal. Houssara really remembers little or nothing. Kilen, even now after all these years, breaks down and weeps so I haven't the heart to ask her too much. That leaves Samreth and Poutherein. They are both articulate, Samreth in broken Italian (strangely after all these years he insists in speaking Italian to myself and John) and Poutherein in fairly good but breathless English. Samreth's story is confused and at times incoherent but rings terrifyingly true. He tells it with intervals of Oriental laughter and with his usual charm. From time to time he says, as he often does 'Cosa potevo fare' or 'perché' (what could I do or why?), as if someone could supply an answer. Poutherein is more self-conscious, her story more organized, her phrasing unique and her acting superb. 'Thank God I was born in a politic family', she says, 'I look those guys in the eye and tell them what they want to hear.' This for anyone from a Khmer Rouge cadre to a Red Cross worker or an American immigration official.

The children were all lovers of truth but in Samreth it was

an obsession. I remember when he first began to understand Italian television. 'Is it true,' he asked, 'that if I eat my *merenda* I will become stronger and wiser?' I explained as best I could that he was watching *pubblicità* (a commercial) and that it was not necessarily 'true'. He was disgusted. What was the point, he wondered, of lying when your life didn't depend on it? When bit by bit he began his story I knew that, although disjointed and sometimes scarcely understandable, it would be 'true'.

When the family was forced out of Phnom Penh into the country, shortly after the Khmer Rouge victory, Samreth was sent to work in the fields. His independent spirit caused him trouble there but his mother's proximity and his own sense of survival kept him going. Early on the 'leaders' in the work camps were benign, almost. They were young, unschooled boys and girls who had spent several miserable years in the jungle and were tasting power for the first time. The degree of power they held corrupted rapidly and the humane were soon replaced. Part of the cadres' duty was to instruct the 'new people' and inform them of the advantages that were to be theirs under the new system, as well as the dangers for those who did not conform. This was called 'political education'. At first there was little of this as teenage semi-literate boys and girls have little to say. Bit by bit they developed their own brand of jargon, a language of their own. Samreth hated it. 'Why,' he asked, 'couldn't they talk like everyone else?' I often wondered if Samreth's disdain for language, any language, didn't come from this period in his life. 'Sorry' was abolished as was 'please'. 'You couldn't be sorry,' said Samreth, 'or sick'. Punishment was announced in jargon as was the rare praise. 'You are responsible for your own safety' was a favorite phrase. What it actually meant, says Samreth, was 'if you don't do as you are ordered, anything can, and probably will, happen to you.' What they all dreaded most was to hear one of the 'leaders' say, 'You're history', or the phrase 'To keep you is no profit, to lose you, no loss'. Everyone knew those phrases meant death.

After some time (he has no idea how long it actually was) he was moved into a group called 'Front Line', and sent about 150 kilometers from his family. He is vague about the location but insists on the distance. 'Front line?' I asked. 'Did that mean they gave you a gun?' 'No, no, they didn't give me a gun until the Vietnamese came.'

Whether it was a spirit of adventure or that he was unaware of the extent of the Khmer Rouge madness and the danger it implied, I don't know, but he ran away and decided he would set out on his own. He was small for his age which was about eleven or twelve, slim, and very beautiful. He was able to slip into, and fortunately, out of, all manner of situations. He was wise with the wisdom of necessity, and sought some form of protection as soon as possible. As he was walking along the road he came upon a family composed entirely of women (mother, grandmother and daughter) and offered his services. They were on their way to try to find the mother's husband, an important general. Samreth knew he was important because they had four cows (I assume he meant bullocks or oxen but he insisted on calling them cows): two pulling their cart and two tied behind – unheard-of wealth. They also had a hidden store of gold and diamonds but it was the cows that held the real value. This 'important' family, like so many other Cambodians, was involved with both sides, or more correctly, all sides, in the conflict. The war in Cambodia was indeed a family affair: Sihanouk had fought his cousin Prince Sirik Matak (an ally of Lon Nol); Matak's brother Prince Sisowath Méthavi went into exile in Peking with Sihanouk; Pol Pot fought against his own brother. The family's grandmother spoke Thai and Vietnamese and worked secretly for the Khmer Rouge while the mother's husband was a general with Lon Nol. Samreth's protection only lasted a short while before the Khmer Rouge reclaimed him and took him into the mountains. He was told that he was near the frontier with Laos. We assume that he was somewhere in the Dangrek Mountain range. Conditions were even harsher than before, the food more scarce. Each soldier had a tube of material, about the size of a shirt sleeve, knotted at both ends. This was filled with rice and worn about the neck and from it a daily ration of rice was taken. To Samreth it was incredible how long one of these sleeves could last, ten days for each sleeve and some of the soldiers had four or five slung about their necks. Samreth, even today, admires the discipline and dedication of these Khmer Rouge cadres, who, hungry as they were, rationed themselves with rice. 'That's why they won the war,' he says. The workers were not entrusted with a sleeve. They were fed rice once a day and potato once a week. Water had to be scrounged from the earth, unless they were fortunate enough to be working near a stream. Samreth was disorientated and unsure of where he was – the Khmer Rouge may have lied to him about his whereabouts to discourage escape. He remembers the back-breaking work of digging a canal out of the mountainside, his perpetual hunger and little else. Although slightly built Samreth has extraordinary strength which he undoubtedly owes to the Khmer Rouge. He also owes them a pair of bandy legs, a product of an overworked, underfed body and a crooked hand, broken when smashed by a rifle butt.

One day the camp was in turmoil, the leaders stopped work and held what seemed to be non-stop meetings. Among the workers, speculation ran high. There were new fears, but the respite from labour was so welcome that they revelled in the unexpected holiday. The workers were assembled and the leaders announced the incursion of the Vietnamese into Cambodia. The meetings had been held to determine future action and it was decided to go deeper into the mountains and build a defense against the invader. The workers were told to prepare to leave camp, nothing else. They were given no indication that the Vietnamese were close by. No one doubted that there was something being planned, but what? They had always gone to work at daybreak and so when they left the camp well past sun-up they were certain something unusual was happening. The unconcealed anxiety of his leaders gave Samreth a particular happiness. They were marched along a river where they were allowed to drink. There were fish in the river, but they were not allowed to catch them. Although the workers were starving and the cadres themselves were hungry, Khmer Rouge rules decreed that if everyone did not fish, no one could. Samreth was once called 'an American' even for asking if he might try to catch some, obviously the lowest form of insult.

As they were marching they heard shots apparently from the approaching Vietnamese. Then, as though by a miracle, a gift of Buddha, Samreth saw a chicken (where it came from he is still uncertain, but there it was) and he refused to go any further. The 'leaders' ordered him to hurry but he refused to obey. 'I'm not going' he said, 'I'm going to eat that chicken.' His leaders were insistent but in such a rush that they left him there swearing to come back and kill him. They obviously did not want to risk revealing their whereabouts with a gunshot then. Samreth does not remember if he figured this out at the time. Nothing mattered any longer. The hope, the chance, the blessed possibility of eating a chicken was the most important thing to a starving boy. He felt strangely free, and no longer afraid in spite of the threats and the sound of approaching gunfire. It felt wonderful to be no longer doing what everyone else was doing, or thinking what they were thinking or eating what they were eating. I found Samreth's spontaneous use of the word 'freedom' interesting under the circumstances: freedom being defined by what one has at the moment. Samreth took a piece of wood and killed the chicken, made a fire to cook it and watched with glee as the 'Pol Pots' fled into the mountains. Still unafraid and gloriously full he was just finishing off the chicken when the Vietnamese soldiers arrived. 'What are you doing, little boy?' they asked in Cambodian. 'Finishing my chicken', he told them, innocently. They were dressed like the Khmer Rouge, although their uniforms were dark grey instead of black, but they were armed with the same guns so when one of the soldiers spoke to him in his own language, he was frightened. Bewildered and confused, he feared a Khmer Rouge trick. He knew he could not try an escape and at that moment he thought himself 'dead, my soul had already gone'. He was reassured when he heard them speaking Vietnamese among themselves. Anything, anything at all, would be better than falling into the hands of the Khmer Rouge again.

The Vietnamese said, 'Come along with us, little boy, it is dangerous here'. So he went with them. 'No one cares what you think, just what you do.' He went with them back to Battambang. Following this move his story becomes confused, and he tells it in a series of disjointed images. Samreth found himself at the train station in Battambang: a train loaded with guns was expected to arrive from Phnom Penh. At the time the city of Battambang was divided between the Khmer Rouge and the Vietnamese. He had been lured back to the Khmer Rouge. (Whether the Vietnamese no longer needed his services or if he left them, I don't know and he is not certain that he remembers.) They played 'love music' (Cambodian pop music, which he says he never liked before) from the old times and promised him that he could go back to the 'old ways', that he could even join his family again. And in his desperate need to believe them, he slipped away and went back.

That is where and when he was given a gun of his own. What they didn't tell him was that the Vietnamese were waiting for the train, too. 'Let us get a gun and kill Vietnamese,' they said and Samreth had the excitement of firing several rounds of ammunition. There were Khmer Rouge on one side of the train, Vietnamese on the other, all dressed and armed in the same manner. Samreth, unknowingly, went towards them to shake hands only to hear them speak Vietnamese. 'Totum tutum totum' went the guns on both sides with a dazed boy in the middle. 'No one knew who was who or what was what,' he said. On one side of the train he saw Khmer Rouge dead and dying: the others had fled. The Vietnamese let him go. His gun was without ammunition so useless now, but they took it anyway. His military career, brief and inglorious, was over. He took to the road again.

In the confusion that followed the fall of Battambang to the Vietnamese, the Khmer Rouge were among the refugees trying to get to the border camps. 'Were they running from the Vietnamese?' I asked. Samreth thought most of them were running from the 'Pol Pots' whom they no longer wanted to follow. Some of the cadres were recognized by the other refugees. 'That one killed my brother,' screamed a woman and one luckless man was knifed to death in front of Samreth. Others were beaten by furious, victimized Cambodians. Samreth recognized one of the cadres who had treated him badly but he said nothing, secretly pleased that he could still feel an 'old feeling' and not give in to brutality. The mayhem continued and Samreth's laugh grew hysterical as he described how ears were cut off, beatings administered and the remaining 'Pol Pots' ran away amid the jeers of their erstwhile victims.

Listening to the children's accounts of the horrors I realized that this was the only time any of them actually saw a killing. Reading other accounts, I find the same thing. There were many dead and dying but the killings took place out of sight. Not out of hearing. So consistent were these reports that it seems to me to be a definite Khmer Rouge policy decision. I have wondered myself, and asked others, why the killings always took place out of sight. Secrecy and mystery are often associated with tyranny, but this sort of semi-secrecy has always puzzled me. Other accounts I have read also mention this. As far as I know none of the refugees actually saw a Khmer Rouge execution although many claim to have seen the bodies of the victims. No one I have asked has either an answer or a theory. The closest to an explanation (for me) comes from a poem by Norman Cameron. Satan finding a rebel devises a horrible punishment and places a vitriol-soaked mask on his face: 'The renegade begins to scream with pain/(The mask is not designed to gag the sound,/which propagates the terror of his reign.) There is still more./Yet Satan has a stronger hold: the fear/That, if his rule is threatened, he will tear/The mask from that pain-crazed automaton/And show his vassals just what he has done.'

On the road he met the family who had protected him before but now the mother's husband was dead and they had only two cows. They were travelling south on their way to Takeo. He went with them to live with the Cambodian soldiers who supported the Vietnamese. He stayed with them a few days as he and the beautiful daughter liked each other very much. 'I knew the mother wouldn't want me for the daughter, I had no money', he said but the first few days were 'almost like old days.' Then the girl met a soldier with a wristwatch and lost all interest in Samreth. Although he understood, his feelings were hurt. His pride was strong and he knew he could never compete with a real wristwatch, so he left them and set off by himself. The mother, who had become fond of Samreth, gave him a piece of a golden ring to help him on his journey. He ran into a group of Khmer Serei soldiers (Free Khmer) and joined them briefly. They gave him a gun but there was so little ammunition he only fired it once or twice. Then one night he dreamed that his mother was alive and needed him. He had no doubts whatsoever that she was calling him and ran away the next day, leaving his gun behind. He cut pieces off the precious ring to buy food and even a bicycle ride towards the Thai border. He moved slowly but steadily.

Further along the road he was picked up by two Russian military advisers in a large black car driven by a Vietnamese who spoke both Cambodian and Russian. The Russians were drunk, boisterous and happy. They were dressed in white, in contrast to the black clothes of the Cambodian cadres or the dark grey of the Vietnamese. Imprinted on Samreth's memory is the first armoured tank that he saw. The top opened and a fair-haired giant with blue eyes climbed out: he was too stunned to be frightened. The Russians kept asking Samreth, through the interpreter, which he preferred – the Soviet Union or America. The driver taught Samreth to say in Russian, 'I love the Soviet Union and do not like America' – his ticket for a ride almost to the border.

I met Poutherein for the first time in San Francisco in 1996 but we had corresponded and spoken on the telephone before this. She and Kilen are both happier in the English language than Samreth or Sary so chatter began at once. She was easy to like. She is without guile, straightforward and generous. Poutherein inherited her father's mercurial and unreflective character. She is wonderfully attractive, not with Kilen's delicate beauty, but slim, taut and explosive. Her large black eyes crackle with spirit. When she is excited, as she often is, her voice grows raucous. She was aware of this as she told her story and apologized but the decibel count grew even louder. The past has done nothing to limit her impulsiveness. Like the good American she has become, she is ready to move on when necessary and she no longer has any fear of impermanence. She seemed happy to tell her story.

Poutherein found Houssara in Battambang after the city fell to the Vietnamese. Poutherein is enterprising, fearless, tense and extremely intelligent. She and Houssara managed to scrounge some salt from houses in the city that had been abandoned: they found nothing else but were grateful for this precious commodity. Together (Houssara was eight and she about thirteen) they set themselves up in commerce. Their salt made quite a nice capital. After days of searching Sary found them at their work and announced her intention to try, with Kilen, to get to the border camp called 07. (Only later did they discover that 07 was a lawless enclave for smugglers and that they would be safe only with the UN at Khao-I-Dang). Poutherein's legs were still swollen (she had never recovered from her severe attack of jaundice) and they were unwilling to leave their thriving business until all the salt was bartered or sold. Poutherein and Houssara promised to rejoin Sary and Kilen within a few days. No one had the remotest idea of the hardships and dangers they might face getting to the camp: vague rumours had reached them about the brutality of Thai soldiers and the mountains to be crossed, but after more than four years of the Khmer Rouge nothing frightened them. Sary left Poutherein and Houssara some rice from her meager supply and the salt was bartered for dried fish and *caramelle* (sweets). They had always been taught not to lie. However, clever as she was, Poutherein soon realized that this was a peacetime rule and both she and Houssara made up some whoppers. Their imagination was as great as their need. Houssara limped while she wailed and clutched her side in pain and a cart stopped almost at once. They were given a ride and even a little rice soup. After the first time it was easy. They met a man who befriended these poor beaten orphans and gave them some 'real rice', rather than the watery soup that they had been living on for over four years. He had a great deal of rice, an amazing amount (they neither wondered nor cared where it came from) and he also knew how to get to the border and promised to take them. But he told them that the border was not open at the moment and they must wait. He had to go back to Siem Riep, his home near Angkor Wat, to get more supplies and told them to wait where they were for his return. They waited and waited, maybe ten days, maybe more but he didn't come back. Any kind of travel was still dangerous so they were not surprised, just disappointed. They decided to leave without him. A brave – or foolhardy – decision. They were unaware of the risks involved but at that stage would probably have taken their chances anyway. Poutherein wrote a letter to thank the man for everything he had done for them – the rice and the encouragement of getting to the border – she hadn't forgotten all her manners or her mother's teaching. She pinned the note on the wall, as they were in one of the Cambodian houses made of straw and palm leaf. They never learned what happened to him, so many people disappeared, dropped out of sight they gave it little thought but they were sorry. They had some food and a small piece of gold earned from their salt-trading and they felt grown-up and invulnerable.

Then one day Poutherein lost Houssara. She had been

taking a nap in their shelter and woke up to find him gone. She looked for him everywhere, she asked everyone she could find but no one had seen him, or would admit to having seen him. She called and called 'Baou, Baou' (little brother) but there was no answer. She went back to the shelter in tears, desperate at the thought of going on without Houssara. There she saw him, sitting in the corner eating rice. It was night by then and all she could see were the whites of his eyes and his teeth. She was incensed. To get the rice he had told an elderly woman he had no mother, no family at all. Poutherein was outraged, she was his sister, his big sister, and the lies were supposed to be hers. He had not even mentioned that he had a sister, which was the final indignity. Sheepishly he offered to share his rice. She grabbed him and tied him to the central pole in their hut. She began to beat him in a blind rage and to choke him. He submitted to the beatings but when she began to choke him he made such horrible noises that Poutherein herself was frightened. 'Never, never leave me again,' she pleaded, and started to weep in distress. He promised and she proudly says she never hit or strangled him again.

They were still miles and miles from the camp, that much they knew. They learned that the land on the way ahead was mountainous and very dangerous, and that close to the border there were threatening Thai soldiers everywhere. Then Houssara went out (with Poutherein's permission) and came back saying, 'I got the news there is another way around.' Poutherein does not remember the name of the place they were headed for, only that the way to it was wild and mountainous. Carefully hiding the tiny piece of gold that was their profit from the sale of salt, they set out. They went up hill, down hill. Houssara at one point had to carry Poutherein she was so weak. Houssara was only eight but years of Khmer Rouge labour had made him strong. There was a vague sort of trail to follow and they went slowly. Neither of them had shoes. They rested until Poutherein regained some strength and then went on. Houssara went ahead at first to lead the way and warn her about ditches, water and other hazards. Then they met 'a guy with a big knife'. As they were so slow he passed in front of them. They hailed him, 'Hey, big guy where are you going?' It was now that her 'politic family' training was an advantage – she began talking and obviously did it very well because the 'big guy' not only offered to lead them but put Houssara on his shoulder as they walked along. When they stopped their new friend cooked rice and gave them some, together with some meat. 'Even meat, meat for the first time in years, dried beef, it was so good, so good!' said Poutherein. They went on until they came to a house like an abandoned temple where there were other people. There was 'another guy' there, a Laotian who spoke Cambodian and Thai and who took people across the border, for a price. Poutherein thought he looked like a criminal and wanted to have nothing to do with him. He asked the children if they wanted to go with them as they were going to Thailand. Poutherein refused saying she wanted to go to her mother who was (she thought at the time) in 07 camp. Poutherein then spotted 'activity' outside the temple. A fairly large group of people had arrived and someone was collecting from them. She asked what was going on and was told these people, too, were going to Thailand and they have to pay 'like two or three ounces of gold'. Ounces in Asia, she insisted, were heavier than ounces in America. There were three or four men organizing the people. The man in charge looked less frightening and friendlier. He came over to the children and told them that they were going to pass 07 camp and when they passed 'we can drop you off.. So Poutherein said OK. They lined up with the others and off they set. There was a trail of sorts but it was heavily mined and totally unusable, so they had to walk through the jungle. Their bare feet bled. Poutherein began to scream in pain. Houssara was stoical but he, too, was covered with blood. The others had shoes or at least rags wound around their feet, the children had nothing. Poutherein cried but after the others told her to be quiet, she cried softly. Houssara endured. He was more like his mother and Kilen, thought Poutherein. Having inherited her father's character she was more inclined to anger, even hysteria; she never weighed the consequences the way her eight-year-old brother did.

Three days and three nights they walked through the jungle, stopping rarely for a brief rest, eating their rice as they walked. They walked in single file through the dense undergrowth which snagged and tore at their arms and legs. At certain points the bushes and trees were so thick that only the head of the person directly in front was visible. They walked close together, as close as possible, the terror of getting lost always present. Poutherein bled so profusely that she gave up, she could no longer stay on her feet. She stopped for a bit to rest and found herself alone. The worst had happened. The others had gone on without her and she was lost. She began to call out for help but at first her voice was so weak no one heard her. She called 'Uncle, uncle' and at last the man in charge heard her and came back. He told her that she would get killed if she stayed there, she must get on her feet and walk but all she could do was nod her head. She was too weak, too exhausted and in too much pain to struggle any more. He was not an unkind man and he wanted to save this poor bloody child. He tied a rope around her waist and dragged her along. She was half-conscious but she felt relieved, someone was taking care of her. She has no idea how long this lasted. Sometimes she managed to stagger along on her feet, sometimes she was dragged along on her back. She was so dazed she no longer felt any pain, just wonder at all the blood oozing out of her.

They finally came to a clearing, the rope was untied and she fell in a heap on the ground to learn that she had been taken all the way into Thailand. Just as they felt the excitement, relief and joy of delivery, gunshots were heard and people began to scream, 'Thai soldiers, Thai soldiers'. It was shortly before daybreak but still fairly dark, and Poutherein could not see Houssara anywhere. She was far more worried about Houssara's disappearance than about the presence of the Thais. The Thais approached and told the whole group to come out and surrender as they knew where they were. Many people began to cry, Poutherein could not understand why. She kept calling for Houssara. 'Baou, Baou, come out, please Baou, come out,' she prayed but there was no sign of him. To this day no one quite knows what happened to Houssara. He remembers that a Laotian man threw him into the undergrowth to hide him from the Thai soldiers. He remembers nothing else until he found himself in one of the small camps at the border. He was with a Laotian family of husband, wife and three small children. They tattooed a number and a sign on his chest (still slightly visible) and used him as a slave. The father was kind but the mother beat him with a big stick. He ran away and somehow made his way to the camp where he found Kilen. At that point remembering and forgetting were all the same to this battle-scarred eight-year-old.

Poutherein and her entire group were ordered into the back of a lorry driven by the Thai soldiers. Several of the adults began to weep and moan. They felt certain that the Thais were going to kill them or send them back. Poutherein had, until then, heard only vague rumours of the Thai soldiers' cruelty. Several people had tried to escape before and had been turned back; they, however, were the fortunate ones as they were at least still alive. There were stories of Thai soldiers who pushed Cambodian refugees from a high cliff into a minefield and of soldiers using the returning refugees as target practice. Poutherein thought that nothing could be worse than Pol Pot and she tried to console some of the others. The lorry in which they were riding stopped at a training camp. Sounds of soldiers drilling at the break of dawn did not sound menacing to Poutherein but the others kept up the wailing. They were unloaded and herded into an enclosure outside one of the main buildings in the camp. The sight of the Thai flag flying over the barracks had a soothing effect on Poutherein. Nothing, nothing could be worse than Pol Pot she kept repeating until the others told her, quite forcibly, to shut up. They remained in the enclosure without food or water from around five in the morning until around three in the afternoon. They were fed minutes before the arrival of the Red Cross. This was obviously planned so that the Red Cross representatives could see for themselves the generosity of the Thais. The food, Poutherein remembers, was wonderful – pork and bean sprouts. Forgetting her manners she pushed her way ahead of some of her elders in order to get to the precious stuff, gobbled it down and asked for more. She no longer cared what anyone thought of her she was so hungry and the food was so magnificent.

The Red Cross nurses cleaned and bandaged her feet and her other wounds. It looked as though they were finally to be cared for and were safe at last. This relief did not last long, as the whole group was put into the back of another lorry and taken to a huge, dank room dug out of the hillside. A low wall of bamboo kept the men on one side and women on the other. Many of the men were wearing leg irons, they were convicted criminals. Poutherein, to her horror, found herself in a Thai jail charged with illegal entry. She felt abandoned. Then the Red Cross came and gave her a spoon, a bowl and a mat for sleeping. She stayed there for two or three weeks until she was taken into the barracks for questioning. There was a Cambodian interpreter who helped her and told her what to say. She insisted that she (a thirteen-year-old child swathed in bandages) did not come to Thailand to spy or to overturn the government, she only came, she said because of the war in her own country. Tense as she was, she remembered being pleased at once again telling the truth. Then one day, she is not sure how many days later only that her wounds had begun to heal, she saw several vans lined up before the prison. Names were called out. The first two vans went to Khao-I-Dang, her name was called out for the third van. It went not to Khao-I-Dang but to the transition camp of Buriram in Thailand, a privilege. Buriram was known as 'the ready camp' and arrival there was almost a guarantee of resettlement. There were sponsors for the refugees in Buriram, sponsors from all over the world, Germany, Australia, France, Italy even China. The refugees shrieked, 'CHINA who would want to go to China?' It was simple, you were registered and then someone came along and picked the orphan he wanted. Everyone thought Poutherein was an orphan (her respite from telling the truth was brief). It was made clear to her by the interpreter and the others that for orphans doors were opened, so she became that much sought-after commodity, an orphan. She still held out hopes of seeing her mother but soon began to believe, as she had been told again and again, the best way to find her family again was to get to a 'third country' herself. Whether this was true or not she did not know, everyone was adamant on the subject. A 'third country' was paradise, surely only good could happen to her there. She was taken into an office to be questioned by an American immigration official, a 'big guy'. Are there no small Americans, she wondered? His head was buried in a series of files, one of which was hers. He spoke a bit of Cambodian but most of the questioning was done through an interpreter. 'You have an uncle in France,' he said, 'Why do you want to go to America?' Then her political training took over. 'My father studied in America and he told me that America was the best place to live.' All this she said through the interpreter. Then she stood up forcing him to look at her straight in the eye as she said in English, as her father had taught her, 'AMERICA is the land of OPPORTUNITY'. 'You,' said the official, 'are going to America.'

She was happy. For several days she ate, slept on her mat, sang to herself and dreamed of her bright future. One day as she lay on her mat day-dreaming she heard her name called out over the loudspeakers. She was given a number – Americans love numbers she thought – and told to get ready to leave. She rolled up her mat and reported for her new life.

Kilen and Sary's stories were inextricably linked and this is what I managed to piece together. With the arrival of the Vietnamese the Khmer Rouge camps were broken up, but the family was so scattered (and communications non-existent) that only Kilen, Sary and Puit, the nine-year-old daughter, were able to find each other at first.

Kilen walked along the only road away from the paddy asking if anyone had seen her mother. An old man told her that Sary had passed him a short while ago and that if she hurried she could catch her. Weak and tired as she was she began to run and soon she saw Sary and Puit ahead of her. She began to call her mother and Sary turned. All she could say was, 'You, you is it really you?' as an exhausted Kilen threw herself into her mother's arms.

They knew that Sarin, Sary's parents and Noi, the eight-year-old boy, were dead but they knew nothing about the others and, quite naturally, they expected the worst. In

Battambang they found Poutherein and Houssara. It was there that Puit, the nine-year-old girl died, apparently from tetanus and lack of proper medication. It happened suddenly and terribly. Her muscles tightened until she had a fixed, joyless smile on her face, then she could no longer breathe. Sary and Kilen were helpless, and within forty-eight hours she was dead. Before she died she asked Sary to remove the elastic from her skirt and give it to Houssara as his shorts were held up with only an old piece of rope. Sary was so distraught she couldn't bring herself to carry out the child's wish. She couldn't even bring herself to look at the child's body and gave it over to be cremated to avoid contamination. The precious elastic was burnt together with the poor, rigid, little body. Only the children cried, Sary was speechless and tearless. Then when food became scarce once again, Sary decided they must try to get to the camps at the Thai border. At first the Vietnamese soldiers had given them food but then their own supplies diminished and were not replaced. There were two choices, says Kilen, stay and starve or try to get to the border. They chose to risk the trip. Poutherein was still very weak and her legs were so swollen she could scarcely walk so they left Houssara with her, together with some of their precious rice. Kilen and Sary set off by themselves, promising to send for the other two when they arrived safely at the border. It was unseasonably hot and Kilen worried about her mother, still dazed after the cruel death of her nine-year-old daughter. Kilen begged rides on bicycles. 'Please sir, uncle,' she would say and when someone agreed, she would call for her mother who would ride as far as she could and then wait for Kilen. They were told the road to Thailand was straight ahead. There was no danger of getting lost. Mostly they walked. Sleeping on the ground was no problem but the meager supply of food they brought with them dwindled daily. They had no shoes and the road was rough, the weather incredibly hot. They wound rags around their swollen feet and somehow hobbled towards the border.

They walked for eight days until they reached the Thai frontier. When Sary finally unbandaged her feet all her toenails came off. They were weary beyond belief, but they felt safe when they saw the many other Cambodians camped there. Kilen says that her first sight of electricity seemed to be a miracle: they had been living in the dark for so many years. She found it hard to believe the extent of her joy at seeing it. When you have nothing, she thought, then you appreciate electricity, even if it is not yours. Then she saw that there was food, bread and ice: people drinking soda pop from bottles. It was almost like her memories of before the war! There were many others camped there but, unlike themselves, they had food and supplies. Kilen and Sary had almost nothing. Terror and deprivation had made others hard, selfish and tight-fisted, says Kilen. No one offered them any food. Their only possession was a teapot, their only food, one can of rice. (The unit of measurement was a can of condensed milk which contained about 250 grams of rice.) Sary was too proud to beg, and although Kilen wasn't, she had little success. Sary went to look for wild leaves to cook with their rice and Kilen wandered around this wonderful, terrible place. She saw people drinking what looked like milk. It turned out to be filthy water. How can they drink that she wondered. It looked so awful, it gave her an idea. She took her precious teapot and found ten empty bottles which she tied, with vines, on to a bamboo pole. These she balanced on her shoulders and set out to find a source of clear water. The teapot was light and the bottles heavy so the pole was difficult to balance and as she walked she clinked and clanked. It was so dry she could not find any water. She came upon some people going the other way who had water, and she asked, 'Uncle, aunt, please tell me where you got the water'. They refused to tell her. They even made fun of her and called her stupid for asking. She looked at the sky and asked why she had been brought this far to starve among these mean people. Why wasn't I killed in Cambodia, she thought, why do I have to go through this? She walked along singing to keep her spirits up but when she found herself singing a Khmer Rouge work song she burst into tears. Suddenly she felt a splash on her face. She had stepped into a running stream. The water was clear blue with the blueness of purity, 'so clear, so clear' she said. She danced in the stream, doused herself in the glorious liquid, laughing and singing at the same time. Then she collected all the water that her bottles and teapot could hold and made her way back to the camp, slowly as her load was heavy. Once in the camp she sat by the road and called out, 'Please, sir, uncle, please, aunt, come buy my pure water, the finest water you have ever had.' She sold her entire stock and earned 15 baht (about 75 cents/45 pence). Never had she felt so proud as when she presented her earnings to Sary. Sary's excitement when she saw the blessed money was another reward, that and the bread and canned fish they bought for their supper.

It was so good, that first meal in their new lives. Kilen went everyday to her stream after this. Sometimes she could not sell the water, when it rained people weren't thirsty. A born entrepreneur, she cast about for a more permanent situation. She found a woman who made and sold rice noodles and asked if she could sit next to her as people were sure to be thirsty after eating. The woman had no time to bring water from the stream and welcomed Kilen: they established a partnership. She exchanged water for noodles: it worked beautifully. After her enterprise had made her almost 500 baht (25 U.S. dollars) she decided to branch out. As she said, 'I do more adventure things.' First Sary paid a man to bring

Poutherein and Houssara from Cambodia. The rest of the money was Kilen's capital. She saw some men with great loads of rice which they sold in the camp. Learning that they had run the risk of entering Thailand proper she determined to join them. 'Sir, uncle, can I come with you?' she asked. She was told it was impossible as she was a woman and women, if caught by Thai soldiers, were raped and even killed. The men were merely robbed and beaten. Undeterred, Kilen wrapped a cloth around her head and posed as a boy (at four in the morning not much is visible). Her clothes were loose, her hair completely hidden, no one could really see her. So, without even asking permission, she got in line and followed the men into Thailand. She went to buy rice, bargained with the Thais, came back to the camp and sold her rice. At the border were those who had made their way there to bring rice back into Cambodia for sale. They were her best customers. If the border was closed the price went up and Kilen became a war profiteer. She got up at four in the morning to cross the border where she bought rice and canned fish which Sary sold and by eight the same morning she was back selling her water. This was the everyday routine until representatives of the Red Cross came to where they were camped and promised to take them to Khao-I-Dang. Two days later a large lorry came to collect them and several others. Some of the people were reluctant to get into the lorry as it was driven by an armed Thai soldier with an even more heavily armed soldier seated next to him. Kilen and Sary were also wary but they scrambled into the back, Sary with her back to the side of the lorry, Kilen seated between her knees. They had been camped by the side of a deeply rutted mud track. The lorry was old, the motor noisy and the load heavy but it managed to chug along. After what seemed like hours they came to a crossroads. The road to the right was another crude track and led to mountains, the road to the left was newly asphalted. When they stopped, one of the soldiers got out and went into the woods. The Cambodians crammed in the back were too frightened to do more than stand up to look out and try to discover where they were being taken. The back of the lorry began to smell of their fear. They had all heard of the dreaded mountain where the Thais had thrown thousands of refugees to their death. There was an unnatural silence as the motor started up again. When the driver turned to the left, there was a collective sigh of relief and Kilen found herself in tears. They soon stopped at Khao-I-Dang and when they saw their first sign of foreign faces they felt that they had at last been rescued. It was here that Sary recognized a picture of Samreth, and they were eventually reunited.

Safe in the hands of the United Nations relief workers, Sary began to dream again: she had not dreamed in years. She dreamed of Sarin, she dreamed of her 'tall brothers' and her dead children. One night she dreamed of Sihanouk. He told her that he would grant her every wish but first Kilen must dance for him. Sary believed this to be a sign and persuaded Kilen to dance again. Sary was criticized by other camp members for keeping Kilen away from English lessons and letting her dance instead. 'The dancing is important, too,' she said, little knowing how true this was to be. Kilen's dancing was to prove a turning point in all our lives.

There were several young girls who danced at Khao-I-Dang. The dancing was the camp's main entertainment. A raised platform served as a stage. Sometimes the girls were sent to outlying camps to perform. On one of her last performances before leaving for Italy – at a small camp near Khao-I-Dang – a larger than usual crowd had gathered and a group of ragged little boys had pushed their way to the front. After the performance the very dirtiest and most bedraggled tugged at Kilen's skirt and said, 'I think you might be my sister'. Kilen recognized Houssara at once, threw her arms around him, running sores, snotty nose and all. When she came back to Khao-I-Dang she screamed for her mother and Samreth. Samreth came running at once but Sary was unable to move, so conditioned by loss and misery she could not bring herself to believe Kilen that Houssara was really there. Kilen and Samreth went to the camp's director, the admirable Tom Generico, and he arranged for Houssara's transfer to Khao-I-Dang the next day. The children were ecstatic but when he arrived Sary could only stare at him in wonder. It was some time before she could bring herself to touch him.

Through Kilen's dancing they also made contact with Poutherein. While dancing in another camp Kilen was recognized as Sarin's daughter by the widow of a former minister who was on her way to the U.S. She promised to look out for Poutherein and indeed met her in Buriram, the transitional camp where people were processed for immigration to the United States. They could make no direct contact with her but at least they knew she had survived.

PART V

They are thriving I see. I hope they always thrive
Whether in Italy, England or France.
Let them dream as they wish to dream. Let them dream

Of Jesus, America, maths, Lego, music and dance.

WHEN OUR FIRST anniversary came around – 19 February, 1982 – we decided to celebrate. Sary was so much stronger and the children well established in school. It was a full year of achievement. We felt we were all owed a party. There was a newly opened Chinese restaurant in Florence, a real novelty at the time. Simon was at Westminster School in London, but the rest of us, dressed in our best, drove into Florence. There were ten of us in all: three Vietnamese, four Cambodians, Lisa, John and myself. Trinh and Tuyen took over the ordering and the Chinese flowed to everyone's amusement. We thought the food delicious although the Orientals had considerable reservations. There was a great deal of laughter, John amazed everyone by touching his nose with his tongue, Tuyen wiggled his ears, Samreth had a beer that went right to his head. We giggled about nothing in particular as though it was a first-time happiness for us all.

Suddenly I saw Tuyen reach across the table to Sary and slap her face. I realized she had had a seizure, her head was shaking uncontrollably and she was unconscious for what seemed an eternity. Samreth began to sob, Kilen turned pale and led Houssara into another room. Lisa called an ambulance and she and I took Sary to the nearest hospital. By the time we arrived at the hospital Sary had regained consciousness and although weak was coherent. The examination found nothing wrong with her so we brought her home shortly before midnight. John had stayed to pay the bill and he and Tuyen drove the children home.

It was as though the euphoria was too much for Sary. She had kept steady for all the years of horror and now at last, when she saw her children safe, an invisible hand had lifted a latch and all the blackness inside of her was released. When Lisa and I got Sary home Samreth stopped sobbing and Kilen made tea for everyone. We did not disturb Houssara who had curled up on the floor and purred himself to sleep. Tuyen picked him up and valiantly carried him the four floors up to his room without waking him. Children tend to have little or no knowledge of life other than their own, nature's protection against the outside world which can so often be baffling, precarious and frightening. When I thought of what these children had seen and known, I would shudder. For most children evil is just a rumour from some strange elsewhere, at most a film or a story. To these children it had a name and a face. There was nothing of the glamour and excitement of imaginary evil for them, just the gloom, the desolation, the slavery of the real thing. I would look at these children, so familiar and so dear, and wonder, try to imagine their other life. Somewhere inside were ghosts of horror, hunger, bloodshed, terror and with all my love I could never reach them. I could listen, I could weep for them, but the burden was theirs. One night we were watching a film on television: the Errol Flynn version of *Kim*. In one of the scenes Kim places a burr next to the skin of an infant to make him cry so that his 'Holy Man' can cure him, and be rewarded by the infant's mother. Houssara, who was nine at the time, groaned. He was visibly upset by the scene. 'He only did it because he was hungry, so it's not really bad,' he said. He was relieved when both Samreth and John agreed (in Cambodian and Italian). He had a highly developed moral sense, especially for a child his age, although, like most children, he could see little or no difference between a great wrong and a small one. Samreth had worried that

148

Houssara would eventually suffer guilt because of his confession to a Khmer Rouge cadre that his father had been a senator.

Samreth was inclined to talk about his experiences with the Khmer Rouge as an adventure. He had us laughing as he showed how he and two friends managed to get an extra ration of the dreadful and sparse food they were given. He treated us to an elaborate performance, placing a series of chairs in a line that led up to the cooking pot – guarded this time by a benevolent Houssara. Then he danced in and out of the line of chairs, a mad, manic, magical version of musical chairs. When least expected he was at the front of the line time and time again. He wept easily, noisily and copiously but never about events in Cambodia – those he spoke of with laughter or rage. He wept excessively when John left home to go on a business trip. He wept when he left for Oxford to stay with James, and wept even more violently when he left Oxford for home. Any parting completely unnerved him. He couldn't bear an unhappy ending in a film or on television and would leave halfway through if he had any suspicions about the final reel. Samreth, who joked about his blood-spattered companions in Cambodia, was appalled at any filmed violence. He would press his hands tightly over his ears and bend his head down as far as possible to escape. Kilen was the same, but about sex. The first film I took the children to see was John Boorman's version of *Excalibur*. I thought a myth about King Arthur and chivalry would be just the thing. Houssara and I were the only ones who actually saw the film: Samreth and Kilen had their heads down most of the time.

The older two were more, not less, afraid than most children of their age, and not at all shy or embarrassed at expressing their fear. At first I put that down to the strangeness of their new world. Certainly in Cambodia each had

149

shown bravery and daring, far exceeding most children's experience and under the most forbidding circumstances. Then, little by little, I came to believe that, unlike more fortunate, protected children, they had learned to trace the consequences of danger to the bitter end. A search for wild oranges could lead to rape and a bloody head. A hand stretched out to help a friend could be shattered by the blow of a rifle butt. They were on the lookout for any portent, any premonitory sign, mystical or imagined or real. Many childhood terrors seem to centre around people: the wicked stepmother, the cruel older sister, the sinister man in black, the bogeyman. To the children the terror was always personified by the figure of 'Pol Pot'. I once asked Kilen what Pol Pot looked like. I had seen only a blurry photograph of him in a newspaper. She had never even seen a picture of him yet she told me she knew his face from dreams and that it never changed. Once she started to draw me a picture of the face in her dreams. She got no further than the cap and the outline of the head when her hands began to tremble so severely that she had to stop.

Change was difficult for them all – even for Houssara who was only eight. Simple things such as using a knife and fork, sleeping between sheets, working to a time schedule, were new to them, and like most new things, bewildering. Houssara still talks about the strangeness of his first night here: the mattress with its magical springs and the fact that he was put to bed with electric lights on the stairway to his room. Unheard of, new and prodigious marvels that he was determined to understand. In the early days I often found him standing as close as possible to the refrigerator, a hand, palm up, against its side, trying, I learned later, to figure out why the cold stayed inside and not out. He was determined to understand how things worked, to learn. He made me realize that for some children intellectual curiosity can be a desire as strong as other more basic drives.

Houssara was the only one who did not suffer in the winter; in fact it was difficult to make him dress warmly enough. He also had a very high tolerance for pain. Falls from bicycles and later motor-bikes distressed him for the damage to the bike, not for the bloody head or dislocated shoulder suffered. He once fell from his bicycle into a field of stinging nettles. Because it was summer he was bare to the waist and was immediately covered with ugly red blisters. I came upon him, in his room, with his face turned to the wall, biting a cloth to keep from crying: he was nine. A psychotherapist who worked with victims of Nazi persecution and their children came to the house as a lunch guest, not in his professional capacity. Naturally he was fascinated by the children. His professional opinion differed from ours. He told us that adjustment would be far more difficult for Houssara than the others since he had no cultural memories to fall back on. The two older children had been to school, spoke and wrote their own language, and had felt part of a nation and its heritage. It is true that Houssara was illiterate in any language until he was nine and never really had a 'first language'. His spoken Cambodian is a family joke (he has never learned to write it). Although he had more trouble forming his letters and never acquired the dexterity of the other two, his social adjustment came much more easily than theirs. Actually, the expert's reasoning did not hold as none of the children had really known Cambodia, they had all been born into war and the Khmer Rouge. They were never homesick. The city of their birth had been abolished. Even Sary dreamed of another world, a life so much a part of the past that she could not communicate it to the children.

Samreth was so full of charm and so romantically beautiful that he had girls beating a path to our front door from the time he was fourteen. Strangely, even this success did not give him confidence. Old superstitions had such a hold on him that he continued to put more faith in amulets and fortune-tellers than in his own talents. He believed that music and art were not serious subjects for a man and that his natural gifts were unimportant. A friend of ours in Florence, Harold Acton, was particularly kind to the children, giving them all lovely presents. He was interested in all things Oriental so Samreth gave him in return a tiny statue of Buddha that he had always worn on a string around his neck. It was a crudely made little figure of no intrinsic value, but Harold was touched. The day after the present giving Samreth took to his bed convinced he was going to die. Doubled up in pain, writhing violently on his bed moaning, his skin the soft grey-green Southeast Asians get instead of pallor, he terrified me. Kilen rescued us both: Samreth from the doctor that I was ready to call, me from the fright I felt. He knew with absolute certainty, Kilen told me, that Buddha and his own good fortune had deserted him since he had given the little figure away. I bit my tongue from saying 'nonsense!' Kilen explained, carefully, softly and painstakingly to Samreth that his Buddha was now in the hands of an old man, a good and kind old man, and that Buddha himself would be pleased as the elderly are more in need of good fortune than the young. Samreth gave one final howl, rushed into the bathroom where he stayed for several minutes and came out, cured. To this day I do not know, nor would I ever ask, how much Kilen believed what she said. What I did believe was that having faced a 'reality' so malevolent and savage, Samreth needed to believe in magical powers that ruled both matter and nature. These beliefs took a long time to disappear, if they ever did completely. He told me of bands worn around soldiers' heads that kept them safe from bullets, of magical hair that kept growing within a tiny vial. I could only listen without comment, and hope my face didn't betray me. He believed with such necessity and force.

Yet it was Samreth who could see clearly the difference between what he considered 'rational' magic and fantasy. Bo and his cousins, Peng and Ang, were convinced that there were 'Germans' hiding in the deep end of the swimming pool (too much television obviously). John and I had failed to prove to them it wasn't so. Only Samreth by an elaborate series of dives and stories allayed their fears. 'You must,' he told them, 'believe only in good spirits in this country.' He was the Pied Piper, children and animals and girls followed him everywhere. (John bought him a recorder which he played by ear and which added to the effect.)

Samreth was on the lookout for *offese*, a wonderful Italian word that has more to do with loss of dignity than an actual insult. I have had experience with Oriental male pride, a universal trait, but never have I seen it stronger than in Samreth. I once jokingly called him 'Signor Samreth' and he was offended: he thought I was making fun of his lack of position. One afternoon in early summer we were all outside delighting in the sun's warmth. Kilen and I were collecting wildflowers; Samreth was high up in the holm oak; Houssara was dashing about on his new bicycle and Trinh was making flower chains in a vain attempt to attract Bo's attention. Bo's only real interest was in Houssara and his bicycle. Wanting to be helpful, Sary picked up a scythe and began attacking some stray weeds. Samreth came down from the tree with a face as grim as stone and grabbed the scythe from her hands. His mother, his father's wife, would never again do peasant's work.

Samreth had many talents: one summer he discovered the piano. We have an upright Japanese model, bought for our son Simon when he was nine years old. It was usually out of tune but for Samreth it was ideal: compact and available. James started him out on a Bach Prelude. Samreth had never touched a piano, had scarcely seen one before, but was musically sensitive and played with manifest enjoyment. We held a family conference with James and decided that he should have proper lessons. Interestingly, he loved Bach and Mozart and simple Bartók but was hopeless with any of the romantics and when he tried Gershwin it was a disaster. We took him to hear Richter play, it was his first concert and he adored it. When Richter concluded a Sonata with a great bravura flourish, Samreth burst out laughing, a proper reaction and one I felt certain Richter would have approved.

All four came to Italy provided with chest X-rays to prove there was no TB and a medical certificate (a printed form with half the spaces blank) that indicated, at best, a cursory examination. They also brought their traditional medication. Their equivalent of Trinh's 'dragon's tooth' was a solid round object, coin-shaped and about two inches in diameter. When any child had a headache, stomach trouble or just general malaise he went to Sary who dipped the coin in oil and scraped lines on arms, legs and back until she raised ugly red welts all over the sufferer's body. Without fail the patient declared himself cured. Sary, however, recognized the limits of her cure when Samreth came down with a severe case of shingles. She was terrified, thinking she could see traces of her nine-year-old daughter's symptoms. The cruelty of losing her first born was a thought too horrible to bear. Samreth was never in any real danger although in acute pain, speechless and numb with fear. Our GP was heroic and not only came to see Samreth twice a day for the first few days but spent time calming Sary's fears as well. After a week or so Samreth declared himself well, and the doctor agreed. The coin cure was never used again.

*

The children made lasting and in some cases passionate, friendships. That, to me, says something for Italian sensibility as well as the children's charm. Like most people confronted by completely different surroundings they were inclined to see only virtues or defects, never a mixture. Kilen thought the girls in her class were all lovely, even the plainest. She loved the way they walked, so different from the flat-footed tread of Cambodian women. What a wonderful and elegant thing a Western instep was. She loved my footprints when I came out of the swimming pool and would place her tiny, completely flat prints next to my enormous ones. She deplored the lack of respect, as she saw it, to old people. One day she came home indignant at having seen an elderly woman cross the street unaided. She admired the freedom of girls her age although she never took advantage of it. She was still terrified of men, not boys her own age, just men. Her shyness was no affectation, her timidity about her body no mere prudishness. When I first bought her a bathing suit she giggled and refused to wear it. Finally, during a very hot summer she came up to the pool but only when there were no males present.

Her fear of men was in a large measure justified and not only by her Cambodian experiences. At Khao-I-Dang she slept under Sary's bed as the Thai soldiers often came into the shelters at night with flashlights on the lookout for pretty refugee girls. She found it difficult to believe she was safe. Once when we were rebuilding a fallen wall near the house, one of the workers, a handsome blue-eyed Sicilian, asked her if she would like to go to the movies with him. She was terrified, shaking her head and staring at the ground. With me she became hysterical, gulping and weeping and saying, 'If my father were alive he wouldn't insult me so.' I felt rather sorry for the good-looking lad. For all the rest of the time he worked at the house he brought her little presents: flowers, chocolates and once a piece of Sicilian pottery which we still have. Fortunately, the wall was soon finished.

Kilen willed herself to be brave during the day but at night the terror took over and many is the time I have gone to her when she screamed and found her face wet with tears. Little by little the fear subsided and she became preoccupied by the kind of worries I could understand. When she first turned to me in acute distress because 'No one understands me', I wanted to kiss her. It was the same story that I had heard from my own children during their teens and I could somehow cope. Poor Kilen, being a teenager is difficult enough under any circumstances. She was a complicated mixture of innocence and experience – mixture that could easily have destroyed older and wiser heads than hers. As time passed her self-confidence increased and with it came a gentle, but determined, calm.

Kilen was a dancer and she performed the Classical Royal Cambodian dances. Sary had begun to limber up Kilen's hands when she was little as required by that exotic art. One of our first purchases in Italy for them was a piece of silver-threaded cloth so that her mother could make her a new costume. The dancing was a delight to us and to our friends. One cynical, and slightly drunken, journalist burst into tears at her performance. Several of Simon's friends were secretly in love with her but were too much in awe to tell anyone but John or myself. Her appalling history and her fragile beauty intimidated healthy, pampered teenagers. Once I told her that one of Simon's friends, a tall, incredibly handsome blond youth was in love with her – I couldn't resist. She answered, 'Oh, no, he is sky and I am earth. It could never be.'

Kilen's shyness disappeared when she danced, but the minute the dance was over she ran from the room. I was fascinated by the way she used her fingers. They could do wonderful things, those fingers, they could see in the dark, explore the world, anything. The dancing itself was exquisite and strangely non-sexual. I once asked her if she danced in her mind as well as her body and she said, 'Of course'. She sang softly as she danced. The words sounded hypnotically similar, the sounds coming from deep in her throat, almost from the nape of her neck in the Oriental manner.

When the Khmer Rouge forced her to work in the rice paddy the dance training helped her. She showed me the rhythmic motions, the bending and graceful hand movements that looked so tender and were in actual fact back-breaking. She sang the songs devised by the Khmer Rouge to lighten her work, or more properly, to speed it up. The songs were unusually musical, not like most work songs that depend entirely on rhythm. She moved her tiny golden hands delicately as she planted the imaginary green shoots, stepping back after each planting so that the entire process became one perfect movement, like water flowing. I found it difficult to believe that anything so aesthetically lovely could be, in reality, a murderous form of labour.

Sary grew stronger during that first year and her depressions weaker and further apart. She had never, even during her extreme lows, lost her dignity. Suffering may indeed ennoble, but the old adage holds true only if there was something worthy to begin with. She was a wonderful cook and often prepared some delicious Cambodian dishes. I was sorry when she gave up wearing sarongs and chose Western dress. She looked so lovely in the draped sarong and seemed to enjoy teaching me how it worked. Practicality took over though and the sarongs were replaced by skirts and later even by trousers. As the months passed the lines around her eyes faded and the sadness in them almost disappeared. Then one could imagine her as the eighteen-year-old bride dressed in her finest, gold-threaded sarong, hair loose and garlanded with flowers as she walked under a canopy through the streets of Phnom Penh.

Through the Red Cross we had learned that her daughter, Poutherein, barely one year older than Kilen, was alive and well and married in San Francisco. She was considered the family intellectual because from her early childhood she had been interested in politics and she was called 'the baby politician'. She was also considered the family beauty because she was slightly taller and much fairer than the others. I have always found this tyranny of skin colour and the widely accepted preference for paleness strange but it certainly exists. Houssara, who is by far the darkest of the family, has always come into his share of teasing. It has, however, remained just that, good-natured teasing without offense received or given. The practice has surprised many of our friends who are accustomed to Western attitudes about colour.

After Poutherein had been separated from Houssara she made the rest of the journey alone. At this point Poutherein had no idea how many, if any, of the family had survived. In the camp she met and married a Cambodian-Chinese, twice her age, whose name was on a list to go to America: she was fifteen. It may have begun as a marriage of convenience but within a short time it turned into a love match. Her first child was born before her seventeenth birthday. Puit, her nine-year-old daughter, had come to Sary in a dream. 'I could feel her soft baby hand', she said. In the dream she told her mother that she was well and in her sister's womb. The birth of Poutherein's daughter, Mary, shortly after, gave Sary great comfort.

Sary had two sisters whose whereabouts were not known until later. We got a suspect letter written in barely decipherable English, postmarked Singapore, from a sailor who claimed to be in touch with them. He could help them, he wrote, if we sent him some dollars or two Swiss watches. How he ever found our address we never learned. All attempts to trace him or them were fruitless. After that first letter we never heard from him again. We finally made contact with the sisters who were still in Phnom Penh. In November of 1991 two great friends of ours, the noted art historians, John Fleming and Hugh Honour, went to Cambodia. It was shortly after the Civil War ended, the peace treaty was signed and UN-sponsored elections were in sight. I asked them if they would mind taking some money to one of Sary's sisters begging them not to put themselves at risk. They went with their driver/interpreter to the address I had been given, a fairly large office building, and sent the interpreter inside to find her. They went at the close of the working day so as not to disturb her too much. The interpreter had no trouble at all and she came out to their car at once. 'What did she look like?' I wanted to know. 'Like an office worker', said John. She took the money and letter I had written, smiled, thanked them and put everything into the basket of her bicycle without any hesitation, fear or fuss, as though it was an expected everyday occurrence, and rode away. Later she even came to their hotel and brought a brief letter and piece of Cambodian cloth as a present for Houssara. 'Couldn't have happened six months ago', said the interpreter. Sary is now in touch with both sisters regularly.

The Cambodians got several letters from friends and relatives who somehow managed to find us. One, for Samreth, was postmarked Moscow where a school-friend was studying engineering. He had fled to Laos and, as a bright student, was sent from there to study in the Soviet Union. Another, for Sary, arrived from the daughter of Son Ngoc Than who was living incognito in Vietnam where her father had died in prison. The letters were always answered but we never heard further. We tried sending money to Sary's friend in Vietnam but this was before the 'thaw': it arrived after a delay of months and such a healthy chunk was taken by the government that there was little left for Sary's friend. All this we learned much later when the friend made her way to Canada and got in touch with Sary through the amazing system of refugee information. Mysteries remain. The mother of a Cambodian friend of ours who had long been thought dead turned up in Washington, D.C., unexpectedly and joyfully. I learned long ago not to question too closely, just to be pleased at any good news.

There was also Sary's youngest brother, Vancy, who lived in Paris. Vancy had been at the Sorbonne when the Khmer Rouge took over and unlike most of his fellow students, refused to go back to Cambodia when Pol Pot urged their return. He had a moment of doubt when he went to the airport to say goodbye to nine of his friends. The enthusiasm with which they left to help re-build their country was almost, but happily not completely, contagious. All nine, including Vancy's first cousin, ended up in the notorious Tuol Sleng prison and were murdered together with other returning 'intellectuals'. Vancy had married a French girl and when Sary first came to Italy we made contact with them and they promised to come to visit with their young daughter. Sary was the eldest of seven, after her were the three 'tall brothers', the two missing sisters, then came the baby, Vancy. His wife, Silvie, was the daughter of a successful doctor and the family spent a month each summer at the parents' villa in the south of France. They drove to Florence from there and arrived late one Friday afternoon, Silvie driving a conservative family car loaded with equipment for two-year-old Jade and presents for everyone. Sary had talked so much about her 'tall' brothers' beauty I wasn't prepared for Vancy. Slightly under six feet, he was incredibly handsome sporting a modified Afro hair style that was then the height of fashion, dressed tastefully in forest green. We learned later that as a student in Paris he supplemented his income working as a photographer's model. Silvie was almost as tall and handsome in a raw-boned way that made me think of Joan of Arc. Jade was a paler edition of her father.

An initial shyness was inevitable: John and I had anticipated it and did our best to keep things moving. Silvie, like Sary, was undemonstrative and Vancy too overwhelmed to do more than hug them all again and again: the real excitement was left to the children who rushed about smoothing cushions to entice the visitors to sit, bringing unwanted drinks and generally screaming their heads off. Late that first night I awoke and noticed lights still on in the *salotto*. Thinking someone had forgotten to turn them off I went upstairs to find Sary seated very close to Vancy, holding his hand as she spoke softly to him. Tears were streaming down his face as she told her story. It was past three in the morning.

Sary went to visit in Paris and returned with an impressive array of cheeses for John. Silvie had gone to a great deal of trouble and there were precise instructions on their proper care and consumption as well as two bottles of wine to be drunk only with two specific cheeses. John and I gorged happily as the Cambodians found the whole thing smelly and disgusting. It was also decided that Kilen and Sary would spend a few weeks with Vancy and Silvie at the sea the following summer. We made rather complicated plans for that summer (their second in Europe). Sary had somehow made contact with a cousin who lived in Paris. I was to drive all four to England with a stopover in Paris to see the cousin whose son had, alas, been one of the nine who returned to Cambodia. I would then leave Samreth and Houssara with

James in Oxford and take the others to the south of France.

Driving through France (back roads, not Autoroute) has always delighted me and this trip was better than ever. It was a treat to see familiar and admired sights through the eyes of sensitive, receptive passengers to whom everything was new and primarily wonderful. The first night we stayed at an inn between Pont Arlier and Ornans as I wanted to show them the Courbet Museum the next morning. There are a few minor works in the museum but its attraction to me is the setting; the clear, pure sound of running water from the wild river nearby, the unspoilt village and the pleasure the town takes in Courbet, its illustrious son. No hushed reverence, no ostentation, only the feeling that this particular boy did well. We wandered into the village with Samreth pointing out a statue of a fisherboy in the main square: it was charming, and a small model statue in his studio suggests that it was inspired, if not executed, by Courbet himself.

Then on to Paris, a part of Paris I nor any of my Parisian friends had ever seen before. Boulogne Brillancourt is a stop on the *périphérique* south of Paris and we found the exit without too much difficulty. Finding the cousin's house, a rather battered building of the turn of the century built around a centre courtyard, required more ingenuity. This particular part of the city seemed to be inhabited primarily by Orientals. The concierge herself was Laotian but her French was fluent and had even acquired the proper churlish tone. Kilen and I climbed the several flights of stairs to the cousin's flat leaving the boys below with a nervous and emotional Sary. There was no answer to our repeated knocking and calling but we were heard by a neighbour. A tiny, very old lady who looked like a benevolent witch told us, in heavily accented French, that the cousin was at work and would be home in an hour or so. All three of us spoke uneasy French as we explained ourselves to each other. 'I, too, am a refugee,' said this minute creature, 'I know what it is like.' She began to cry, with joy she assured us, as she would be able to see us happily reunited. She had escaped with her parents when the revolution swept Czar Nicholas from the throne and was finishing her days with her great-grand-daughter here in Boulogne Brillancourt.

The Cambodians are a bit vague about family relation-ships, husband and wife call each other brother and sister and full names are not always known. Villages were not organized the way they were in China and Vietnam and even in the cities few records were kept. Ancestor worship did not exist, only the nuclear family was important. So I am still not certain of the exact degree of relationship of the three family members we met; Sary's cousin, the cousin's cousin and his wife. That night we all ate at the local (delicious) Vietnamese restaurant. They were dignified, courageous, considerate and utterly charming. Kilen assured me that the tears each shed wouldn't last long and she was right. It was an exquis-ite banquet with each offering dishes and compliments to us all. An evening full of pale noise and nostalgic, bitter-sweet laughter.

We were lucky with the Channel Ferry. We found a place on the first one we tried and everyone was brave, silently so, during the adventure of parking in the echoing, crowded hold. We found a table in the top deck bar where Sary and Kilen sat rigidly during the entire voyage refusing drink, food or toilette. First Houssara and then Samreth explored the ship, each in his own way. Samreth struck up a conver-sation with two pretty girls who bought him sandwiches and drinks. Houssara climbed up and down the stairways noting with interest the different vibrations the motors made on each deck. Then he discovered the slot machine. I confess to a weakness for the damned machines myself and had been playing, unsuccessfully, when Houssara asked for a go. I gave him two of my last tenpenny pieces. He hit the jackpot on the first try. Business at the bar came to a standstill and the bartender came running out with a plastic sack to catch the money – £150 in tenpenny pieces makes quite a racket as it jumps out at one. Houssara was calm and dignified as he brought his sack to the table where Sary and Kilen sat, unlike Samreth and myself who made no effort to conceal our excitement.

We had four days in London. The 'whiteness' of the city disturbed Samreth; Kilen called the parks 'tame jungle'; Houssara was miffed that the Queen was not at home when I took them to see the changing of the guard. Then on to Oxford where all five of us crowded in on James. After three busy days, seeing friends, punting on the river and wandering about the university, we left the boys with James and took off for France. I knew that Samreth who spoke passable English would have no trouble but I worried, needlessly, about Houssara. He made friends with the talkative, enthusiastic mother of an English friend. He couldn't possibly understand what she was saying (even I had trouble) but her goodness was clear to him, or maybe it was her loneliness.

His great friend however was Danuta, the beautiful young Polish wife of Tim Garton Ash. Danuta knew no more English than Houssara and neither Italian nor Cambodian. He had neither of her languages, German nor Polish but their friendship was real and they seemed to understand everything the other said. 'She looks like Danuta' was for years Houssara's highest form of praise. Both boys had very definite ideas about female beauty. Only Kilen wasn't interested: she seemed almost to dislike or at least to be afraid of her own beauty.

At first only Samreth was curious about Florence so John took him to see the city. John was fascinated by Samreth's uneducated but nearly unerring eye. The simple Renaissance lines and the coolness of the Pietra Serena appealed to him in the same way as Mozart and Bach were to do. Without any prompting from John he disliked the façades of the Duomo and Santa Croce. And when John took him to the Pazzi Chapel he sat down, crossed his legs and pressed his hands together in the attitude of Buddhist prayer. John went outside so he would not disturb Samreth and came back after a few minutes to find a radiant boy whirling around with outstretched arms.

When Samreth finished Middle School he wanted to follow his friends into the Liceo Scientifico which, as we feared, turned out to be a mistake. He did his best, but understood little of what was expected of him scholastically. He did well in English lessons and excelled in technical drawing. He failed everything else but here again he became the special 'pet', even of the teachers who despaired of him in class. It was through the drawing teacher that we got him accepted at the Scuola d'Arte di Porta Romana (the Art School at Porta Romana) where he really belonged, and where he went on to get his *Maturità*, the Italian equivalent of a Baccalaureate, so much more than a high-school diploma. His drawings were delicate, intimate and extremely skilful. I have in my bedroom one of his first efforts, a copy of a De la Tour portrait from the Louvre which, although accurate, looks surprisingly like a lovely Oriental girl.

Kilen's obsession with food continued. She became plump, too plump for her tiny frame. She seemed destined to put on weight until she burst, until one night watching television in our bedroom where we all piled on our huge bed, she saw a classical ballet and was enchanted. She started to diet and began dancing lessons the next week. Classical ballet did not work with the flat heel and toe movements of Cambodian dancing but she kept at it with dogged enthusiasm. A Western instep was indeed a great and wonderful thing she told me but the other girls used their fingers foolishly.

Houssara meanwhile was enthralled constructing buildings and machines with his newly acquired Lego. I regret that I did not keep at least one or two of his most imaginative inventions. To Sary he became her engineer brother although she had to bend a Buddhist rule or two to make the dates match.

'Not yet, not yet . . .' I kept saying to myself by the third summer. It was clear that some changes would come, must come, should come but exactly what I wasn't sure, and, frankly, I was in no hurry. About the others I couldn't be sure. Sary was so much stronger in every way and Samreth felt himself a man. They would soon, if they hadn't already, feel it necessary to make their own decisions, to feel that they could no longer pledge their futures to us. It was natural for them to wish for a life that no longer depended on our powers but on their own. Would our family bond dissolve, our union end, when there was no longer any need for it, I wondered? Today I know my worries were needless. A genuine love on both sides and common goals still pull us together although 'distance and duties' do indeed divide us.

That summer Kilen went to the south of France alone to stay with her uncle Vancy and his family. We sent Samreth to the sea as a paying guest with an Italian family to improve his Italian, took Houssara with us to Istria and sent Sary to San Francisco to see her other daughter, Poutherein, and to meet her granddaughter. Since the older children were still away, Houssara and I were to drive to the airport in Rome to meet Sary on her return, and bring her back to Florence. Monday evening we were all, together with our friend Elizabeth, in our bedroom watching a re-run of *Roman*

Holiday on television. John was explaining to Houssara about the scene of *La Bocca della Verita* when the phone rang. It was Sary in her halting Italian. I told her that Houssara and I would be waiting for her when she stepped off the plane. She hesitated and then put Poutherein on the line. 'My mom,' said an Americanized Poutherein, 'was married today and won't come back.' 'Married!' I shrieked as Houssara turned grey. 'His face, dear God,' said Elizabeth, 'the look on his face!' None of us could find anything to say, we were all struck dumb by the astonishing and unexpected announcement. John, as usual, came to the rescue. He went downstairs and opened a bottle of champagne we happened to have in the refrigerator and we all drank to Sary's health, even Houssara. The champagne improved our spirits and sent Houssara to sleep, as intended.

Poutherein had arranged everything: Sary had married a green card. It was up to us to tell the others. Two days later Houssara and I drove the six hours to the sea to tell Samreth in person. In the throes of first love and sexual experience Samreth seemed to take it well and some of his coolness rubbed off on Houssara. Kilen was due back from France within a few days so we decided to wait until then to tell her. She was appalled. Fortunately school started soon after her return and she began her last year at Middle School with her usual consuming interest. A few weeks later I came home to find Samreth, tears streaming down his face, on the phone with his mother. She had just told him that she was arranging for the younger two to come to America but that she preferred that he stay in Italy.

What followed was not easy for anyone. A struggle began between Sary and ourselves for the children. I think you could say we all gained a bit and lost a bit. We were respectful of one another and the true affection was as strong as ever but the struggle was real. She, naturally, wanted the children to join her in California. We made a sort of compromise: I began working on the papers that would allow Kilen to emigrate to California. Her mother wanted, and needed her the most.

The fourteen months that elapsed between Sary's marriage and Kilen's departure were difficult for us all, but also personally rewarding for me as Kilen and I became very close. Truthfully, I never worried too much about Kilen in America, knowing her strength of character. What I perceived as the dangers of America wouldn't apply to her. I did worry, desperately, about the boys, especially Houssara. Chameleon that he was (by necessity in the past), to be thrown into an alien and perhaps violent atmosphere without adequate protection seemed to me a prescription for disaster. For a twelve-year-old with his history, without a language of his own, to start all over in school, abandoning what he had learned with such difficulty and leaving his devoted friends was too much to ask of him. True, he would be within a loving family, but a family that was itself struggling to get to grips with yet another world. Samreth's talents were obvious, Houssara's less so. He was good at mathematics though not instinctively brilliant the way Samreth was. He was a builder, a fixer, a theorizer: he was searching for his own special path which led eventually to computer science. He was a natural athlete, although small for his age, and ran much faster than boys older than himself and won all the Middle School prizes. He had the family charm, though his was more aggressive than the others and he got upset if there was no reaction to his efforts. Neither of the boys had Kilen's steadiness.

In the end affection, good sense and the boys' wishes prevailed. Samreth stayed until he finished his studies here and Houssara has remained with us. His rapport with computers is nothing less than brilliant. He is now *consulente* (trouble shooter really) for an ever growing group of clients. It is almost like having a doctor in the family – he gets calls for advice and help at all hours. He has just been responsible for the installation of a complicated new communication system connecting the University and the Observatory of Florence to the biggest hospital complex in Tuscany.

The immigration papers were complicated and abysmally bureaucratic but we finally managed them. Kilen and I went to Genoa, the closest American Consulate where she could be 'processed'. It was a three-hour drive, during which we both indulged ourselves in the mixture of tears and excitement that marked the months we had to wait until she actually left. In Genoa we stayed at a small, respectable hotel within walking distance of the Consulate. I decided we must have a grand celebratory dinner but after what seemed hours of searching, we ended up eating Nouvelle Cuisine (or the Genoese idea of it), which left us considerably poorer and still hungry. 'Memorable' was Kilen's description of that night.

We arrived at the Consulate before it opened the next morning and found that the 'processing' would take all day. It did, although most of the day was spent in killing time from one appointment to the next. We walked around and around the not very interesting zone where the Consulate was, we squeezed each other's hands, chattered about nothing in particular and somehow the time passed. There was one particularly considerate member of staff, a young and attractive Italian woman, who allayed Kilen's fears a bit. The Consulate doctor, seeing Kilen's nervousness, allowed me to stay with her during the physical examination, which was a big help. The Consul himself was efficient and kind when we finally got to his office, the last moment in a tense and tedious day. He congratulated Kilen and told her she had gained a great deal: she answered 'We shall see.'

After Kilen and I had finished with the Consul, we went to a Genoese 'alimentari', stocked up on local delicacies such as *torta pasqualina* (a Genoese Easter cake made with artichokes) and *Cima* (stuffed, cold breast of veal) and drove home, arriving just as John and the boys were finishing dinner. John gave Kilen a huge embrace and she and Samreth both began to sob.

Kilen was the only one of the children who was neither frightened nor intimidated by America. Puzzled, curious perhaps, but always certain of how she felt and of her right to express herself. It was as though she had vowed to herself that she would set her own standards, make her own rules, determine her own behaviour. She somehow managed to keep America and American values at arm's length. Kilen knew, from bitter experience, that men are not naturally good: she was never guilty of the dishonest rationalizations she deplored. She observed (carefully and dispassionately): she interpreted. She never confused the two. I suppose that is why she loves the country more than the others do.

On Samreth's first trip to America he was cheated out of his wages. He had taken a temporary job picking grapes but after a month when he expected to be paid he was told that he had no proper papers and couldn't possibly expect to be paid like an American. Since he had, in fact, no proper papers, he had no recourse. Houssara was even more upset on his first trip when he approached a group of fellow ten- and eleven-year-old boys on a playground only to be turned away for being 'not American'. Young as he was he recognized this as a synonym for 'white'. He said that during his almost two-month visit the only white people who talked to him were in the shops. Coming as he did from the small friendly zone where we live, this was a shock.

Transatlantic telephone calls, the occasional letter and the even rarer visit kept us informed and aware of Kilen's progress. She has employed those extraordinary hands as a dental assistant and has worked, happily, for the same dental surgeon for eight years now. By hard work, frugality and steadfastness she bought her own house. Sary wanted her to marry 'within the culture', so she submitted to a series of courtships by fellow Cambodians. A stunningly beautiful Cambodian virgin with a steady, well paying job, who owned her own house in a pleasant area of San Francisco, was what my mother would have called 'a catch'. Many attempted. Not a single one came anywhere near success. Once she lost patience with a bumbling, terrified suitor and said 'Let's not waste time, what do you offer?' Sary despaired. Then she met Gary. After a rather tumultuous engagement they married in 1993. She is blissfully happy in her marriage. Gary is a Japanese-American whose father was interned during World War II. His widowed mother has preserved many of the traditions, or at least what we think of as the traditions, of Japan, where she was born. She is a meticulous housekeeper, a devoted mother and grandmother, a talented gardener and speaks very little English after forty years in California. Gary is attractive, honourable and just right for Kilen. Last year she produced a gorgeous, healthy boy whom I call 'The Samurai'.

When Samreth had *fatto la Maturità* (passed his Baccalaureate) with above average marks, we cast about for further educational possibilities. He had been to see his mother and sisters the summer before and found what seemed to be an admirable solution. The San Francisco College of Art offered a three-year course with a degree in such subjects as industrial design, book illustration, advertising and so on, and, as all such colleges do, dangled promises of work after graduation. We all agreed on the choice, said we would pay the tuition if he could support himself, and after bureaucratic wrangles about documents, he went off. He completed the course satisfactorily. I have a photograph of him in mortarboard and robe at his graduation – the only unattractive photo of him I have ever seen. His fellow students seem intent on the proceedings while Samreth looks out at the camera as if to say, as he often does 'What could I do?' The promised jobs were few and more than once the promised wage was not paid. He tried several different things and places. At one time he found himself in Texas where he had gone for a promised design job, and where he ended up shining shoes to get enough money to go back to California. Small wonder that when he discovered, almost by accident, he had a talent for salesmanship, he was pleased. He still has an impressive portfolio of his designs and showed it to me with justifiable pride but he realizes that selling Hondas brings in more needed money than designs.

A letter from Poutherein told me that Sary's husband was not an educated man like her father and when in Cambodia he had been a professional soldier (for the Khmer Serei). He was also, in the Southeast Asian tradition, an inveterate gambler. Therefore I was not unduly surprised when Sary divorced him. She kept the green card and is now an American citizen. Belonging in the bureaucratic sense was not enough for her, even the common memories she shared with her fellow refugees were not enough. The friendship with the other victims she found in California was not enough either. The new life in America seemed to have little effect on her, as it was a world so distant from anything she had ever known and believed in. She couldn't, wouldn't measure herself against these new experiences, conditions for success or failure no longer existed for her. That they existed for her children was all she wished. What she needed for herself was security and solace. She had no use for a 'clever God', one who wrote and said things she couldn't understand in a language not her own. What she wanted was something to which she could give her full and impassioned attention, to the exclusion of all thoughts about herself, her past and her problems. What she yearned for was a protective presence, to keep her from drowning. Buddhism made no promises, particularly Theravada as practised in Cambodia (only a Buddhist monk could achieve Nirvana), nor did it make any threats which seemed somehow important to her. She needed assurance. She never knew where she stood, within Theravada the system of merits and demerits was never made clear. Her old beliefs were still strong and the mixture led her in the direction she felt she must go. Her dreams became visions, her constant companion and protector, Christ, her favorite phrase 'In the name of Jesus'. She became a born-again Christian and in true matriarchal fashion took her entire family with her into the Voice of Pentecost Church.

When tragedy struck the family yet again, Sary's faith helped enormously. Poutherein's husband Chap Tim, father of her two children, was diagnosed with lung cancer. 'But this is America,' said a bewildered Poutherein. 'How can this happen here?' The cancer was brutal but quick and Chap died a few months later. He was forty-two. Samreth rang me in tears with the news of Chap's death. 'When did it happen?' I asked. 'About ten minutes ago,' he said, and hung up.

They had all lived together in the house bought by Kilen and Poutherein as the two fully employed members of the family. Samreth had just come to California to go to Art School, Poutherein's children (Mary and her brother David) were in elementary school. Sary was not able to work as she suffered from fainting spells, so she stayed at home and attended to the day to day running of the house. Chap was a goldsmith and had his workshop at home so that he and Sary spent a great deal of time together. As far as it was possible to ascertain, Chap had no family left alive. He became dependent on Sary. She began to teach him to read and write Cambodian, which he had never learned. Their attachment to each other was strong and shortly before he was taken to the hospital Chap was baptized in the bathtub giving great comfort to Sary and, I trust, to the others as well. As a Buddhist Sary had dreams of gold. As a Christian, she told me, she had visions and saw great swathes of purple cloth with the outline of a figure inside them.

After a long and painful period of mourning Poutherein began to smile again. She had interrupted her work as an accountant only briefly and the demands of a daily routine and two enchanting children to raise brought her back to her old self. Last year she married her former boss. Her husband is a fine-looking, blond American who towers over them all like a gentle giant. The children adore him.

Trinh, Tuyen and Bo prosper. They have had their troubles, too, but the troubles for the most part had little to do with exile. Last year Trinh and Tuyen opened the first Vietnamese restaurant in Tuscany. The hours are long, the work hard and there is considerable strain but they are established now and are, justifiably, proud of what they have accomplished.

A few years ago, after a bureaucratic hassle, we brought over Trinh's youngest sister, the only unmarried one. Lively, intelligent and full of natural charm she is a great help at the restaurant. She is now engaged to the chef whose name (Phuk) is always good for a giggle.

Bo does very well at the Liceo Scientifico. His marks are good under a demanding educational system, his friends are many, his tastes, for the most part, are Italian. He has just turned eighteen and is tall and handsome. I realized just how grown up he was when he received a notice to report for a physical examination for military service. He and Houssara have grown up as brothers, quarrels and all. They are, most of the time, devoted to each other.

Recently I called on Don Luigi whom I hadn't seen in years. He had been transferred to a Parish north of the city in a working-class suburb quite a distance from us. His church, San Martino, is not a tourist attraction and is in the town of Brozzi, a medieval *borgata* with fortifications constructed to protect the north side of Florence from invasion. There are a few traces of the old walls left, impressive even as ruins. San Martino and the cemetery nearby were begun in the eleventh century and suffered various restorations and serious damages during the Florence flood of 1966. The actual damages have all been repaired, the aesthetic ones have not. The Bell Tower rebuilt in the Renaissance still stands, untouched and unruined, as well as two Romanesque doors together with the splendid cypress grove. The Parish house is large, spotless and sunny: the courtyard a jumbled jungle of growing things. Don Luigi looked much the same as he had some seventeen years ago although he seems even larger (taller not heavier) than I remembered. He has a wonderful voice, gentle and powerful at the same time, useful in his profession no doubt. He no longer wears the *soutane* but was dressed in what the Italians call 'clergyman' trousers. I noticed with pleasure a slight vanity: he practiced what is known as the *riporto* – some long strands of hair combed over to hide a bald spot. We reminisced with mounting pleasure. The arrival and placement of the Asian refugees was the period of his greatest happiness he told me. He had taken care of over two hundred and swears there was not a negative experience in the lot. His Parish house is now home to six

Italian children that have been given over to his care (aged six to twenty-one). What began with the Oriental refugees has given him a vocation within a vocation. Priests are often described as 'serene', Don Luigi is more.

EPILOGUE

IF THIS WAS a story with a moral it would have a particular kind of ending, just to teach us our lesson. In fact the story is more complicated than that, it doesn't really have an ending. Whatever purpose or plan we might have had, the reality was, as it tends to be, different.

I wanted to hear more of their stories and perhaps tell some in their own words. I wanted to see at first hand how they coped with the contradictory colossus that is America. With this in mind I flew to San Francisco in February. When I arrived, after an eleven-hour flight non-stop from Paris, I was still dazed by the time change and Veuve Cliquot (I had flown Air France). To my delight and surprise, Samreth was waiting for me. He looked wonderful, handsome as ever and no longer vulnerable in Western clothes, a little heavier or perhaps just more mature. With him were his year-old son, his wife and her mother: the mother spoke no discernible English; the wife a few phrases; the baby had the romantic, deep-eyed beauty of his father. Samreth took charge of my luggage and me with admirable efficiency and in no time at all we were in his shiny new Honda on the way to Kilen's house, where I stayed and where Sary also lives. I met Gary, Kilen's husband, and the ten-month-old Samurai. I saw a great deal of Samreth and his wife and son and met Poutherein, her husband and children for the first time. How we talked and wept and talked. How clear the memories were. There were no longer the strange, and I suppose inevitable distortions that come from obsessive memories.

The past seemed at last, the past. Kilen confessed to me, in tears, that she had lied about her age. They all took wonderful care of me, Samreth took two days off work and guided me around the city; Sary made me Cambodian dishes that she knew I liked; Poutherein and Kilen took me to their favourite restaurants. I went to Church with Sary, Kilen and Poutherein on Sunday. I was passed from one to another with such thought and care for my wellbeing that I was touched.

We sat in the kitchen drinking innumerable cups of tea, talking and talking – of the past, of the promises kept and to be kept still. One night, returning from an elegant Cambodian restaurant (named, of course, 'Angkor Wat'), we all squeezed into the kitchen for our last cup of tea. Kilen began to sing and Samreth's wife began to cry. The tears were therapeutic, washing away the past to make room for newer wisdom. I could almost feel Sary's approval.

Samreth and Poutherein are on the surface more 'Americanized' than the others, although Samreth yearns to come back to Italy. He is, however, the only one who does. Samreth who played Bach and Mozart and read Dante now sells cars in San Jose, California. He does well financially, his natural charm has come in handy. His fellow salesmen tease him, I assumed good-naturedly, until Samreth told me there was nothing 'good-natured' in the jealousy he found surrounding him. The salesmen wonder how he does so well without speaking English any better than he does. Those without charm can never recognize its appeal, I suppose. He complains that he has no friends, no one to talk to about things that really interest him. He misses those long night sessions around the dinner table where the world was saved and set right. He misses his two great friends and his first great love and spends far too much money on transatlantic phone calls. Samreth had always been restless. He is married to a beautiful, silent, Cambodian girl: they married on the day after their son was born. His attachment to the baby is deep and his mother and sisters hope that, with time, he will settle. I have formed no opinion.

When the phone on my bedside table rings on Sunday mornings I know instinctively who it will be.

The Secrets of Merebank Bay

Jo Harries

Grosvenor House
Publishing Limited

This book is published by
Grosvenor House Publishing Ltd
Link House
140 The Broadway, Tolworth, Surrey, KT6 7HT.
www.grosvenorhousepublishing.co.uk

This book is a work of fiction. Any resemblance to
people or events, past or present, is purely coincidental.

A CIP record for this book
is available from the British Library

ISBN 978-1-78623-694-4

To Helen

Acknowledgements

My thanks to; Val Jennings. Sue Barker. Hepzibah Harries-Pugh M.A. B.A.(Hons). Terry Wright.

Prologue

On a beautiful September week-end, in the quiet sea-side resort of Merebank Bay, Amelia was married in the family's prestigious hotel, The Portland Arms. Unfortunately, things didn't go to plan when a long-held secret was broken, and a family was torn apart.

When a convoy of inexperienced fishermen arrived to take advantage of the newly opened cockle beds, it meant almost certain disaster. Five years later, things have changed, but secrets remain. In this pacey sequel to The Cockles of Your Heart we are re-introduced to the believable characters in a gripping novel with many interwoven strands. And Bryony is back!

Chapter 1

The gliding, upward spirals of seagulls rising on the thermals of warm air were mesmerising and soporific, and soothed by the murmur of voices, Sharon found herself drifting between sleep and wakefulness. Roused by Tom's laughter, she pushed herself into a sitting position, and looked over to the barbecue where he was placing the king prawns on the grill. Always the last to be cooked, it was a sign for her to bring out the salads and dressings.

When he was satisfied everything was under control, he rubbed greasy hands down the front of his apron and picked up two bottles of lager from the improvised ice bucket. Holding one in his outstretched hand, he passed it to Damian while simultaneously tilting the other to take several deep gulps.

'So, how does it work then?' she heard him say, as he wiped frothy lips with the back of his hand, 'do they actually give you a pile of pornographic magazines, and leave you to get on with it?'

Sharon held her breathe. The couple had made no secret of their desire to start a family but this wasn't the appropriate time to discuss it, especially with Tom's typically blunt approach. Damian seemed quite relaxed about explaining how he hadn't needed any assistance, but a bloom of pink was already deepening Louisa's sun-tanned face.

'I'm so sorry about that,' Sharon said, 'to say Tom doesn't always think before he speaks is an understatement.'

Don't worry,' Louisa replied, 'I know it's silly, but I can't help being a bit embarrassed at the thought of what Damian has to do. I prefer to think of it as a simple medical procedure instead of the image which immediately jumps to everyone's mind. Damian doesn't seem at all bothered.'

Sharon wriggled her toes into the flip-flops by the side of her sun bed. 'I'm quite sure I'd feel the same as you, but Tom wouldn't be fazed at all. It's a man thing I suppose. Just look at them now, fooling around, they're worse than the kids.' They both watched as Tom speared a large sausage with the long- handled fork and held it up in the air. Sharon groaned, guessing what might be coming next. 'Does this remind you of any-one?' he asked. Putting her head to one side she pretended to give it serious thought. 'Not really,' she replied, 'it looks a bit puny to me.' It was the kind of answer he was looking for and his reaction had them all laughing again. She turned to Louisa and said wryly, 'Now that definitely is a man thing.'

Fortunately, neither of Damian's parents appeared to be aware of the gist of the men's tomfoolery; Marie was concentrating on the elaborate sandcastle she was building with Lily and Ben, and Stuart was immersed in the local newspaper. Since Sharon and Tom had come to live in Merebank Bay, Marie and Stuart had taken them under their wing and become like grandparents to the children, a role which was welcome on both sides.

Picking her way across the improvised patio, she went towards the house which bore more resemblance to a building site than a home. Swallowing her frustration, she tried to imagine the state-of-the-art kitchen, which Tom assured her would soon be filling the empty space where the newly plastered walls were a dusty shade of pink, and the air was heavy with the smell of dampness.

In the place designated as the utility room, but which temporarily housed an oversized fridge-freezer, she was surprised to see Sam haphazardly shuffling things around in the fridge. He'd left the house earlier, on his way to play in the school football team. At his previous school he'd been one of the star players, and everyone had expected an easy transition to the team in his new school, but it hadn't happened. Although he'd been picked for the squad, he spent all his time as a substitute sitting on the bench.

'Hi, love,' she said. 'what are you looking for?'

'Hi, mum,' he mumbled, 'something to eat, I'm starving.'

Putting the bread and a selection of salads on the trays ready to take out, she tried to keep her tone casual. 'I didn't expect you back so early. Aren't you supposed to be playing football?'

'Mum, you know I am, don't pretend you've forgotten.' Shrugging his shoulders dispiritedly, he added, 'I didn't get picked again. So, I left.'

Sharon knew he hadn't helped his cause by leaving, but there was nothing to be gained by telling him what he already knew, so she decided to leave it for now. 'There's plenty of food out there,' she told him, but he shook his head. 'Why?' she asked, 'you like your dad's barbecues.'

'I do,' he said, 'and I like Louisa and Damian, but it's boring when all you talk about is babies.' Sharon laughed. 'That's not strictly true, but I understand what you mean.

I'll bring some in for you.' Before he had time to reply she hurried outside with the tray. He gave her a weak smile of thanks when she returned with a large plate piled up with food, before turning to go to his bedroom. 'Do you want me to get you a drink?' she asked.

'No thanks, I'm fine.'

Sadly, she watched him go. He was clearly not fine, and his misery snagged her heart. The happy, carefree boy of the past was no longer happy or carefree, and she knew it wasn't all down to the hormones charging round his body. He turned back. 'Don't say anything to dad, will you? I don't want another lecture.'

Sharon rose to Tom's defence, he was as worried about Sam as she was, they just had differing ways of showing it. 'It's only because he cares about you. He's on your side in all this,' she told him.

'Yeah but dad makes it worse by going in to school complaining all the time.'

Fighting the urge to go and hug him as she used to when he was a child, she tried to reassure him instead. 'I'm fairly sure I've managed to get that over to him.'

Sam shrugged. 'He's probably forgotten about it anyway.'

It upset her seeing him like this, but she felt so helpless. He'd been opposed to the idea of moving from the place where he'd been born, and he'd pleaded to be allowed to stay with his grandparents until he left school. That had been out of the question, but he was finding it hard to settle here, and the football issue was making the situation even more difficult for him.

The men's conversation had effortlessly swerved from fertility to football, giving Sharon and Louisa time to catch up on some gossip. Louisa was always fascinated by the latest goings on at The Portland Arms Hotel, but Sharon couldn't understand why everyone found it amusing she was working for the notorious Bryony Portland. She didn't mind, because she enjoyed the job, and despite her boss's reputation she'd found her to be fair if you pulled your weight, and they'd got on quite well up to now. Colin Portland, despite his wife's low opinion of him, was popular with the staff and the local people, and she found him quite pleasant and funny to be with. Their nephew Justin was the manager of the hotel, and his wife Ellie was on maternity leave and due to return in a few months time.

Having almost read the print off the pages, Stuart closed his newspaper and carefully straightened it, before holding it up and tapping the front page. 'This nonsense about the proposed development on the mere isn't going away,' he announced, 'I can't imagine how anyone could even contemplate suggesting such a thing.' He took off his reading glasses and after rubbing the indentations on the bridge of his nose he replaced them with his regular spectacles.

Tom's manner was casual as he piled onions onto his burger. 'Why are so many people against it?' he asked, taking a hefty bite out of his towering bun. Sharon wasn't fooled, she could read his expression and knew he was more interested in Stuart's reply than he was letting on.

'You haven't lived here long enough to be aware of the importance of that area,' Stuart said. 'It's the home and breeding ground for many species of birds and lots of other forms of wildlife, and it hosts overwintering swans, geese and oystercatchers, to name but a few. Nobody in their right mind would even contemplate submitting such a plan.'

'Even if they were promising to build affordable housing for local people?' Tom asked.

'Not even then.'

If Tom replied, it went unheard during the commotion which ensued. Rusty was racing round the garden, barking loudly as he ineffectually tried to chase off the seagulls which, lured by the smell of food, were hovering unnervingly low. Lily was in pursuit and making even more noise than the dog. Sharon was grateful for the diversion, but she was filled with a deep sense of dread. There had been a small, but vocal opposition when Tom had bought the land with the intention of building their house here. But as there had been no legitimate reason for his application to be turned down, most people had accepted it. But this was different, and opposition to a housing estate on the Mere was gaining momentum.

Most residents were vehemently against it, and Tom, not having been born here, or a 'coaster,' as they called themselves, it would anger them even more. Stuart would be at the forefront of any campaign to prevent it happening, and she hoped with all her heart it wasn't going to be a bone of contention between the two families. Marie and Stuart were so dear to them; it would break her heart if anything happened to spoil their friendship. They'd had enough turmoil in their lives already, the last thing they needed now was everyone falling out.

Chapter 2

Despite the last-minute panic, searching out the various cardboard tubes, rubber bands, and pieces of string, which Lily insisted were her contribution to the improvised school band, they arrived at school with time to spare. Sharon stood near the gates, ready to make a quick getaway, but it was a few minutes before any of Lily's friends came and whisked her away. An animated discussion was being had by a group of parents nearby, and one of the men broke off from what he was saying to glance in Sharon's direction. Realising she was watching him; he gave a surreptitious nod before quickly turning away.

Normally she wouldn't have thought anything of it, but she was convinced it was because of the gossip surrounding the proposal to build a new estate. If this was a sign of how strongly people were already reacting, there was no way of knowing where it could lead and she wanted to have no part in it. Tom was obviously intending to get involved, and she knew she needed to persuade him to change his mind. She decided to have it out with him as soon as possible.

She strode briskly towards the promenade where her steps slowed to a more leisurely pace. She loved this start to the day when she was alone with her thoughts, it gave her time to clear her head of the chaos at home and prepare herself for the more structured situation at work. Most of the time she was able to compartmentalise the two but sometimes there was inevitably a cross over. For her, family would always come first.

A short distance away, a group of women she recognised from the school playground had gathered around the fountain. Some of them were struggling to prevent their toddlers from getting wet as they teetered on tiptoes, leaning precariously over the edge of the ornate bowl, dabbling little fingers in the water. One by one their resisting, wriggling bodies were forced back into their buggies and securely fastened, accompanied by wails of protests from the children and promises of treats from the mums. They were familiar faces to her, members of a fluid group of young women who gathered together at the school gates to stroll along the sea-front and enjoy a coffee in one of the cafés.

Walking slowly along the promenade she breathed in deeply, savouring the salty, fresh air of the place she'd loved for as long as she could remember. This was the place Tom had proposed to her, and she'd always dreamed of living here. Sometimes, she couldn't believe it had come true, but it had come at a cost and there were still little niggles to be dealt with.

Glancing at her watch she broke into a run as she neared the hotel. Punctuality was demanded by Bryony Portland and she cursed herself for losing track of time. Puffing slightly as she hurried up the steps of the hotel, she resolved to take more exercise; these relaxed strolls to work did nothing to keep her fit and she was slowly but surely putting on weight. Tom, with his delicious, fattening barbecues, was no help at all, and when she moaned about getting fat, he told her he loved her curves and called her bonny. Instead of reassuring her, this had the opposite effect, and although she had no wish to return to the skinny specimen she'd been reduced to during the food bank days, somewhere in-between would be nice.

Patting her new shorter hairstyle into place she sighed as she felt her natural curls begin to spring back, but there was no time to do anything about it now, so she spun through the revolving door into the rarefied world of The Portland Arms.

She'd been surprised and flattered when Mrs. Portland had added the role of Wedding Organiser to her new remit, but Justin had brought her down to earth by pointing out the reasoning behind it.

'She's the Mayoress and thrives on all the glamour that goes with it,' he said, 'and she can't possibly do herself justice without shedding some of her workload here. But watch out - when Mr. P's year of office ends, she'll soon be sticking her oar in again.'

'I don't care,' Sharon replied, 'I'll just enjoy it while it lasts.'

And she was enjoying it, but with reservations. Mrs. Portland had given her the responsibility for wedding planning, but seemingly couldn't quite bring herself to relinquish all her involvement, and already she'd interfered in some of Sharon's plans. There was the potential for friction, which was something Sharon was desperate to avoid. There would only be one winner if that happened.

Fortunately, the meeting she'd arranged for this morning was straight forward and she didn't anticipate any problems. The young couple had chosen to stretch their budget to the limit to enable them to hold their wedding at the hotel, but it meant there was very limited money available for all the extras and Sharon had been tasked with coming up with some original and inexpensive ideas. The only thing they'd set their heart on was a spectacular start to their first waltz, and Sharon had spent a lot of time negotiating a price they could afford.

Justin was in his usual place behind the desk in reception, and she returned his friendly welcome as she passed on her way to collect a file from the office. When she returned, she laid it on the desk to flick through the pages and do a quick mental assessment of what had been agreed, and what still needed to be done.

'They've got an idea for their first dance,' she said to Justin, 'look, it's an enormous balloon filled with tiny lights and hung over the ballroom where....'

'Balloons! What do you mean balloons?'

Sharon spun round; she had no idea Mrs. Portland was standing behind her. 'It's just one balloon,' she explained, 'I know you don't like them on the tables and around the hotel, but I thought you wouldn't mind just this one.'

Sparks glinted in Bryony Portland's eyes. 'Then you thought, wrong, didn't you?' she said icily. 'We do not *do* balloons at The Portland Arms. I thought you'd be aware of that.' Turning on her heel she began to walk away, and then pausing for a moment she added. 'You'd better find a suitable alternative. Quickly.'

Stunned, Sharon watched her walk towards the lift. 'Oh my God, where did that come from?' she muttered. Placing his index finger on his lips, Justin slowly shook his head until Mrs. Portland was out of sight. Sharon waited; she'd learned from experience her boss's hearing was as well-honed as her ability to appear from nowhere.

Justin watched the lift doors slide together 'Actually,' he said thoughtfully, 'I think I probably know the answer to that. I'm fairly sure the appearance of Greg Robson is the reason behind her bad mood.'

Sharon was puzzled. 'Greg, what has he done to upset her?'

Justin hesitated. 'This is absolutely top secret,' he said, 'you mustn't repeat it to anyone. It seems there's going to be a meeting here this morning, a very private and confidential meeting, and even Mrs. P. didn't know about it until just now.'

'And where does Greg fit into this?'

'Ah, that's what I'm coming to. Greg is coming to the meeting and I guess that's why she's in a tizzy.'

Sharon shrugged her shoulders dismissively. 'I really don't know what all the fuss is about, it sounds ridiculous to me.'

Justin nodded. 'I know what you mean, but I don't think they've met very often since Amelia's wedding and you know what happened that day.'

The memory of the day Justin was referring to was imprinted on her brain. Tom's brother and best friend had almost lost their lives at sea, but she knew he wasn't referring to that. 'Many things happened that day,' she said, 'but I suppose you mean when Greg found out he was Amelia's father.'

'Yes, and I don't think he's forgiven her.'

Sharon flicked through her file and frowned. 'Greg isn't the type to make a scene,' she said absentmindedly, 'and he's been with Katy for years, so Mrs. P. should get over it and get on with her life. With all her money it shouldn't be too difficult.'

Justin nodded. 'I suppose so,' he agreed, 'but I don't think she has got over him.'

'Well I haven't got time to stand here gossiping, the happy couple will be here soon.' Sharon closed her file in frustration. 'What on earth can I offer them instead of the balloon, I've looked on the internet and everything decent costs more than they can afford.'

Justin turned to her with a smile. 'Ellie and I got married here, and we must still have the lights...'

He was just about to lift the phone when a well-known local councillor entered the foyer and walked towards them. Justin positioned himself to greet him, but his welcoming smile froze on his lips as the visitor walked straight past and hurried around the corner towards the small meeting room.

'Well,' Justin huffed, 'manners don't cost anything, as my mum always says.'

Sharon frowned. The man seemed vaguely familiar, but she couldn't place him, and she certainly couldn't remember his name. When she asked Justin, he said it was better that way and to forget whoever she saw coming in that morning.

'You make it sound as though someone's been murdered,' she said, 'you obviously know more than you're letting on, so you'd better tell me, or I'll spill the beans.'

'It isn't all that important,' he told her, 'Just an unofficial meeting about building a housing estate, I think. Personally, I don't see what all the fuss is about.'

Sharon felt as though she'd been punched in the stomach. If meetings were being held to discuss the development, even if they were unofficial, it turned rumour into reality. How did she not know about this meeting? There was only one reason for Tom's silence; he knew how she felt about him being involved. He was either siding with the developers or even worse, he was behind the proposal.

'What's Greg's opinion?' she asked, 'is he in favour of it?'

Jason shook his head. 'I've no idea who thinks what. From what I can gather these people today are from all sides of the debate. Anyway, I'd better ring Ellie about those lights before your clients come.'

'Too late,' Sharon groaned, 'they're already here.'

'Keep them occupied, get them a coffee or something. I'll be as quick as I can.'

Sharon walked over to the couple who were holding hands and smiling as they looked around them. They still couldn't believe they were lucky enough to have their wedding in The Portland Arms and they radiated happiness at the anticipation of it. She would do all in her power to make it the perfect day for them.

Chapter 3

Bryony closed the door and took several deep, calming breaths before walking towards the window. She looked out at the familiar view of the bay where yachts moved smoothly along the water and fishing boats were silhouetted on the distant horizon. Vision below the window was restricted due to the room's position at the top of the building, but the view of the promenade and beyond was clear. The holiday season wasn't yet in full swing, but there were plenty of tourists taking advantage of the mild weather, and local parents with pre-school children mingled happily with those who were enjoying the freedom of retirement.

One of the couples caught her attention and she recognised Stuart and Marie walking leisurely along the promenade. Occasionally, Stuart stopped to look through his binoculars while Marie carried on alone, until they reached their favourite shelter where she lost view of them. She guessed they were sitting inside facing the sea. Marie was her oldest friend, but they had fallen out at Amelia's wedding. They'd patched things up over time, but things had never been quite the same since. To say it had never been the same between her and Greg was an understatement of the century; they had barely exchanged more than a few sentences in the space of five years.

Any initial hope of a reconciliation had been ruined by his unexpected relationship with Katy Sheridan, and the shock of that had catapulted her into the arms of Ethan Denning. When his wife made her presence known and Bryony discovered he'd lied to her about being divorced, she used it as the reason she'd been looking for to return home without losing face. Arriving back in Merebank, she soon discovered that for the first time in its history, The Portland Arms Hotel was experiencing financial difficulties. She approached her father-in-law Ralph and offered to take up her previous position as the manager of the business, to which he readily agreed. Colin was doing his best but Ralph admitted finances and management were not amongst his son's best skills. After she resumed her role in the business, things began to improve.

Unfortunately, neither Greg nor Amelia had been able to find it in their hearts to forgive her, despite the fact she'd only kept the secret to protect them, but while she was desperate to restore her relationship with her daughter, time had helped to erase Greg from her heart.

When she suspected Colin was hoping to resume their marital life, she quickly put him right. He must have known it was impossible after everything that had happened, and anyway their marriage had been over long before that. In order to keep up appearances she'd agreed to return to their home at The Lodge for the duration of their term of office as Mayor and Mayoress, but she was adamant it was for twelve months only. When it came to an end, they would have to reconsider their living arrangements.

Most of the time she was content to let him run his own life, but when he told her about the meeting, he'd arranged for this morning she was furious and told him he was an idiot. It was stupid getting involved in such a controversial issue while he was Mayor, and nothing he said on the contrary would convince her otherwise.

'Don't get out of your depth, and don't say I didn't warn you,' she'd cautioned him, convinced he was being used, and terrified he was jeopardising his position as Mayor. If he did anything to cut short her reign as Mayoress she would never forgive him. She was determined to enjoy her time in the public eye, and was willing to go to great lengths to prevent him making a fool of himself.

Learning that Greg was attending the meeting had caused a momentary tingle of anticipation, not least because she'd heard a rumour that he was single again. For years, she'd hoped there was a chance for them to be together, but that was all behind her now and she'd moved on. The expensive and exclusive 'Select Dating Agency' had proved very rewarding and she'd enjoyed several relationships, one of which was looking very promising. Unfortunately, she'd had to put things on hold during her term of office, but she couldn't wait to pick up where she'd left off. She'd barely tolerated the physical side of her marriage to Colin, but even the more appealing brief affair with Greg paled into insignificance compared to some of these exciting romances.

Unable to resist, she opened one of the doors of the wardrobes lining the wall, and a small sigh of pleasure escaped her lips. This was her compensation for what she was missing, a full array of all the designer clothes and gowns she would be wearing as the Lady Mayoress. Despite Colin's reservations she'd already spent far more than the allocated allowance for their year in office, but most of this had been paid for out of her own pocket, together with a little help from the business.

She had no qualms about what she was doing, after all it was a once in a lifetime experience and she was determined to make the most of it. Colin acceded when she explained the benefits it would bring to the business, and she did genuinely believe it would prove to be the best publicity that money could buy. If she acquired a few new clothes in the process it was a small reward for all her efforts, and the hotel and town would both benefit.

If only she could overcome the one thing overshadowing everything, her satisfaction would be complete, but no matter how much she tried she couldn't conquer her fear of public speaking. In her imagination, she could visualise herself addressing rapt audiences, but unfortunately the reality was very different, and the act of standing up to speak to even a small number of people was enough to send her into a panic. The speaking course she'd purchased online had been virtually useless, and the shock of her cleaner's reaction when she'd unwittingly walked in on Bryony practising voice projection still had the power to mortify her. Unable to contain her laughter, Angela had clapped her hand over her mouth and backed swiftly out of the room, leaving Bryony humiliated and angry.

It was made even more frustrating by Colin's ability to stand up and give a half decent performance interspersed with humorous anecdotes, while she was a bag of nerves. She was working on a strategy which would enable her to fulfil the role without the need for many speeches, and she was convinced most of her audiences would be grateful they didn't have to listen to the dull ramblings of some boorish official. There would of course be times when she would have to say something, but she was confident of her ability to keep the women's organisations interested with her knowledge of fashion and her role in business.

She decided to make a quick visit to see Ralph. He'd always recognised her skills and was the only person who'd shown a thread of compassion when she'd come back home again. It was a combination of his belief in her business acumen and a genuine, mutual fondness for each other which had eased her return to the family and the hotel. Colin had acted as though her return was inevitable, which irritated her greatly, but at least it meant he hadn't put up any barriers to prevent her taking up her previous position.

It was only a few steps along the corridor to Ralph's room but the contrast between hers and the penthouse was remarkable. When he'd retired from running the business, he'd chosen to leave the Lodge and make his home at the hotel. Sparing nothing, he'd ensured the conversion was stunning and a lovely place to live. Although he'd made a good recovery from several small heart attacks, Bryony still worried about him, and was relieved that by living here he had someone on call day and night. She was careful not to mention this to him.

Entering his apartment, she was met by a very familiar scene. He was sitting in his favourite chair, a book on his lap and coffee and a plate of biscuits on a small table by his side. Although he was looking older, he'd retained his suave demeanour, aided by his handsome face and full head of thick, silver hair. He was the smartest and most honest man she'd ever known, and she respected and loved him more than almost anyone else in the world.

'Good morning father-in-law,' she said before dropping an affectionate kiss on his cheek, 'how are you this morning?'

'I'm fine thank-you,' he replied, 'and you, how are things with you?'

'Not too bad,' she replied, sitting in the chair on the other side of the small coffee table, from where there was a breath-taking, panoramic view of the whole bay. At Ralph's request, the window gave an unrestricted view of the promenade, the coastline opposite, and the horizon where the sea met the sky. On a clear day like this everything was thrown into sharp focus and it was a scene she never tired of seeing. 'It's beautiful isn't it?' she murmured, not really expecting a reply, and Ralph nodded his agreement.

The sound of voices below the window caught her attention. 'The men are putting up the bunting for the carnival already,' she said, 'it seems to come around very quickly, I can't believe it's almost twelve months since the last one.'

Ralph chuckled. 'The years get shorter as you get older. Wait until you're my age, they simply fly past.'

She shuddered at the thought of him getting old and changed the subject quickly. 'I've ordered some lights for the front of the hotel this year,' she said, 'I've never done it before as you know, but I thought it would be nice and welcoming for the dance we'll be holding for the carnival on Saturday.'

Ralph looked thoughtful, and she was surprised when he appeared less than enthusiastic about the idea, but she was even more taken aback when he told her he'd heard murmurings of discontent amongst some of the locals.

'Apparently not everyone shares your enthusiasm for two separate events going on at the same time,' he told her, 'and I must admit I have some misgivings myself; it will split the occasion into two groups instead of the one traditional disco in the Memorial Hall.'

Bryony dismissed the criticism with a flutter of her fingers, but she was shaken by Ralph's lack of support. 'There will always be some stick-in-the-muds who find fault with anything new, but if we listened to them nothing would ever change. What are they objecting to anyway?' Without giving him time to reply she carried on speaking. 'How can they complain when I'm offering the ballroom as a venue for the ball? Free of charge don't forget.'

Ralph waited a few seconds before replying and his voice was measured. 'I don't think it's anything to do with that, they feel you're dividing the community and in a way they're right, because after all, the Mayor and Mayoress have always joined in the fun with everyone else.'

Bryony rapidly considered her options. It was true the traditional climax to the carnival had always been in the Memorial Hall, but the type of celebration had sometimes varied, and having a dance in different premises was only a small step away. No-one could object to that, but she had to convince Ralph, who was steeped in tradition and loyalty to the residents.

'We are hoping to make a lot of money,' she said quietly, 'not only from the tickets, but we're holding an auction and I have a few other things in mind. Surely they will understand it's all for a good cause.' She took a deep breath and after a swift debate within herself, she voiced her own secret ambition, to help him understand what she was doing.

'The final figures for last year's appeals have just been announced, and they've not only broken all records, they've done it by a mile. I've got to set my sights higher and I'm sure this will help,' she said, 'do you understand?'

Ralph smiled. 'I thought I knew you very well, but you can always surprise me,' he said gently, 'Bryony I know you mean well, but from now on I suggest you take other people's feelings into account and that way you'll keep them on board. Have your dance, and I hope it's a success, but from now on I'd set your sights a little lower if I were you, and that way you may be surprised just what you achieve.'

Sensing there was a double meaning to his words which she was unable to fathom, she thanked him. 'I knew you'd understand,' she said, 'now I must go, but before I do, there is something I want to ask you.'

Ralph nodded, but when she still hesitated, he asked gently. 'Is it something I can help you with?'

'I don't honestly know. I'm thinking of inviting Amelia and Piers to stay with us at The Lodge for the weekend of the carnival. What do you think?'

'I never ask how things are progressing between you,' he said thoughtfully, but I've been hoping they're improving. I know you meet occasionally, but I think that's mostly when you are with Colin, and of course on the rare occasion with me.'

'She never answered my calls for a long time, but I never give up trying,' she replied, 'but recently I've sensed a little softening in her response to me on the odd occasions we have spoken.' She stood and looked out of the window. A local school was holding its sports day on the beach while their playing fields were being prepared as a running track for the carnival. The triple glazing and distance blocked out the sound, but the children's expressions and antics clearly demonstrated their excitement and determination to win. In contrast she felt sadness seeping through her veins, all she wanted was to have her child back.

'I sometimes wonder if she will ever forgive me,' she said, 'Oh Ralph, I do miss her so much.'

His face reflected her sadness, with the added sorrow at the collapse of his family, and he had no idea how they would ever heal the breach. 'I don't think it would do any harm to invite them,' he said, 'after all, Colin is the Mayor and she'll probably want to share the weekend with him.' His words hurt, but she knew he was speaking the truth. 'I'm sorry Bryony, but that is the reality and nothing I say will change it. Do you wish me to have a word with Colin and together we'll try to persuade her to accept your invitation?'

Bryony shook her head. 'Thanks, but I feel I must take advantage of this opportunity to contact her. But if she declines, I'd be grateful for your help.'

'And Colin's,' he replied, 'don't forget him.'

'Of course not. After all, she is still close to him.'

Reluctant to leave, she slowly walked over to him, and Ralph began to speak, his voice so low she thought for a moment he was talking to himself.

'It was a terrible shock for Amelia, and indeed all of us, when we found out that Greg was her father, and I fully understood why she rejected you. But the bitterness has gone on long enough and it is benefitting no-one, including Amelia. I think the time has come for more understanding and forgiveness on all sides and if there's anything I can do to help, please ask.' Bryony put her arms round him, and they embraced each other affectionately. 'I love you Ralph, and so does Amelia,' she said, 'if anyone can do it, you can.'

'I'm making no promises,' he replied, 'but I want my family whole again.'

Chapter 4

The boy was standing alone, his eyes fixed on the horizon. Every now and then he bent down to pick up a pebble, examine it, and then throw it in a desultory fashion into a rock pool. Stuart watched from a distance before joining him.

'Hi Sam,' he said.

'Hi Stu.'

'Do you mind if I join you?'

'No.'

In silence Stuart raised the binoculars to his eyes and tried to pick up a sighting of any rare visitor to the bay. Oyster catchers proliferated as usual, but he glimpsed the black-tailed godwits and a curlew was silhouetted against the sky.

'What can you see?' Sam asked.

'Just the usual,' Stuart replied, 'do you want to have a look?'

Wordlessly, Sam took the binoculars and with Stuart's help he adjusted the lenses to his eyes. 'Wow,' he said, 'I've been standing here for ages and never realised how many birds were out there.' After a few moments, he lifted his chin and peered across the water which stretched into the distance until it disappeared over the horizon. 'My uncle nearly drowned out there.'

'Yes,' Stuart replied, 'it's quite true, and he wasn't the only one in danger that night. Luckily, and because of the lifeboat crew, no-one lost their life.'

'What were they doing?'

'They had no work, and they were desperate to make some money, so they went out to fish for cockles. Unfortunately, they were ill equipped and inexperienced.'

'So why would mum and dad want to live here?'

'They've put those memories aside to try and give you a better life, I suppose.'

'Well, they needn't have bothered, I was happy where I was.'

'It must be difficult leaving all your friends behind and trying to settle in a new school. I've always lived around here, so I suppose in a way I was lucky, although I didn't always feel that way. Sometimes I envied boys who came from exciting sounding places.'

'Like Bolton and Burnley?' Sam asked ruefully.

'No,' Stuart laughed, 'a little bit further afield than that.'

'Manchester then.'

'I suppose this place seems a bit boring at first for a lad of your age, but given time I'm sure you'll find things to interest you. What's your favourite subject at school?'

'I like biology and I think I'm going to study the environment.'

'Well, you couldn't be in a better place than this to study that subject,' Stuart said. They stood in silence before Stuart asked impulsively, 'are you doing anything next Sunday?'

'No. Why?'

'I'm going up the estuary, there's something happening I like to go and watch. It is not what you call exciting, but you might find it interesting.'

'Is it birdwatching?'

'Not exactly, its more about fishing in a way.'

'Yeah, cool. At least it will get mum and dad off my back.'

'Ok. I'll pick you up about ten.'

'No. I'll come to yours.'

'Ok. See you then. I'd better get back before Marie sends out a search party.'

'Me too.'

They reached the top of the steps where their journeys diverted and Stuart had walked a few steps when Sam called his name. 'Stu, is it okay for me to call you that? No-one else does and Mum says it's disrespectful.'

Stuart laughed. 'Of course, lad, you're more than welcome. It was the name everyone used until I married Marie, and then she insisted I changed it.'

'Why?'

'She said a stew was something you made in a pan with meat and vegetables, and she didn't fancy being married to one.'

Laughter filled the air as they went their separate ways.

Chapter 5

The call from school sent Sharon into a panic. She left it to Justin to find Mrs. Portland and explain why she had absented herself from work. The headmistress chose her words carefully, but all Sharon needed to know was that Lily had fallen, or been pushed. The bang to her head had resulted in a cut above her eyebrow. The staff member in charge of first aid had advised that Lily should be taken to hospital due to the blow to her head, and an ambulance had already been called.

Sharon told them not to wait for her, she would make her own way to the hospital. She ran home to pick up the car and by the time she got to the hospital Lily had been examined and was ready to have the dressings applied to the cut. Although a much simpler procedure than having stitches in, it had been decided to wait for Sharon before proceeding. She'd been very brave, the teacher explained, but as soon as Lily saw Sharon the floodgates opened, and she burst into tears. 'It was all Liam's fault,' she sobbed, 'he pushed me.' Mrs. Banks smiled and gently suggested she didn't think the scuffle had been all one sided and Sharon nodded her understanding while commiserating with her indignant daughter.

When Lily was discharged, Mrs. Banks declined Sharon's offer of a lift home, explaining she had organised a taxi, and after saying goodbye to Lily the two women shared their feelings of relief that no serious damage had been done.

'We will have a word with Liam, and indeed all the children,' the teacher told Sharon, but it's very difficult to prevent these little altercations.'

'I know,' Sharon said with feeling, 'it's bad enough at home, and there are only three of them. Don't worry about it.'

Sharon took Lily to the café close to the maternity and childrens unit but instructed her not to go into the play corner in case she banged her head again. Lily took one look around and decided it was too babyish for her anyway and chose a book from the mini library instead. Sharon was just finishing a call updating Tom on what was happening, when she felt a tap on her shoulder and with surprise saw Louisa standing there. Lily proudly showed off the sticker she'd been given to prove how brave she'd been, and after giving Louisa a hug she settled on her seat to drink a hot chocolate smothered in tiny marshmallows and concentrated on her book.

Sharon asked Louisa to join them, and after giving a brief description of what had brought them there, she waited for Louisa to explain why she was in this part of the hospital. Judging by her red eyes and blotchy face she didn't have anything to celebrate today and knowing how desperate Louisa and Damian were to start a family she hesitated before saying anything. They chatted about inconsequential things for several minutes, until Louisa, told Sharon she'd just had an appointment with her gynaecologist. 'I came for the results of the scan and laparoscopy,' she whispered.

Sharon watched as Louisa dabbed her eyes. It was obvious the outcome wasn't good, but she was shocked when Louisa told her just how bad it was. 'The endometriosis is worse than they thought,' she explained, 'it's already spread inside my womb, much more rapidly than they expected.'

Sharon was puzzled. 'I thought your inability to conceive was due to the damage to your ovaries, not your womb.'

'It was, but it's more serious now, because even if I could conceive, this means there is no possibility of me carrying a child full term.'

Sharon was stunned. To be told there was no possibility of carrying a child was unimaginable. Thrashing around in her mind for something supportive to say, all she could come up with sound so futile.

'Surely, there must be something they can do,' she said lamely. She listened in disbelief when Louisa briefly explained what had happened.

'Apparently not,' she said, 'in fact, it's just the opposite, Mr. Clarke recommends I have a hysterectomy as soon as possible, and there's nothing more final than that.'

Feeling so inadequate, she took Louisa's hand and pressed it between her own. 'Why isn't Damian with you?' she asked softly, 'you shouldn't be here on your own.'

'I know, but I'd convinced myself there would be some positive news today, so I decided to come alone. He's already taken so much time off work to be with me, I decided against telling him about this appointment. I don't know what I was expecting to hear, but it certainly wasn't this.'

Sharon glanced at Lily to check she was still engrossed in her book, before mentioning something which was puzzling her. 'Louisa,' she said gently, 'I don't quite understand why you've been having IVF treatment before you knew the extent of the problem. Why have they been putting you through all that trauma? Surely they should have waited until they'd confirmed exactly what was wrong?'

'That's my fault,' Louisa said, 'and that's what makes it worse.' She was weeping silently now, and Sharon waited patiently. 'Mr. Clarke said we could start IVF on the NHS if it proved necessary after the investigations were finished, but I was worried about losing time and persuaded Damian it would speed things up if we went privately instead. Now it means it was all a waste of time and money.'

'Oh, Louisa, I'm so sorry, but you didn't know it would turn out like this.'

'I know, but I should have been more patient instead of becoming obsessed with getting pregnant. I feel so bad about it now.'

'No, you have no reason to blame yourself,' Sharon said emphatically, 'you only did what you felt was right at the time and Damian knows that.'

'Maybe, but he didn't expect this when he married me, and now he probably wishes he hadn't.'

Sharon tightened her grip. 'Louisa, you mustn't talk like that, Damian adores you, everyone knows that. He married you because he loves you, and yes, he may have wanted you to have children together, but I'm sure he'll never regret marrying you.' When Louisa lifted her pale, tearful face, Sharon added, 'you'll break his heart if he hears you saying that.'

'I know,' Louisa replied, 'but I love him so much I just wish I could do this one thing for him.'

Lily was starting to become restless and Sharon guiltily scooped her onto her lap. Her face was drained of colour and she looked very tired as she pressed herself into Sharon's breast. 'I want Bear,' she whimpered. 'Of course, you do sweetheart,' Sharon said, kissing the top of her head, 'we're going home now, and you can stay on the couch all afternoon and watch a video with him.'

Lily came to life and looked at Sharon in surprise, 'Aren't I going back to school?'

'No, of course not, you're a very brave little girl but that nice doctor said you had to rest today.'

Louisa stood up and stuffed the leaflets she'd been given into her bag. 'I'm sorry,' she said, 'Lily's the real patient here, and I've made you neglect her.' Sharon smiled. 'Lily is fine,' she said, 'we'll be home soon and reunited with Bear. I have a feeling she is going to enjoy the rest of her day.'

In the car park, Sharon hugged Louisa. 'Be strong, and don't completely give up hope, there are lots of things they can do these days and hopefully even more in the future.'

'I know. Thanks for everything Sharon, I am so sorry I burdened you with this, especially with Lily there.'

'I told you not to worry about that, she's okay. Keep in touch and we'll have a coffee together soon.'

Sharon drove out of the car park and they were soon on the way home. Lily was able to see out of the car window from her elevated position in the car seat, and in the middle of pointing out things which caught her interest, she asked casually. 'Why was Louisa crying?' Wondering how much she'd heard of the conversation; Sharon was taken by surprise.

'Err. Because she's got a poorly tummy and she's got to have an operation,'

'Grandma had an operation and she didn't cry.'

'No, you're right, she didn't.'

'The doctor put a new knee in her leg, didn't he?'

'He certainly did.'

'Why did she want two knees in the same leg?'

'Oh, I don't think it works like that sweetheart,' laughed Sharon.

Tom was already there when they arrived home and he swept Lily up in his arms. 'How's my little soldier?' he demanded, 'I believe you were incredibly brave.'

'I never cried once,' she replied proudly and then glanced towards Sharon. 'Well maybe just once, but that was when mummy came.'

Tom burst out laughing. 'Well, mummy has that effect on me sometimes, but I'm sure she doesn't mean it.'

Sharon faked a frown. 'Very funny, but don't push your luck just because you feel safe hiding behind your daughter. I'll deal with you later.'

'Promises, promises,' he chortled, as he settled Lily on the couch and sat next to her, one arm gently resting around her shoulder. Lily instinctively leaned into him, and watching them, Sharon felt a sense of relief that things had turned out so well. It could have been so much more serious, a bang to the head and all the many potential repercussions didn't bear thinking about, so she pushed them to the back of her mind and thought about Louisa who hadn't been so lucky.

As if reading her mind, Lily suddenly said, 'We saw Louisa at the hospital today,' and without taking her eyes from the screen added, 'she was crying.'

'I guess she was upset about something then,' Tom said, looking questioningly at Sharon 'sometimes that happens, just like you were upset after your little accident today.'

Lily looked at him indignantly. 'It wasn't an accident, Liam pushed me.'

'Well he'd better not do it again or else he'll be in trouble,' Tom said.

'It's alright,' Lily replied, 'I'm going to push him tomorrow.'

'That's my girl,' Tom began, but Sharon's warning look cut him short and he corrected himself. 'Perhaps that isn't a good idea, you might end up hurting someone or getting hurt yourself, in any case you've got to be very careful not to bust your stitches.'

'They're not stitches,' she replied adamantly, but with Bear once more firmly secured under her chin, she turned her attention back to the television and the princess with icicles for fingers.

'I'll explain later,' Sharon mouthed, and he nodded. 'At this rate, we are going to be very busy later.'

Sharon phoned the hotel and was able to speak to Mrs. Portland, who showed a certain amount of understanding, while at the same time pointing out how these kinds of emergencies involving children very often turned out to be grossly exaggerated minor incidents. Sharon came off the phone not knowing if she should feel reassured or reprimanded, but by this time she was beyond caring. Mentally exhausted, she decided to have an early night and she was pleased when Tom said he would join her. Discussions about Lily's accident and Louisa's bad news dominated their conversation, but it puzzled her how he'd managed to return home so quickly from Benton, where he was working.

Slipping under the duvet, she broached the subject as casually as she was able. 'I thought you were very busy,' she said, 'how did you manage to leave work so early?'

'We are busy, but I had a meeting to go to and it finished early. When I came back to change into my working gear, you phoned, so I decided to stay here and wait for you to come home.'

'You seem to be having quite a few meetings, are you having problems?'

Pulling her close he held her tight and stroked her hair. 'There are no problems,' he murmured, 'now what about your promise to deal with me later.'

'Don't change the subject.'

'Why?' he asked, 'this is far more enjoyable than work.'

'You will tell me if there's something wrong? You promised there'd be no more secrets between us.'

'Sharon there's nothing to worry about, and there are no secrets, it's just the usual day to day business. Now let's get sleep, I've got a busy day tomorrow.'

'So, have I,' she replied. She knew this uneasy feeling would be waiting for her the following morning.

Chapter 6

Bryony mixed herself a smoothie and carried it to the gazebo at the bottom of the garden. The sound of the gardener's activity in the orchard on the other side of the fence was strangely soothing and relaxing. Colin had been trying for years to persuade Rupert to retire so he could replace him with someone younger and more energetic, but he resisted all the incentives and Colin could do nothing about it.

If it wasn't for her, there would be no orchard now. When she'd returned, he'd been on the verge of selling all the land belonging to the estate to keep the business afloat, but with some help and financial assistance from Ralph she managed to rescue it. Colin had felt mildly put out by his father's willingness to support Bryony instead of himself, but they all knew the reason, and he was reluctant to force the issue.

When Bryony returned to Merebank, Ralph hadn't hidden his hurt and disappointment in her, but he'd always admired her competence and flair in running the business, and under her renewed management, he'd made the funds available to retain the land. Although it wasn't technically a part of the business, Portland Lodge had been built as a home for the founders of The Portland Arms and Bryony believed the land was also an integral part of it. After all, what was the point of having a beautiful home like Portland Lodge without the privacy provided by the grounds surrounding it.

It was the one place she could come and completely relax away from the demands of work, and it almost made up for living under the same roof as Colin. If only she could persuade him to take up permanent residence at the hotel she would live here permanently, but she couldn't envisage that happening in the foreseeable future, and hopefully she would be living a different life by then.

She was enjoying a wonderful sense of achievement following several successful events during the last few days. The official visit of the Mayors from the surrounding Boroughs had gone down very well indeed and at its conclusion she'd been showered with praise for her very imaginative itinerary. Strictly speaking, the visit to the famous Merebank Golf Club had been Colin's idea, and to her surprise had proved to be the most popular by far, but the ladies had also enjoyed afternoon tea in the café overlooking the sea.

Her fascinator had not only drawn complementary comments, it had also remained securely attached despite the strong winds, unlike the wide brimmed hat of one of the visiting ladies which flew off and skimmed through the air like a frisbee. As they were at the Lifeboat shop at the time, there were many amusing suggestions involving the crew setting out to rescue it, and Marie who was serving had joined in the laughter, but then Bryony overheard her, true to form, effusively sympathising with the woman in question.

Her visit to a primary school had been even funnier, when some of the children had mistaken her for the Queen and insisted on curtsying to her. The teacher went to great lengths to stop them calling her Your Majesty, by pointing out that The Mayoress wasn't as important as the Queen. The children enjoyed trying on the things she'd taken and were reluctant to part with them when she was leaving, so Bryony left some of the hats and beads as a donation to their dressing-up chest. She made sure she packed every one of her pashminas safely back in their boxes. She hadn't been called upon to make a speech apart from a short introduction to the class to explain who she was, but it had boosted her confidence ahead of her forthcoming solo engagements.

Remembering why she was here, she picked up her bag and took out a cigarette case and the gold lighter Ethan Golding had given her. They were the only things of value to come out of the disastrous affair and she was reluctant to throw them away; at least they were proof he'd had some feelings for her. They'd been celebrating her birthday in the restaurant of a lovely hotel in the French Alps when he'd given them to her, but neither the romantic setting nor the jewel encrusted gifts could ease her pain. Her thoughts were far away in England. Months had passed since the debacle of the wedding, and she was hoping Amelia would have forgiven her enough to at least text or email her, but she'd received nothing. Now, five years later she was still trying to pluck up courage to ring her own daughter.

She rarely smoked these days and never in public, but occasionally it helped to calm her nerves and today was one of those times when she needed it. Her hand shook as she flicked the lighter and held it to the cigarette between her lips, but she only inhaled a few times before grinding it out underfoot and putting her finger on the speed dial to Amelia.

She held her breath. Amelia obviously had caller recognition and most of Bryony's previous calls had been ignored. She knew Amelia had read her text messages and discussed them with Colin, as he sometimes inadvertently told her how Amelia had responded to them. He didn't realise what he was doing of course, but it gave her a small measure of comfort to know they were being read, and so she never missed the opportunity to tell her daughter how much she loved her. She was just preparing herself to leave another voicemail when the sound of Amelia's cautious voice reached her.

'Hi mum, is everything okay?'

Bryony exhaled, trying to calm herself, but her heart was beating fast. 'Hello Amelia,' she said, 'yes I'm fine, everyone's fine.'

'How's granddad?' Amelia asked tentatively, 'you're not ringing to tell me he's ill, are you?'

Bryony tried to ignore the implication her call had only been answered by Amelia because she was worried about Ralph. 'Your grandfather is very well,' she said, 'why are you so concerned?'

'Oh, it's just that he was feeling a bit under the weather when I last spoke to him.'

'Really?' Bryony stopped herself just in time from adding she was unaware of anything wrong. He hadn't said anything to her, but she didn't want to admit that to Amelia. 'As far as I know he's fine, and the reason I'm ringing is to talk about the Carnival weekend and to ask if you will come this year. It is of course quite important to your father as he's the Mayor,' she added for good measure.

'Of course, we're coming. I've hardly missed one apart from the year we got married. There's no way we'd miss it with dad as Mayor.'

Bryony couldn't believe what she was hearing. 'Did you come last year?'

'Of course, and the year before that, and the year before that.'

'I didn't know you'd been at all since you got married.'

The few seconds of silence were broken by the sound of the electric trimmer starting up on the other side of the wall and Bryony had to strain to hear Amelia's reply. 'You weren't around for the first couple of years, and then when you came back you didn't come to the carnival anyway.'

Bryony had been determined to avoid any discussion about her time away from home and she wasn't going to let it get in the way of these first steps in making things better between them, so she ignored what Amelia had said. 'Well, we're both going to be here this time, that's what's important now,' and feeling courage deserting her, she blurted, 'do you want to come to and stay at The Lodge? You're very welcome.'

She regretted the words as soon as they were out of her mouth. How formal they must sound to her daughter when all she meant to say was please come home. She waited with bated breath while Amelia considered what she'd said, and she sighed with relief when there was no sign of outright rejection in her voice as she replied. How long would it be before she didn't feel as though she was walking on eggshells every time she spoke to her daughter.

'Is the spare room on the top floor of the hotel available by any chance?' Amelia asked.

Bryony was stunned. Obviously, Amelia didn't regard either the hotel or The Lodge as her own home anymore.

Trying vainly to keep the hurt out of her voice she said sadly. 'That is your room Amelia. It hasn't been used by anyone else and it is exactly as you left it. You never need to ask if it's available, I thought you knew that.'

'It's just never felt right, although dad has tried to persuade me many times. I might just take you up on the offer this time. I'll have a word with Piers and let you know, if that's alright with you.'

It wasn't very much, but it was progress of a kind and she would have to be satisfied with that for the moment. At least she hadn't been rejected again, and Amelia seemed more open to contact between them. But there was still a long way to go. She was intrigued about where Amelia had stayed on previous visits and she couldn't help wondering if she'd been with Greg. If so, she would know the truth behind the rumours of him being single again, but she didn't dare risk the consequences of asking her. Instead, she said simply. 'Of course, that's alright,' but then couldn't resist asking, 'just as a matter of interest, where have you stayed previously?'

'Oh, usually with Damian and Louisa, but it's a bit of a squash for them and they've got quite a lot going on now. I know they wouldn't mind, but just this once I think they need their own space. We'll be with them all weekend anyway. Damian and Piers are in the tug-of-war as usual, but this year they're on opposing teams. Damian is on the lifeboat crew team of course, and Piers is on the open team. They're both playing in the five aside football competition as well, so it will be great fun. They're regular fixtures now those two.'

'That's nice,' murmured Bryony, wondering what Damian and Louisa had going on. She couldn't ask

Amelia, but she would soon be seeing Marie and it shouldn't be too difficult to winkle it out of her.

'I must go now; I'll ring you soon and let you know what we're doing.'

'Thanks darling. Please keep in touch.'

'I will. Mum?'

'Yes?' Bryony replied.

'We must have a talk sometime.'

'Yes, we must,' Bryony agreed.

She climbed into the hammock and rocked gently as she went over the conversation. Clearly, Amelia hadn't tried to avoid her completely over the last few years; she'd obviously expected Bryony to be at the Carnival but it hadn't discouraged her from coming. The thing that really hurt was finding out her daughter had been visiting Merebank regularly and she'd had no way of knowing, which added to her feelings of rejection. Probably everyone in Merebank knew more about her daughter's life than she did, but hopefully that was about to change. She would have a little rest before ringing Ralph to tell him the good news.

Chapter 7

Marie would have skipped her way to the gift shop if it wasn't for the twinges of pain in her back, but after the news she'd received that morning, nothing was going to cloud her day. She'd deliberately set off early, to allow time to walk through the Square where the annual floral displays were being put up. Once again, it was a joint effort between the Council, the Civic Society and residents, who gave both money and their time towards making the town so lovely each year.

Stuart had been there since early morning, helping to erect the frames and supports that had to be in position before the gardeners could start filling them with hundreds of plants, but when she arrived, he was on a platform, hooking a magnificent hanging basket onto a lamp post. Gardening wasn't his best talent, but this was one of the highlights of the year and he was an enthusiastic volunteer. The competition for the best street display had already taken place, and after losing last year, the street they lived on was once again the winner.

The Square thronged with people, some watching the structures being erected, while others were happily appreciating the formations emerging from the multitude of colours. Although most people kept a safe distance, some were obviously getting in the way of the workers, but the atmosphere was genial and pleasant. The cobbles underfoot made walking and working a little tricky for some, but the residents had always fought off any suggestions of paving the road.

The bunting, unsullied yet by wind and rain, was strung between the Victorian style lampposts, adding a cheerful aspect to the whole thing, and a few speciality market stalls were already being erected in readiness for the big day. Marie made her way slowly around the perimeter of the square, looking with interest at the shops which had been entered in the Window Display competition. There were some very imaginative ideas, but she was delighted to see the trophy had been awarded to the book shop which had eye-catching displays all year round. It was one of Lily's favourite places and Marie took pleasure in buying her a book whenever they were in town together.

The carnival procession didn't come through the Square; the streets leading to it were far too narrow for the large vehicles making up the floats, and it was too bumpy anyway, but Marie was pleased it remained the centre of attraction despite that. The procession was a big attraction and great fun, but it was over very quickly in relation to the rest of the celebrations which lasted all weekend. The fun-fair, which was held on the downs, went on well into the following week.

She was just about to resume her journey to work when Sharon almost bumped into her as she jostled her way through a crowd of people.

'I'm so sorry Marie,' she said, shaking her head, 'I don't know if I'm coming or going today. Lily would not get a move on this morning and I only just got her to school on time, and then I remembered Mrs. Portland had asked me to pick up some things from the 'Let's

Party' shop, and so here I am. Out of breath and stressed.'

'You mustn't let her put on you.' Marie said, looking at the bags at their feet. 'She takes advantage of people, but she must remember you have a family to consider as well as being at her beck and call.'

Sharon put her bags on the floor and shuffled them around to spread the load. 'I know,' she replied, 'but you know what's she's like. Anyway, you haven't heard the worst of it. She told me yesterday that I've been given a temporary promotion to the position of secretary to,' she made a parenthesis with two fingers from both hands to emphasise her last two words, 'The Mayoress.' When I told her it simply wasn't possible because of the extra work and child-care involved, she pointed out how *everyone* had rallied round the day I rushed off when Lily was taken to the hospital, and that's what she expects from all her staff. Apparently, it won't involve much more work because she'll attend to most of it herself, but I'm not holding my breath on that score.' She hugged Marie. 'Sorry, but I must go or else I will be really late. Bye' She picked up her bags and hurried away as fast as the crowds and her bulky purchases would allow.

Marie stood for a moment, considering the implications of what Sharon had told her. There was no doubt this latest development would impact on her. Sharon had no-one else to rely on, so any extra hours she had to work meant Marie would have to step in to look after the children. She loved them dearly, but their energy was boundless and she struggled to keep up. A few hours a week was fine, but any longer would be a struggle and she knew what Stuart would say about it. Seeing his platform was on the move, she decided against trying to pass on the good news about Damian until later, so she set off to start her shift at the gift shop.

She arrived to find Claire busily pricing up the latest batch of merchandise which had been delivered that morning, so after putting her bag in the small room behind the counter she went to join her. 'How can I help?' she asked, as Claire expertly fired the stickers from the pricing gun onto the backs of a pile of children's notebooks.

'You could unpack a couple of those parcels please,' Claire replied without breaking her rhythm, 'and then a cup of coffee would be very welcome.'

'No sooner said than done,' Marie replied with a smile as she carefully removed the brown paper wrapping from a few parcels, before folding it neatly to save for future use. Claire grinned at her and Marie shrugged her shoulders. 'Waste not, want not,' was her predictably cheery reply as she went to put the kettle on. By the time she returned with the drinks and two chocolate biscuits, Claire was already arranging the gifts on the shelves. 'The roll has run out,' she laughed, 'I don't suppose you could put a new one in.'

'That's very convenient,' Marie replied, 'it just so happened to run out as I came in. How did you manage that?' Without waiting for an answer, she good-naturedly began the fiddly procedure of putting a new roll of labels into the old-fashioned pricing gun. With a sigh of satisfaction, she laid down the gun and looked around at the well stacked and tidy shelves.

'I'm surprised you had the time to sort all that stock,' she said.

'I know,' Claire replied, 'but it's been very quiet this morning, despite the lovely weather.'

'That's probably because most people have been drawn to the Square.' Marie said. 'The flower displays are being put in place and the bunting is going up. I must say it was already looking lovely when I left. The Council seem to have pushed the boat out this year despite their lack of money.' Chuckling to herself she added, 'I'm sorry, that was an unintentional pun.' Claire frowned questioningly over the rim of her coffee mug until Marie reminded her of the impressive boat shaped exhibit forming the central display.

'Ah, that probably explains it,' Claire replied, 'hopefully most of them will make their way down here after lunch. That reminds me, have you heard the rumours about the extra money being spent on the Square and the adjoining streets, particularly the boat you mentioned?'

Marie had heard nothing, but she had a feeling it was going to involve Bryony, and she soon discovered she was right. No,' she replied, 'what rumours?'

'I don't know if there's any truth in it, but I've heard there's been an anonymous donation from a prominent business-person in the town. It doesn't take much to guess who that is.'

'But what would she gain from that? The procession doesn't go down there.'

'That's what I thought at first, but when I heard she's trying to arrange for the car carrying the Mayor and Mayoress to pass through there on its way to join the procession, it all fell into place. A photo opportunity to publicise the RNLI is how she's selling it apparently.'

'Oh no,' Marie said, 'Damian told me they are already feeling they're being hijacked by the rolling publicity machine of The Mayoress; this is going to make things even worse.'

Claire nodded. 'Do you realise we both knew who we were talking about without even mentioning her name? That must say something about her and her devious ways. By the way, before we leave this boring topic, Her Ladyship was in here earlier, looking for you.'

Marie groaned again. 'What did she want this time?'

'It was far too important for a minion such as me to hear, she's going to get in contact with you soon.'

'Not if I see her coming first,' Marie replied with feeling, 'now come on let's finish these parcels before a rush of customers pile in, I can see quite a few people heading in our direction already.'

They were kept busy for the next two hours and when the relief volunteers arrived Marie and Claire decided to walk to The Sands café before heading home. Stuart and Russell were going to yet another meeting about the proposed development before taking part in a practise session at the bowling club, so Claire texted Russell and arranged for them all to meet later. Marie was happy to leave the arrangements to them, as Stuart was still getting used to his phone. If he heard even the single ping of a text alert while on the green, he would probably panic or at least lose his concentration. That was, of course, if he even had his phone switched on.

They chose a table facing seaward and both ordered herbal tea with one of Billy's famous scones served with strawberry conserve and clotted cream. Claire came back from placing the order at the counter and Marie returned the cheery wave from the affable owner. 'He hasn't lost any weight, has he?' Claire commented as she moved her chair round to give herself a better view of the bay.

'No, but he hasn't put any on either,' Marie replied. 'Why are you looking at me like that?' she asked, wriggling uncomfortably under Claire's scrutiny.

Claire tilted her head slightly. 'I don't really know, it's just that there's something different about you. You seem to have been buzzing all day, as if there's something going on that I don't know about.' Marie grinned and Claire immediately pounced. 'I knew it, there *is* something! Now come on, spill.' To her irritation Billy arrived with their order and she was forced to listen to the small talk before finally rounding once more on Marie. 'So, what's happened?'

'Damian's been asked by the skipper to become a deputy coxswain. He's so pleased, and I'm over the moon because it's such an honour, oh of course he deserves it, but nevertheless it shows how highly they think of him. I suppose you think I'm over-reacting, but I can't help it.'

Claire shook her head vigorously. 'No, I don't. No-one knows better than we do, the time and energy those lads put in, including your Damian, and I'm thrilled for him and you. No wonder you're excited and feeling proud of him.'

'I've been wanting to tell you all day, but the time never seemed right. I haven't had chance to tell Stuart, he'd already left when Damian rang, so please don't say anything until I do.'

'Of course not. That shouldn't be long anyway, because here they are.'

Both men were satisfied with their efforts on the bowling green, but when Claire naively enquired about the meeting their moods changed. They'd learned the rumours were now reality, and plans were about to be submitted for a housing development on, or close to, the Mere. Despite the poll carried out in the local newspaper, which had indicated a large percentage of the population were against the development, it had done nothing to deter the still unknown developer behind the proposal.

Stuart was incandescent with indignation and Marie urged him to keep his voice down as people around were looking over with interest. It was unusual for him to vent his feelings like this, but she knew how strongly he felt about what was happening. Even so, he nodded and when he spoke again, he had dropped his voice.

'The good thing is,' he told them, reading from a scrap of paper in his hand, 'the Local Planning Committee have told the applicants to engage with the community in the pre-application stage. Apparently, they feel this will add value to the process and outcome.'

'Well, that's positive, surely?' Marie exclaimed.

Stuart and Russell reluctantly concurred, but Stuart wasn't totally convinced. 'I suppose so,' he said forlornly, but the final decision will probably come down to a few councillors on the Committee, and what do they care a small bit of land that rightfully belongs to wildlife?'

You're being a bit presumptuous,' Marie said boldly, 'after all, nothing's been decided yet and you never know, the planners may be bird lovers themselves who'll see sense and listen to the voices of the people they are there to represent.'

Stuart couldn't keep the exasperation out of his voice. 'Do you *honestly* think it would have escaped my notice if they were?'

'No, but maybe they will be inclined to save the environment - you don't have to be a bird enthusiast to do that.'

'I hope you're right,' Stuart replied.

'So do I,' Marie whispered under her breath to Claire, 'and not only for the birds sake.'

'Amen to that,' Claire replied as they all stood up to leave. When the men started to plan to meet later for the drink, by unspoken agreement both women declined on the grounds of lacking energy after a busy time in the shop. They knew the conversation would be dominated by the latest turn of events, and the celebration of Damian's promotion would be better left to another time. Marie would choose a moment to give Stuart the news, when he was calmer, and able to enjoy it.

Chapter 8

The Carnival was the largest event of the Mayoral calendar and Bryony was determined to make it the most impressive weekend anyone could remember. Despite strong opposition, she'd insisted on leading the parade from the comfort of a limousine instead of walking with the other officers and leaders of local organisations and charities. When Colin had tried to dissuade her by pointing out she would be more on show to the crowds if she was on foot, she'd come up with a spontaneous and perfect riposte; they could use his prize possession, the open topped Rolls Royce.

Initially refusing on the grounds that it would be liable to get marked or damaged, she managed to cajole him into it by pointing out this once in a lifetime opportunity to show it off. She'd been surprised how quickly he'd capitulated considering the car rarely saw daylight apart from when Colin brought it onto the driveway of the Lodge for its regular clean and polish.

There was no possibility of walking all that way in the shoes she'd bought to go with her outfit for the day. But it wasn't just about shoes; waving from a car was much more dignified than tramping through the streets. She wasn't being unreasonable, she was quite prepared to stand up all the way if necessary, so she couldn't understand the reasoning behind the objections which had been raised. Fortunately, everyone had eventually come around to her way of thinking.

After taking part in the parade, she would crown the local Rose Queen in the park and present the prizes for the best floats and the winners of various sporting competitions. The finale to the day was the disco in the Memorial Hall, but this year, in a break with tradition, she'd organised a dance in the hotel ballroom as well. She'd been surprised at Ralph's unexpected reaction on hearing about it, but she was convinced he would think differently once he was there enjoying himself. It wasn't as if she was suggesting it as a regular feature, so no-one needed to worry about its effect on the regular disco in future years.

This was her day, and she was determined to make the most of it. She'd struggled to hide her disappointment when Amelia had rung to decline her invitation to stay for the weekend, but she reluctantly accepted the decision. It was normal for young people to want to be together, and she presumed they were staying with Damian and Louisa, despite what she'd said previously. Bryony had taken comfort from Amelia's positive response to the suggestion that she and Piers join her parents and grandfather for a meal at the hotel sometime over the weekend.

A small part of her wished she could invite Greg, but she knew it was a vain hope. He would never agree to share a social occasion with her, especially in public. It had been so different when they were young and enjoying the Carnival, especially when they reached their teens and fell in love. She couldn't recall a time when she hadn't loved Greg, and she'd been so proud when he'd chosen her. Their engagement had been the happiest day of her life, but when Colin had unexpectedly declared his love for her, the appeal of becoming a member of the Portland family had proved too strong and she'd made the biggest mistake of her life. She'd paid a high price for status and wealth, and she'd lived to regret it.

Sharon had taken a message from Greg to say he wouldn't be bringing a partner to the evening dance at the hotel, but to Bryony's annoyance Sharon couldn't remember much more about the brief conversation, but after some gentle prompting from Bryony she concluded he'd probably meant he would be unaccompanied all day. He'd given no reason, and of course Sharon hadn't thought to ask why.

As far as Bryony was concerned, there could only be one reason for him coming alone. Greg must be single again, and if so, she would make the most of her opportunity to remind him of what might have been, if he hadn't been so stubborn. As soon as Colin's term of office finished, she intended to tell him she wanted a divorce, but until then she was determined to keep the affair with her latest conquest a secret. It was frustrating, but a harmless game of cat and mouse with Greg would make an amusing diversion until she could pick up her life again.

The procession had been assembling since early morning, and arrangements had been made for them to take their place at the head of the parade as it was about to start moving. Officials had decided the route from the hotel was the preferable option, giving people gathered on the promenade and downs an opportunity to see The Mayor and Lady Mayoress. Some of the roads into town were cordoned off to prevent traffic getting in the way and delaying their arrival, which was being timed to perfection.

Glancing at her watch, Bryony decided she had just enough time to pop in to see Ralph before she needed to go downstairs and join Colin. Standing for a few moments in front of the mirror she felt her confidence rising. It wasn't always easy performing some of the official duties, but today was special, putting her in the spotlight for a whole day. She was aware of the scrutiny she would be under, and for the most part she could cope, but one slip on her part would be remembered for years.

Running her hands down the side of her body, dipping into her waist and over the curve of her hips, she breathed a gentle sigh of satisfaction. The crimson dress and hat were a departure from her normal choice of colour, but she could see they suited her and for this occasion they were an unexpected success. Very opportunely, she'd read an article about how the Queen chose hats which didn't hide her face when she was wanting to be seen by crowds of well-wishers. This one fitted the bill exactly, and Bryony was pleased.

She was truly delighted with the overall effect and when she walked into Ralph's apartment, he confirmed how right she was to feel this way. 'You look absolutely stunning,' he said to her, 'no-one is going to miss seeing The Mayoress today, that's for sure.'

'I wasn't convinced about it at first,' she said, 'it isn't normally my choice of colour and it isn't recommended to go with blonde hair and blue eyes, but I must say I really like it.'

Ralph nodded, 'So do I. Colin must be very proud of his consort. Where is he by the way? He said he would call in before you leave.'

Bryony looked out onto the downs where a small crowd were beginning to gather. When she saw some of the people on the promenade stop to look over to the hotel, she glanced down and saw Colin standing by the side of the car. He watched apprehensively as a group of people approached, but when he realised, they were genuinely interested in the car, he relaxed and became animated as he pointed out various features.

'He's just arrived back with the Rolls,' she said, 'he'll probably come up to see you now, if he can tear himself away.'

Ralph joined her at the window and smiled. 'He's always been that way about cars. Ever since he was a little boy collecting models, he's loved them.'

Not wishing to spoil the moment, Bryony resisted pointing out that that was all very well, but he was an adult now and needed to start acting like one. They watched him leave and hurry up the steps to the hotel and a few minutes later he came into the room. 'Is it alright?' he asked, 'it's a magnet, people can't stop touching it!' He hurried towards the window and looked down, before even greeting his father.

'It's fine,' Ralph said, 'and just in case you're wondering, so am I.'

Colin grinned and went to embrace him. 'Sorry dad, but I'm a bit on edge about leaving the car there.'

Ralph looked affectionately at his son, who although he wasn't the most successful businessman in the world, his heart was in the right place. Unfortunately, he was married to a woman who didn't return his love and Ralph felt sorry for them both.

Bryony accepted a small glass of wine from Ralph, her feeling of confidence and optimism were quickly evaporating since Colin's arrival, leaving her in need of something to calm her nerves. She looked impatiently at Colin who was glued to the window. 'For goodness sake, come away from there, she exclaimed, 'Nobody is going to do anything to your precious car.'

Colin didn't move. 'As a matter of fact,' he said slowly, 'I'm not looking at that, I'm watching out for the car bringing our chains, they said they'd be here by now.'

Bryony gasped, for some reason she'd never given a thought to the official chains. 'Where on earth are they?' she demanded 'If they don't come soon, we'll be late, and the whole procession will be delayed! Or worse still, if they start without us, we'll miss it altogether, because there's nowhere else we can join it!'

Colin turned to face her. 'Calm down,' he said, 'they're on the way. I've given the responsibility for making sure they're where they should be to Janet Bancroft, today and every occasion in the future for the rest of my term of office.' He puffed out his chest with pride. 'She's already contacted me to say they will be here soon. In fact,' he added as he turned back to the window, 'there they are, arriving at this very moment.'

'Thank goodness for that,' was all Bryony could say, but Ralph was genuinely impressed and congratulated Colin for his foresight.

'It seems sensible to make one person responsible for them,' Ralph said, 'that's one less thing to worry about before all your official appointments.' Bryony was left with no option but to agree when Ralph turned to her, waiting for her to say something. After a slight nod she couldn't resist adding, 'I just hope she's up to the task, she seems a bit unreliable to me.'

'Oh, come on Bryn,' Colin protested, 'you've no reason to say that.'

'Well, we'll see. Anyway, all this just proves I was right all along. We ought to be able to keep them here. They would be perfectly safe.' It still rankled her that they couldn't keep them in the hotel safe simply because, in a neighbouring borough the previous year, the Chains of Office had been stolen from the Mayor's home. They'd quickly been recovered, presumably because the amateur burglars had soon found there was no ready market for them, but now they all had to be kept in the relevant Town Halls and only taken out for official business. She'd tried to tell them that security at the hotel was equal, if not better than at the Town Hall but they wouldn't listen, so they were reduced to having to wait for them to be delivered every time they were making an official visit.

Before they went downstairs, Bryony kissed her father-in law affectionately. 'Have a restful day, then you'll be able to enjoy the dance this evening.'

'I will, I'm quite happy to miss the day's activities, but I'm looking forward to the dance and the disco tonight.'

Bryony stiffened. 'Surely you're not going to the disco?'

Ralph smiled. 'I rarely miss it and I've no desire to start now, if I did people will think I'm getting too old.' Bryony nodded, unsure if that was the real reason, but she couldn't believe he would choose to go there instead of staying in the comfort of the hotel with some of his friends.

'We'll talk about this later,' she said, closing the door before he had time to reply.

In the small meeting room, they stood while the chains were placed round their necks and when Janet Bancroft stood back to check Bryony's were lying perfectly straight, she nodded with satisfaction. 'The colour and simplicity of your dress sets them off beautifully,' she said, and Bryony nodded with satisfaction. 'Thank you,' she replied, 'of course it takes a certain amount of flair to carry off a look like this.' As she moved away, she detected the beginnings of a smirk on the woman's face, and when she heard her call her name, she was tempted to ignore it, but Colin put a restraining hand on her arm. 'At least hear her out Bryn,' he said.

'Mrs Portland, can I make a small suggestion?'

Bryony hesitated, 'You can make it I suppose, but I won't necessarily act on it.'

'I wondered if it might be a good idea to take a pair of comfortable shoes, for when you're walking on the field.'

Bryony laughed in disbelief, and without turning around she muttered under her breath that in future she'd better keep her suggestions to herself. Colin edged round and gave an apologetic smile to the embarrassed woman, but Bryony, full of confidence now, pulled herself to her full height and with Colin following behind, she walked outside and down the steps to the waiting car.

Chapter 9

Marie had been helping with the floats since early morning; she was beginning to flag and needed a rest. Glancing around at some of the other helpers she could see they were feeling the same, and as soon as the procession started to make its way along the street, they would all be taking the opportunity for a rest and a welcome cup of tea or coffee. Fortunately, the initial spots of rain hadn't developed into a full-blown shower and the sun was succeeding in its efforts to break through the clouds.

Lily was on the Rainbow's float and she and some of her little friends had giggled with delight when they felt the drops of rain and looked up to see the glimmer of sunshine.

'Look, Nana Marie!' she called. 'There might be a real rainbow in the sky soon.'

Marie laughed. 'You may be right but keep those umbrellas handy just in case there's a downpour.'

The float, true to its name, was one of the most colourful in the line-up and whoever was responsible for the design this year had done the group proud. The children were divided into three categories, the sun, rain, and rainbows. Lily was in the latter group, and as usual she was unable to remain still for more than a couple of minutes at a time, making the chances of the rainbows staying fastened to her front and back very small indeed.

Even so, she would still look fantastic in her colourful, floaty dress and glistening headband. 'I'm every colour of the rainbow!' she'd told Marie earlier as she twirled round to show the effect of the dress from every angle.

'That is spectacular,' Marie said, and Lily rewarded her with one of her widest smiles which stretched her lips over her perfect little teeth.

Sharon was helping to repair the damage to one of the cloud costumes and after urging the children to stay in their designated places, she climbed down and joined Marie. 'They're starting to get fidgety now, she said, 'and you can't blame them, they've been here for a long time.'

Marie nodded, 'What's the delay? The bands in position and all the people leading the procession are there.' Tired and thirsty, she stood on tiptoe and peered between the heads of the parents and helpers who were waiting impatiently for the floats to start moving away.

'All the dignitaries seem to be there,' she said, moving her head from side to side to get a better view, and then she groaned. 'Oh no, I can't see Colin and Bryony. They're supposed to be leading the procession in one of Colin's cars, but I'm sure it isn't there.'

'Trust her,' Sharon said under her breath, 'Marie, you look done in and there's no reason for you to stay. Why don't you go and sit down, and we'll meet up again later?' When Marie started to protest, she held up her hand, 'I won't take no for an answer. Just think about it, you won't be able to enjoy the rest of the day if your back starts playing up.'

Marie reluctantly agreed, but as she walked towards the sea, she became aware of several groups of people hurrying in the direction of The Square. Intrigued, she turned to follow them and abruptly came to a halt when she saw what had drawn them there. The attraction for most of them was the car parked close to the central floral display, but her eyes were fixed on the tableau set out next to it. Colin was standing in all his regalia and Bryony was blatantly posing, turning one way and the other for the benefit of the photographer from the local paper. An adrenalin surge propelled her forward and she marched towards them, but before she could speak Bryony fixed her with a look fit to kill and for a split second she forgot where she was and spitefully demanded, 'Marie, what on earth are you doing?'

Tired as she was, all Marie could think about were the children and helpers who were being held up while Bryony behaved like a prima donna. She was furious and oblivious to the small crowd who'd gathered round. 'More to the point,' she demanded, 'what are you doing? Don't you realise there are lots of people, including many very excited children who've been getting ready from early this morning, and they are all being kept waiting by you?'

Colin looked at his watch and gasped in dismay. 'Oh, bloody hell!' he exclaimed, 'we're late, we should be there by now.' He walked over to the car and turned to see Bryony setting herself up for another photograph. 'Bryn, for God's sake hurry up, we've got to go.' Indignant and irritated, she joined him, but as they drove away, she took the opportunity to give a royal wave to onlookers gathered around.

Marie turned and walked towards the café; Stuart would be at the park helping to set out the tracks for the children's races and making sure all the equipment was in place for the different events to be held during the day. She could go home and snatch an hour of peace and quiet, but she was tempted to rest her feet in the café close by and enjoy one of their special cappuccinos. The café wasn't packed, as most people were in town waiting to watch the procession, but Janet Bancroft was sitting near the window and asked Marie to join her.

Slipping her shoes off under the table, she breathed a sigh of relief. 'Oh, that's better, I only hope I can get them on again when it's time to go.'

Janet grimaced. 'I wish that was my only problem, I've a feeling it's going to be a tricky day for me.'

'Are you working?' Marie asked, 'I didn't think you worked at the weekend.'

'I'm sort of working,' she explained, 'but it's in an unofficial capacity.' She shook her head and smiled apologetically, 'I'm sorry to be so vague, but it's a bit awkward for me really.'

'Well, don't worry,' Marie replied, if it's a private matter I don't wish to pry.'

Janet glanced around warily. 'No' she explained, 'it's nothing like that, but I'll have to be careful no-one can hear, gossip travels fast in this place, but also, you're a friend of Mrs. Portland and I don't want to speak out of turn.'

'In that case, there's nothing you could say about her that would surprise me.'

'Are you aware she refused to accept the services of a secretary during her term of office?' Janet asked.

Marie nodded, but with all the noise from the coffee machine she could hardly make out what Janet was saying, so she leaned closer. 'It seems she hasn't been as efficient as she ought to be and mistakes have happened, some to do with double bookings, but more problematically some official procedures haven't been adhered to. Apparently, she's now enlisted the help of one of her own staff at the hotel, but unfortunately, although she's very willing to learn, she isn't au fait with procedures either.'

'Poor Sharon,' Marie said, 'she didn't want the role or the extra work, but Bryony didn't give her a choice. So, is that why you're here today?'

'Yes. Mr. Portland has asked me to go along to important events and gently guide Mrs. Portland in the right direction. Unfortunately, today hasn't gone to plan as I upset her first thing this morning and she almost gave me my marching orders.'

Marie raised her eyebrows. 'What did you do?'

'I delivered the chains of office to the hotel as Mr. Portland had asked me to do, and when they were almost ready to leave, I suggested she put a spare pair of flat shoes in the car, to wear when she has to walk on the grass in the park.' Marie stifled a laugh and Janet grimaced before adding. 'To say she wasn't very pleased is an understatement, and Mr. Portland suggested I take the rest of the day off and said they'd manage the day by themselves.' She sighed. 'Now I don't know what to do, because we'd previously agreed that whenever his wife gets stroppy with me, I'm to keep out of her sight but carry on helping in the background.'

'It's a great pity you weren't with them when they arrived in The Square then,' Marie said with feeling. 'I'm afraid I might have shown myself up having a go at her.' Janet listened with frustration as Marie described Bryony's selfish behaviour and her own reaction to it.

'Oh dear,' Janet said, 'that's exactly the sort of thing I'm supposed to ensure doesn't happen. I'm surprised Mr. Portland did that because he knew time was short when they left the hotel.'

'I suppose she insisted on going there as she'd planned, and when people were admiring his car, he must have lost track of time. Anyway, there's no point in worrying about it now, I can hear the band playing so the procession must be getting near the park. I must go, I promised a little friend I'd wave to her.'

Marie walked back in the direction of the park and was able to see most of the floats as they followed each other through the ornate gates. Some of the characters were still throwing sweets to the watching children, who eagerly darted about trying to catch them before they fell to the ground. The float of the local bathroom business was proving very popular. Sitting in an impressive Victorian bath was a young lady wearing a frilly bathing cap, surrounded by enormous, colourful bubbles which floated tantalisingly close to the watching crowds. Children demanded to be lifted so they could reach and pop them, and laughter ensued when some of them were successful.

Collecting buckets were very much in evidence, and Marie surmised the final figure would be an improvement on the last few years when money had been tight. The year they'd first met Tom had been a particularly difficult one for him, and it was amazing to think how he'd managed to turn his life around since then. She just hoped he wouldn't forget the people who'd helped him, otherwise he might alienate himself and his family from the local community.

The Rainbows entered the park and Lily's voice could be heard above the cacophony. 'Mummy, mummy!' she shouted, 'Nana Marie, I'm here!'

Sharon had pushed her way through the crowd to stand by Marie and position herself to take charge of Lily. 'Well, you could have fooled me,' she called back, and they both laughed. Some of the costumes were still intact, but others, like Lily's, were a little worse for wear. It didn't stop them winning the massive rosette for third place, but the children had little interest in that, they'd been confined long enough and were raring to go and see all the attractions.

Marie went to find Stuart who was helping to organise the relay race, and she waved to Ben who was standing in line, ready to take part. In the distance she saw Sam with a small group of friends. Knowing from experience that teenagers didn't appreciate greetings from golden oldies, especially when they were with friends, she refrained from waving, but she was pleased to see Sam with a group from school, he was obviously getting over his initial problems of mixing in. Stuart would be glad to know; he'd seemed quite worried about the lad after he'd met him on the beach.

Chapter 10

Bryony stood on the podium and placed the tiara on the shimmering hair of the Rose Queen elect. The large crowd had been waiting patiently for the ceremony to begin, and showed their appreciation by a surge of cheers, whistles and applause which raised Bryony's headache to another level. The retiring queen looked as if she had somewhere more interesting to be now that she was no longer the centre of attraction, and Bryony knew exactly how she felt.

Piers was taking part in the tug of war, and knowing Amelia would be watching him, she longed to make her way over to where it would be happening, but she couldn't get away from this interminable succession of prize giving. Added to which, her feet were throbbing and the walk to the field where sporting activities were taking place was uneven and damp. Maybe Janet Bancroft's suggestion hadn't been so ridiculous after all, but it was too late to think about that now; she would just have to manage, and if her shoes got ruined, they got ruined.

Just when she'd decided she'd been forgotten, one of the officials came to take over while she went to have a break and something to eat.

'The leaders of the smaller groups will present their own awards,' he explained. 'Thank you very much for everything, now I suggest you take a well-earned rest.'

She set off in the direction of the loud roars which meant the tug-of-war was already underway, but she was impeded by her heels, which kept sinking into the grass. Walking as fast as she was able until she reached the circle of noisy spectators, she was pleased, when as if by magic the crowd parted to let her through, but to her dismay she found herself standing next to Colin.

As the cheers thundered around her, she stood glued to the spot as the opposing team were being slowly but surely pulled towards the dividing line. As the front man, Greg strained and pulled with all his might, and as she watched, Bryony was transported back to the time when she was still a girl, and then later, a young woman. How she'd loved him then, and how long that love had lasted. From this distance he seemed hardly changed by the years between, his bone structure retained his good looks and although his fair hair had darkened slightly it showed very little grey. His physique was still impressive and judging by the size and strength of his muscles, it was obvious he still worked out in the gym. As she watched him, straining with effort against the opposite team, somewhere deep inside her she felt the stirrings of sensations she'd long forgotten.

She was brought back to reality by the plaintive sound of Colin's voice. 'I wish I could have taken part.'

'Why didn't you?' she asked vaguely, having no interest in the reason.

'Apparently it's not the done thing for the Mayor,' he replied, 'and anyway, there's the problem of what you do with the chains.'

He was just about to say something else when an enormous cheer drowned him out as Greg's team pulled the opposition over the line. Catching sight of Amelia, she was about to go to her, when someone unexpectedly placed a small trophy in her hand to present to the losing team. As quickly as she could, she handed it to the leader, but was again prevented from moving away when she was given the winner's trophy. When Greg walked forward to accept it, she congratulated him and his team and without thinking she leaned forward and kissed him on the cheek. Quickly glancing round to check if anyone had noticed anything amiss, she saw to her annoyance that most people were wandering away or gravitating towards Colin.

She'd wanted to announce her intention of repeating the presentation of the trophies at the dance later and in desperation she called to Greg and asked him to pass the message on. She listened with disbelief when he said he'd be spending most of the evening at The Memorial Hall, as that was where all his friends would be. When Stuart nodded his head vigorously in agreement Bryony was livid, but she was determined no-one would know what she was feeling. Surreptitiously prodding Colin in the back, she hoped he would understand the message she was trying to get across, but as usual it was to no avail, so she was forced to play her final card, the charity appeal.

'The dance is in aid of Colin's charities you know,' she said, in her most appealing voice, while laying a hand on Colin's arm, in an obvious display of affection and support. 'We're depending on your support.'

Greg's smile still had the power to make her heart beat a little faster, and her skin tingled under his gaze, even though she was wilting in the heat. He promised to spend the first part of the evening at the dance, but it seemed nothing was going to change his mind about also supporting the disco at the Memorial Hall.

'I've paid for my ticket, and given a donation,' he said in a low voice, 'so you won't lose out by me not being there.'

She nodded graciously. 'We're grateful for your generosity, it's just that we'd appreciate the pleasure of you and your friends' company. As a matter of fact,' she said, desperately casting around for something to catch his interest, 'I've got an important announcement to make, regarding The Lifeboat Association.'

'Oh, I'll look forward to hearing it,' he replied, 'now I must go, I've promised to meet someone.'

It seemed there was no way she could change his mind and the successful outcome of the dance depended on keeping as many people there as possible. Greg's group included many respected people, and if they left early, the knock-on effect could be potentially disastrous. She had no option but to seek out the only person who could persuade him to stay, but it would have to be handled with care. 'Stuart,' she called, 'have you any idea where Marie is? I need to speak to her about something, and I haven't seen her all day.'

Stuart was vaguely aware that Marie was feeling annoyed with Bryony about something which had happened earlier, but when wasn't she annoyed with her? Bryony Portland seemed to possess a gift for irritating people. He thought for a few moments before replying. 'She was with Sharon the last time I saw her,' he said, 'but I've no idea where they are now. Somewhere near the children's activities I guess.'

When Colin suggested a visit to the beer tent, she accepted out of desperation simply because she was thirsty and didn't know what else to do. She'd spotted Amelia's crowd disappearing into the distance, and there was no way she'd be able to catch them up, so reluctantly she slid her arm through his for support, and together they went towards the marquee. As they approached the entrance, she caught sight of Janet Bancroft sitting at a table with a group of friends. Having endured her condescending attitude once today she was determined to avoid any opportunity for her to gloat. 'I've changed my mind,' she told Colin, 'I need to find Marie urgently.' Spinning around, her high heel snagged in the soft earth, sending her completely off balance and straight into Colin's arms.

Mortified, she brushed him aside and walked away with as much dignity as she could muster, but the image of Janet Bancroft's false expression of concern would stay with her for the rest of the day. Thank goodness she'd turned the woman down when she'd offered to be her secretary during her year as The Mayoress.

Determined to salvage something out of the day, she went in search of Marie to ask her to use her influence on Greg. She was still fuming at Marie for her unprovoked outburst in the Square earlier, but she was the only person Greg might listen to, so she had no choice but to ask her a favour. The sooner it could be achieved the better the chance of success, but the problem was, she couldn't find her.

It was becoming increasingly difficult to maintain her composure and she was aware the image of the self-contained Mayoress was slipping. She was just about to give up, when she caught a glimpse of Marie standing by the running track, cheering and urging on one of the runners. Her obvious delight in the result was something beyond Bryony's comprehension, she had no recollection of ever experiencing it even when Hugh and Amelia were competing in school sports days. Who on earth could Marie be supporting now, at her age? As she edged nearer, her question was answered when Sharon entered the frame, her camera aimed at a boy with tousled hair standing in the centre of the winner's podium.

After giving the young winner an obviously unwelcome hug, Sharon turned to throw her arms round Marie and as they stood in an affectionate embrace, Bryony watched, isolated and alone.

Chapter 11

Sharon tightened her grip on Lily's hand. 'Mummy, your hurting me,' she complained, trying to wriggle her fingers free.

'Well you shouldn't have run away from me Lily. I thought I'd lost you,' Sharon said, her body still shuddering from the heart stopping moment of panic when Lily disappeared.

Lily was indignant. 'I didn't run away from you, I ran to Sam,' she said, her bottom lip trembling.

Sharon bent down to wrap her in her arms. 'Oh sweetheart, I'm so sorry I was cross with you. It's because I was worried.'

'It's okay,' Lily replied chirpily, 'now please can I have an ice-cream?'

'You certainly can, and I think I'll have one as well.' Before moving away, she stood and looked across the crowds of people, hoping for a glimpse of Sam, but he was nowhere to be seen. He'd been with a group of friends who'd carried on walking away while he was bringing Lily back to her, but once the confusion of Lily's whereabouts was settled, he went to catch them up. Sharon was hoping he wouldn't lose track of them, but he was unconcerned. 'Don't worry,' he said, 'I'll leg it across the field, I know where we're heading.' She'd missed a golden opportunity to meet his new friends, but Sharon knew he'd be embarrassed, so she satisfied herself with the knowledge that he was one of a group again.

'Let's go and buy an ice-cream, and then we'll look for daddy,' Sharon said to Lily, 'you've had a very busy day and I think it's nearly time to go.'

Tom proved difficult to track down and when Lily began dragging her feet, Sharon decided to ring Tom to tell him she was going home. Just as she was pulling her phone out of her pocket, Lily squealed with delight at the sight of Marie approaching, and with a sudden surge of energy she lunged herself straight into her arms. When Marie told them she was on her way to the bandstand, all signs of tiredness were forgotten as Lily jumped up and down with excitement, so Sharon capitulated, and they all set off together

'I saw Sam with some friends,' Marie told Sharon, 'they seem very nice, and there were a couple of girls with them. Do you think Sam's got a girlfriend?'

'No, I shouldn't think so, he doesn't seem interested,' Sharon said, and Marie burst out laughing. 'Since when have teenage boys not been interested in girls? Get real, as Ben would say.'

Sharon could see the funny side of what she'd said and joined in the laughter. 'Okay, I suppose you're right, but I'm pretty sure he hasn't got a girlfriend, I'd know if he had. I haven't seen Ben for a while, he was a bit miffed because Sam and his pals were going to the funfair and they wouldn't take him.'

'Oh dear, poor Ben,' Marie sighed.

'Mummy hurry up,' urged Lily, 'I can hear the music.' Sure enough, the sound of the brass band tuning up was being carried across the field, so they hurried towards the seats. They were just in time to get the only two remaining on the front row, where they were able to watch Lily at the bottom of the bandstand steps, jiggling in time to the music.

Marie watched her with amusement, she was such a happy, smiley child, and she was a pleasure to be with. 'Louisa told me she's spending the evening with you, thanks for doing that, I know she really appreciates it,' she said during a pause between tunes.

'You don't need to thank me,' Sharon said, 'we're friends and I enjoy her company. She's doing well after the hysterectomy, but she seems very down.'

Marie nodded. I'm very worried about both of them. Damian is trying to be strong for her, but I know he's as devastated as she is.'

Sharon looked at Lily and tried to imagine a life without children. 'Is there absolutely nothing else they can do?'

'It seems not,' Marie replied sadly.

Sharon saw Bryony Portland in the distance, obviously enjoying her day in the spotlight. 'Look at Mrs. Portland,' she said casually, 'she enjoys being the centre of attention, doesn't she?'

'Yes, she does,' Marie replied, following the direction of Sharon's eyes until she picked her out in the middle of a group of people, 'but then she always has, even as a girl. Is she being difficult at work?'

'She's not being difficult exactly,' she replied tactfully, 'but she is expecting more and more effort from all the staff. For example, she's expecting everyone to work this evening, even though normally they'd all be enjoying themselves at the Memorial Hall.'

'Ah, yes of course, the dance. It's causing problems all round. She's putting pressure on friends and even business people, to attend her function, when they really want to join the fun in the hall as usual. I'll give her the benefit of the doubt and accept that it's because she's raising money for charity, but I don't know why she didn't leave that to all her other fundraising events.'

'Which one are you and Stuart going to?'

'Goodness knows. We've got official invites to the dance, but Stuart is adamant we should do what we want, and for him especially, that obviously is not The Portland Arms. I suppose, in the end we'll go to both. Did she try to get you to work?'

'She tried, but I refused.' Choosing her words carefully she said, 'Marie, you know the businessmen you spoke about, are they in any specific kind of business?'

Marie was puzzled. 'When did I mention businessmen?'

'When we were talking about raising money for the charities.'

Marie bit her lip thoughtfully. 'I don't think so,' she replied, 'I can't think of anything that's common to them all. Why do you ask?'

'Please don't say anything to anyone, but I'm worried about Tom.'

'Why, how is Tom involved?'

'That's the point, I don't know. Normally, he would avoid occasions like the dance at the hotel tonight, but he's mentioned more than once that it would be a great opportunity for networking. I really hope I'm wrong, but I've suspected for a while that he's involved in the proposal to build on the mere.'

There was no point in denying her own suspicions when they were both thinking the same thing, so Marie reluctantly agreed. 'Stuart has reason to believe he is, but we've been hoping the feelings of the local people would change his mind before he takes serious action. Obviously, you don't think it will.'

Marie's words stung. The reference to local people being on the opposing side to Tom was the reality, but it hurt and confirmed her own fears. 'I'm afraid,' she murmured, 'of how it will impact on us. Everybody's been so lovely and welcoming, but this could change everything.'

'Try not to worry,' Marie said, 'I'm sure it will all sort itself out, and remember, we will remain friends whatever happens. You're like family now.'

Sharon squeezed the arm looped through hers. 'Thanks Marie, that means a lot.'

'Now it's my turn to ask you a question, and it concerns our mutual friend. Has Bryony tried to persuade Greg to go to the dance tonight?'

'Well, that's an easy one,' Sharon giggled, 'yes, she has. Why do you ask?'

Marie shrugged her shoulders. 'I have a feeling she's up to something. Oh, don't worry, it's nothing for you to be concerned about, but I suspect she's got him in her sights again.'

Marie's words triggered something in Sharon's memory. 'That's strange,' she said, 'Justin made a similar comment recently.'

'Oh dear,' sighed Marie, 'that would explain a lot. Now I know why she's been pestering me, and I'm so stupid not to have realised it sooner. The most annoying thing is the way she's used Damian to get to me. The pretence about wanting to put the life-boat crew in the spotlight, when all the time she was desperate to get

Greg to her wretched dance. She's up to her old tricks again, but thanks to you I'll be ready for her this time.'

Sharon was puzzled by Marie's harsh opinion of Bryony, but they had known each other all their lives and she probably had good reason for thinking what she did, but even so she found herself defending her employer. 'She's desperate to make sure the evening is successful and I suppose she believes Greg's presence will help,' she said, 'anyway Greg's in a relationship with Katy, so what could she hope to achieve?'

'She may not know why they are living apart I suppose.'

'Well,' Sharon replied, 'if she's unaware of it, she must be the only person in Merebank who doesn't know, and I find that hard to believe.'

'I agree,' Marie replied, 'but if she's desperate, she won't care if they're still together or not. Anyway, that's enough of Bryony Portland, let's not spoil the end of a lovely day thinking about her.'

Sinking back into their deckchairs, they joined in the chorus of voices singing to the medley of popular songs being played by the band. The sun was setting, and Sharon caught sight of a dark cloud hanging over the sea in the distance and she hoped it wouldn't rain and spoil the evening's entertainment.

Chapter 12

Once again, Luke had excelled himself and produced a wonderful buffet of delicious and beautifully presented food. His expertise, combined with the tradition of sourcing local produce helped to keep the hotel's reputation alive and she never resented the regular increases to his salary, it was a price worth paying to keep him there. By tacit agreement, his bargaining power was never mentioned, but they both knew he would be snapped up by any one of several rival establishments if he ever left The Portland Arms.

The hotel looked glorious; the outside was illuminated with lanterns while fairy lights shimmered discreetly throughout the interior. Reluctantly, in response to Ralph's misgivings she'd made some minor changes to the programme for the evening, but she'd resisted the urge to make clear her feelings on the matter. If some of the invited guests would really prefer to be elsewhere it was their choice, but she had a sneaking feeling if she voiced her opinion some would be only too pleased to take advantage and she couldn't take that risk.

Justin had volunteered to work and oversee the evenings activities, and together they quickly went through the checklist until satisfied everything was in order. 'I do appreciate what you are doing,' she told him, 'You're an invaluable member of staff and I will make sure you are suitably reimbursed.'

Justin's eyes shone. He thrived on the infrequent but in his opinion, fully warranted snippets of praise, but things were getting tight at home and if Mrs. P didn't turn some of the extra payments into a permanent increase in salary, he and Ellie would be really struggling. He loved his job, and Ellie wouldn't listen to any suggestion of him leaving, reminding him he was part of the Portland family and things were bound to come good in time. But he'd done a bit of checking and knew he could make more money working somewhere else.

Bryony went to her room to shower and change, before walking down the corridor to check on Colin. He'd overcome his reliance on alcohol, but at times like this when it was accessible all day, he was still very vulnerable. He was sitting on the edge of the bed, trying to put a cufflink in his shirt sleeve.

'Ah, you're just in time,' he said, 'to help me with this bloody thing.' Her eyes swept the room. The clothes he'd been wearing were strewn across the floor, but apart from that it was reasonably tidy. A whisky bottle and a half empty glass were on a bedside table, and judging by his slightly slurred speech, it wasn't the only drink he'd had. Irritably, she secured the link, but when he unexpectedly leaned towards her, she recoiled.

'You can't even bear to be close to me, can you? he said wearily, but without waiting for her to reply he turned away and shrugged his shoulders. 'Don't worry,' he said, 'when this is all over, you won't have to.'

'When what is all over?'

He stood up, tucking his shirt into his trousers. 'I think you know what I mean, all this palaver of being Mayor. When it comes to an end, we'll have to sort things out once and for all, and then you'll never have to put up with me again.'

Instinctively, she moved round the room picking up the discarded clothes and throwing them on the bed. 'I don't know what you mean, as far as I'm concerned things will simply go back to how they were before.'

Colin moved to the table, and lifting the glass he put it to his lips and in an act of defiance, drank it down in one gulp. 'There's no need to look at me like that,' he told her, 'I'm not going to do anything to jeopardise your precious year as the *Mayoress*.'

'It's not just me you'll be showing up,' she replied, 'but please, just try and stay sober while you're in public.'

He shook his head and locked his eyes into hers. 'You haven't even noticed, have you? I haven't been drunk once since the day after Amelia's wedding, but you are so wrapped up in yourself you can't give me credit for anything. Never mind, as I said before, we'll soon be able to get ourselves sorted out.'

'Stop talking in riddles, what exactly do you mean by that?'

There was something about his expression which made her uneasy, and for the first time in their married life he appeared to be taking the initiative about their future instead of it being securely in her hands.

'I'm not completely stupid Bryn, despite what you believe. I know what you think of me, and I have no intention of living like this for the rest of my life.' He turned to look at himself in the long mirror standing in the corner of the room, and she noticed for the first time how trim he was. With surprise she could see that not only had he lost weight, but he was firmer and almost toned, and she remembered he had mentioned visits to the gym. Not being in the slightest bit interested in him she hadn't noticed, but now she realised he was looking much better and healthier.

'I wish I didn't have to wear this tonight,' he grumbled, 'I should be in my casual clothes ready for the knees up in the hall, and I know for certain I'm not the only person who's feeling like this.' He shrugged, and without looking at her he added, 'I believe some of your chosen elite are prepared to break your dress code and come ready to make a quick getaway.'

The setbacks and rejections had taken their toll during the last few weeks and suddenly she felt overwhelmed and isolated. If she could turn back the clock there would be no dance tonight, but from the very beginning it had been all about making money for the charity and she couldn't understand why people didn't recognise that. Unlike everyone else, she'd have no opportunity to go to the disco, she would have to stay at the hotel until the very end of the evening and suddenly, she felt trapped.

'Why are you doing this?' she asked Colin, 'you seem determined to hurt me.'

'I'm sorry if I'm coming across like that, because I'm not doing it deliberately,' he replied, 'but I suppose I'm fed up with the endless criticism, and the constant dirty looks. Even when you came in the room just now, your eyes were all over the place looking for something to find fault with.'

Suddenly she felt like running away, and for the first time she resented all the restrictions which came with her year in office. She was tired of trying to win over her unforgiving daughter and even Ralph was beginning to question her decisions, and now Colin was talking in riddles about their futures.

'I don't want to talk about this now,' she said, 'can you be ready in a quarter of an hour? I think we should be together to welcome our guests.'

Colin nodded. 'I'll give you a knock on my way down. Before you go,' he said, 'I just want to say, you look great. I love the dress; it really suits you. Brings out the blue of your eyes.'

Her smile was spontaneous. 'Thanks. You're looking pretty good too. Have you lost some weight?'

'Yeh. I'm still going to the gym regularly,' he replied proudly, 'who would have believed it a few years ago? Colin Portland keeping fit.'

'I used to encourage you to do that, but you just didn't want to know. What's changed?'

He stood up to look at his reflection in the mirror. 'I think it's partly being in the public eye,' he replied thoughtfully, 'but as you know, a lot of the weight was my beer belly, and I've lost most of that.'

'Good,' she replied, 'keep it up.'

The auction had gone far better than her most optimistic expectations, giving a massive boost to the current takings for the charitable funds. She was confident the final figure would be the highest recorded, meaning the charities would receive more money than ever before. She could have raised more, if Geoff Hayes had agreed to her suggestion to make the top prize a trip in the lifeboat, but he'd adamantly refused. She could understand his worry that an emergency could arise while it was out at sea on a jaunt, but secretly she didn't think bringing the winner back to shore would cause a significant delay. Fortunately, Geoff appreciated the benefits of being one of the mayor's chosen charities, and he'd come up with an agreeable alternative suggestion. The winner would spend a day with the crew, watching or taking part in duties in the station and on the lifeboat itself. It had been very well received and topped the takings of all the other prizes.

Desperate to keep Greg's group at the hotel, she was considering announcing free drinks later in the evening to celebrate Damian's recent promotion to deputy coxswain, but Marie's reaction to the suggestion was swift and unequivocal. 'Why would you even consider doing that?' she demanded, 'it won't benefit anybody, and you know Damian would be embarrassed.' Shaking her head, she asked pointedly. 'What did you hope to achieve Bryony? Did you think by doing that, Stuart would want to be here, and then obviously his friends would want to stay too? Including Greg, of course.'

Bryony snorted with derision, but she was so shocked by her earlier reaction to him, she was afraid Marie was getting too close to a truth she herself, couldn't comprehend. 'Don't be so ridiculous,' she snapped, but her attention was diverted by the sight of Tom Lester with a group of people gathered near the door, and she knew instinctively they were planning to leave. It would only take that to happen, and it would be the start of a mass exodus, which she had to prevent at all costs.

Suddenly, she saw Greg break away from the group and her heart thudded when she thought he was coming towards her, but instead he turned a corner and began to walk down the corridor. Without stopping to think, she hurried after him, calling his name. He stopped and turned and reaching him, she put her hand on his arm, and before she could stop herself, she slid her hands around his neck, pulled his head down until his face was close to hers, and kissed him. For a split second, she felt him submit and she thought she'd succeeded, but he pushed her away.

'Bryony, what are you doing?' he demanded, but before she could reply, they both heard a sound, and turned to see Marie watching them. Greg's head dropped back, and he stood perfectly still, with his eyes fixed on the ceiling. A loud groan came from somewhere deep inside him. 'Oh my God,' he said at last, straightening up and looking from Bryony to Marie.

Bryony was filled with overwhelming anger, because despite his reaction she was convinced it would have taken only a little more time to for him to reciprocate. Now the moment was gone, simply because of virtuous, boring Marie.

Greg walked slowly towards Marie and Bryony followed. 'I suppose it's clichéd to tell you nothing happened, despite how it may have looked to you,' he said to Marie. Bryony's resentment grew, she didn't share his obvious sense of remorse or regret, and if Marie had caught them in an embrace so be it. They were adults and free to kiss who they chose.

'You don't have to explain anything,' Marie told Greg, 'because I saw it with my own eyes. Bryony held her breath, dreading what Marie might say, but after a scathing look, she turned and walked away with Greg following swiftly behind her.

Bryony waited a few moments before following them back down the corridor to the ballroom. It wasn't proving to be quite as easy to attract Greg's attention as she'd thought, but it only made the pursuit even more of a challenge. She'd never intended to go as far as kissing him, and her own actions had taken her by surprise, so she would have to be careful to keep her guard up if ever that happened again. When she reached reception, people were drifting towards the door and she looked round in disgust at the depleted number of guests who were enthusiastically trying to keep up an impression of jollity. When Colin came over and told her some of the people leaving had promised to return soon, she couldn't trust herself to reply.

Suddenly, a spectacular flash of lightening lit up the room, followed by a deafening crack of rolling thunder, causing some of the guests to run towards the nearest windows, while others crowded round the revolving door to go outside and watch the unexpected spectacle lighting up the sky.

Amongst the animated chatter, Bryony heard someone say their indecision about the rest of the evening had been resolved, as no-one would be going anywhere tonight.

'Well you won't be staying here,' she said to herself, as she slipped out of the back entrance to stand in the torrential rain while the sky tore itself apart.

Chapter 13

After all the day's excitement, Lily had finally settled down and gone to sleep. Sharon tiptoed along the landing to ask Ben and his friend Toby, who was sleeping over, to keep the noise down. They nodded their assent, but when she began to give instructions about the time they had to finish and get ready for bed, they were so engrossed in their game they didn't even hear her. She had no idea where Sam was, but having seen him with friends earlier she tried not to worry. If only he would ring, or at least put his phone on so she could contact him.

The disco in the Memorial Hall would be fun, but she was quite happy to stay at home with Louisa who was still recovering from her recent operation. When Mrs. Portland gave her an invitation to the dance, before casually mentioning that Sharon's presence on the night would be useful, she realised she would be called on to help and in her capacity as secretary would be unable to refuse. After giving it some thought, she declined on the grounds she couldn't get a babysitter. Mrs. Portland tutted with irritation, until Sharon innocently mentioned Marie's offer to change her plans and look after the children in order to allow Sharon to attend.

Instantly, her boss's demeanour completely changed. 'Oh no,' she exclaimed, 'you mustn't let her do that.

I know how much she's looking forward to the dance and she'd be so disappointed.' Curiously, it seemed that Marie's attendance was far more important than her own, but Sharon didn't spend much time wondering why because it had helped her out of a tight corner.

After taking a last peep at Lily to satisfy herself she was deeply asleep, she was halfway down the stairs when the hallway was illuminated by a blinding flash of lightning, followed immediately by a booming crack of thunder. After only a few seconds it happened again, and when rain came lashing down, she realised it was a storm of epic proportions and it was very close to home. She spun round to run back upstairs, and as she turned, the next flash illuminated the figure of Louisa standing wide-eyed in the lounge doorway.

'Are you afraid?' she asked, but Louisa shook her head. 'Not normally,' she replied, 'but I've never experienced anything like this before.'

'Me neither,' Sharon replied, 'I'm just going to check Lily.'

Running up the stairs, she listened for any sound coming from the bedroom, but the rolling thunder was drowning out all other noises. At first, she thought the bed was empty and her heart lurched, but as she crept closer, she saw the familiar sight of Bear squashed beneath Lily's chin and her thumb, which had almost completely slipped from between her lips. A feeling of love, and an urge to protect her sleeping child surged through her, as she gently pulled the duvet over Lily's exposed legs. Before leaving the room, she turned once more, and was just in time to see Lily's legs lift in the air and form an arc as she brought them down again, leaving her legs completely uncovered, exactly as before.

Leaving the door ajar she went to check Ben and Toby, who despite the noise going on around them were still engrossed in their game. The only way she could gain their attention was by standing directly in front of them, and she gave strict instructions they were to be in bed in half an hour, and that included any time spent getting something to eat.

The storm seemed to be abating, but rain was still beating against the windows, and as she walked back across the hall, the front door burst open letting in a deluge of water as Tom and Damian almost fell across the threshold. Calling unintelligible reasons for their unexpected appearance, the two men went upstairs to shower and change into dry clothes. When they reappeared sometime later, Damian was wearing a pair of Tom's jeans and a tee shirt.

'I'm surprised you can squeeze your pecs into that,' Sharon said to Damian, nodding towards the shirt and ducking to avoid the cushion flying in her direction from Tom's hand. 'Anyway, what made you two decide to walk home in the rain, instead of waiting for it to ease off a bit?'

'That,' Tom replied, 'is easy to say with hindsight, but the situation was a bit more complicated.' Looking at Damian, who nodded in agreement, he carried on. 'We decided to go to the hotel first and get that over with before going on to the shindig at the hall. We'd had a bit of a struggle making our get-away from Bryony who was trying to get us to stay there, and we'd only just set off from the hotel, when the rain started pelting down. We had to decide quickly whether to go back to the hotel and her clutches, which to be honest, wasn't an option, or run all the way to the hall and spend the rest of the night soaked to the skin. Neither of us fancied that, so here we are, home and dry.'

Sharon felt a tinge of sympathy for Mrs. Portland, who'd invested a lot of time and energy trying to make sure the dance was a success, but as usual she'd refused to listen when anyone dared to offer their advice. Instead, she'd forged ahead with her own plans, when a few little tweaks to the arrangements might have made a big difference. She asked Tom why they'd been so desperate to get away.

'I can only speak for myself,' he replied, 'but there was no atmosphere. Bryony seemed satisfied with the auction, I reckon she made a tidy packet from that, but she was trying too hard to keep everyone there after-wards, instead of just leaving them to enjoy themselves.' He paused and pulled his eyebrows together in a frown. 'Now I come to think about it, there was a slight com-motion, but I don't know what it was all about.'

Damian was sitting next to Louisa, and he turned his face to her and grimaced. 'Oh, that would be my mum,' he said, 'I have no idea what it was about either, but apparently she and Bryony had a few words. That's nothing new, but mum does sometimes get her knickers in a twist about things Bryony does. I don't know why she bothers when she knows better than anyone what she's like.'

'To be fair to Marie, that's probably why she reacts like she does,' Sharon said. A shiver rocked Louisa's body and Sharon asked Tom to plug in the heater beside the sofa. 'It warms up quite quickly, she said, tucking a blanket around Louisa's legs, 'but the temperature has dropped a lot with the storm so it's chilly in here now, especially near these windows. I'll be glad when we can decorate and put some curtains up,' she added, 'speaking to no-one in particular.'

Damian raised an eyebrow and looked at Tom. 'That sounds very much like a gentle hint. When do you expect to be finished?' he asked.

Tom pulled down the sides of his mouth, his jaw jutting out as he concentrated. 'Most of the outside work is finished, so we're not reliant on good weather and hopefully we can concentrate on the inside now. I'd say it will be complete in a couple of months, and then Sharon can go to town on the decorating and the furnishings. That is of course, if she has time to spare, after she's finished running around after her boss.'

'It isn't just that,' Sharon protested, 'I don't know where to start.'

'What do mean?' Tom asked, 'you didn't have a problem with our other house, and that was fantastic. Everybody said so.'

'I know, but it was so much smaller than this. I'm out of my depth here.' She could see the hurt on Tom's face, but it was true, she was overwhelmed by the thought of what would be involved. 'Actually' she said turning to Louisa, 'I've been meaning to ask if you'd help me. Your flat is beautiful, and you obviously have a really good eye for putting things together that I wouldn't even think of.'

'Hang on a minute,' Louisa replied, holding her arms out and looking round, indicating the size of the room, 'there is a world of difference between our tiny flat, and this.'

'But it's not just that,' Sharon protested, 'it's your flair and taste, and we could have such fun.'

'Don't get carried away,' interjected Tom, who was beginning to look apprehensive at the way the conversation was going, 'it's a family home, not a show house.'

Sharon ignored him and turned back to Louisa. 'Will you do it, will you help me?' she pleaded, and Louisa nodded. 'I'd love to, it's something I really enjoy doing. I only wish,' she added pensively, 'that we could buy a house of our own.' Sharon sensed she was keeping her eyes averted from Damian who was looking at her with concern, but Tom didn't notice anything and carried on obliviously.

'Why don't you buy a house closer to town?' he asked Damian, 'that flat of yours is way out and must be very inconvenient.'

'It's actually only minutes in the car,' Damian replied, 'but yes, I agree it would be better if we could move nearer to town.'

'So?' Tom said, missing the glare Sharon was sending in his direction, 'what's stopping you?'

'Tom!' Sharon cried, 'it's nothing to do with us.'

Damian shook his head and smiled reassuringly in Sharon's direction before turning to answer Tom's question. 'It's okay, it's quite simple,' he replied, 'we simply can't afford it. The price of property has rocketed in this area, putting it way out of reach of the likes of us.'

Sharon was still fuming at Tom for being so insensitive, but she was also aware of the reversal of their situations. It wasn't that long ago when she and Tom were scraping pennies together while Damian and Louisa were very comfortable, and she couldn't help feeling embarrassed on their behalf. 'That's not right,' she protested, 'you've lived here all your life.'

Damian nodded. 'I know, but so many of the smaller properties are being bought by speculators as an investment, as well as a few being purchased as holiday homes. Most of them are empty for half of the year. It makes my blood boil at the injustice of it but there's nothing we can do to change it.'

Sharon bristled indignantly. 'Surely someone could stop it happening?' she said, 'it just doesn't seem fair.'

Damian's face clouded over. 'Unfortunately, life isn't always fair.'

Louisa had been silent during the exchange and was barely audible when she said softly. 'That's very true.'

To break the uncomfortable silence, Sharon made an excuse to leave the room to get more nibbles and suggested to Tom he might want to bring some drinks in. 'Why did you have to do that?' she muttered through clenched teeth, 'you know how vulnerable she is at the moment.'

'Sorry,' Tom replied, 'I didn't realise it was such a touchy subject.'

When they returned, Sharon was pleased to see Louisa looking cheerful again, and she surprised them all by returning to the previous conversation by telling them of a property she'd seen, which would be perfect for the two of them. Damian pulled his arm from around her shoulder to look at her in amazement.

'It's one of those fishermen's cottages just off the high street,' she continued, 'it's very like your parents' house, but a bit smaller of course.'

Damian was stunned. 'Have you been inside?' he asked her, 'you seem to know a lot about it.'

She explained she'd been passing when the Sale sign was being erected in the garden, and she was simply standing for a moment looking at the property, when the lady who lived there came out and asked if she wanted to see inside. When Louisa explained she'd often wondered what those cottages were like inside, the owner had insisted on showing her round, even though Louisa made it clear she wasn't in a position to buy.

'It was lovely, absolutely lovely.' Louisa told them wistfully, unable to keep the longing out of her voice. 'Despite being quite small it's all oak beams and inglenooks, but it could be a family home because the garden is bigger than you'd expect. I suppose it's because it's on the corner,' she added enthusiastically.

Damian was lost for words and obviously shaken by Louisa's interest in the cottage, which he knew would be way out of their league. Tom was the first to break the silence. 'The sooner the powers that be give their permission for the new housing development the better, then young couples like yourselves will be able to buy their first home in a place where they really want to live.'

Damian reluctantly dragged his eyes away from Louisa to answer Tom. 'We're not that young in relation to buying our first property,' he pointed out, 'and I'd give anything to buy the cottage Louisa is talking about, but out of principle I wouldn't touch a property built on the mere.'

Sharon watched Tom's reaction closely and detected a slight but recognisable change in his expression. Whatever his position she hoped he wouldn't instigate a discussion now, it certainly wasn't the right time when Louisa was so sensitive, and obviously she and Damian had a lot of talking to do. Unfortunately, Tom, deliberately or unintentionally missed her attempts to catch his eye, and persisted in questioning Damian.

'I don't understand,' he said, 'you're saying you can't afford to pay the market price for a house here, yet you're against more properties being built. Don't you think' he asked, 'that it will benefit the local community to have some affordable housing available?'

Damian smiled weakly. 'I very much doubt they will include many affordable properties, but that isn't the point, it's where they're building them. There are other, less damaging sites, and anyway, it would be far better if our local councillors and planners spent more time protecting the homes we already have, instead of letting them go to people who see them only in terms of investments. When mum and dad got married, those cottages Louisa was talking about were within the reach of first-time buyers, but now, the prices are sky high.' He grinned at Sharon and Tom. 'Sorry, I'll get off my high horse now, but you'll never convince me to change my mind. The mere is a bird sanctuary, which means it should never be built on, for any reason.'

'Sometimes needs must,' Tom said stubbornly, 'and things change.'

'Not an estuary and its wildlife, nothing must change such an important part of our surroundings, especially a developer from out of town who'll make his money and then leave, not caring what damage he's done.'

Ignoring the strength of conviction in Damian's voice, Tom fired one last shot. 'Come on mate, you and Louise are more important than some birds, surely they'll fly off and find somewhere else to settle.'

With relief Sharon watched Damian's face crack into a smile. 'Oh Tom, you're an unbelievable townie, when you've lived here a bit longer you might adapt to the sea-siders' way of thinking. Anyway, I've told you, you'll never convince me, so don't even go there.'

Sharon jumped in and passed the nuts and crisps round, making more effort than necessary to point out the choices and different flavours before Tom had an opportunity to respond. With everyone's glass replenished, the conversation turned on the lighter aspects of the Carnival and each one of them had different tales to tell. Quite a few of the anecdotes centred around Bryony Portland, until Sharon asked if anyone had witnessed the episode in The Square, and they all shook their heads.

'I didn't see it myself,' she explained, 'but Marie told me when we were listening to the band. Apparently, Bryony insisted she and Colin went through The Square on the way to join the procession. Marie, on my instruction, was on her way to have a cup of tea and a rest, when she saw them there, posing and having their photographs taken. Knowing they were late and everyone was waiting for them, she marched up and told them off. Colin was apologetic, but Bryony was fuming.' She turned to Damian. 'Marie is worried, because the official photographer was there.'

Damian burst out laughing. 'Oh, that's my mum alright, act now, worry later. Sometimes she can't keep her nose out, but she does everything with the best intentions.' All the previous tension seemed to drain away as he chuckled at the antics of his mother and Bryony. 'I don't know what we would have done without your mum and dad,' Sharon said to him, 'they've been great since we came to live here, and the children adore them.'

'Well mum has always loved kids,' he told her, 'and they've never seen enough of my sister's two, so I suppose she's making up for not having grandchildren around.'

Louisa visibly stiffened and Sharon cursed herself for bringing up the subject of children. She watched helplessly as Damian took Louisa's hand. 'I'm sorry, that was so thoughtless of me.' he said, shaking his head. 'I'm such an idiot.'

'No,' Louisa told him firmly. 'We can't avoid the mention of children for the rest of our lives. I'm okay.'

Tom was puzzled, looking from Sharon and back to the where Damian and Louisa were sitting.

'I take it you know what we're talking about?' Damian asked him, and Tom nodded. 'I guess I do. I know Louisa can't have a baby, but that's about it.'

'Well, that's all there is to know really, but it's taking a while to accept this is really the end of the line.'

'But unfortunately, that isn't all,' Louisa said, 'it's also the reason why we can't buy a house because we've used all our savings on the IVF treatments, leaving us with nothing. No baby, no home, and no money, just because I was so desperate to try anything to have a child.'

'That's not true,' Damian protested, 'I wanted a child just as much as you and we made all our decisions together. None of this is your fault.'

'Damian's right,' Sharon said, 'you can't blame yourself, after all the IVF was a success. You couldn't possibly have known that you wouldn't be able to carry a baby.' Sharon looked on helplessly as Louisa's face crumbled.

Tom stared at Sharon and raised his eyebrows. 'I think I am missing something here; did you just say the IVF treatment was successful?'

She nodded and looking towards Louisa she was just about to try and explain when Louisa stopped her. 'That's the most difficult thing to accept,' she told Tom, 'knowing there is a perfect little baby just waiting to grow, and I can't carry it. I'm it's mummy, and I can't carry it.'

Tom listened; his eyes wide in disbelief. 'I'm sorry to keep banging on,' he said, 'but let me get this right, do you mean you've got as far as having your very own embryo, but you can't use it?'

'That just about sums it up,' Damian said.

'Is it frozen?'

'Tom,' exclaimed Sharon, but both Louisa and Damian started to answer him.

'Yes,' Louisa replied, 'but actually, it's 'them' not 'it'. We were told we're very lucky as there are several viable embryos. I don't know about being lucky, it seems to make the situation worse now we can't use them.'

Tom looked at Sharon, a frown creasing his face. 'What was that programme you were watching on television a while ago? Don't you remember? You should do because you were in tears by the end of it.' Suddenly she remembered, her memory jogged by the mention of her crying. She'd thought about Louisa at the time, but it had completely slipped from her mind because then, they were still optimistic they'd have a child. 'Yes, I remember now, she said, 'you mean the one about couples using a surrogate to carry their child.' She smiled. 'You're right, I was in bits by the end of the programme.' Tentatively she looked at Damian and Louisa. 'Could that be an option for you two?' she asked gently, and she was shocked when Damian told her they'd already considered it.

'Regretfully, it's not for us,' he said.

Louisa's head dropped, suggesting they weren't in complete agreement about the decision and Sharon, even at the risk of upsetting at least one of them, asked why they had decided against it.

'All these tests and procedures - and now the hysterectomy - have been very gruelling both mentally and physically and it's taken a lot out of Louisa. I don't want her to go through any more disappointments,' Damian replied firmly.

'What kind of disappointments?' she persisted, 'you've already got the embryos.'

'From what we've learned, surrogacy is a minefield where lots of things can go wrong. Sometimes the womb doesn't accept the foetus, or the pregnancy fails, but the worst-case scenario is when the surrogate mother won't give up the baby when it's born. It's perfectly understandable, but can you begin to imagine what that must be like, and what it would do to Louisa? I'm not prepared to even consider her having to endure that.'

'A miscarriage can happen to anyone,' Sharon said, 'that's no different from any pregnancy, but I'm sure the cases where surrogates refuse to part with the baby are few and far between. Most have happy endings, surely?' Knowing she was treading on dangerous ground when Damian had firmly stated his views, she needed to know what Louisa really felt. 'How do you feel about it Louisa?'

'Damian's right, I honestly don't know how I'd cope if that happened, but I'm so desperate for a baby I think it might be worth the risk to try. Anything is worth a try.'

Tom, wishing the subject had never been brought up and feeling totally out of his depth, made what he hoped would be his last comment. 'You'd have to make certain you picked the right person in the first place, that's for sure.'

Damian nodded. 'Yes, but how can you do that? It's impossible to predict how any woman might act after she's carried a baby for nine months.'

'Well, I suppose there's the chance the women might ask for more money before they'll hand the baby over,' Tom said, 'but that's a risk you'd have to take.'

'No,' Damian said, 'that's one problem you don't have in this country, because it's illegal for the surrogate mother to be paid. The only money she receives is a small amount to cover her expenses. In other words, she does it out of the goodness of her heart, so I suppose in a way that's why it's so difficult to find one. It's a massive undertaking.'

Tom whistled through his teeth in amazement and looked at Sharon. 'Did you know that?' he asked, 'did it say that on the programme?'

'I don't remember,' she replied, 'but don't forget, it was in America, they do things differently there.' Louisa's growing distress was obvious, but Sharon sensed she hadn't given up the hope of surrogacy being an option, and she impulsively asked how far they'd investigated the possibility of using a surrogate. 'It just seems such a shame when you've already got the embryo,' she said diffidently, with her eyes firmly fixed on Louisa and away from Damian. 'You seem to have given it serious consideration before deciding against it.'

'We did for a little while,' Louisa replied, 'but Damian is terrified of what might happen.'

'You'd have to have confidence in the surrogate, that's for sure,' Sharon agreed, 'it's tricky, but not impossible.'

'How do you figure that out?' asked Tom.

'You need someone who's already got the family they want, had relatively trouble-free pregnancies, and preferably a member of the family or a very close friend. That way they won't let you down at the end.'

'But where do you find someone like that, we certainly haven't got anyone in either of our families who would fit the bill?' Damian looked at Louisa. 'Can you imagine our Debbie's response if I asked her to carry a baby for us?' Louisa's face broke into a weak smile despite herself, and she shook her head disconsolately.

'Right,' Sharon said, 'not family then. It's going to have to be a friend.'

'That's very helpful, Sharon,' Tom said sarcastically, 'and where does that leave Louisa and Damian?'

'I think I know the very person,' Sharon said, 'and I can guarantee she won't let you down.'

'Who do you know?' Tom asked. 'Sharon stop it, this is not funny.'

'I'm being very serious,' she replied, I do know someone who fits the bill exactly.' The silence in the room was broken by a distant rumble of thunder, followed by Rusty's answering grumble from where he lay in the safety of his bed, close to Sharon's feet. Hesitantly Louisa began to speak. 'Sharon, do you really mean you know a surrogate mother?' Sharon held her breath as all three faces, with differing expressions of disbelief or expectancy, turned to her.

'She isn't a surrogate yet,' she explained, 'but she's willing to be.'

'Who is she, do we know her?' Louisa asked, and suddenly Sharon's face lit up. 'It's me,' she said, 'I'll carry your baby.'

A stillness filled the room. Tom's breaking voice disturbed the silence. 'For God's sake Sharon, what the hell are you talking about?'

She barely knew herself, so how could she explain how the germ of an idea had taken hold and grown, almost without her being conscious of what was happening. She hadn't expected the words to come out now, but she truly believed she could do this thing which would transform her friends' lives. Looking only at Tom's bewildered face, she apologised gently for not discussing it before blurting it out like this, but he was hardly listening.

'Sharon, don't joke about this, it's not fair. You know it's impossible.'

'I'm not joking,' she said gently, 'and it isn't impossible, I've had babies before.'

'That's just the point, you've had three and we agreed there wouldn't be anymore.' His voice was beginning to rise while Louisa and Damian watched in stunned silence. 'For Christ's sake Sharon, I had the snip to make sure it didn't happen again.'

'Tom, you're missing the point, that was because we didn't want any more children. This won't be our child; it will be theirs.'

Damian found his voice and urged them to stop. 'Please don't argue about this,' he begged, and turning to Sharon he shook his head, 'I know you meant well,' he added, 'but you spoke without thinking. Don't worry, we'll forget you ever said it.'

Sharon levelled her eyes to his. 'I don't want you to forget it, I want you to think about it, because I am serious about this.'

There was no mistaking the conviction in her voice and Tom slumped forward with his head in his hands, while Damian looked at Louisa who was sitting motionless, her eyes riveted on Sharon with a mixture of disbelief and hope. Tom lifted his head. 'Sharon, I can't let you do this. You've already had three kids and you're not as young as you used to be.'

'I'm thirty-eight, some women don't even start having babies until much older than that,' she told him.

Louisa was visibly shaking and Damian put a protective arm around her. 'Sharon, please drop the subject, surely you can see you're upsetting Louisa. It's unbelievable for you to even consider it, but we can't ask you to do this.'

Sharon glanced at Tom, but he held his head in his hands and she could only imagine the look of despair on his face. She was going against his wishes, but it was too late to back out now. 'You didn't ask me to do it,' she said to Damian, 'I offered, and I mean it. If you want me to carry your child, I will.'

Louisa's eyes were brimming when she turned expectantly towards Damian. 'Oh, please don't say no,' she pleaded, and to her surprise he shook his head. 'Why would I do that darling?' he asked. 'I want us to have a family too, remember, and Sharon's offer answers all our worries about being able to trust a surrogate who's a stranger to us. It's an amazing turn of events, I only hope Tom will agree.'

Tom, who'd at least been hoping for some support from Damian, raised his eyes to the ceiling. 'Heaven help me. Do my feelings count for nothing here? We have a situation developing which is fraught with disaster, can no-one else see it?' Dragging his eyes away from Sharon and Louisa who were locked in an emotional embrace, he shrugged his shoulders. 'Don't get me wrong mate,' he said to Damian, 'I feel really sorry for your situation, but I have to say I do not agree with what Sharon is proposing.'

'I don't blame you, but it was said in haste and...' he glanced in Sharon's direction, 'and she is a bit...'

'Drunk,' volunteered Tom and Damian nodded.

'I think Sharon should sleep on it before you get too concerned.'

Tom's voice lifted in anger. 'You don't know my wife as well as I do, and I'm pretty sure her mind is made up.' They both looked at the two friends who were embracing, and Louisa's face was giddy with happiness.

'Oh God,' Tom said despairingly, 'am I the only one here who's terrified? If you ask me, this is a disaster in the making, but then again, nobody is asking me.' Springing out of his chair, his foot caught the leg of the coffee table, sending glasses, drinks and nibbles flying across the room. Angrily kicking them out of his way, he stumbled towards the door where he turned to face them. 'I just want you all to be very clear about this. I do not agree with it and never will.

Chapter 14

The long-awaited announcement had been made and it was now unavoidable. A site visit had been undertaken and an Environmental Impact Assessment had been made, following which, the applicants had made several proposals they were prepared to compromise on, to lessen the impact on the environment. The public were being given an opportunity to voice their opinions and participate in the decision-making process. Plans were being prepared and were due to be submitted to the Planning Committee in the near future. Emotions were running high as more and more people joined the debate. When the local paper published the results of a poll they'd carried out, it left the older residents reeling to discover it was more evenly balanced than their wildest fears. They were prepared for some dissenters amongst the young people, but nothing had prepared them for this. A shortage of affordable homes was impacting on the younger generation, and they were now beginning to make their voices heard. It was causing friction within families and Marie was afraid her own family was going to be affected.

She tried to put it out of her mind by keeping busy at the shop all afternoon, stocking shelves and sweeping the small forecourt in front of the building. She was just about to put her coat on to leave when she heard her mobile ringing in her handbag. Thinking it was Stuart she replied. 'Hello love,' only to hear Sharon's voice instead. 'Oh, I'm so glad I caught you before you left, Stuart told me you might already be on your way home. I don't like to ask you this, but is there any way you can pick Lily up from school? There's a bit of a crisis here and Mrs. Portland doesn't take kindly to me refusing to stay.'

Marie's heart sank. All she wanted to do was go home and get her feet up. 'Of course, I will,' she replied, 'but what about Ben?' Although he insisted, he was old enough to walk home with his friends, Sharon always kept a surreptitious eye on him.

'He's already arranged to go back with Jacob to his house for dinner,' Sharon explained.

'That's fine, do you want me to give Lily something to eat?'

'I'll see how it goes here; can I ring you later?'

'Of course, don't worry we'll be okay.'

Marie walked through into the shop. 'That bloody woman,' she exclaimed, 'I swear she's stalking me.' Claire closed and locked the door and they began walking together along the promenade. 'Which woman?' she asked, 'I thought it was Sharon who rang.'

'It was, but only because she needs me to pick Lily up from school. Bryony needs her to work late again. It's getting more and more frequent.'

'You must be careful you don't overdo it,' Claire cautioned, 'we're not getting any younger.'

'Tell me about it,' Marie laughed.

Things were so chaotic in the Lester household there was no guarantee of finding something suitable for Lily to eat, so she called in at the mini supermarket to pick up a few things. Pasta shapes were a favourite, although

Marie always struggled to pick out the crowns and carriages illustrated on the tin, much to Lily's disappointment. Some strawberry yoghurts and a packet of chocolate biscuits would suffice, but she added a loaf and a packet of ham, in case there was nothing in for tomorrow's packed lunches, together with a healthy option snack for Lily.

It was a short walk to the school where she joined the other parents and grandparents waiting on the perimeter of the school yard. Lily was one of the last of her class to appear, but when she saw Marie, she flew towards her with arms opened wide. 'Nana Marie, Nana Marie!' she called, before flinging herself at Marie and nearly knocking her to the ground. Marie hugged her and caught the picture Lily had dropped. 'Why have you come to pick me up?' Lily asked.

'Because mummy's working a bit late,' Marie explained, 'but she'll be home soon, don't worry.'

Lily skipped along, calling to her friends. 'I'm not worried,' she said, 'I like it when you pick me up.'

Marie suddenly felt lighter. 'Well that's very kind of you to say so,' she replied.

'You're welcome,' Lily chirruped. 'Nana Marie, what have you got in that bag?'

Marie made no effort to control the laughter that burst from her lips. 'Don't be so nosy, now come along cheeky madam. Would you like to go to the park?'

Without a pause Lily raced over to the gate and was already on a swing by the time Marie reached a bench where she could rest her feet and keep a close eye on her. Lily was a daredevil and had no real concept of danger, a combination which had resulted in many minor scrapes and occasionally potentially serious ones.

Marie was determined to make sure nothing happened on her watch.

The day was still warm and as she sat watching the children playing, her body was suffused with a feeling of well-being. Having Sharon and Tom and their children living here had enhanced her life, and Stuart's. If only Damian and Louisa could have a child, things would be almost perfect.

There was no-one home when they reached the house, and after she'd given Lily her tea Marie made two packed lunches and laid out Lily's reading book and the picture she'd done at school for Tom and Sharon to see when they got home. It was Tom who arrived first and after a quick change he took Lily into the garden and put her on the trampoline. Sharon trudged in, as Marie was putting on her coat, so she gave her a quick embrace and left them to sort themselves out. She turned down their offer of a lift home, they had little enough time together as a family these days.

Stuart had a glass of wine waiting as Marie walked in the door. 'I expect you're ready for that,' he said as he took her coat and hung it up. 'Everything is ready and being kept warm so you can relax before we eat. I presume Sharon was later than she'd expected to be.'

'Much later, as far as I'm concerned. I don't mind helping her out, but it irks me when it's Bryony who's keeping her back. Especially, as it's all to do with her elaborate arrangements for some official event or other.'

Stuart's opinion of Bryony had never changed over the years and nothing in her behaviour ever surprised him, but he had expected a slight mellowing as she got older, which up to now had never materialised, leading him to believe it never would. 'It's Bryony all over,' he said, with an air of resignation.

'Oh, she'll be lapping all this up, but I'm beginning to think she's asking more and more of Sharon because she's fully aware it's me who has to help out.'

Stuart laughed. 'Now I believe you are getting just a little bit paranoid.'

'You're right,' she sighed, I'm tired and hungry. Not as bad as Sharon though, she looked worn out.'

'Well,' Stuart said, 'she's sandwiched between Bryony at work and those live wires at home, I don't envy her.'

'She's young, she'll cope,' Marie replied, taking a sip of wine before she slipped off her shoes and wriggled her toes. 'That's better,' she sighed, 'much better.' Stuart was holding the local newspaper and from his barely suppressed look of excitement she guessed he was impatient to tell her something. The only thing he was passionate about was the housing development, and as she had very mixed feelings about it, she knew she wouldn't share his satisfaction if it had been turned down, but for now she would keep her thoughts to herself. 'Is there some good news in there?' she asked, 'is it about the houses?'

Stuart couldn't stop grinning. 'Well, there is an item about that,' he told her, 'but it's been buried by something far more interesting. Look.' He folded the paper to one of the inside pages and handed it to her. 'It's the caption competition love,' he told her, 'but with a rather interesting subject.' She stared at it, gasping in astonishment. Instead of the usual small picture, this was a half-page spread showing Bryony and Stuart posing in the Square on their way to joining the procession. The only problem was, the photographer had captured the moment when Marie had stood with her finger pointing towards them in a gesture, leaving readers to speculate the meaning of what she was saying. The funniest caption entered would win the prize.

'Oh no!' she gasped, 'how could they do this?' The paper slipped from her fingers and bunched around her feet. 'Bryony will never speak to me again,' she said forlornly, 'this is truly awful.'

'I wouldn't say it's that bad,' Stuart said, 'it's only a bit of fun and everybody just takes it as that.'

'I know,' Marie replied, 'but she is the Mayoress, and you know how important appearances always are to her.'

Stuart began picking up the discarded newspaper and placing the pages back in chronological order. 'It might not be a bad thing to bring her down a peg or two,' he said, 'and it wouldn't do her any harm to see the funny side of things for a change.' When Stuart held up the offending picture again, she started to turn her head away, but then she sneaked another look and couldn't help smiling. She had to concede it was funny, but she knew Bryony wouldn't see it that way.

'Funny?' Stuart laughed, 'it's hilarious. Anyway, she can't complain too much, look at this.'

Reluctantly she looked to where he was pointing. In addition to the usual prize for the funniest caption, for one week only, the entries had to be accompanied by a donation to the Mayor's charities. 'I've just been on the website, and the money's rolling in,' Stuart told her, 'it's captured everyone's attention I can tell you, and there are some hilarious entries. The best one up to now, in my opinion is---,'

'I really don't want to know now' she said, 'Tell me when I've had something to eat and a bit more to drink, I'll be in a better frame of mind to appreciate it then.'

Stuart couldn't stop grinning. 'I'm with you,' he said, 'because they really are funny.'

Chapter 15

Ever since the day she'd made the promise to carry the baby, her moods had swung from excitement to apprehension. What had seemed like a mad, spur of the moment suggestion, wasn't the impulsive gesture the others believed it to be; it had taken hold on the day Louisa had confided in her at the hospital. Even so, she hadn't given it enough serious thought before blurting it out under the influence of a few glasses of Prosecco. If she told Tom she'd been considering it beforehand, he'd be hurt and annoyed that she hadn't discussed it with him first. He still hadn't come around to the idea and had flatly refused to meet Damian and Louisa to discuss the first steps they would need to take.

'Please come,' she begged, 'all we're going to do is chat about what we've been able to find out about surrogacy.'

'The only things I've found out have confirmed what I already knew, that it's the most stupid offer I've ever heard in my life. If you want to take my suggestions to your meeting, you can tell them I think it's outrageous you are even thinking about it, and nothing is going to change my mind.'

'Not even the look on Louisa's face when she thought she may be able to have a baby of her own?'

'I'm not stopping her having a baby.'

On the evening they'd arranged to meet, Tom settled himself in front of the sports channel, a glass of beer in his hand and a look of determination on his face. He scarcely acknowledged her farewell kiss and made no attempt to accompany her to the door when Damian and Louisa arrived to pick her up. She offered no excuses for his absence, they were all aware of the magnitude of what they were contemplating, and they understood Tom's very real misgivings and respected his decision not to be involved.

The enormity of what they were going to discuss fuelled their anticipation, which simmered under the surface. As the evening progressed, Louisa could hardly contain her excitement, and her face glowed with barely concealed happiness. Damian was more circumspect, but even he found Louisa's mood infectious, and by the time they were ready to leave all three of them were smiling.

'Before we go,' Damian said, 'we should consider the possible effects of Tom's objections to what we're planning.' Sharon had avoided any reference to Tom's defiant stand, but she knew it would have to be addressed before any further decisions were made, so she braced herself and waited for Damian to continue. 'Despite our hope to continue with the surrogacy,' he said, 'it must not come at the expense of your marriage. Do you think there's any chance Tom will change his mind, or at least, not object so strongly?'

Sharon shared the anxiety clouding their faces, and she fervently wished she could give them the reassurance they were looking for, but this wasn't the time for raising false hope. 'I honestly don't know,' she said at last, 'we always try to discuss important issues before making decisions, and I know he isn't happy that I'm considering doing this. I'm just hoping he'll accept it, despite his reservations. Nine months is a long time to hold a grudge, I'm sure he'll come around by then.'

Instead of entering into a discussion, she stood up, ready to leave. Keeping her voice low, she told them to contact the clinic and set the wheels in motion. 'Obviously, they'll want to see me,' she said when they were in the car, 'but I suppose they'll also ask to see Tom?'

'I know,' Louisa said, 'That's what worries me. What will happen if Tom refuses to get involved? I do hope it won't complicate things too much.'

'It could put an end to everything,' Damian said, 'we've got to be prepared for that.'

'Stop worrying,' Sharon told them, as they hugged each other when Damian parked outside her house 'everything is going to be alright.'

Tom was watching a documentary they'd previously recorded, intending to watch it together, but to her surprise, he switched it off when she entered the room and fixed his eyes on her as she crossed the room.

'Isn't it very interesting?' she asked.

'Yes, but not, I imagine, as thought provoking as *your* evening. Did you make any decisions?'

Sharon took a while to reply. 'No, not exactly. It was more of a general discussion, but I know they are desperate to give it a try. Even though,' she said firmly, 'they are adamant they don't want it to cause trouble between us.'

'You've got a problem then, haven't you? Because it already has.'

'Tom, please tell me why you are so dead against it, because if I can understand, I'll probably have to tell them I can't do it.'

'Where do I begin,' he asked crossly. 'For one thing, I'm worried about you going through another pregnancy, because no matter what you say, it may not be as easy as you think. I'm also worried about the effect on the children, and, I don't believe you will find it easy to give away a child you've carried for nine months. You get clucky every time you see a new baby in a pram.'

Of the several reason's she'd guessed would constitute Tom's objections, she hadn't considered this one. 'I never guessed you would be worrying about that,' she said, with a weak smile, 'but I suppose you do have a point, I love babies. The thing is, I don't want any more children, we've got enough to do with the three we already have. If that's your biggest fear you can put your mind to rest, this will be Louisa's baby, not mine. However, if you feel so strongly against it, I won't go ahead.' Pushing the image of Louisa's face to one side, she added, 'I mean that.'

Putting an end to the discussion, he pointed the remote towards the television to resume watching his programme, but Sharon asked him to listen to what she had to say. Reluctantly, he did as she asked and turned half-heartedly to face her. 'What now,' he asked, 'I thought we'd said everything there was to say.'

'Not quite,' she replied, 'you see I don't think there's much substance to your objections, at least, not sufficient enough to take away Louisa's only chance to have a child.'

'Sharon, I am not stopping Louisa from having a child, surrogacy is still an option. I just don't want you to be the one providing it. Now can we drop it, you know how I feel.'

Wearily she stood up. He was obviously not willing to discuss it further, so nothing would be gained by trying to pursue it tonight. 'I'm going to bed,' she said, 'tomorrow, I'll tell Louisa and Damian that I can't go ahead without you agreeing to it.'

Tom groaned. 'And then I lose the only real friend I've made since we came to live here, thanks for that.'

She dragged herself through the following day, torn between letting her friends down or causing a serious rift between herself and Tom. When Justin studied her after she'd snapped at him for several times with no good reason, she apologised and explained she wasn't feeling very well. 'Why don't you go home?' he suggested, 'Their Lordships are not expected back for ages and no-one will be any the wiser.'

It was a very tempting offer, but regretfully she declined. 'Knowing my luck, Mrs. Portland will come back unexpectedly and catch me out,' she sighed, 'she hasn't forgiven me for going to the hospital with Lily, so there is no way she would condone it if I simply skive off.'

Justin shrugged his shoulders. 'You're not skiving if you feel ill, but have it your way,' he said. 'but don't say I never offer.' Nonchalantly tidying an already imm-aculate desk, he added under his breath, 'I can't believe you are so intimidated by her, I thought you had more pluck than that.'

'I've got plenty of that, if you must know,' she retorted, 'but I want this job and I can't rely on being related to the boss to keep me out of trouble, like someone I could mention.' Justin dramatically clasped his hands across his belly and groaned, 'Ouch, that was a bit below the belt. Now I know you are not yourself, so off you go before I change my mind. If she does come back early, I'll tell her you might have caught a tummy bug, you know how paranoid she is about that.'

'I'm sorry,' she said, 'I'll return the favour, I promise. I do appreciate it, it's just been...' Justin stopped her. 'No explanations needed, just go.'

She was surprised to find Tom already home when she got there, and once the normal chaos of dinner time and getting the two youngest off to bed was out of the way, she raised it with him.

'Was it something to do with work?'

He shook his head. 'I had an appointment this afternoon,' he replied. 'I went to see a solicitor.'

Chapter 16

The man and boy lumbered over the mud of the estuary towards the edge of the water where a group of men were working together.

'What are they doing?' Sam asked.

'Wait and see lad,' Stuart answered, 'we're nearly there now.'

As they approached, Stuart called a greeting while Sam tried to make sense of the scene in front him. At first, he thought they were picking something off the rocks, but as they came closer, he realised they were collecting shells. He'd been to lots of gift shops selling souvenirs made out shells but couldn't remember any in Merebank. 'Why do they want shells?' he asked Stuart, 'do they make things with them?'

Stuart's laugh was warm, he had no desire to humiliate Sam. 'Not just shells lad, they're mussels.'

'Are they picking them for shops and restaurants?'

'No,' Stuart told him. 'They're collecting the smallest, the ones not yet ready for eating.'

'That's cruel,' protested Sam.

'No, not at all, it's quite fascinating really. All the seeds, as they're called, are taken to a mussel farm on Anglesey and transplanted onto ropes suspended from rafts in the sea. They have more room to grow, you can see how tightly packed they are here.'

Sam peered at the nearest rock and nodded. 'More importantly,' Stuart continued, 'if they are left here, they spend a lot of time out of the water, but over there in the clean fresh sea they build more muscle and end up fatter and tastier.'

Sam sighed with relief. It seems a lot of work for a few mussels,' he said, and Stuart chuckled. 'I suppose you're right lad, but it can be quite a lucrative business, and anyway lots of people love eating mussels.'

Ugh,' Sam groaned, 'they must be mad.'

'I suppose it's an acquired taste, but most local people and a lot of holidaymakers love them, so long may they stay. They are under threat of course.'

'From what?' Sam asked.

'The proposed housing development. It wouldn't extend this far, at least not at first, but it will destroy this environment for ever.'

Turning his head, Stuart scanned the estuary and its banks. The sky was noisy with the screeching of opportunist gulls looking for easy pickings; a statuesque heron stood silhouetted on the horizon, and dunlins and redshank dipped in and out of the reeds and grasses searching for their own choice of food.

A flock of godwits probing the wet sand for lugworms were disturbed by a helicopter crossing the estuary. They flew away, yelping their sharp pip-pep calls and leaving a maze of footprints on the sand. With an effort, Stuart tried to lift one of his feet, but his boot had sunk into the mud. As he pulled, it came out with a wet, sucking sound and he set it back on firmer ground. He pointed to where the godwits had been feeding. 'This sand and mud,' he said, 'is packed with shellfish and worms, and masses of other things that give a never-ending supply of food to the birds.'

Sam was impressed, but when Stuart added, 'to put it in to modern jargon, every square metre of the mud under our feet contains the equivalent nutrition, for wildlife, of twenty large Mars bars.' Sam was even more impressed. 'Wow, 'he exclaimed.

They stood together, deep in thought, silently watching the activity all around them.

'In the autumn,' Stuart said, 'you won't be able to see a scrap of mud around here, because it will be teeming with birds refuelling before they set off on their way to places like Russia and Siberia. Sometimes there can be a quarter of a million of them at any one time. We'll come to see them if you like.'

Sam nodded his head vigorously, and then said thoughtfully. 'My dad's in favour of the development, but I'm sure he doesn't know about all this. I think I'll tell him; it will probably make him change his mind.'

'Let's hope so lad, we certainly must try and change some minds before it's all lost.'

Chapter 17

Tom had flatly refused to discuss his appointment with a solicitor, conceding only that he wanted time to think about what he'd learned before telling her about it. She could only guess it was about the surrogacy, but he adamantly refused to either confirm or deny. A severe migraine had rendered her incapable of any meaningful conversation, so she'd taken medication and fallen into bed exhausted. The following morning, she forced herself out of bed to get the children off to school, and as it was her half day, she was back home by lunch time.

Relaxing with a cup of tea and a sandwich, she unfolded the local newspaper and stared with horror at the headlines emblazoned on the front page. The speculation was over and the culprits were revealed. The banner headline left no doubt as to who was responsible for the proposed planning application, and amongst the list was a builder, who has only recently become a resident in Merebank. Making no direct accusations, they suggested his acquisition of land for a family house posed a question. Was it a deliberate move to place him in a strong position, for obtaining permission for this much bigger proposition?

The story continued inside the paper but Sharon let it drop to the floor without opening it. Her fears were realised with it the sickening realisation that Tom hadn't been honest with her. It threatened to undo everything they'd achieved to feel settled here; they'd be perceived as outsiders who put their own interests before their new community and the local environment.

Later, when Tom walked in wearing a beaming smile, Sharon couldn't trust herself to look at him without yelling or bursting into tears. Did he have no idea what he'd done, or didn't he care? When Lily came into the room and he swept her up into the air she almost screamed at him. Lily, who'd earlier caught her mummy crying, wriggled in his arms until he was forced to stand her on the floor. 'Mummy needs Bear, she's upset,' she said indignantly, and sensing this was a grown-up problem, she scuttled over to thrust the bear into Sharon's grasp, before running out of the room and up the stairs to her bedroom.

Tom watched her go before turning to Sharon. 'What's happened sweetheart, is it one of the boys?' Unable to speak to him she shook her head and pointed to the newspaper on the floor. After skimming the front page, he reacted angrily. 'What the hell is this?' he exclaimed, 'what are they going on about, you'd think I'd committed a murder.'

'I think you may just as well have done,' Sharon replied furiously, 'for the harm it will cause us.' Tom looked genuinely puzzled but she pulled away when he tried to put his arm round her. 'Don't touch me,' she said, 'you'll ruin all our lives, how dare you act as though nothing's happened.'

Tom stood up and scanned the paper again. 'I don't know why you think I've ruined our lives just because I'm going to build some houses. I'm not the one who's buying the land or applying for planning permission, they've got this all wrong, I'm just a builder trying to earn a living.'

'But I told you this would happen! Why do you never listen to me?'

'I listen to you all the time and you know that, but sometimes I have to make my own decisions, and this was an opportunity too good to miss. Greg is more involved in this than I am; it's more his project than mine, and you know how well respected he is round here.' He moved close to her, and this time she didn't move away. 'I didn't say anything because it's been pushed from pillar to post and I didn't want you to worry unnecessarily. Greg still isn't confident it will get through and nobody expected it to come out like this. I'm sorry babe, I was trying to protect you, but it seems I've done just the opposite.'

A sob shuddered through her body and she dabbed her eyes as she leaned into him. 'I'm weary.' she whispered. 'I feel so stressed all the time with the worry of the surrogacy, and then this happens. I'm dreading going into work and facing them all. I can just imagine what kind of response I'll get. But it's not just me; the children will be affected as well, especially Sam.'

Tom stroked her hand. 'I wouldn't worry too much about what other people think,' he said, 'you'll be surprised how much local opinion is divided, not everyone is against the idea, in fact there are a lot of people very much in favour.'

'Not Stuart.' Sharon said, 'this could ruin our friendship.' Tom shook his head, 'I think our friendship is too strong for that to happen.'

Sam came into the room. 'Are you talking about Stuart and the houses?' he asked, 'because if you are, I can tell you he's dead against it, and he'll stop at nothing to prevent it from happening.'

Tom glanced at Sharon, who was nodding in agreement. 'I think we know that son,' he said, 'all I'm trying to say is I don't think it will make any difference to our friendship.'

'I wouldn't be so sure about that,' Sam replied, 'I don't think you realise how strongly the people round here feel about it. It's a very important site for all kinds of things, not just birds, and they won't give it up easily.'

Tom held his hand up and stopped him. 'Okay, I give in, but since when have you become an expert on the environment?'

'Since I took it as one of my options, but you probably don't even know that do you?'

'What's that supposed to mean?'

'You haven't a clue what I'm doing, all you're interested in is upsetting people and building houses where they don't want them. You didn't even discuss it with us, even though everybody is talking about it and asking me if it's true.'

Tom pulled away from Sharon and shot to his feet. 'I'm trying to do the best for my family, is that so wrong? When this place is finished, we'll be living in a fantastic big house at the seaside, that's a big step up from where we were a few years ago.'

'Big deal!' Sam shouted, 'You don't get it do you? I liked where we were living, and I never wanted to come here.'

'Well, it's not just about you, we made the decision to come here for the benefit of all the family. I thought you were settling down and making friends.'

'Yeah, like you care.' Sam shouted, as he turned and stormed out of the room, giving Tom no opportunity to reply.

'Wow, where did that come from?' he asked Sharon.

'From his heart probably,' she replied, 'and he does have a point. Out of interest, *do* you know what subjects he's studying at school?' Tom shuffled uncomfortably.

'Okay,' he conceded, 'I haven't kept my eye on the ball, but I've been busy!' When Sharon didn't reply he stood up and walked away. 'I'm doing it for all of us you know,' he muttered, but Sharon had already slumped onto the sofa and closed her eyes, so he went upstairs to change out of his work clothes and have a shower.

'Are you going to explain why you went to see a solicitor?' Sharon asked later.

'I wanted to find out about the legalities involved in this hairbrained scheme of yours,' Tom replied, 'because I don't think you've given enough serious thought to all the complexities.'

Sharon bristled. 'I'm not going into it without having done a lot of research, if that's what your implying.'

'I didn't suggest you were, but for instance, do you know who the child's legal parents are when it's born?'

Sharon hesitated; she had a good idea where the conversation was leading. 'The surrogate mother and her husband,' she replied.

'That means me,' Tom said, 'but I don't want to be its father.'

'I know you don't, but there is a way round that.'

'Yes, but the alternative is no better as far as I'm concerned. If I refuse to go along with it, Damian will be named as father.'

'Why do you object to that?'

Tom was beginning to get angry. 'Is that so difficult to understand? There will be a child with you and Damian named as the parents on its birth certificate. I'm not exactly over the moon about that prospect.'

'It's only until the parental order is obtained about six weeks later, then a new birth certificate is issued with Louisa and Damian named as the parents.'

Tom dropped his head into his hands. 'Which brings us neatly back to what I was saying earlier.' Letting his hand fall, he directed his eyes to Sharon. 'We will be up shit creek, if you can't hand over the baby. There will be a baby in our family, with Damian's name on the birth certificate.'

Sharon's voice broke with emotion. 'But it would be changed with the new birth certificate, and anyway I don't know why we're discussing this, because I won't be keeping the baby.' Thinking she heard a noise outside the room, she shook her head and whispered. 'Tom, we must keep our voices down, or discuss this later.'

'Okay,' he agreed, 'I'll just tell you this. I went to see the solicitor today, to try and make sense of what we might be letting ourselves in for. It seems we can't enter into any legally binding arrangements, but we can draw up some agreements in writing between us.'

Sharon strained to hear. 'If it isn't legally binding, what's the point?' she asked. 'Surely we can trust each other?'

'It can't do any harm to agree a few guidelines and put them in writing.' Tom replied firmly.

She could barely breathe. 'Does this mean you're happy for us to go ahead?' she asked.

'Happy comes nowhere near to how I feel, but if I do agree for you to go ahead, and it's a big if, I must be on the birth certificate with you. It frightens me to death, the thought of being legally named the parents of a child who isn't ours, but the alternative is even worse. The solicitor was very reassuring, but she doesn't know you. Sharon, promise me you'll hand the baby over when it's born.'

'I promise,' she said.

Chapter 18

The screening procedures had been complex and thorough, and once or twice she'd been concerned that Tom would object to the intrusion into their private lives, but thankfully he'd made no real objections. Following the positive results concerning the reasons for the surrogacy and the mental state of all participants, Sharon attended the clinic for her last appraisal before any final decision was made.

She hadn't told anyone about the appointment, as it was only to get the results of the tests she'd had a couple of weeks ago. She wasn't anticipating any problems, but it was strange to know that other people were waiting for news of how her body was functioning.

Becoming a surrogate mum wasn't proving to be quite as simple as she'd thought it would be; some of the questions were very personal, delving into her relationship with Tom, and the physical tests were invasive. In her more rational moments, she knew it made perfect sense. The medical professionals needed to be satisfied that she was emotionally and physically fit to see it through successfully, but she wondered how anyone could possibly be certain how they would deal with it emotionally until it actually it happened

The walls in the waiting room were covered with a collage of babies conceived through IVF. She noticed one particularly happy baby who was the outcome of a successful surrogate birth. She had no time to read any more, as she was called into the consulting room where Mr. Janus was waiting for her. After exchanging greetings, he rolled the computer screen, glanced at some papers on his desk, and turned to her with a broad smile.

'Well, Sharon,' he said, 'I'm pleased to tell you, all your results have come back positive, you are a very healthy specimen both mentally and physically, and there is absolutely no reason why you can't be a surrogate mother for your friend.'

'Good,' she said, 'that's a relief, even though I wasn't expecting any problems. I'll let Louisa and Damian know the good news, and then we can start looking ahead. What is the next part of the process? I must admit I haven't given a lot of thought about what comes next.'

'As far as we're concerned, there is no reason why we can't get started immediately,'

Sharon felt her pulse race. 'Oh,' she said, 'I'm sorry, but I wasn't quite expecting that. I didn't think we would be starting so soon.'

'I know, it comes as a bit of a surprise to us sometimes, when everything happens so smoothly.' He glanced at a chart on his screen. 'Luckily, your cycle is so regular there is no need for you to take any drugs to regulate it, so whenever you're ready we can go ahead.' When he started to consult his calendar Sharon began to panic, and she breathed a sigh of relief when he pushed it away. 'There's no hurry,' he said kindly, 'talk it over with your husband and Louisa, and when you're ready to proceed, just let us know.'

'Yes, yes I will,' Sharon replied, and the doctor looked at her, his expressive face filled with understanding.

'Sharon, there's no rush,' he said quietly, 'and there is still time to change your mind. You mustn't feel you're being pressurised into anything.'

'I don't,' she replied, 'I was just a bit taken by surprise at the speed of it, but I'm happy and determined to go through with it.'

'Good for you,' he said, holding out his hand, 'and give my regards to your husband, it can't be easy for him.'

'Thank you,' she replied, 'I will.'

Unfortunately, the timing was all wrong as far as work was concerned. When Mrs. Portland had told her she was the unofficial secretary to the Mayoress, she had no idea how much work was involved, but she'd wrongly believed the term of office would be almost over before the pregnancy began. If everything went according to plan, that was now seeming very unlikely.

After browsing the women's clothes shops and the large Department Store, she went into the designer outlet shop and picked out a couple of items that caught her eye. They fitted perfectly and she decided to buy them, but eying herself in the changing room mirrors it suddenly occurred to her that they may not fit for very long. She would save them as an impetus to regain her figure after the birth; she'd done that with her own babies, and it had worked every time.

On the way to the car park she found herself veering towards a mother and baby shop filled with everything an expectant mum could wish for. She lingered over the tiny dresses she'd longed to buy when she was expecting Lily, but hand-me-downs from friends and charity shops had been all they could afford at the time. That was in the past and nothing would persuade her to go through it all again, what she was proposing to do for Louisa and Damian was altogether different. Nearing home, she was tempted to go and break the good news to Louisa, but she wanted to tell Tom first, to confirm he hadn't changed his mind. He'd promised to support her when she was ready to go ahead, and at this crucial stage she needed his assurance that he still felt the same way.

Chapter 19

Damian had seemed oddly excited on the phone, but he'd refused to explain the reason for the unexpected proposed visit, and Marie was impatiently trying to figure out what it could be. The one thing that sprang instantly to mind was the possibility of them buying a house, but the last time they'd discussed it, both Louisa and Damian had been adamant it wouldn't be on the agenda for some considerable time. Starting a family had unfortunately been ruled out, which left Marie none the wiser, so she would simply have to wait and see.

Stuart returned home from his game of bowls in a funny mood and barely registered the news that his son and daughter-in-law were due to arrive shortly. All her enquiries regarding the health of his friends, the state of the green, and how many games he'd won, were all met with a mumbled, unintelligible growl. After he'd hung his coat up and taken off his shoes, he apologised and told her he would explain when he'd washed his face and changed his clothes in readiness for Damian and Louisa's arrival.

Marie filled the kettle and put a bottle of white wine and some lagers in the fridge, which she thought would cover every eventuality by way of a celebration, and then she sat down to wait.

I'm sorry love,' Stuart said, coming into the kitchen and taking a beer from the fridge, 'I shouldn't take it out on you I know, but I'm absolutely fuming.'

'About what?' she asked, as he poured the beer into a pint glass and tasted it. 'This pesky planning application, apparently someone's submitted the plans.'

Marie ran her hands down the front of her dress. Smoothing out invisible creases gave her time to try and compose herself. If Damian had heard the news and was hoping to buy one of the properties, there would be no celebrations here today. Stuart was looking at her, waiting for a response. 'You're very thoughtful.' he said.

'Sorry, I'm still trying to take it in. I heard about it on the local news but surely everyone knows the planners won't allow it.'

'Let's hope you are right, but if the rumour about Tom, turns out to be right, he'll feel the lash of my tongue I can tell you. He's done very well for himself since Greg helped him out, but even so I can't imagine he's got the wherewithal to finance a project this big.' Running his fingers through his hair he looked distracted and let down. 'I know you won't want to hear this,' he added, 'but if it is Tom, I don't want anything more to do with him. After all we've done to help him, and then he betrays us like this, I'm finished with him.'

'I think you're jumping the gun a bit,' she protested, 'you said yourself you don't know if it's true. Let's wait and see before we start saying something we may regret later.' Her instincts told her she was about to hear some good news and she didn't want it spoiled by discussions around a problem that may never happen. 'I don't think we should talk about it today,' she told Stuart, 'let's keep the conversation light.'

'Are you joking?' he laughed, turning on the television, 'there will be a rumpus here when this gets going.' The local derby football match had completely escaped her mind, but it could provide a useful diversion, and it would cause far less aggravation than a possible housing estate, even though on the surface, they were all in agreement about that.

Damian and Louisa arrived promptly, and both were exuding an air of suppressed excitement. Louisa was positively glowing as she handed her coat to Stuart, and Damian was grinning like a Cheshire cat. Marie had already given up trying to second guess them, but if by some stroke of good fortune, they were buying their own home, she prayed it wasn't to be on the proposed new estate.

With her mind deep in thought, she watched Damian raise a bottle of champagne, and slide his free arm lovingly around Louisa's waist. 'We have something very important to tell you,' he said, pausing just long enough to take a deep breath. 'We are going to have a baby.'

Clasping her hands, Marie gasped in amazement, before moving towards Louisa to envelope her in a breathless hug while Stuart pumped Damian's hand up and down, repeating, 'congratulations son' over and over again.

'Oh, that's wonderful,' Marie exclaimed, standing back and holding Louisa's hands. 'I'm so glad you've decided to adopt. I thought you'd come around to it eventually, but the sooner you make the decision, the better. I suppose it will take a while, but at least now, you've got something to look forward to.' Puzzled, she watched Damian shaking his head, his face split through with a smile.

'No, mum,' he said, 'we're not adopting, we are having our own child.'

Silence stilled the room. 'How can that be?' Marie whispered, struggling to make sense of what she'd heard. How could this be possible? Louisa had already undergone a hysterectomy, making it impossible for her to bear a child. Once the decision had been made it had all happened very quickly. Marie had shared their sadness and had helped and supported them as much as she could during Louisa's emotional and physical recovery. She struggled to make sense of what they were saying and looking from one to the other, her glance settled on her son.

'I don't understand,' she said, 'how can you possibly be expecting a baby of your own?'

Damian apologised. 'I'm sorry mum, we got a bit carried away there. We should have explained before we dropped a bombshell like that. Let's sit down and we can fill you in with the details.'

Shaking, Marie allowed herself to be led to a chair and Stuart followed suit and sat next to her. Damian looked enquiringly at Louisa who gently nodded. 'The thing is,' he began, 'as you know we've already got an embryo, well more than one, so we are going to have a surrogate mother carry it for us. This way, when the baby is born, it will be completely ours.'

Stuart was the first to respond. 'You'll have to bear with me on this one,' he told them, 'I know a bit about IVF obviously, well to be fair everyone must know a bit about it, but I don't understand the first thing about surrogacy. How does that work?'

This time it was Louisa's turn to speak, and she began to explain. Marie and Stuart listened intently while Louisa explained the details of their intentions, and neither of them interrupted until she concluded by saying, 'Unfortunately, I can't carry a child, but some-one else could do it for us, and unbelievably we've found some-one who will.'

'Is it very expensive?' Stuart asked, and when he learned there were no costs involved, he shook his head in disbelief. 'You mean this person is doing it out of kindness? She must be one hell of a lady.'

'She certainly is,' Louisa said.

'How did you find her?' Marie asked, 'are there agencies for this kind of thing now?'

'Not exactly, but in fact she found us.'

Damian hesitated in his search for champagne flutes until Stuart pointed out they now resided on the bottom shelf of the display cabinet. 'Your mum has developed quite a liking for bubbles, so now, the glasses have to be within her reach,' he said, with an apologetic nod for interrupting.

'A slight exaggeration,' Marie protested, under her breath, 'but I must admit I have grown to enjoy a glass of bubbly.'

'Well, fancy that,' Stuart declared, 'grandma and granddad yet again. I don't suppose it will happen for quite a while though, I should imagine you've got a lot to sort out first. Damian and Louisa fidgeted uncomfortably, making Marie uneasy. 'You'd better tell us everything,' she told them, you're beginning to worry me now.'

'The thing is…' Damian began, and when he faltered, Louisa took over from him.

'Actually, we do know when it's going to happen, we know exactly when our baby is going to be born. That

is of course, if everything goes according to plan.'
Damian agreed. 'Of course, it's early days yet.'

Marie was getting increasingly puzzled, but she tried
to remain calm. 'We can go into details later,' she said,
but we're not celebrating too soon are we? You said
you've found a surrogate mother, which couldn't have
been easy, but surely you now have lots of hoops to
jump through, like medical tests and other procedures.'

'Finding a suitable surrogate for our child would
have probably been very difficult, but some-one we
know has offered. It was she who suggested we take this
step, by offering to do it herself. The reason we know
when the baby is due, is because the embryo has already
been implanted in her womb, and up to now it seems to
have been a successful start to pregnancy.'

Marie took a gulp of champagne and sat back in her
chair, her head was already spinning and this time she
didn't even attempt to disguise it. Stuart was looking
from one to another, saying nothing, simply trying to
make sense of what he'd heard. 'You are the first ones to
know,' Louisa explained, 'but we couldn't say anything
until we had some real news to tell you. I hope you don't
feel hurt, because we have been longing to tell you, but
we were afraid to until we were sure. Sharon's had a scan
and there's no doubt about it, we're going to be parents.'

Marie was fighting back tears as she pulled her son
close and Stuart shuffled with embarrassment as Louisa
unashamedly did the same to him. 'I'm so happy for you
both,' Marie said, before pulling away to look at him
questioningly. 'Did I hear you right, did you just say
Sharon's had a scan?'

Damian moved his head slowly up and down. 'I
wondered if you'd noticed my deliberate mistake,' he

said, 'and yes you are right, it is Sharon who's carrying our baby.'

The room again fell silent as Marie and Stuart processed this latest, overwhelming news. Marie's first reaction, after the shock of hearing it, was to marvel at Sharon's willingness to go through a pregnancy for someone else when her life was already so full. Stuart gave up trying to work out how a child being carried by Sharon, was going to end up being born looking like Damian and Louisa.

'I still can't believe it's really happening,' Marie said, 'and for once I'm glad you didn't tell us until it was confirmed, because I would have had sleepless nights worrying about it.'

Damian looked anxiously at his mother. 'We can't tell anyone else yet,' he said earnestly, 'it's very early days for a surrogate pregnancy and something could still go wrong.'

'Don't worry son, your secret's safe with me,' Marie said, 'now let's talk about what will happen in the next few months and all the lovely things we can look forward to.'

'Oh, baby talk,' grumbled Stuart, 'I suppose there's going to be a lot of that from now on.' He looked at Damian. 'How do you fancy leaving them to it while we go to the pub and watch the match?'

'Sounds good to me.'

'Well son, you may as well take advantage now, because when the baby comes, it won't be this easy to get time off. Mark my words.'

While Damian and Louisa were chatting in the hall, Stuart leaned towards Marie and muttered.

'This is great news, but it doesn't change my feelings towards Tom, so don't expect it to.'

'Alright, but don't say anything to Damian.'

'I won't,' he agreed, 'at least, not today.'

Chapter 20

Everyone filed out of the building in an orderly fashion, some trying to hide their feelings of satisfaction and optimism and others mumbling and shaking their heads in disbelief. Stuart, making no effort to conceal his delight, grinned and beamed at anyone his eyes alighted on regardless of which side of the argument they supported. Turning down Russell's invitation to join him in a game of bowls, he made his way to the café where he'd arranged to meet Marie on her way back from her reading group in the library.

After a lot of nagging, he'd finally given in and learned the basics of his mobile phone, and now he was able to keep in touch with Marie and change or confirm their arrangements any time he wished. He still had a bit of an issue with remembering to keep it switched on, but by and large it was proving very handy. She was sitting by the window gazing out over the horizon, and as he approached, she turned towards him anxiously.

'How did it go?'

Stuart's arms folded across his chest as he breathed a deep sigh of satisfaction. 'Better than we hoped, it was a unanimous vote against, thank God.' He looked speculatively across the bay before turning his smiling face towards her. 'In the end, it all came down to the pink footed geese, the need to protect them, helped to sway the decision.'

'So, what happened?' Marie asked, filling up the teapot from the jug of hot water.

'Basically,' Stuart said with satisfaction, 'the Officers advised the councillors to turn down the application on the grounds that the impact on the environment was too great to be acceptable. The only problem now is the need to identify some land so they can solve the problem of meeting their housing targets. That can wait for another day.'

Marie was genuinely pleased for Stuart, and in her heart, she was glad, so she pushed her own feelings of disappointment to one side. The problem facing Damian and Louisa would have to wait, but the expected arrival of a new baby made the situation even more pressing, and she couldn't stop worrying about it. She took his hand and smiled at him. 'That is good news, and such a relief that it's all over.'

Stuart shook his head. 'Oh, it's not over yet love, I suppose the developers will appeal, and it could even go down to the Secretary of State, but for now we can breathe again.'

'I thought it was too good to be true, so it's still a waiting game.'

'Afraid so, but at least we're over the first hurdle, and it was encouraging to hear the committee backing the local people and not the ones trying to destroy our environment.'

Marie nodded in agreement, there had been a few issues during the last few years when the local planners had seemed out of tune with the wishes of the residents. It was generally accepted they were sometimes bound by rules and regulations beyond their control, and she hoped this wasn't going to be one of them, or at least that's how she felt most of the time. She couldn't help noticing that Damian had become very guarded whenever the subject was raised, and she was beginning to wonder if his desire to buy a home was over-riding his objections to the development. If it ever came to the point where he and his father were at loggerheads, she would have to support one over the other, and that would be catastrophic and didn't bear thinking about. The community was already being split down the middle by the effects of the proposal, now families were at risk as well.

If only a way could be found to solve Damian's immediate problem, she could support Stuart's campaign unreservedly. In a moment of inspiration, she'd come up with a possible way to help them, but it was going to be tricky persuading Stuart and she would have to choose her time for broaching the subject very carefully. For the moment, she was happy to share his pleasure and satisfaction with today's result.

'Were there many people there?' she asked.

Stuart's face creased into a grin. 'There were too many to get in. Apparently, more members of the public turn up for the Planning Committee meetings than a full council meeting.'

'Were they all against it?

'It was difficult to tell, you can't speak or comment, so it's the groans and mumbled cheers that give you away.' His face turned bleak. 'I tell you what though, it didn't take much imagination to guess which side of the fence Tom is standing, at least we know now for sure he's involved in this. Unfortunately, this looks like the end of a friendship.'

It always seemed to come down to this, Tom's role in the proposal and the effect on their respective families.

She hoped the time would arrive, when one could be separated from the other. 'Surely, it doesn't have to mean that, we could agree to disagree. That's what friends do.'

'No, we can't agree to disagree, at least not about this, and anyway that's just the point, he's thrown our friendship back in our faces.' Seeing the look on her face he relented a little. 'Don't look so worried love, it may never happen, especially after what happened today. I'm sure Tom won't bear a grudge if he loses.'

Marie forced a smile, but she couldn't help wondering if he too would be magnanimous in defeat. Did you speak to Tom?'

'No, he left in a hurry, I suppose he was in a rush to get back to work. I hope this doesn't adversely affect him, because I'm full of admiration for everything he's done to get himself back on his feet. I don't wish him any ill, no matter what the outcome is.'

Marie seized on that. 'I know you don't, so please don't be too hard on him Stuart, I don't want any trouble.'

'Don't concern yourself, there won't be any trouble of my making, it's up to him now. He's made of pretty stern stuff that lad and he didn't give any signs of being put out by anything.' Stuart paused. 'It was quite the opposite, now I come to think of it.'

'What do you mean?'

'Well, you'd expect him to have been a bit put out at the decision, but he seemed quite relaxed and not in the least concerned. So, you see' he added, 'there is absolutely nothing for you to worry about.'

Marie smiled in agreement, but it still didn't stop her worrying.

Chapter 21

Sharon leaned over the toilet and retched. Morning after morning, before she'd even eaten anything, she was sick. Even when there was nothing left to come up, she couldn't stop this horrible heaving. After a few minutes, she stood up and gently rubbed her ribcage beneath her breasts before moving her fingers to where her back felt so sore. She had never experienced anything like this during her three previous pregnancies, maybe a slight nauseous feeling occasionally, but this was relentless vomiting which sometimes carried on intermittently throughout the day.

It was getting more difficult to hide her condition, and she was grateful for Mrs. Portland's total absorption in her duties as The Mayoress, which made her less observant than she was normally. There was a downside of course; she was piling more and more work onto Sharon, who was then forced to ask for more support from friends and family.

Tom was already making comments about how tired she was looking so she tried even harder to keep up appearances as the last thing she wanted to do was give him ammunition to fuel his objections. Sharon stroked her belly and whispered softly, 'stay safe little baby.' She was petrified of something going wrong, despite the doctor's assurances that the baby would be getting all the nourishment it needed, even if its mother was being sick all the time. She'd turned down his offer of a prescription to reduce the nausea, she was adamant nothing would pass her lips that had the potential to harm the baby.

It was turning out to be a bigger responsibility and more complicated than she'd imagined, but she just had to get on and do it. Maybe it was a good thing she hadn't known what was coming, because she might have thought twice about it, but every time she saw either Damian or Louisa, she was convinced it was the right thing to do. It was a strange feeling, knowing you held the happiness of two people in your hands, well actually your womb, and it made it all worthwhile. She would appreciate a little break from this wretched feeling though, especially when trouble was erupting downstairs.

'What is going on?' she demanded, going into the kitchen where chaos reigned, 'why aren't you all getting ready for school?'

'Sam won't reach my cereal down for me,' wailed Lily, 'and I can't reach it by my own.'

'By myself,' Sam corrected her impatiently, 'and you didn't even ask me.'

'Yes, I did,' she insisted, 'you know I did.'

'Mum, do you know where my football kit is, I can't find it,' Ben called, 'I'm going to be late.'

'That's my fault, is it?' Sharon asked crossly, 'honestly, you are just like your brother was at your age, he never knew where things were, and I'll tell you again, as I used to tell him; if you put them in the dirty linen box to be washed, they will be in your bedroom drawer, clean. If you didn't, they'll still be in your sports bag, dirty.'

'I've looked, and they're in neither. I don't know where they've gone.'

'They haven't gone anywhere,' Sharon replied, 'they can't walk, so they will be where you left them.' She felt like screaming, but managed with difficulty to control her temper, it wasn't their fault she was feeling so out of sorts and stressed.

'Look,' she told them, 'I'm going to work and I'm running late, so can you please stop bickering and help me by getting yourselves ready. I don't think it's too much to ask, you're old enough now.'

A small, plaintiff voice piped up. 'I'm only five,' and Sharon dropped onto the chair beside her. 'I know you are poppet, and I'll help you. Which cereal would you like?'

'I'll get it,' offered Sam, 'I know which one she wants.' Sharon threw him a grateful smile and when Ben called out he'd discovered the kit in his bedroom, she almost fainted with gratitude.

'Bunches or plaits?' she asked, trying to save time by brushing Lily's hair while she was eating her cereal. Lily pondered, holding a spoon halfway between her mouth and the bowl. 'Plaits please, and can I have those pink ribbons with hearts on?'

Sharon didn't have a clue where they were so she tried to change the subject and hoped that Lily might forget.

'I'm off,' Ben called, 'see you later.' Sam put his head round the door. 'See you mum, don't forget it's parents' evening, will you?'

Parents' evening, where had that come from? Leaping up she ran to the door and called to him. 'Sam, I don't know anything about this.' Sam turned without halting his steps. 'I brought a letter home last week. It's on the pile where you told us to put everything important.' Sharon groaned; she hadn't had time to go through any correspondence for days now. Rusty suddenly shot past her on his way to attach himself to the boys. 'Mum, can you get him I'm going to be late,' Sam called urgently. 'Well at least stop walking away from me,' she replied. Bending down to hold the dog's collar she enquired if either of them had thought to take him for a walk, knowing what the answer was even before she asked it.

Sharon scooped the dog up and ran back into the house. She'd arranged time off to keep an appointment this afternoon, so she'd already asked Marie to pick Lily up from school, and now she needed someone to watch her while she went to the parents' evening. Tom would go of course, but they'd always tried to go together and now it was even more important for them both to attend while the boys were settling in their new schools. Apart from that, she and Tom had different priorities, while Tom was more interested in their sporting abilities, she concentrated on their academic and wellbeing issues. Having become aware of Sam's problems, she was keen to know if he was showing any signs of stress, while Tom would probably tell him he needed to 'man up'.

At last they were on their way. Lily was skipping along with her friend, the red ribbons at the end of her plaits bobbing in rhythm with her steps. At the school gates, Sharon bent down to kiss her. 'Don't forget, Nana Marie is picking you up this afternoon.' Lily wriggled out of her grasp and zoomed towards her friends. 'Okay,' she called, 'bye!' For a few precious moments, Sharon watched as Lily was enthusiastically embraced by a circle of girls, and when it became obvious there was to be no backward glance, she turned to make her way to work. At least the smallest member of the family was giving her no cause for concern.

She walked through the square to pick up some things Mrs. Portland had asked her to buy on her way to work. These small errands were occurring more frequently and encroaching on Sharon's own time, but she was reluctant to complain. Mrs Portland's comment about everyone pulling together was still ringing in her ears, and the unspoken insinuations had made her feel less secure.

Earlier, she'd heaved at the sight of the children's breakfast and for the first time in her life even the aroma of the coffee in the pot didn't appeal. Now, the smell of baking bread wafting across the square made her stomach lurch, so she hurried towards the 'Let's Party' shop, which thankfully was on the furthest corner from the bakers. She had never suffered from morning sickness before, but she was certainly making up for it this time. Desperately trying to think where the nearest toilets were in case of an emergency, she didn't see Marie who was standing beside her.

As they walked together towards the party shop Sharon found herself instinctively increasing speed until she realised Marie was struggling to keep up. She'd left home in plenty of time but suddenly it was running away from her and although the nauseous feeling had eased a little, she still felt a bit squeamish. 'I'm sorry,' Marie said, I don't want to make you late, you go on, I'll get there in my own good time.' They said their good-byes, but Marie looked at Sharon's drawn face with concern. 'Are you alright dear?' she asked, 'You look a little peaky.'

'I'm fine, I'm just a bit tired that's all.'

'I'm not surprised, you mustn't let Bryony put on you. She will do if you let her, but you've got to look after yourself, it's more important than ever now.' Sharon nodded, anxious to get away, but Marie held her arm. 'Are you going to tell her soon?'

'I can't yet, not before we've told the children, but I don't think it will make much difference, my problems aren't high on her priorities.'

'Other people's problems have never been of much concern to Bryony I'm afraid, but that is no reason for letting her take advantage of you now. She deserves to be pulled into line every now and again.'

Wondering if she was going to make it in time, Sharon hurried to the back entrance of the hotel and ran into the nearest lady's room where she retched repeatedly until her ribs felt as though they were going to crack. After it had subsided, she waited for a few moments for the nausea to pass, and then she splashed some water over her face and made her way towards reception.

Justin greeted her from behind the desk as she passed on her way to the office. 'Good morning Sharon,' he smiled, looking up from the computer. 'There are a few messages for you, wedding related I believe, I've put them in a pile in the office.'

'Thanks Justin.'

'My pleasure. Oh, I nearly forgot, Mrs. Portland was looking for you.'

Sharon glanced at the clock. 'Looking for me, when? I'm not due in until nine.'

'Oh well, you know what Mrs. P's like…' Justin was looking past Sharon who jumped at the sound of Mrs. Portland's voice.

'No Justin, I don't know actually, but I'm sure you're going to tell us,' she said. 'Good morning, Sharon, are you well?' Sharon didn't miss the darting glance at the clock or the hint that only illness should make her late. 'Yes, thanks,' she replied, 'but it took a little longer than I expected to get these things you asked me to buy.'

'Oh, I'm so sorry, I completely forgot,' Mrs. Portland said, peering into one of the bags. 'Before I look at everything let me make us both a nice cup of coffee. We'll go into the office.' She filled the kettle and put three mugs on the tray. 'I may as well make Justin one at the same time, and we can all have a piece of this lovely cake Luke brought in for us to sample. It's a new recipe he's trying out.' She put a slice of cake and a coffee on the table in front of Sharon before taking a tray out to Justin in reception.

The smell of the coffee triggered another sweeping wave of nausea rising to her throat, and holding her breath, she hurriedly broke off a piece of her cake which she wrapped in a tissue and stuffed into her bag, and with one eye on the door, poured half the coffee down the sink. With a bit of luck Mrs. Portland wouldn't notice.

Wiping a few crumbs onto her lips she smiled and pretended to be swallowing a mouthful of cake and lifted the coffee to her mouth. 'Mm. Delicious,' she said, 'but if you don't mind, I think I'll save this piece until lunchtime. I'll appreciate it then, when I've got more time. I must go, I'm expecting the man who's coming to discuss the possibility of us hosting another wedding fair here.'

'Of course,' Mrs. Portland said, 'I won't keep you. Oh, Sharon,' she added, 'thanks for getting these things for me.'

'It's a pleasure,' Sharon replied, trying to get away as quickly as possible without causing offence.

Sharon became acutely aware that all their plans for keeping things secret for as long as possible were not going to work, and unless they broke the news to immediate family there was a possibility other people would guess first. That would be catastrophic so she would have to act quickly. Drat this completely unexpected morning sickness.

She'd been determined to keep her condition secret until she was into the second trimester when they could be more confident of her going full term. It was nothing short of a miracle that the first implant of an embryo had been successful, but as they'd been reminded, there was no certainty of success. At the beginning, she'd confidently assured Louisa of her determination to carry on trying until all the embryos had been used if this one didn't work out, but now she wasn't so sure. She hadn't bargained for being so ill, and she didn't think she could face starting all over again.

'Before you go,' Mrs. Portland said briskly, 'we've got a busy day ahead of us. I'm up to my eyes with the arrangements for the Charity Ball, so I want you to take charge of some of the smaller events. I know you are busy this morning, but I thought we could get together after lunch and make a start on prioritising them.' Sharon's mind raced, searching for a way out of this dilemma, but it seemed the only way to handle it was head on. Mrs. Portland was watching her reactions closely. 'Is that a problem? 'she asked.

'Yes, it is I'm afraid, I've arranged to have the afternoon off for a doctor's appointment. I did put it in the diary.'

'I see. I haven't noticed it, but maybe it hasn't been there very long.' Before Sharon had chance to correct her, she went on, 'well it can't be helped I suppose.' Tapping her nails on the desk she scrutinised Sharon as though trying to decipher what was ailing her. 'It must be a long appointment,' she suggested, 'if it's going to take a whole afternoon.'

'It's at the hospital, and I thought it would be better if I did it in my own time rather than just taking it out of work time.'

'Very thoughtful, but it still doesn't help me.' Sharon again began to move away, but before she'd reached the door to the office Mrs. Portland's voice halted her. 'I don't suppose you could give me a few hours this evening?'

Sharon counted to ten. I'm sorry, but it's parents' evening at the school and I have to be there.' There was no way Tom would condone her returning to work in the evening. That had been part of their agreement when she took the job and it was even more important now.

'Very well,' Mrs. Portland huffed, turning on her heel to go to reception where she went over to rebuke the window cleaner who was chatting to a group of visitors near the door.

Sharon sent him a silent apology for having turned her boss's mood, but to her amusement he was unruffled, and having resumed his job was whistling merrily.

Chapter 22

To save time, Louisa was picking Sharon up from work on their way to the hospital. Sharon had suggested the staff entrance at the back of the building would be the safest place to avoid prying eyes, and when she pulled the door behind her, she saw Louisa waiting anxiously in the car. Despite the precautions, Sharon couldn't help feeling she was being watched, but glancing up at the building as she fastened her seatbelt there were no signs of anyone at any of the windows. Not that it mattered, it was her official half day off, so she was doing nothing wrong. The fact she was attending a hospital appointment was of no concern to anyone else and everything would become public knowledge soon anyway.

Louisa edged the car out into the traffic on the inner promenade. 'I can't believe this is happening, I had no idea I would be coming with you for the scan.'

'Well, you are the obvious choice,' Sharon replied, 'as long as it doesn't make it difficult for you at work.' She thought it best not to mention she'd discussed it first with Tom, who'd categorically declined. His initial squeamish reluctance to being present at the births of their own children had eventually been overcome, but he had no desire to attend the birth of a baby who wasn't even his, and she'd made no attempt to persuade him to change his mind.

'No-one at work knows what's happening, but there's no problem getting time off,' Louisa told her, 'I'm owed plenty of holiday leave, but of course it is a bit difficult...' Her voice dropped, 'we are under a bit of pressure due to the sad situation with Paul Sheridan.'

Sharon knew a little about Louisa's past involvement with her boss and how it had all come to a head five years ago, but a lot had happened since then and she couldn't remember quite how it had ended. There was currently some gossip going around about him, but the only thing she could remember was that he was ill. 'How is the situation now?' she asked gently.

'I'm not sure exactly, but not good.'

Sharon couldn't think of a suitable reply in the circumstances, so she simply said, 'I'm sorry.'

Louisa paused for a moment. 'Yes, so am I,' she said, 'it's very sad, and I think Katy is being incredible.' They were both quiet as Louisa drove past the main hospital car park and parked in front of the maternity block. Sharon linked her arm through Louisa's as they made their way towards the waiting room, making Louisa shudder with excitement. 'Oh, this makes everything seem more real somehow, I can't believe we are actually going to see the baby live, on a screen!'

'Your baby,' Sharon reminded her, 'not *the* baby.'

'My baby, my baby,' Louisa breathed, 'oh how wonderful that sounds.'

The waiting room was busy, but while Sharon was signing in, Louisa found two vacant seats in the corner. Most of the women were accompanied by their husbands or partners, and although she felt quite ambiguous about the idea of having someone present at the birth, she wanted to give Louisa the choice of being there. 'I'll soon be asked for the name of my birthing partner. Would you like to be with me when the baby is born?' she whispered.

Louisa gasped; the answer was written all over her face as she turned to look at Sharon. 'Oh, I would love to be there, but I tried not to think about it. I didn't know how you felt, it is a very personal thing and I didn't want to intrude.'

'Oh, you won't be intruding, it is your baby after all, and as I'm going to need someone, I can't think of anyone I would rather have.'

Louisa hugged herself with excitement. Oh Sharon, I'm so happy, thank you so much.'

Sharon smiled. Louisa understandably had no idea what it would entail, but then neither did any other first-time mum. 'You may not thank me when the time comes,' she warned, 'but I'm really glad you'll be there. I was lucky that all my labours were quick and trouble free, so there's no reason to think this one won't be the same.'

'It must be pretty hard, bringing up three young children,' Louisa said. 'Did you plan it so they were evenly spread out?'

Sharon chuckled, shaking her head vigorously. 'No way. Our plan was to buy a house and get everything we needed before starting a family, but Sam came along before we had chance to even get the deposit. We decided to wait a few years before we had another and by the time Ben was born our little family was complete and we'd moved into our new house. When he started at primary I went back to work, and we had a decent quality of life. Then of course it all went pear-shaped when Tom lost his job in the recession.'

'It must have been very difficult for you.'

'It was, and it certainly wasn't the best time to fall pregnant again. Still, we managed, and I can't imagine life without Lily now.'

'She was only a baby when we met,' Louisa said, 'how quickly the time has gone. I can't believe she's already five and going to school.'

Sharon was fighting back an urge to go over to rescue a toddler trying to follow his older brother up the climbing frame. Their mother was engrossed in a conversation with the heavily pregnant women next to her and seemed oblivious to what was happening. Fortunately, someone else intervened and lifted him down, so she was able to regain concentration on what Louisa was saying. 'It seems to happen when you have children,' she said thoughtfully, 'just wait till you have one of your own.'

'I can't wait,' replied Louisa, her eyes sweeping across the room. 'Do you remember the last time I was here? It was the day I met you and Lily after she'd fallen at school. It was also the day I was told I would never be able to carry a baby and I was absolutely devastated.'

Sharon pressed her hand in sympathy. 'Yes, I think I can understand how you must have felt; it must have been awful for you. Luckily that's all behind you now and soon you are going to have a baby of your own.' Louisa didn't reply, and when Sharon turned to her, she was clutching her hand to her mouth, choking back her excitement.

'I'm sorry, but it's all because of you, and I'll never be able to thank you enough.'

'That's alright then, because I don't want any thanks. Oh, that's my name they're calling out, let's go and have a photograph taken.' Following the nurse down a short corridor towards the room where the radiographer was waiting, Sharon whispered to Louisa. 'This hasn't come a moment too soon, if I don't empty my bladder soon there's going to be a torrential waterfall.'

They were still giggling when Sharon lay on the bed as instructed, but they were silent as the radiographer squeezed the blobs of jelly on Sharon's tummy and slowly moved the probe, pressing gently. Sharon concentrated on the screen until the image of the baby emerged and for a fleeting moment she was drenched in a rush of maternal tenderness, oblivious to her surroundings. Louisa's sudden intake of breath brought her back to reality and recovering quickly she viewed the scene impartially, as if she was on the outside looking in, and it really was Louisa's baby she was looking at.

Louisa was sitting perfectly still, fighting back tears of joy. Her glistening eyes were riveted to the screen. 'I have never seen anything more beautiful in all my life,' she breathed. The boom of the tiny heartbeat seemed to fill the room as the miniscule creature swam in the safety of Sharon's womb. Sharon's previous experience helped her to recognise the parts of the baby, but Louisa was transfixed as the radiographer explained and pointed out the organs and limbs of the tiny child who would soon belong to her. When the image was finally switched off, Louisa had to be coaxed out of the room, her reluctance finally being overcome by the promise of printed photographs of the baby.

Sharon gave all the images of the baby to Louisa, and when they were parked outside Sharon's house, Louisa couldn't resist taking one out of her handbag again. 'It really is the loveliest thing I've ever seen,' she said, 'and I'm longing to show Damian.'

Sharon took a last look at it and smiled. 'It's like a little shrimp swimming around,' she replied, which prompted Louisa to burst out laughing. 'Don't you dare call my baby a little shrimp,' she protested, and they both fell silent, recognising the significance of the moment. It was the first time Louisa had spontaneously referred to the baby as hers. Louisa leaned towards Sharon and as she laid her palm gently on the curve of her stomach, she whispered, 'thank you.'

Sharon smiled before easing herself out of the car.

When she let herself into the house there was no sign of activity, even Rusty's boisterous and noisy greeting was absent. Presuming Marie had taken Lily and the dog out for a walk, she made herself a cup of tea and went into the lounge where she slipped off her shoes and sank into the comfy depths of the old, familiar settee. They had plans to change it when the house was finished but until then it provided a feeling of security whenever home-sickness threatened to unsettle her.

Moments of peace were rare, so she decided to take Marie's advice and grab every opportunity to rest. She was feeling mentally and physically drained. It had been a difficult morning at work, and then at the hospital she'd been surprised by her reaction to seeing the baby during the scan. It had made her feel far more emotional than she'd expected, and the most difficult part was trying not to show it. Resting her head on the cushions, she persuaded herself it was probably normal to feel like this with all the hormones surging through her body, and the memory of Louisa's ecstatic response made everything worthwhile.

When Rusty's yapping and Lily's excited chattering disturbed the quiet, she came to with a shock at the realisation she'd been sleeping. Hurriedly combing her fingers through crumpled hair, she swayed backwards as Lily ran into the room, propelling herself into Sharon's lap. In her attempt to relate what she'd been doing, the child's words tumbled out over each other. 'We've been to the beach and I paddled in the sea and Rusty went into the sea, actually into the sea and...' Sharon was puzzled, Marie was so afraid of any mishap befalling the children, she never allowed them anywhere near the sea. 'Hey, calm down. I hope you were good for Nana Marie and did as you were told.'

Lily's laugh tinkled from her wide smiling lips, in a way that brought a lump to Sharon's throat. 'Not Marie, it was daddy who took us. Nana Marie's gone home.'

'Daddy took you?' Sharon looked up as Tom walked through the door and picked Lily up before throwing her in the air. 'We had a fun time didn't we munchkin?' Lily squealed with delight, 'Yeah.'

'Why were you home so early?' Sharon asked.

Tom started tickling Lily and mumbled something inaudible about a meeting, so she decided not to ask anything more until later when the children were in bed. She didn't feel like provoking an argument and she had a feeling she wasn't going to like what she was going to hear. Ben arrived back from a school football game, and later when he and Lily were settled in bed Sam came down from his room to discuss a school trip to London.

By this time, Sharon and Tom were feeling weary and ready for bed themselves.

In the bedroom, Sharon debated with herself whether to broach the subject of the meeting, and when Tom folded back the duvet inviting her to join him, she slipped into bed beside him. Curving herself to his shape, she felt the comforting strength of his body as he pulled her gently into his arms. 'I love you,' he told her, 'you know that, don't you?'

'Yes,' she murmured, and I love you.'

'I can feel a 'but' coming on,' he said sleepily, 'something's bothering you, I can tell.'

'It's the meeting you went to. What was it about Tom?'

'The proposed housing development.'

'On the mere?'

'Yes.'

'Oh Tom, not again. I wish you weren't involved with that! So many people are so against it, they may well turn against us too. I thought when it was turned down that would be the end of it?'

He tightened his hold on her until her face was pressed against his chest and she could barely breath. 'Sharon, while I was at the meeting you were at the hospital.' She could feel the rhythm of his heart beating against his ribs, lulling her to sleep. 'Well, I wish you hadn't got involved in that, because it scares me, in fact it scares the hell out of me.'

'There's nothing to fear and it'll soon be over.'

Cupping her head in his hand, his words were muffled by her hair. 'Not soon enough. Anyway, it's what might happen in the meantime that bothers me.'

'I'll carry the baby until I give birth, it's as simple as that.'

'I'm not so sure it is going to be as simple as that.'

Sharon shivered with apprehension. 'What's that supposed to mean?' she asked.

'Only that in an earlier life I'd sometimes wondered if you might be a potential baby-snatcher, it was almost impossible to walk past a pram without you cooing at it.'

'Okay, I love babies, I admit it. But this one belongs to Louisa and Damian and I certainly don't want any more children; I can hardly cope with the ones we've got.'

Tom loosened his hold and tilted her face towards his and she could see her own fears reflected in his. 'Did you see the baby today Sharon?'

'Yes, and it was perfect, which was a relief I must admit. I'd been a bit worried before the scan, because after all, it did start out as a tiny frozen embryo.'

'Was that all you felt?'

'Yes. Now are you satisfied?'

'No way,' he replied, 'but there is something you can do to remedy that. Do you love me?'

Wriggling away from him she told him 'yes', but still he pursued her, 'how much?'

'A lot,' she whispered, folding herself into him.

'Show me,' he said, caressing her body.

Chapter 23

Bryony replaced the phone angrily. She couldn't believe this was happening, especially after the fiasco of the Carnival dance when everything that could go wrong, had gone wrong. She had to admit it had been a huge success as a fund raiser, the auction particularly had brought the money rolling in, and the first prize, consisting of a day's visit to the lifeboat house and meeting some of the crew had definitely been the biggest draw. Ironically it was the same people who were now letting her down.

Geoff Hayes had just rung with some cock and bull story about Damian having to attend a training course in Poole for newly promoted coxswains, which unfortunately coincided with the Mayor's Charity Ball where he was to be the guest of honour. Knowing how reluctant Damian felt about being in the spotlight, she believed he would be secretly relieved about the clash of events, but she didn't believe he'd done it on purpose and Geoff Hayes was totally wrong to say she'd implied that. She couldn't understand why members of the RNLI were so reluctant to put themselves in the limelight. Geoff's explanation that there were acceptable ways of doing it seemed so out-dated when just about everyone was on social media.

She was reluctant to ask Marie for help, but this was an emergency, so as a last resort she took a deep breath and rang her number. Stuart answered and told her Marie was working at the gift shop all morning, so she thanked him and sat down to consider her options. She wanted to talk to Marie in private but that would be impossible at the shop, and she was reluctant to visit her at home, where she'd have to suffer Stuart's condescending attitude which always made her feel as if he found something about her faintly amusing. Calculating that if Marie was working a morning shift, she would finish at lunch time, she waited until the appropriate time and set off at a brisk pace towards the boathouse and shop.

The sky was bright but there was a distinct chill in the air and the walk along the seafront was unexpectedly exhilarating and enjoyable. A few local people passing by recognised and greeted her, and the downs and the beach were scattered with a few visitors and holidaymakers taking the opportunity of the last school break before Christmas. Children were enjoying the freedom of racing across the sand, while parents struggled to erect windbreaks and build the castles which were springing up everywhere. The muscular young man hiring out the windbreaks was a member of the family who'd supplied the donkeys and windbreaks for as long as she could remember, and probably a long time before that. The animals would be enjoying a well-earned rest from walking up and down the beach all summer, but the windbreaks were still very much in demand.

It was a sobering thought to realise he was probably the grandson of the boy who gave them free rides at the end of the day or provided them with windbreaks without a ticket, when she was a teenager. With his tanned and well-honed body, he'd been admired by most of the girls in her group, but he was older, and he'd shown no interest in any of them. She'd pretended to share her friends' fascination with him, but from a very early age she'd had eyes for no-one except Greg.

She'd timed it perfectly; her arrival coincided exactly with Marie's departure from the shop, and after a few brief words with the incoming staff they set off by mutual consent to The Kings Head for lunch. Marie had to ring Stuart of course, to tell him about her change of plans, but apparently, he'd been very agreeable.

'What are Stuart's feelings about the new houses being built?' she asked casually, unfolding her napkin and placing it on her knee.

Puzzled, Marie looked at her and frowned. 'You're not seriously asking me that, everyone knows what he thinks about it. I should think he's had a letter published in the local paper almost every week since it all began. Hopefully it's been sorted out now, and it won't happen.'

Bryony flicked her hand disdainfully. 'I can't say I bother with that rag very often these days, it can be helpful sometimes when you want to advertise events, but as far as news is concerned, they just seem to trade in gossip.' For some reason, Marie started choking on her soup so Bryony waited until she'd recovered before bringing up the subject of Damian, who she was sure Marie would prefer to talk about.

'I'm hoping you can help me out,' she said. 'You see, I was relying on your son to be the main attraction at the ball, and now I'm being left a bit high and dry, and at the last minute too.'

So, this was what the meeting was all about, it hadn't taken Bryony long to divulge what was on her mind, but Marie was relieved. They could get it out of the way, and relax and enjoy her lunch. 'It's not for a few weeks yet, surely you can find a replacement before then,' she replied. Bryony tried to remain calm, but she was surprised by Marie's reaction, she'd expected a bit of sympathy and a more apologetic response. 'It's not as easy as that,' she said, 'there's all the publicity to sort out for one thing. Couldn't he just arrange to go another time.?'

'To use your own words,' Marie replied, 'it's not as easy as that. The courses are planned in advance and it's very important for him to go.'

'Why exactly *does* he have to go? I would have thought he'd already know all there is to know about being a member of the lifeboat crew.'

Marie sighed. 'That's just the point,' she said, 'he does, but now he's been made a coxswain and he'll be responsible for all the operations when he's in charge, safeguarding the crew and rescuing the people in danger. It's not just that though, his duties don't finish when he's not at sea, he has to help promote the organisation in the community amongst other things. It carries a lot of responsibility, and he needs all the help he can get. So that's why he must go. Anyway, I believe it's mandatory.'

Bryony was only half listening, but she picked up on some of Marie's words. 'I can't think of a better way to promote themselves than playing a prominent part in The Lord Mayor's Ball.'

'Bryony, I don't think you've been listening to a word I've said, but if you brought me here to try to persuade to get Damian to change his mind, you've been wasting your time.'

'Of course, I didn't,' she replied shortly, 'since when did it become a crime for friends to have lunch together?'

'I'm sorry,' Marie replied, 'but Bryony, I hope you don't mind me saying this, but I think you're trying a little bit too hard.'

Bryony stiffened with resentment at being given advice, especially from Marie. 'You sound just like Ralph,' she said. 'Why are you all suddenly being so critical, don't you think I'm doing a good job?' Anyway, what exactly do you mean?'

Marie sighed. 'It's difficult to explain, but you just seem to be striving to improve on well-established customs and do everything differently, or better. And don't look at me like that, people don't like change, especially when it concerns local traditions. You're only making things more difficult for yourself.' Bryony couldn't believe she was being challenged by someone lacking in imagination, and anyway, advice of any kind was not what she was after. If Marie couldn't or wouldn't try to change Damian's mind, she was wasting her time.

'Nothing's written in stone,' she maintained, 'so is it wrong to inject a bit of originality to enable us to raise more money for the charities?'

'No of course not,' Marie conceded, 'forget I said anything.

'Going back to the topic of the new houses', Bryony said randomly, 'I must say I'm a bit surprised Greg is on the side of the developer.'

'Oh, I think you've got that wrong, I'm sure Greg doesn't support it. Who told you that?'

'Greg did.'

Bryony was amused by Marie's reaction, but she didn't know what had surprised her the most; the position Greg was taking, or the fact that he and Bryony had discussed it. 'We had an interesting discussion about it,' she said, slightly stretching the truth, 'but he made his opinion very clear. Now I must go and try to catch Sharon before she leaves, we'll need to talk about changing the publicity leaflets.'

Marie was still frowning as they left the restaurant, but she didn't comment any further and Bryony linked her arm through hers, pulling her close. 'Let's walk through the square,' she said, 'just like old times.'

Apart from a few hardy customers sitting outside café's and coffee shops, most were inside, occupying the window seats, and illuminated by the soft lighting indoors, they looked warm and snug. It was nearing closing time and one or two shopkeepers were starting to dismantle the Halloween window displays. Soon it would be time to start on Christmas decorations, a thought which had filled her with dismay ever since her rift with Amelia.

'We had happy childhoods,' Marie reflected, 'but of course we didn't know how lucky we were. Growing up seemed simpler then, or am I romanticising it all?'

'I don't know, maybe every generation feels the same, but you're right, things were less complicated then.' When they reached the end of the street where Marie lived, Bryony looked at her watch and pecked Marie on the cheek. 'I'm sorry, I really must go otherwise I won't catch Sharon before she leaves.'

'Oh, please don't ask her to work more hours,' Marie blurted out impulsively, and ignoring Bryony's flare of annoyance, she muttered, 'otherwise it will mean I have to look after the children even more than I'm doing already. It affects me too, you know.'

Bryony shrugged her shoulders. 'She knows the terms of the job, and it's no concern of mine how she arranges childcare. I do try not to expect too much of her as I know what it's like to hold down a job when you've got a young family. She's a nice enough girl, but a bit, shall I say, feisty.'

Marie couldn't help herself. 'Nice enough?' she repeated, 'she's a lovely girl, and I think you do sometimes ask too much of her, but you won't be able to soon, not now she's...' Bryony's perfectly arched eyebrow shot up, catapulting Marie into a tizzy of agitation.

'Now she's what, exactly?' Bryony asked.

'Oh, I can't tell you, but she's doing something amazing,' she blustered, 'please don't try to get it out of me.'

Bryony's eyes were cold. 'I'm not forcing you to say anything, but as you've already indicated, Sharon is doing something which will affect her work, so as a friend I think you owe it to me to say what it is.' Marie drew away, shaking her head. 'It's not my secret to tell. I've already said more than I should and if it gets out, they'll never forgive me.'

Bryony was getting impatient. 'Marie, who am I likely to tell? I'm not close enough to anyone who'd be the slightest bit interested in Sharon's affairs. Come on,' she coaxed, 'I promise I won't say anything, but if you don't tell me, I may just have to ask Sharon myself.'

'No, please don't,' Marie said, 'I'll tell you if you promise to keep it to yourself.' Bryony tutted impatiently and Marie continued. 'You know Louisa can't have children, well, Sharon is being a surrogate for them. She's carrying their child.'

Bryony stared at her in astonishment. 'Are you telling me Sharon is pregnant with someone else's baby, that she's actually pregnant now? And she hasn't even had the decency to tell me!'

'Nobody knows yet, it's only just been confirmed, and Sharon's children have to be the first ones to know. I'm certain she intends to tell you once they've done that.'

Bryony turned to leave, and without commenting on the selfless thing Sharon was doing, she said irritably. 'It will be interesting to see how she reconciles it with a full-time job. Now I really must be going.' A casual air kiss and she was gone, leaving Marie feeling manipulated and used.

Chapter 24

It happened so softly, she sensed rather than felt it. Sharon leaned against the kitchen table, motionless and silent, holding her breath and waiting. There it was again, tiny, popping bubbles, deep inside her belly. Laying her hands protectively across her womb she swayed slightly. This was nothing new, she'd experienced it with her other three babies, but it never failed to surprise and thrill her. When she was expecting Sam, she hadn't recognised what was happening until the midwife told her it was the baby moving. Now she knew she'd felt the very first stirrings of the baby growing inside her.

Picking up her mobile intending to contact Louisa, her finger remained poised over the number. She'd promised to let her know when anything significant happened, and this they'd agreed would be a very major development. Louisa was avidly following all the stages of pregnancy, looking online and buying books, and she was desperate for this milestone to happen, and might even be getting anxious about not hearing news from Sharon. It must be horrendous to be in that position, but still she hesitated, telling herself it would be better to wait until both Louisa and Damian were home from work and together when they received the news. She started to clear away the breakfast things but resisted the temptation to throw the remains of the toast and cereal onto the lawn for the birds. When they first came to live here, Marie had warned her about the problem of enticing gulls down, but she'd learned the hard way when she'd found the habit hard to break and had thrown some bread out.

The gulls, majestic and graceful in the air, were enormous and scary close up. Their size and massive wingspan scared off all the smaller birds and sent Rusty scarpering back to the security of the kitchen, where he barked incessantly until the last one disappeared. Lily knew no fear and was likely to walk out with bread in her hand, with potentially dangerous repercussions, so the rule was; no food of any kind must be taken outside. The exception of course, was barbecue time when adults would be present. After checking the peanut and birdseed feeders were full (the gulls didn't have the agility to access the food in them), she set off for work.

The town was busy with holidaymakers and when she reached the hotel, she had to wind her way through the guests moving up and down the steps leading to the entrance. The feeling of pride when she first started working here had never left her, and she felt a buzz every time she entered the foyer. Mrs. Portland's recent attempt to get every member of staff to use the rear entrance had been met with derision, and she'd joined the other staff in ignoring it.

Tom's recollections of the night he spent here, following the rescue of his brother Danny and his friend from their ill-fated cockle fishing attempt, were hilarious. Only a deluxe room was available and he'd taken advantage of all the fantastic facilities. Greg Robson had taken care of him during the frightening episode, and she would always be grateful for that, but she hoped he wasn't encouraging him now, to get involved in things which would bring them trouble.

Justin appeared to be in control at the desk, so she went straight through to the small office at the back of the reception and closed the door. Going through a pile of paperwork she'd left from the previous day, she heard Mrs. Portland talking to Justin and her tone suggested she wasn't in the best of moods, but there was no sign of anything wrong when she entered the room clutching the post. Sharon greeted her before checking the calendar for her day's appointments and meetings.

After flicking through the envelopes to satisfy herself that nothing intended for her personal attention had slipped through, Mrs. Portland placed them in a neat pile on the desk. 'We are going to have a busy time leading up to, and during the Ball,' she said casually, 'I hope you are still happy to work all the extra hours you'll be needed.'

Sharon paused before answering. She had to strike the right balance because there was no way she could take on more hours. If she made out it was no problem, she had a feeling Mrs. Portland would take advantage and pile even more work onto her, but on the other hand she didn't dare say she couldn't cope. Tom and Marie had promised to help, and even Sam had volunteered some support, but happy wasn't the word to describe how everyone, including herself, was feeling. Before she had time to gather her thoughts Mrs. Portland sighed heavily and casually asked, 'how's Marie? She must be such a help to you, and like a grandmother to your children.'

Instinctively, Sharon felt very cagey. Why was she suddenly showing interest in her family and Marie's place in it? She had no time to ponder however, because this time Mrs. Portland was waiting for an answer. 'Yes, Marie does help,' she agreed, 'but it's much more than that. It's lovely for the children, especially Lily. I miss my mum since we came here and I know the rest of the family do, but Marie is just like a second mum and grandma. If it wasn't for her,' she added cautiously, 'I wouldn't be able to do all this overtime.'

'I see. It's lucky for you she's been willing to step in then, for me too of course, you are proving invaluable as my social secretary during my year of office. I hope you don't mind stepping up like this.'

Wondering where all this was leading and vainly hoping it may involve a pay rise, Sharon shook her head. 'Not at all, it makes life very interesting and I'm pleased to be helping.'

Mrs. Portland turned away and moved a few folders around while Sharon watched out of the corner of her eye. 'Yes, I've heard you like to help people. In fact, I believe you are in the process of doing something for someone, now let me get this right, I think the word used to describe it was, amazing.'

Sharon froze. This could only mean one thing, but they'd all agreed to keep the surrogacy secret until Sharon was ready to reveal it. Fortunately, by the time she'd come up with a vaguely credible answer Mrs. Portland had turned away dismissively. 'It's of no importance. Now I must get on, I have work to do.'

With relief Sharon smiled and watched her go, but she was left with an uneasy feeling that Mrs. Portland either guessed or somehow knew what was going on. Things were becoming more complicated by the day and if she wanted to stay in her job, she was going to need some cooperation from her employer regarding her pregnancy and birth. In the meantime, no matter how hard it was she would have to do whatever was necessary to keep her happy. Struggling to concentrate, she was glad when the day was over and she could try to get things clear in her head.

Tom had texted to say he was home and Marie had already left. Lily was already in bed asleep, and Ben was doing his homework. She didn't ask about Sam. He was guarded about what he was getting up to and she didn't want Tom getting irritated if he had to tell her he'd no idea where his son was. The golden opportunity for a few precious moments alone drew her towards a shelter on the promenade where she sat for a few moments looking across the bay. She never tired of this view, but rarely did she have the chance to enjoy it quietly on her own. It was one of the places which helped her adapt to living here when she felt homesick and lonely. Despite everything they'd achieved, she sometimes longed for the familiarity of friends and family and the place where she'd grown up.

In the distance, she could see two men peering through binoculars looking out to sea, and she wondered what there was to see with the light falling. They were too far away for her to be able to see them clearly, but they seemed vaguely familiar and she wondered if one of them was Stuart. How uncomplicated his life seemed to be compared to hers, but to be fair, she knew he'd had plenty of problems to contend with in the past. Her own quandaries were here and now, and needed instant attention. Even if Mrs. Portland had been referring to something else, which was highly unlikely, it didn't really matter because the outcome was the same. The time was swiftly approaching when it would all have to come out into the open, and that scared her.

On her way home, she phoned Louisa who reacted to the news about the baby with squeals of excitement, and Sharon could hear Damian in the background demanding to know what was going on. When they asked if they could come around to feel it, Sharon laughed. 'You wouldn't be able to feel anything yet,' she told them, 'it's not strong enough to be felt on the outside. Imagine being tickled for a few moments by a feather inside your tummy, and you don't know when it's going to happen again. That about sums it up, but I promise to let you know when it gets stronger.' They agreed to get together soon, and with her resolve bolstered by their happiness she walked home and entered the house refreshed and full of optimism.

'You look happy, have you had a good day?' Tom asked, kissing her lightly on the cheek.

'Not particularly,' she replied, pulling a face. 'The boss was in a funny mood, but I managed to keep out of her way. There was one nice thing that happened today though, but it was before I left for work.' Unsure how he would take the news, she tried not to sound too excited. 'I felt the baby move.'

'Oh,' he replied, 'how did that make you feel?'

She hesitated, how had she felt? 'A bit weird actually.'

He nodded and moved towards her. 'Yes, I expect it would,' he said with feeling, and she leaned into him and hoped everything was going to be alright.

Chapter 25

The developers hadn't given up trying to win over opinion in their favour, but when it was announced they were setting up an exhibition in the Memorial Hall, it was greeted with dismay.

'It isn't just the display we're worried about,' Stuart told Marie. 'They're now promising to include other amenities, premises for a health centre and shops and such like. It's barmy, when shops have been closing in town. Who do they think will take them on? The rents will be sky-high, and they'll just stand empty. That's if they build them of course, promises come cheap.'

Marie did her best to hide her feelings, but she needn't have worried, he was so worked up he wouldn't have noticed if she'd had a gun in her hand. He went out of the room, chuntering under his breath, and when he returned with his coat and scarf on, she asked him where he was going.

'To the pub, we've got to decide what to do next.'

Marie looked at the clock, as a rule nothing interfered with the timing of his midday meal. 'It's almost lunch time, 'she said, 'why don't you have a bite to eat before you go?'

'Don't worry about me, we'll probably get a pie or something at the pub,' he replied, planting a kiss on her cheek.

'Well keep it legal,' she warned, 'I don't want to visit you in prison.'

'Desperate times demand drastic action. See you later love.'

Marie was restless and needed to talk, but there was no-one she could safely confide in. She had a suspicion that Claire was becoming more ambivalent about the issues, but she was keeping her thoughts close to her chest, and anyway she was visiting her mother-in-law today. Sharon was working, and as usual Bryony was indifferent, her opinion flitting about like a leaf in the wind. She was convinced Bryony had initially been against the plan until she learned of Greg's involvement, so she would have no sympathy with Marie's guilty vacillations.

Exercise seemed the best remedy, so she put on her warmest coat, pulled her woollen hat over her ears, and slipped her hands into the sheepskin gloves Stuart had given her last Christmas. It didn't take long to reach Sharon's house where Rusty greeted her with enthusiasm and affection. They set off in the direction of the sea and were soon leaving the promenade to take the path along the edge of the dunes. She was wearing her high, fleecy boots so she walked without care on the deep, firm sand.

Rusty was frolicking up and down the undulating dunes and through the clumps of grass, but he quickly reached the limits of his lead and pulled to free himself from his restraint. She'd never risked letting him off the lead and she wasn't tempted to try today, despite being reassured by Tom and Sharon that he would always come back, even if it was sometimes on his own terms. There was no way she could chase after him, so she wasn't prepared to take the chance. Eventually he accepted his limits and as usual adapted his exercise to match hers. In lots of ways he was a sensible dog, if a little boisterous.

The wind off the sea got stronger, gusting and whipping up clouds of the drier sand from the valleys of dunes, and it was carrying Rusty's ball well out of reach. Apart from adding to the dog's frustration at being unable to retrieve it, she was struggling to keep it in view, so after two forays into the dunes, she decided she'd had enough.

'Come on pal!' she called, 'It's time to call it a day and get home into the warmth.' For some inexplicable reason, the restlessness hadn't left her, and she was reluctant to return to the empty house, so making a spur of the moment decision she turned into the side road just off the edge of the dunes and headed for the small, popular fish and chip shop. 'We're going to have a treat,' she told the dog, as she ordered from the pleasant young man who was serving her. Pulling a nylon bag out of her pocket and remarking casually that she had a little way to walk, he placed the fish and chips in a tray and wrapped them in several sheets of paper to keep them warm.

Making her way to the nearest shelter, she sat on the bench seat facing inland to take advantage of the protection it offered from the cold wind. Taking one glove off, she broke some small pieces of fish and a couple of chips to give to Rusty, before tucking into her own lunch. She'd just finished and was gathering the wrappings together to put in the litter bin, when she heard people arrive and sit in the section behind her, facing the sea. The wind drowned out their voices and

Rusty was so busy sniffing around for any morsels he may have dropped on the floor he obviously didn't hear them.

Marie was just about to leave, when in a sudden lull, she recognised one of the voices and thought she knew the other, but she could hardly believe her ears. Snippets of the conversation became audible, and although she couldn't make out exactly what was being said, it was obvious it was no ordinary meeting, but a romantic liaison. Conscious of a similar occasion when she'd misconstrued a conversation with serious consequences, she had no desire to hear what was going on at the other side of the shelter. But how could she get away without being seen or heard, and if they became aware of her, they would naturally think she'd deliberately eavesdropped on them.

Fortunately, the decision was made for her when the couple decided it was time to go, and she pulled her hat firmly over her ears to block out the sound of their parting. When she was sure they'd left, she leaned cautiously round the dividing section of the shelter to watch them walk away. Despite being hampered by their thick, warm clothing, they couldn't resist stopping for a passionate embrace before reluctantly breaking away to take different routes. She was left in no doubt. Her suspicions were confirmed, and she was utterly shocked.

It was a short walk taking Rusty home, but tired and in need of a warm drink she intended to simply let the dog in the house before making her own way home. When she approached the house and saw a light on, she inwardly groaned and instead of letting herself in she rang the bell. As soon as the door opened, she was nearly pulled off her feet as Rusty catapulted himself through the door, and when Sharon wouldn't take no for an answer, she found herself being ushered through into the hall. 'You needn't have rung the bell,' Sharon said, 'just let yourself in with your key.'

'I do when there's no-one in,' Marie replied, 'but I don't like to when someone's home, I never know if I might be intruding. Or what I might find,' she added miserably.

'Well, I don't think you'll encounter anything unusual here,' Sharon laughed, 'unless you count the children. Here, this'll warm you up.'

'You're home early, I didn't expect you to be here,' Marie said, warming her hands on the mug of hot chocolate.'

'I know, but for some reason Mrs. Portland told me I could leave early. I know it's quiet at the hotel, it always is at this time of year, but in the past, she would have found something for me to do. She seems to have mellowed a bit recently, I don't know why, but I'm not complaining.'

'She's not all bad,' Marie heard herself say, unexpectedly rising to Bryony's defence, but her voiced tailed off as she added defensively, 'she can be quite thoughtful at times.'

Sharon's eyes widened, understandably puzzled by Marie's uncharacteristic behaviour. Marie fidgeted with embarrassment. She was still feeling shaken by what she'd seen, but after all it was nothing to do with her and she decided to put it out of her mind before she said something she shouldn't. It wouldn't be the first time her tongue got her into trouble. 'Are you alright? Sharon asked gently, 'you seem a bit upset about something.'

'I'm fine,' she replied, 'I'm sorry I snapped at you, but things seem to be getting me down just now. I'm a bit tired that's all, but this business about the housing application doesn't help. I've never known Stuart get so worked up like this about anything before, and I wish it would all come to an end, whatever the outcome.' Sharon looked uncomfortable and Marie felt instantly sorry for blurting it out without thinking. She knew better than anyone how fearful Sharon felt about the possible effects on her family and she had no wish to make it worse than it already was.

'I'm sorry love,' she said, 'I'm not blaming Tom in any way. In fact, if I am totally honest, and you must not breathe a word of this to anyone, my views don't necessarily correspond with Stuart's.'

Sharon was shocked, but listened sympathetically, as Marie began to explain how her loyalties to Damian and Stuart were tearing her apart. Sharon was baffled. 'I thought Damian was strongly opposed to the scheme, like his father. What made him change his mind?'

'Oh, I don't know if he has,' Marie said, 'I'm just guessing that if the opportunity arose for him to be able to buy a house, especially now the baby is coming, he would. Even if it was on the mere.'

'Well, I wouldn't be so sure,' Sharon said, 'he was implacably opposed when we were discussing it, and I wouldn't think he's changed his mind so completely. I think you're worrying unnecessarily, but even so, what a lot of heartache it's causing, and here was I, thinking it was only my family who were being divided by it. Still, that's beside the point, and you're right about the difficulties of having a baby in that tiny flat, especially with it having no garden. There's a bus route close by though, and you can take buggies on the buses now, they even lower the step to make it easier.' She smiled ruefully. 'I'm sure she'll be fine.'

'She'll have to get the buggy up and down the stairs to the flat though, and you know how narrow and steep they are.'

'Of course, I'm forgetting that,' Sharon replied thoughtfully, 'yes, I agree with you, it isn't going to be easy. It's strange really, but Louisa has never mentioned the difficulties she'll have in that respect.'

'I think that's because she's so excited about having the baby. She's not given a thought to the practicalities of living in a flat. I'm just hoping against hope that something will turn up.' Marie stood up and shrugged her coat on. The light was already fading and she didn't want to walk home in the dark, in any case it was almost time for Sharon to pick Lily up from school, and as much as she loved to see her, she was in no mood to face the happy exuberance of the child today. Sharon was eyeing her up quizzically. 'Are you sure there's nothing wrong?' she asked, 'you don't seem quite yourself today.'

'I'm fine,' she replied, 'don't worry about me.'

Picking her way down the temporary path, she was aware of Sharon standing at the front door waiting to make sure she made it safely to the end. When she turned to wave goodbye, she could see the look of concern on her face and she regretted having left so abruptly with no explanation for her subdued mood. It was too late to make amends now, and anyway, there'd been enough confidences shared for one day, but she resolved to contact her as soon as she reached home to apologise.

Reaching the Square, which was busy with the activities of shopkeepers decorating their windows now that the Christmas lights were already strung from buildings and lampposts, she paused for a moment to savour the atmosphere. The weeks leading up to the festive season was one of her favourite times of the year, and already she could feel her spirit rising. Impulsively, she turned and walked towards the library where she received a warm welcome from the staff. She was a regular visitor and her preferences were well known, but today she walked past the fiction section to choose some books with a Christmas theme.

She was determined to make this one as special as possible in anticipation of the new arrival to their family. The enormity of what Sharon was doing overwhelmed her, so she hurried home and picked up the phone before even removing her coat.

Chapter 26

Sam clambered up the rocks and focused the binoculars on the distant view, scanning the horizon before zooming in onto the mud and sand closer to where he was standing.

'Can you see anything?' Stuart called from his position on the lower, more accessible ground.

'No, not yet,' Sam replied, 'give me a few more minutes.'

'Alright, but it's getting a bit cold and the light's falling fast.'

Sam climbed down and they both fell into step as they made their way by mutual consent towards the steps leading up to the deserted promenade.

'I'm getting binoculars for Christmas,' Sam said, 'I want good ones but not too expensive, which do you think I should get?'

'Well, that's a bit tricky because I haven't bought any for a long time, but Harpers are very good, and they'll be able to advise you.'

'I know, I've already had a look in their shop, but my dad says we'll get a better bargain on the internet.'

'Ah, well, I can't help you there son. I suppose I could have a look on our iPad, but I don't think you can tell which is best for you without holding them in your hand and trying them out. It's a very personal thing choosing binoculars.'

'I suppose I could try some in the shop and then look them up on the internet.'

Stuart was quiet. 'I suppose you could, but it doesn't seem fair to use their expertise and then go off to buy them somewhere else.'

'I never thought about it like that. Everybody does it all the time.'

'I know, but that doesn't make it right.'

'I'll buy all my Christmas presents in the local shops, I promise,' Sam laughed, 'not that I buy many. Mum and dad are already arguing about what we're doing at Christmas. Dad wants to stay here and invite all the family over, but mum wants us to go to grandma's house.'

'What do you want to do?'

'That's a no-brainer, go to grandma's of course.'

'What do you think you will do?'

'I've no idea.' They walked in silence, 'Stu?'

'What?'

'Can I tell you something I don't want anyone else to know?'

'Of course, but I hope it isn't something you've done wrong.'

Sam shook his head. 'When I go back to stay with grandma or my old mates, well, one of my friends there is a girl.'

'Do you mean she's your girlfriend?'

'Yes, we've been going out for ages, since we were thirteen actually.'

'Why don't you want your mum to know?'

Because she'll tell dad, and then every time I say I'm going over he'll make a big deal about it, and anyway mum wants me to make friends here so she wouldn't be happy about it either. Mum saw me with them when they came over for the Carnival, but she thought they were friends from Merebank High, and she wouldn't stop going on about it for days after.'

'I don't understand, what did she keep going on about?'

'Oh, you know. How lovely it was that I was settling in and making friends here, and the girls I was with were lovely. That kind of thing.'

'Oh, I see. Do you see your girlfriend often?'

'No not really, only when I go to stay at grandma's or Max's house, or sometimes when my mates come here for the day. We've all got exams coming up, so we won't be able to do it as often now. She's one of the reasons I want to go there for Christmas.'

'I think it's a great shame you don't want to tell your parents, but your secret's safe with me son.'

'Thanks Stu.' He slipped the binoculars off his shoulder and handed them to Stuart, who took them reluctantly. 'You know you can keep them as long as you want,' he said.

'I know, but I'd have to explain where I'd got them from, and I don't want to.'

'Where do your parents think you are, when you're with me?'

'With mates, from school. Cheers,' he said before loping off into the darkness.

Chapter 27

Marie was being pulled in all directions until she didn't know what to believe or how to feel. She was loyal to Stuart, and in truth she shared most of his reservations about the houses, but at the same time she was sympathetic to Sharon who found herself in an even more difficult position. Since the application had been turned down, the applicants had published a statement saying they were taking advice about the decision. The national policy stated that local plans must identify land for housing and employment uses, and a five-year supply of specific housing sites should be updated annually.

The whole town was holding its breath. Unless the local policy was up to date, and the committee could prove they had approached the application with an open mind and were able to show they had given it detailed consideration, it could leave the decision susceptible to challenge by a judicial review.

Conversations now centred on the which sites might be suitable to develop, but it was all useless gossip until the councillors and committee produced the necessary information.

The RSPB information centre next to the lifeboat shop had set up an informative display pointing out the importance of protecting one of the most important sanctuaries in the country and a site of special biological diversity. This meant she was faced with reminders whether at home or at work, especially as most of the visitors to the information centre made their way into the gift shop afterwards. She and Claire had heard both views discussed, as everyone seemed to have an opinion which they weren't afraid of expressing, and they'd reached the conclusion that most local people were against, while a slightly larger percentage of the visitors were in favour of the proposal.

At first, they'd been surprised by this, until they overheard a couple discussing their dream of retiring to the coast and how the plan to build more houses here might help them achieve it. Claire and Marie nodded to each other and smiled. 'There's always more than one side to an argument' had become their mantra over the years.

Despite all the protests, the signs were showing a growing number of residents who were beginning to support the development, but Marie was keeping her feelings to herself. The worry about Louisa and Damian was still uppermost in her mind, but an idea which wouldn't be affected by the outcome of the plans had taken hold in her head. Over and over, she rehearsed how she could put it to Stuart, but every time she tried to pluck up courage something happened to stop her.

'Can you believe it?' he'd said that very morning, 'if they do build those houses, they are going to pile the ground, in other words build them on stilts. They'll probably sink into the ground in a few years.'

'Surely they know what they're doing,' she said, which brought a deep groan of disbelief in response.

'They said that before they built the estate near Merebank park, and look what happened to that,'

Stuart pointed out. Marie nodded. Sometimes she wished he didn't have an answer to everything she said. It seemed to be happening more and more these days.

She'd been on edge since telling Bryony about Sharon's pregnancy, worrying if she might let it slip, or even worse, confront Sharon directly. Marie knew from bitter experience that Bryony was invariably pragmatic about facing the consequences of her actions, and the possibility of Marie's anger wouldn't trouble her in the least. The news was bound to come out soon, and though it would undoubtedly bring some very mixed reactions, hopefully the majority would appreciate it as an unselfish and wonderful act. She couldn't help wondering how the children would take it, especially Sam who was no longer a child and would probably react more strongly than his younger brother and sister. At his age, even the thought of his parents having a baby in the normal manner would probably be a source of great embarrassment, but goodness knows what he would feel about this.

When her shift was finished, she made a detour and walked towards the Memorial Hall, where the presentation of the proposed development was being displayed. Marie couldn't help feeling it would have been taken down if the developers believed they had no chance of changing the decision, and now curiosity overcame her. After a quick look around she climbed the steps to the elaborately carved door and hurried inside. Most people had already seen it, so it was quiet in the large entrance hall where pictures of the development hung on the wall. She made her way towards the glass covered model displayed in the middle of the floor.

It was a 3D model of the proposed development and she gazed at it in amazement. Houses and bungalows of all shapes and sizes were arranged around ponds and amongst landscaped green spaces planted with shrubs and ornamental grasses. The much talked about road was shown leading to a new roundabout which was carpeted in wildflowers where it joined the existing thoroughfare. Sculptures of herons and cranes were dotted in the rushes around the ponds in what she felt was a pathetic and somewhat ironic nod to the wildlife being displaced by the developers, and far more likely to provoke the protesters than placate them. Even so, it was a fascinating display, and difficult to imagine anyone, even doubters of the scheme, being immune to this impressive exhibition.

She dragged herself away to look briefly at the sketches and read the promises being made concerning the environment, but she knew the claims that the small section of the mere being taken wouldn't have an impact on the environment. She didn't need anyone to tell her the noise of a building sight followed by the encroachment of people living there, would have a massive impact. Even so, this was an impressive exhibition and likely to have made a big impression.

She walked to the square and bought the few things on her shopping list, but just before she turned down the street leading to home, she impulsively changed direction and went to sit in the shelter on the promenade. The bay stretched before her and although she couldn't pick out many seabirds, she knew they were there, camouflaged by their plumage and the colours of the estuary. Sometimes Stuart would hand her his binoculars, pointing out a bird and even then, she had difficulty picking it out, but she knew how important they were to the ecology of the place. She couldn't rid herself of the guilty feeling that for the first time in her life, she was questioning whether it could be justifiable to claim some of the land - or was Stuart right in believing it was totally immoral?

Finding herself shivering and no nearer to clearing her mind, she tightened her scarf and set off for home wondering how she was going to keep her thoughts to herself. One thing was certain, it wasn't the best time to tell Stuart about the idea she'd been considering for a little while now. It was imperative she chose the most opportune moment.

Chapter 28

Sharon and Louisa took their places in the waiting room and looked around them at the women in various stages of pregnancy, some so big they could hardly fit on the seats. Sharon had never carried excess weight with any of her other children and she hoped she wouldn't this time, but for some reason this pregnancy had been different from the others, so she had no idea what was around the corner.

This scan was to check for abnormalities of the foetus, making her very nervous and for the first time she wished Tom was with her. If anything was wrong, she didn't know how she would cope, and instead of having Tom there to support her she would be the one trying to be strong for Louisa. Suddenly, she was hit by the possibility of choices having to be made and agreed by mutual consent. Having satisfied herself they'd covered all eventualities at the beginning of the process, she was now assailed by doubts and fears.

Louisa was anxiously fidgeting and shifting on her seat, which was understandable, but it wasn't doing anything to help calm her nerves. 'If they don't call me soon there'll be an accident,' she said to herself, but the heavily pregnant girl next to her smiled and said she could sympathise. Fortunately, after a few minutes a nurse came out of a nearby room and called Sharon's name.

The radiographer introduced herself as Kelly as she helped Sharon onto the bed and uncovered her tummy. Before Sharon could prepare herself, a splodge of cold jelly landed on the middle of her bump making her catch her breath with shock. At first Louisa, who hadn't been watching, panicked until Kelly explained what had happened, and with a look of relief Louisa turned her attention back to the screen and stared at it with a fixed expression.

Sharon focused her eyes on the ceiling and listened as the boom of the baby's heart resonated around the room. 'Don't you want to see your little baby?' Kelly asked, and Sharon apprehensively turned to look at the image on the screen. It was much bigger than last time and resembled a baby. 'Is it alright?' she asked, and Kelly smiled as she moved the instrument across her tummy. It's absolutely fine,' she replied, putting a little more pressure on, 'all the measurements are correct, and everything is perfect.'

Tears were running down Sharon's cheeks and Louisa was unashamedly crying. 'Do you want to know the sex of your baby?' Kelly asked, looking directly at Sharon, but Sharon turned towards Louisa. 'Do you?' she asked.

Louisa looked bewildered, 'I don't know, what do you think?'

Sharon smiled, 'it's entirely up to you. It's your baby.'

'Oh,' Louisa said, 'I wasn't expecting this. No, let's keep it a surprise because I don't mind what it is. It's a miracle to me whatever sex it is.' When it was over, they went to the machine to print off copies of the scan and before Sharon had chance to hand them to Louisa, she felt someone tap her on the shoulder. Turning apprehensively, she found herself face to face with Selena, the mother of one of Lily's friends and the biggest sharer of gossip in the town.

'Hi, that was a surprise hearing them call your name,' Selena said, eyeing Sharon up and down, 'I didn't even know you were pregnant. Where's your husband, isn't he with you?' Sharon was tempted to tell her it was none of her business, but this called for some swift and careful damage limitation. Stupidly she hadn't given any thought to the chance of this happening, so she was totally unprepared. 'No,' she said, thinking quickly, 'he couldn't make it, so Louisa offered to come with me. It's very early days so I hope you'll understand; we don't want it to be public knowledge yet.' Selena smiled, she loved nothing better than a conspiracy. 'Don't worry, your secret's safe with me, and I can understand why Tom's got more important things to do. Anyway, I must go otherwise I'll miss my turn. Nice to meet you,' she said to Louisa before waddling back to her seat.

'Oh God,' Sharon breathed, 'that's really put the cat amongst the pigeons.'

'She promised not to say anything,' Louisa said hopefully.

'Maybe she won't, but I'd put a bet on it being all over Merebank by the weekend. There's nothing I can do about it, but it means I must break it to the children soon, and I've no choice now but to tell Mrs. Portland, and I'm definitely not looking forward to that.'

By the time Sharon dropped Louisa off, she'd learned everything there was to know about the colour scheme of the nursery, which mobile was hanging over the cot, and the style of the pram Marie and Stuart were buying them, to name but a few things. It was as if the confirmation of the health of the baby had released Louisa's suppressed emotions and anxieties and she was bursting with excitement about everything.

In contrast, Sharon felt relief and an overwhelming feeling of tiredness, and the headache which had started earlier in the day was building up to a migraine which she was desperate to avoid. With reluctance, she took a couple of painkillers before sinking onto the sofa and promptly falling asleep. Marie had arranged to take Lily back home with her after school so by the time they returned Lily was tired and Tom took her upstairs to get her ready for bed.

Marie was just about to leave when Sharon thanked her and told her the news from the hospital. 'Here,' she said, handing her the image of the scan, 'take this, a photograph of your perfect little grandchild, you keep it.'

Marie looked at the image and caught her breath. 'I've never seen one of these before. Is this really your baby?' Her eyes sparkled with happiness, but when Sharon told her it belonged to Damian and Louisa, Marie was lost for words, and simply held Sharon in a warm embrace. Tom insisted on driving Marie home, and on this occasion, she gladly accepted the offer.

Sharon gathered her thoughts and prepared herself for Tom's reaction to the incident with Serena at the hospital.

'She is the biggest gossip ever, she told him, 'if you want to spread the news about anything, forget the local paper, just tell Serena.'

Tom rubbed his fingers up and down his cheek, his expression thoughtful. 'Unfortunately, it looks like the day of reckoning is here. I must say I've been dreading the time when we must tell the kids, but obviously we have no choice now. When and how do you think we should do it? You're better at these things than I am.'

Sharon pressed her fingers on her temples, trying to ward off the impending pain. At least Tom was treating it as a joint problem, which took some of the pressure off her. 'I think Friday would be the best day,' she said, then they'll have the weekend to get used to it before going into school. I'll tell Mrs. Portland tomorrow, the sooner I do that the better. I don't know what I'm worried about really, because the worst she can do is sack me, and she'll be in a bit of a pickle if she does that.' At that precise moment, resting her head back with her eyes closed, she wouldn't give a damn if she did get the sack.

'She'd be on a very sticky wicket if she sacked you simply because you're pregnant,' Tom replied.

'She's cleverer than that,' murmured Sharon, 'she'd manoeuvre it somehow, without actually giving that as the reason.'

Surprisingly, although Mrs. Portland was at first tight lipped when Sharon told her of the pregnancy, there was no immediate suggestion of terminating Sharon's employment. but the puzzling thing was, she didn't appear to be very surprised at the news. It was almost as if she was half expecting it, although Sharon knew that was impossible. 'I presume you intend carrying on with your work,' she said, 'but what about when the child is born, how soon will you be returning?'

Sharon told her she had every intention of working as long as she could before the birth, but when she told her she intended to return as soon as possible after the baby was born, she was shocked by Mrs. Portland's cool response.

'Well there's no reason why you shouldn't do is there?' she asked, and when Sharon didn't reply, she continued irritably, 'in view of the fact you won't be looking after the child.' Sharon stared at her. Surely Serena's grapevine wasn't this efficient, but how else could she have found out.

'In case you're wondering,' Mrs. Portland said tetchily, 'I already knew about the surrogacy and that it's Damian's and Louisa's baby, and although it's a very commendable thing you're doing, I can't help wondering when you were intending to tell me. After all it does affect your work here.'

Sharon began to feel lightheaded and asked if she could sit down. 'I decided to wait until I had confirmation that the pregnancy was safe and the baby perfect, and that only happened yesterday,' she replied.

'So, the hospital appointment was due to your pregnancy, and all the previous ones you've had recently I suppose.'

'Yes,' she agreed, 'but they've all been taken in my own time, I haven't taken any time off work even though I'm entitled to it.'

'But what will happen if you become unwell or need time off? How am I supposed to manage?'

'I've had horrendous morning sickness, but I haven't taken any time off and I'm not expecting any more problems. Obviously, I'll work if I can, but if anything unexpected happens I presume I will be entitled to sick leave and maternity leave, just like anyone else. Being a surrogate mother doesn't affect my entitlements.'

Mrs. Portland arched her professionally shaped eyebrows. 'Really? Well, I'll have to review the position. You see, you haven't signed a legal document of employment, so I doubt I'll be under any obligation to pay you during your absence or maternity leave.'

'When I started work here, you promised it would happen after my six months' probation period,' Sharon pointed out calmly.

'But it never did.'

'No,' Sharon replied bitterly, 'it never did. Now I must go, I'm due to meet a couple finalising their wedding plans, but after that I think I will need to consider my position, whether to continue working here or not.' They both stood up at the same time and Mrs. Portland walked towards Sharon. 'Let's not do anything hasty,' she said, 'I'm sure we can sort something out between us.'

'Maybe,' Sharon replied and walked towards the door without looking back. Once outside the room she hurried through reception and down the corridor towards the toilets, where she heaved and vomited until her ribs and throat were sore.

Chapter 29

The crashing door rattled the crockery on the makeshift kitchen shelves and Sharon braced herself as Sam marched in and threw his bag to the floor. 'Is it true?' he demanded, staring at her defiantly, 'are you pregnant?'

'Oh God. Sam, let me explain,' she cried, but he shook his head fiercely. 'Just tell me the truth. Are you pregnant?'

Sharon nodded her head, but before she could say anything, he spun round and ran upstairs. 'Thanks for telling other people before me,' he shouted, 'you've made me look a real idiot.' He slammed his bedroom door and when she followed and begged him to let her explain, he told her to go away. After a few moments, the heavy beat of his music drowned out her words and she gave up trying to communicate with him and went back downstairs.

Dreading his reaction to her pregnancy, she'd kept putting off the ordeal of telling him, but it had only made things worse, because now, he was angry and hurt at the way he'd had to learn it from some-one else. There was nothing she could do while he was like this, he was better left alone to cool down.

She sank onto a chair and held her head in her hands as she tried to figure out who could have told him, and then with a sinking heart she remembered the look of delight on Selina Proctor's face at the hospital. As well as the child in Lily's class, she also had a daughter in the same year as Sam, and she must have gone straight home and told her the juicy piece of gossip. Obviously, she in turn had wasted no time in sharing it with Sam, so his anger at finding out that way was perfectly understandable.

Having a pregnant mother was bad enough, but carrying it for someone else was unchartered territory altogether, and she was at a loss how to explain that. She wished Tom would come home from work and was tempted to ring him. Hearing a movement behind her she turned to see Ben and Lily edging tentatively into the room. 'Mum,' Ben said, 'are you pregnant?'

She stood up, holding out her arms to them, and Lily, sensing something was wrong, ran straight into them, but Ben walked slowly towards her and stood uncertainly, his eyes locked into hers. 'Yes, I am,' she said to him.

'What's pregnant?' Lily demanded.

'Don't be stupid, it means she's having a baby,' Ben snapped.

'Don't say that to your sister, she certainly isn't stupid and don't forget she's only five.'

Lily pulled away from Sharon and puffed up with indignation. 'I'm nearly six,' she said, and gazing at Sharon's stomach, asked, 'is the baby in your tummy?' When Sharon nodded, she jumped up and down with excitement. 'Am I going to have a baby sister? I want a sister, not another brother.' She ran out of the room shouting, 'I'm going to tell Bear I'm having a baby sister!'

The tears Sharon had held back welled over, startling Ben. 'Why are you crying mum?' he asked, 'is it because Sam's mad with you?'

Sharon shook her head. 'No, well yes in a way. Oh Ben, it's all so complicated, but your dad and I will try to explain it to you later.'

Ben nodded apprehensively. 'What's complicated about having a baby, is it really bad news?'

'No, not bad, just a bit confusing. You've got absolutely nothing to worry about.'

'Okay,' he said, but it was obvious he wasn't convinced.

Sharon crept out of Lily's room and stood outside the door listening to her steady breathing, until she was satisfied she was fast asleep. Every now and then an involuntary sob shuddered her body, but fortunately it didn't wake her.

They'd both agreed Lily was too young to understand the IVF process and Sharon was the best one to explain what was happening in simple terms. What they hadn't expected was the explosion of grief when she was told the baby wouldn't be theirs, and there was to be no little sister. All the promises of being able to see the baby regularly, pushing the pram, and even maybe feeding it made no difference, and it had taken over an hour to calm her and get her to sleep.

Feeling exhausted, she dragged herself downstairs and went into the lounge where Tom and Ben were sitting looking like prisoners awaiting execution.

'Why is Lily crying? I thought you said it was nothing to worry about,' Ben said.

'I know,' Sharon said, 'she's upset about something that I don't think you'll be bothered about, but you'll know as soon as Sam comes down.'

'He said he won't come down.'

'I'll go up,' Tom said, 'I'll just go and get a beer first. Maybe I'll make Sam a shandy.' He looked at Sharon questioningly. 'I think you deserve it, surely, one wouldn't do any harm?' She shook her head, although she would have given almost anything for a whisky right then. Tom returned with a tray of drinks before going back upstairs to talk to Sam. 'He's coming down in a minute,' he said, when he returned.

'What did you say to him to change his mind?'

'He told me he felt an idiot because other people knew about it before him, and after I apologised yet again for that, I also told him there was something about this baby that no-one else knew, but if he didn't come down to hear it, he'd be in exactly the same position again, only worse.'

Ben groaned. 'Now you're really scaring me.'

'Don't worry son, here comes Sam, so you'll soon know everything.'

Ben shivered with apprehension. 'I'm not sure I want to,' he told them, looking away.

The intricacies of what they were doing were far more difficult to explain than Sharon had expected, but not in the way she'd been prepared for. Sam was fully conversant with the IVF process and even Ben had a limited understanding of it, but it was the surrogacy which presented all the misunderstandings.

'So, you're giving your baby away,' Sam said distastefully.

'It's not my baby,' Sharon explained again, 'it's Louisa's and Damian's. I'm just carrying it for them because Louisa can't. It started out as an embryo in a test tube formed from Louisa's egg and Damian's sperm.'

That was more than Ben could take. 'Ugh. That's disgusting,' he groaned.

'When do you give it to them, will it live here at first?' Sam asked.

Grateful for Sam's practical nature, Sharon shook her head. 'No, I'll give the baby over as soon as he or she is born.'

'But what if you don't want to, what happens then. Is it yours really?'

'Legally yes, but morally no. I am doing this so they can have a child of their own.'

Sam stood up. 'Right, I presume that's everything, I'm going to bed,' and without another word he walked out of the room. Tom put his arm round Ben's shoulders. 'That just leaves you. How are you feeling about it all?'

'Muddled up. I don't know what to tell people. Mum's having a baby but she's giving it away, I've never known it happen before. Can I finish Sam's shandy?'

'No, you can't,' laughed Tom, 'now off you go to bed.'

Ben leaned over to kiss his mum goodnight and she pulled him into her arms. 'If you want to talk about anything come to me or dad. Some people might be a bit mean when they first hear, but they'll get used to it. I'll have a word with the teachers, so they know what's going on.'

'Okay, 'he said, pulling free, 'goodnight mum, night dad.'

'Well, I'm glad that's over,' Tom said when they were alone, 'It was even worse than I expected and I didn't think they would all react so differently, that was quite surprising.'

'With different ages and gender, they were bound to I suppose, but I was totally unprepared too. Lily's reaction was out of the blue. I felt sorry for Sam hearing it from someone else first, even Serena Proctor excelled herself this time. I feel like giving her a piece of my mind when I see her, but I don't have the energy for that.' Tom joined her on the couch and pulled her close, and for the first time without being prompted, he lay his hand on her tummy. 'I think I can feel it moving, yes I can.' He turned to her and she nodded. 'Yes, he's getting quite active now, I think he's going to be a footballer.'

Tom moved his hand round following the movements. 'You know the sex then,' he said quietly.

'No,' she replied, 'Louisa decided she wanted it to be a surprise when the baby's born, and it's her choice. You know what I was like with our three, I just don't like calling the baby it, so I make up a sex for the length of the pregnancy.'

Tom laughed. 'If I remember correctly you were wrong every time.'

'Yes, I was. Now it's time for bed, I'm going to need my wits about me tomorrow when I face all those teachers. I hope it'll be easier explaining it to them than it was to our children.'

'I'm coming with you, it's not fair for you to do it on your own. I'll ring Danny, so he'll know not to expect me. Come on, you look very tired, let's go to bed and try to rock this baby to sleep.'

Chapter 30

Bryony walked slowly through the public rooms to satisfy herself the Christmas decorations were up to her own high standard. She had great faith in the florists' work but liked to be sure everything was finished to her satisfaction. Greenery interwoven with berries and discreetly placed muted baubles were her theme for this year, and as usual they'd carried out her instructions perfectly. It would be perfect for the Christmas Charity Ball and she'd been assured the numerous large boxes of oasis would keep everything fresh until after New Year.

In the last few years, the approach of the festive season had filled her with more apprehension than pleasurable anticipation, and this year was no different, especially as Amelia had been very vague about what her plans might be. At first, she'd been disappointed when Amelia told her they were going to visit Piers' family, but during a phone call recently, she'd casually mentioned the possibility of coming to Merebank. Bryony was secretly hoping in the event of that happening, a family get-together could be arranged. But that was still in the lap of the gods.

When she went into the office to arrange the payment to the florist, she was surprised to see Colin sitting at a desk looking intently at the computer screen. 'What are you doing?' she asked.

'Just checking a few things,' he replied without looking up.

'Can't you be a bit more specific, what things?' she asked, as she moved towards him, but he closed the computer down and leaned back in his seat to look at her.

To her annoyance, Colin refused to be intimidated and he turned to her amiably. 'Aren't I allowed to check my own business records? he asked. 'You don't ask *my* permission every time *you* use the computer.'

'Because I run this business and you know it,' she snapped.

'Indeed, you do,' he replied, gathering some sheets of paper together. 'For now,' he added under his breath.

'What did you say?' Bryony demanded, but he stood up without responding, a secretive smile playing on his lips, which infuriated her even more. 'I'm too busy to play your little games' she said, with more than a hint of sarcasm, but undeterred by her little show of histrionics he slowly spun the seat around, so he was facing her.

'I think we need to have a little chat,' he said, 'should we go and have a drink in the wine bar?'

Looking down at him, she replied, 'It's too early, and anyway I'm busy.'

'In an hour then, I could fit you in, but after that *I'm* busy.'

Seething, Bryony went to her room and poured herself a gin and tonic to calm her nerves. She'd already had a session with Sharon to sort out her maternity leave and pay, which hadn't been as easy as she'd thought it might be. In the end they'd both made compromises; Sharon would take as little time off as possible after the birth, during which time she would receive statutory maternity pay. As her employer, Bryony had agreed to pay for time taken for future hospital and doctor's appointments, and in moderation any time Sharon was off sick due to the pregnancy. Bryony was confident Sharon wouldn't abuse the concession, but it still irritated her that really, she'd been left with no choice.

Neither of them had shown any burning desire to change the status quo, and Sharon didn't realise she'd done better out of the deal due to Bryony's reliance on her in the role of secretary to the Mayoress rather than her job in the hotel. It wasn't good policy to encourage a member of staff to feel they were indispensable in any way.

Before she went to meet Colin, she slipped unobserved into the office and switched the computer on. The screen filled with the file she'd been working on earlier in the day, nondescript and of no interest to Colin whatsoever. He must have used the private facility to prevent her seeing what he'd been checking. But why?

On her way to meet him, she was startled to hear his voice behind her, 'Were you looking for me?' he asked. Keeping her composure, she replied. 'Of course not. Why would I be, when we've arranged to meet?' They were walking side-by-side now, and she sensed rather than saw, his childlike smug expression when he replied. 'Even so, you weren't expecting me to be behind you. I wasn't checking up on you,' he added when she didn't respond.

'I didn't think for a moment you were,' she replied, 'after all, I've got nothing to hide.'

He mixed her gin and tonic exactly how she liked it, that at least was something he could do right, and she sipped it gratefully. 'Let's sit in the corner,' he said, carrying both drinks, 'then if anyone else comes in we'll still have some privacy.' He didn't sit next to her as she expected, but instead he pulled out the seat opposite and she watched as his act of bravado drained away. Tapping her foot impatiently, she waited for him to explain what had brought them here.

'I won't beat about the bush,' he said, 'but, I've decided we can't carry on as we are.' Bryony met his nervous, unblinking stare with a nonchalant blank expression, but her heart was beating fast. In all her plans, she'd never considered the possibility of Colin taking the initiative. 'What exactly do you mean by, as we are,' she asked.

'I think you know what I mean,' Colin said sadly, 'all the pretence trying to give the impression we're a normal married couple, when in reality we're living entirely separate lives. Nobody is fooled, the whole town knows it's a sham.'

Bryony took a sip of her drink, thinking fast. It had taken some time for the local people to accept her back in the community, especially taking over the business again, and if Colin instigated a separation now, he would receive undiluted support. On its own, that would be immaterial to her, but she already felt isolated, and the prospect of being shunned even more filled her with an unexpected sense of dread. As much as she couldn't bear the thought, she had to accept that Ralph wouldn't always be here to support her, and the little goodwill she did enjoy, was mainly given out of loyalty to him.

'What are you proposing we do?' she forced herself to ask, 'the current arrangement seems to work very well I think.'

'For you maybe, but I must say,' he said, watching her closely, 'I really didn't expect you to be so surprised.'

'Of course, I'm surprised. I had no reason to expect this. Why…why now?'

Thoughtfully, he ran his thumb down the condensation on his lager glass, while he considered her question. 'I suppose I'm fed up of all the subterfuge and animosity. I can't meet Amelia without feeling guilty and you've come between me and Greg until it almost ruined our friendship. But most of all, it's the mockery of the thing we call our marriage, we neither live together nor apart.'

'It was you who wanted us to give the appearance of us living together at The Lodge while you're the Mayor,' she pointed out testily, desperate to gain the upper hand in the discussion. It was a long time since she'd known him to be so sure of himself, and she didn't like it.

'I know,' he replied, 'but that just illustrates the mess we're in, we have to pretend all the time.'

'I don't see why we can't just go on as we are, when your term of office finishes,' she said, 'nobody's going to be the slightest bit interested in us.'

Colin laughed mirthlessly. 'Bryn, you know that's not true, for some reason the whole town is fascinated by our marriage. You know they are.'

'Well, maybe,' she said, 'but I don't see what it's got to do with anyone else, it's entirely up to us how we live our lives.'

Colin's face fell sadly. 'Yes, I agree, and that's why I want a separation. I want to move on without having to explain myself to anyone. I've made my mind up, so I hope we can keep it amicable.'

'Do you mean now' she asked, 'while you are still Mayor?'

'No,' he replied, 'but I wanted to give you fair notice so we can take action and start the proceedings immediately after it finishes.'

'Is there any reason for all this haste?'

'No, but now I've made my mind up, I want to get it over with.'

Bryony took a long gulp of her drink and tried to steady herself, it was important not to show how shaken she was, so she had to choose her words carefully. 'I suppose you're right,' she said at last, 'we've been pretending for too long, but there's no reason to fall out about anything, we've both got more to lose than gain if we get into a dispute about things.'

His body sank with relief. Obviously, he'd been expecting her to react differently, which was probably why he'd chosen this place to tell her. It was a shock, but she could handle it, she'd simply have to play her cards right to ensure she would come out of this with everything she wanted and deserved.

'Is that all?' she asked, and when he nodded, she stood up. 'I suppose all we're doing is making our separation legal,' she said.

'Exactly,' he agreed, 'I'm sorry Bryn, but it's for the best.'

'I know,' she replied. 'does Ralph know anything about this?'

'No, I wouldn't tell anyone before discussing it with you, and anyway, I think it will be better to leave it until after New Year.'

'What about Amelia and Hugh?'

Colin's features folded into a grimace. 'I'm not looking forward to that, and we can't tell them before dad. So next year it is.'

'I think we should be together when we break it to Ralph, then he'll see we are approaching it without any animosity. We don't want him to have another heart-attack.'

Colin nodded. 'Yes, I suppose you're right,' he said.

Bryony paused, reluctant to ask about Hugh and give Colin the satisfaction of knowing more about their son's future plans than she did. 'That reminds me,' she said casually, 'when I spoke to Hugh, he said he might have a surprise for us soon. Do you think he might be coming home?'

'I've no idea, but when he face-timed me recently it looked like a very decrepit place he was working in. Surely, he'll give up all this unpredictable work some time, he can't spend his life in run down, remote orphanages surely.' He glanced at his watch. 'I must go, I'm off to the golf club.'

She nodded and watched him leave. There was something different about him, but she couldn't put her finger on what it was. An added air of self-assurance maybe, or a sense of satisfaction because he had instigated their separation. Whatever it was, she found it very unnerving, but it made her all the more determined to fight for her own rights. Showing an amicable front to the family was all very well, but keeping what was rightfully hers was worth fighting for. Not that she was expecting Colin to put up much resistance, he didn't have the mettle for that. For a few moments, she'd panicked thinking he was going to suggest a divorce which would have far reaching repercussions, but a separation would be much easier to manage.

Chapter 31

Marie got off the bus and walked down the high street to pick up the ingredients for dinner and a few bits and pieces for Christmas day. The cake and pudding were ready and sealed in airtight containers, and she was going to make the chestnut stuffing and cranberry sauce to put in the freezer. It was promising to be an especially happy time this year, when they would be celebrating the expected arrival of Damian's and Louisa's baby in the spring.

Damian was a fully-fledged coxswain and had led the successful rescue of a fishing boat and fishermen in the recent storms, so although he didn't like any fuss, she and Stuart had decided to have an extra little celebration in honour of that.

It was lovely to share in his and Louisa's happiness, and they all had so much to thank Sharon for, but the whole thing was so incredible Marie couldn't help worrying that even now something could still go wrong. The scans were all reassuring, but somehow the thought that it had come from a tiny frozen embryo grown in a test-tube made her very uneasy, and she still couldn't forget Tom's light-hearted comment, about the possibility of Sharon being unable to part with the baby once it was born. She was sure he hadn't meant it, but a curious, fleeting look had passed over Sharon's face when she heard what he'd said.

What she found even more concerning, was that Sharon would have legal right to the child until a parental order was made six weeks after the birth. Louisa's face was glowing when she explained the process. 'This will act in the same way as an adoption order and pass the parental status to us,' Louisa said, 'we then get a new birth certificate, naming us as the parents. I still can't believe this is happening, in a few months we'll have our own baby.'

Marie couldn't stop herself fretting about the time scale, there seemed to be so many hazards to negotiate on the way and she was hoping and praying Sharon would have the strength to go through with it.

Putting all the negative vibes to one side, she stopped to look in the window of the exclusive children's wear shop where she saw an exquisite and totally impractical outfit for a new-born baby. Impulsively, she went inside and bought it, to add to the growing pile of clothes and soft toys building up in their spare room.

As usual, she'd invited Debbie and her family to share Christmas with them, and once again she'd been turned down. Marie hadn't been surprised when Debbie started reeling off the reasons, or as Stuart succinctly put it, 'the excuses.'

Damian and Louisa had asked Marie and Stuart, but when the practicalities had been discussed, Marie tactfully negotiated the difficult subject of space. Their flat didn't have a dining room and there was only enough room in the lounge for a very small table, which would be very cramped with four people crushed around it. Everyone agreed it made more sense to spend the time together here, but Louisa insisted they share the preparation of the food between them. The invitation to stay the night was accepted, meaning they didn't have to worry about getting a taxi to take them home on Christmas Day.

Sometimes she wondered how two children from the same parents could be so opposite. Negotiations of any kind with Debbie were fraught with problems, but Damian, although he possessed the same strong will, would at least listen and usually things could be sorted out without rancour. Louisa was of a similar nature and she was looking forward to having them around at Christmas.

Just when she thought everything was sorted out, another problem presented itself when Damian asked if Amelia and Piers could join them for Christmas dinner. They'd planned to spend it with Greg, but he'd had to make a different arrangement. They were still staying with him but didn't fancy being on their own on Christmas day.

Marie had no objection whatsoever, in fact it would make it a very merry affair to share it with the young people who were so much fun, but of course there was a stumbling block. Bryony would be hurt and furious. Marie tactfully tried to find out why Amelia wasn't going to be with Bryony, or at the very least Colin, but neither Louisa nor Damian seemed to know, or felt able to say. This made it very difficult, knowing whichever decision she made would end up offending someone. She still hadn't decided, but a decision would have to made soon, and knowing Damian it wouldn't surprise her if he'd taken it for granted that they could come.

'I don't understand what you're worried about,' Stuart told her, 'if it's a case of upsetting one of them I know who I'd pick, and I don't think I need to tell you who that is.'

Flicking through the supermarket magazine, she waited for him to finish reading the newspaper, but then he picked up a pen and started to do the crossword. Knowing this could take some time, she stood up, but before she began to move, he laid down his paper and reading glasses, and with a look of resignation, motioned for her to sit down again. 'Come on, out with it, there's something buzzing round in that head of yours.'

'Am I that obvious? she asked.

'To me you are. I can read you like a book Marie, and I've been aware for a while that something's bothering you.'

'Promise you'll think about what I'm suggesting, before you shoot me down in flames.' She waited until he nodded his head. 'I'll think about it,' he said, 'but I'm not promising anything else.'

'While we've been talking about our Christmas arrangements, it's highlighted how cramped Damian and Louisa are in that tiny flat. They can't even entertain friends or family, and I'm worried about what will happen when they have the baby.'

'Go on, Stuart said, 'I've got absolutely no idea what's coming next, but you'd better tell me.'

'They've used up every penny of their savings on the IVF treatment so they're not going to be able to buy a property for years, if ever.' Stuart nodded, 'Yes it's crossed my mind too, but there are millions like them.'

Marie nodded. 'But love, they're expecting a baby now and that place is barely big enough for the two of them.' She took a deep breath. 'I'd like us to help them with a deposit to buy a house.'

Stuart whistled through his teeth. 'Well I never expected that. How do you suggest we do it, you're talking an awful lot of money?'

Marie nodded. She hadn't expected Stuart to be angry, that wasn't his way, but she'd expected his initial reaction to be more negative than this. For some reason she hadn't considered that he might also be worried about the situation, especially when he'd been so obsessed with the proposed new build. 'I know,' she replied, and the only way I can think of, is to give Damian the money he'll get when we pop our clogs.' She almost laughed out loud at the shocked expression on his face.

'My God Marie, you have given this some thought.'

'I have, because I can't bear the thought of them paying all that money out each month to live in a pokey flat above a shop. Where will they keep all the baby's things and how will Louisa get a buggy up and down those stairs?'

Stuart put his hands up to stop her. 'All right, we'll give it some thought and look into it, but I'm not promising anything. There are lots of things to consider and it won't be as simple as it sounds. Don't forget that money is there for our needs as we get older, and I'm sure there are restrictions on what you can give away, so don't go saying anything yet. I mean that Marie.'

She hadn't expected him to capitulate easily, so his response was a pleasant surprise. He was prepared to give it some consideration, and at this stage that was all she could hope for. 'I promise I won't say anything,' she told him, 'but surely we can do what we want with our own money?'

'I'm not so sure about that,' Stuart replied, 'anyway, before we go any further, what do think our Debbie will say about it?'

'I've thought about that and decided she doesn't need to know; she'll get her share when the time comes. She certainly doesn't need it now and we did set up those trusts for the children.'

'That's true,' Stuart said. 'Obviously, you've considered this in some depth, so have you any idea how much they'll need for a deposit?'

'Not really,' Marie replied, 'but I do know they've been offered a mortgage, but they are struggling to raise the deposit. And then of course there's a shortage of affordable properties suitable for them.'

'Here we go again, trumped-up promises of providing 'affordable' houses.'

'I never said that, I just mean it won't be easy to find a house near town that they can afford. Forget the new houses for once.'

'Sorry, it's just that I'm sick of hearing it, even from people I thought were my friends, I can't believe Greg's involved, and I could willingly ring Tom Lester's neck, I'm definitely finished with him I can tell you.'

'Stuart, you must keep things in perspective, I know you've got strong views and mostly I agree with them, but Greg's entitled to his and Tom is only a builder doing a job, he hasn't got any other investment in it. Don't forget,' she added gently, placing a hand on his arm, 'his wife is carrying our grandchild, and you can't put a price on that.'

Stuart set his chin stubbornly. 'I won't sell my soul to the devil,' he replied.

'I'm not asking you to, but please don't upset Tom I beg you, because I'm so afraid something might go wrong with this surrogacy.'

'I know, but I can't change my feelings and I can't promise to keep them hidden from him, but for your sake, I'll try.'

'Thank you,' she said, reaching up to kiss him.

Chapter 32

At least this was making up for the boring Christmas she'd spent with Colin and Ralph at The Lodge, where most of the food they'd eaten was pre-prepared by Luke at the hotel, and they'd spent most of the day falling asleep in front of the television. Knowing Amelia and Piers were at Marie's had added to her feeling of isolation, until the unexpected call from Amelia, asking if she and Piers could attend the New Year's Eve party at the hotel, and then spend the night there. This marked such a breakthrough in their improving relationship, Bryony could hardly believe it, but she took a deep breath and replied calmly so Amelia had no idea how much she was shaking.

The annual party was as popular as ever and the tickets had quickly sold out. The live band was always a big draw and the food was plain and simple, usually burgers and hot dogs as no-one wanted formality after Christmas. Everyone was enjoying themselves, and Amelia and Louisa had been together most of the evening, radiating happiness and fun.

She'd tried her best to winkle an update of Greg's current love life or hopefully lack of it, out of Marie, but she'd been tight-lipped as usual, telling Bryony to leave him alone as he didn't need any more hassle in his life. Alluding to a problem could only mean one thing, and it had strengthened her belief that he was single and available once again, but she knew it was futile to press Marie further.

She watched her talking animatedly with Janet Bancroft, who seemed to be the centre of attention and was kissing everyone in sight. How dangerously close she'd been to having her as a secretary, it didn't even bear thinking about. Sharon had her failings in the role, but at least she wasn't bossy, and, in a way, she wished she could have been here to enjoy the results of all her hard work. Apparently, she was having a quiet evening at home with her family.

When it became obvious Greg wasn't going to come after all, she took her drink and without drawing attention to herself she found the quietest place she could think of, away from the noise and clamour which seemed to permeate the whole building. In the small meeting room, she sat on one of the easy chairs arranged around a low table in the corner of the room and closed her eyes. Having decided to put her membership of the dating agency on hold during her time as The Mayoress, the prospect of winning Greg's attention had been intended as an amusing diversion to pass the time, but it had quickly begun to pall, and she was missing the excitement of meeting new partners.

When she heard the door open and close quietly, she remained very still hoping the intruder would go away, but instead the footsteps came closer until they stopped close by and she opened her eyes and saw Amelia standing there. Her mouth was smiling but her voice was tentative.

'Hi mum, am I disturbing you?' she asked.

'Of course not,' Bryony replied, 'I only came in here to have a break from all the noise. It's funny really, because I used to be making it, not complaining about it.'

'I suppose you were a real raver in your time, but you're not passed it yet you know.'

'I feel it sometimes. Is your dad still behaving himself?'

Amelia smiled. 'He is, he's with Stuart and a few of their old friends. They do get on well. I sometimes envy them, there's a lot to be said for staying in the town where you were born and having your friends for life.'

Bryony was unconvinced but kept her thought to herself. 'I suppose so,' she replied.

Amelia tucked a stray blonde curl behind her ear. Her upswept hairstyle had fallen into disarray during the twelve o'clock mayhem, but she still looked beautiful. They sat in silence for a few moments, with only the background sound of the music coming from the ballroom. Amelia reached over and took Bryony's hand. Her voice was low. 'Mum, I'm so sorry,'

'For what?' Bryony asked, 'You've got nothing to apologise for.'

'Yes, I have. I still think it was understandable for me to react the way I did when I found out about Greg being my father, it was such a shock and I felt my whole life had been built on a lie. But there's no excuse for the way I've rejected you for all this time, and I am really sorry.'

Bryony was moved, it had taken a long time for Amelia to forgive her, but at last it seemed she had. Reluctant to upset her, she chose her words carefully. 'I think it's time to put it all behind us. We can't forget it happened, but hopefully we can move on.'

Amelia's eyes were brimming with tears and she stroked her finger along her cheekbone to wipe them away, but it was a futile gesture as more sprang up to take their place. 'That's what Piers has told me, but I wouldn't listen to him. Actually,' she said, 'it was Marie who finally got through to me, on Christmas day.'

Bryony was stunned. Marie was the last person she would have expected to act in her defence. 'I am surprised,' she replied, 'and intrigued, what did she say?'

Amelia looked away thoughtfully, as if trying to remember Marie's exact words, but Bryony suspected she was figuring out a way to express them without offending her mother. She was just about to reassure her, when Amelia began to speak. 'She told me I should give you some credit for what you've been through, instead of blaming you for everything. She still believes you made the wrong decision in keeping it from us, but said I should try to understand how difficult it must have been for you at the time, and that you probably thought you were doing the right thing.' Amelia hesitated. 'She also pointed out, how unfair it is, to treat you as the only guilty one, when Greg isn't entirely blameless himself. She believes he might even have put two and two together if he'd really tried.'

'Well, I appreciate Marie's concern, but she's definitely wrong about Greg. He's always loved you so much, there's no way he wouldn't have claimed you if he'd thought for one moment you were his.'

'That's what I said to Marie, and she agreed that was probably true.'

'You seem to have had a very in-depth conversation.'

Amelia nodded, with a smile. 'It helped to clear my head.'

'Good. Have you ever had any chats like this with Greg?'

'Not really, and certainly not for a long time.'

Bryony sighed. 'We've barely spoken for the last few years, but I'm sorry it's all over between him and Katy Sheridan.'

Amelia pulled her hands away and stared at her. 'What do you mean?' she asked.

'Well, it's common knowledge they've broken up. Surely you of all people must be aware of that.'

Amelia was staring at her in disbelief. 'Mum,' she said, 'you do know why she's not there, don't you?'

'There can be only one explanation, as far as I can make out, and that's because they've split up.' Bryony said, shrugging her shoulders.

Amelia slowly shook her head. 'No, that's not it, but I can't believe you don't know,'

Bryony's voice rose, but she quickly checked herself. 'For heaven's sake Amelia, please stop talking in riddles.'

Amelia's eyes misted over as she looked at her mother. 'It's about Paul,' she explained, 'he became ill, terminally ill. Their two children live away and at first, they came back as often as they could to help look after him, but as time went on it became necessary for Paul to have full time care. He didn't want to go into a hospice as he didn't know how long he'd got, so Katy offered to look after him, and with Greg's support she moved back to be his carer. He died just before Christmas and it's the funeral next week. After that, she'll be going back to Greg.'

Bryony was stunned, at a loss as to how she could have been so totally unaware of what was happening, but her overriding feeling was one of relief. In ignorance of the true facts, she would have made an absolute fool of herself in her pursuit of Greg, especially as everyone would have believed she still loved him.

'I can't understand how you didn't know this,' Amelia said, 'everyone in town must have heard except you.' Bryony shook her head slowly from side to side. 'I can only presume no-one thought to tell me, knowing I have no interest in them.'

Amelia smiled. 'I'm so pleased to hear that, because Greg loves Katy very much, and she loves him. They are truly happy together; I've seen it, so I know.'

Bryony stood up and was surprised when Amelia spontaneously threw her arms around her in the first genuine show of affection for years.

Chapter 33

'This feels really weird,' Sam said, as he grabbed the trunks of two Christmas trees and began to pull them over the sand dunes.

'Yes, I know,' Stuart agreed, 'it is a funny thing to do, but it's proved to be very successful, so every year we come to plant dead trees in the sand. You're doing something to help your local environment, and I'm sure that's a good thing for a student of ecology and environmental change.'

'Yeah, I suppose it is. There was a poster up at school asking for volunteers, but nobody took any notice of it.'

'Never mind, you're here now.'

A group of energetic men were digging sand and throwing it into a heap which was gradually forming a ridge along the beach. After watching Stuart and the other workers lined up alongside it, Sam copied them and pushed the trunks of his trees into the side of the incline, before bedding them in firmly by packing them with more sand. You had to dig down a bit to get at the firmer, damp sand, or it simply blew back at you in the wind. Stuart had told him the idea was to stop the dry sand blowing off the dunes into the coastal road and over into the gardens of the houses on the other side, but the main purpose was to keep it on the dunes to prevent the loss of the flora and fauna.

When Stuart began to flag, Sam told him he'd go and bring a few more trees up, as that was the heaviest work. After another hour had passed, they decided they'd done enough, and they trudged back towards the road where the car was parked. Sam heard someone calling his name, and he turned to see a group of boys from his school.

Stuart urged him to go over to see them. 'I'll keep walking slowly towards the car and you can catch me up,' he said.

Sam ran over to the where the small group were enthusiastically forming a kind of conveyor system of collecting trees, digging them in and firmly fixing them in place. As the wind was blowing the sand up the beach, it was collecting in the branches and Sam began to see how it would eventually form a natural barrier. The beginnings of a sandbank.

'Why don't you join us man? We could use a bit of help if we're going to beat that gang up there.'

Sam looked in the direction where he was pointing and was surprised to recognise another group from school, but they weren't so well organised.

'Right, I'll just go and tell Stu,' he told them, 'I won't be long.'

He caught Stuart up before he reached the car and explained what was happening. Some of my mates are there,' he explained, 'and they want me to help. Is that okay with you?'

'Of course, it is son. You see you were wrong about nobody reading the poster. As a matter of fact, we get quite a lot of help from your school, there are usually some volunteers here every year. Now hurry up and get back to them before you're too late.'

'Thanks Stu,' Sam replied, before striding off, swinging the spade in his hand.

'It's a pleasure son,' Stuart said, turning to watch him as he joined his friends digging and planting. It was a cold wind coming off the sea and he could feel it in his bones, but at least he'd done his bit, in more ways than one.

Chapter 34

Marie approached the hotel with trepidation. She'd arranged the meeting knowing Sharon wouldn't be in work today, so she was hoping that whatever the outcome, Bryony wouldn't tell her about the visit. Justin greeted her with his customary friendly smile and offered her a drink while she waited, but Marie declined, hoping that she would be having one with Bryony.

She'd noticed quite a change in Bryony's attitude towards her, which seemed to stem from the Christmas or New Year period, and although she had no idea why, she was glad. As she'd told Amelia, it was time to put all the animosity behind them and start afresh, but it was easier to say than do.

Finding herself in a warm embrace when Bryony arrived, she hoped that what she was going to do wouldn't cause yet another rift and when Bryony asked if she'd prefer the wine bar or her room, she gladly chose Bryony's room which would be cosier and quiet.

'Good choice, Bryony replied, 'I'm far less likely to be disturbed there.' The room had changed little since she was last there when she'd visited Bryony on the morning of Amelia's wedding. The effect of the copious amount of the champagne they'd drunk on that occasion had been quite amusing in some respects, but Marie still remembered the headache which followed her round all the next day. As if she were reading her mind, Bryony held up a bottle.

'I think we could have a small liqueur with our coffee,' she said, 'for old times' sake.'

'I think we could,' Marie agreed, 'but seriously, I really mean it, only a small one.'

Bryony produced two elaborate coffees and placed them within reach on the bedside table. 'I've missed our friendship,' she said thoughtfully, 'and I'm so glad we've made up again. I hope what you've come to see me about isn't going to change that.'

Marie hoped so too, but she was determined to go through with it whatever the outcome, the trouble was, Bryony was so unpredictable. 'There's no reason why it should,' she said, 'but that's entirely up to you. It's about Sharon, I want you to be a bit easier on her.' Bryony's eyebrows lifted and there was a subtle but noticeable change to her expression. 'How do you mean, exactly?'

'Just don't keep asking her to do more hours than she should. I'm worried about her.'

'Has Sharon asked you to do this?'

Marie took a large sip of the liqueur and coughed as it burned its way down her throat. 'Of course not,' she said indignantly, 'she has no idea I've come to see you. I made sure I arranged it for a time when I knew she wouldn't be here.'

'A hospital appointment I believe,' Bryony said, 'one of many.'

'No more than any other pregnant woman,' Marie replied, 'but you shouldn't be asking her to do extra hours at this late stage in her pregnancy.' Look Bryony, I know you probably think it's nothing to do with me, but I look after the children and I see her when she comes home after she's had to stay late, and she's absolutely shattered.'

'Why has she never said anything to me?'

'Because she's conscientious, and loyal to you.' Marie replied carefully. If she was to achieve what she'd set out to do, it wouldn't help to tell her Sharon was afraid of her reaction.

'And Sharon has absolutely no knowledge of this conversation?'

'Absolutely none, and I hope you won't say anything about it because I know exactly how she will react if she finds out.' Marie moved to the window and looked out to where she could just make out the lifeboat house and charity shop in the distance. There were a few people milling around, but it was a dull, miserable day, and most people were staying indoors to keep warm. 'I'm asking you to do this, because she's carrying my grandchild,' she said, 'it's such an incredible thing she's doing, but I can't help feeling concerned about the impact it's having on her. Mentally and physically.'

'What do you mean, mentally.'

Marie cursed herself, she hadn't meant to say that, but it was playing on her mind, and in a way, she felt a sense of relief. 'You must promise me you won't repeat this,' she said, 'but I'm afraid she might not want to give the baby up when it's born.'

'Have you any reason to think that?' Bryony asked, and Marie shook her head. 'Not really, it's just little things like seeing her stroke her tummy in a protective way, and one day she said, 'my baby,' not 'the baby,' as she normally does.'

Bryony's brows drew together, 'There doesn't seem much wrong with that, probably just a slip of the tongue. If the embryo is from Louisa and Damian, as you said it is, then it's biologically theirs. I think you are worrying needlessly, neither Sharon nor her husband are going to want to bring up someone else's child.'

'I hadn't thought of it like that, but you're right of course. I'm just being silly as usual.'

'Getting back to why you are here, I'm sorry Sharon didn't feel able to speak to me, but obviously I'll bear in mind what you've told me. It won't be easy cutting her hours without her noticing, but I'll manage it somehow. The biggest problem will be finding someone suitable to step in for the few weeks remaining, especially to do the secretarial work.'

'How about Janet Bancroft?' suggested Marie impulsively.

'Are you mad?' Bryony exclaimed, 'she'll take over the place, and she'll be telling me what, and what not to wear.' Bryony poured two more shots of liqueur and waved Marie's refusal away.

'Actually, I'm glad you came, because I've got something to tell you,' she said, 'Colin and I are separating.'

'Well' Marie replied, 'I'll believe that when I see it. You told me you were leaving Colin years ago, and look what happened, here you are, still together.'

'I did leave, but I chose to come back, but this time it will be different, because Colin is the one who's leaving.'

Marie choked and the liqueur slipped down, burning her throat. She was never surprised when Bryony threatened to leave Colin, but she'd always believed Colin loved Bryony too much to leave her. 'Colin?' she asked, shaking her head, 'are you sure?'

'Of course, I'm sure. It's surprising I know, but nevertheless, it's true.'

'Why now?' Marie asked, 'isn't it going to be awkward while he's the Mayor?'

'Oh no, he's waiting until it's over before we make it public, but he's already consulted a solicitor, so he seems pretty determined to go through with it. It's ironic really, I've always believed I would be the one to instigate the end of our marriage, and then he suddenly drops this little bombshell.'

Marie was puzzled, but remembering who she'd seen in the shelter, or who she thought she'd seen, nothing would surprise her anymore. Every day since it happened, she'd told herself she'd imagined it, but she knew she hadn't. 'Have you any idea what's prompted it?' she asked, but Bryony shrugged her shoulders. 'None at all, but it isn't a surprise really, we live apart most of the time and we haven't slept together for years. Before you ask', she added with a wry smile, 'there's no-one else involved. Unfortunately, as far as I'm concerned. And you can probably guess what Colin's like, he's probably forgotten what it's for.'

Marie was beginning to feel uncomfortable, and she tried to deflect the conversation away from Colin. They'd all grown up together, and he was one of Stuart's best friends, so she'd always tried to discourage Bryony from divulging details of their personal lives. 'What about the hotel?' she asked, 'and where will you live?'

'I don't know for sure, but he can't run the hotel alone, so probably I'll still be in charge here. It isn't a divorce, which could get quite messy, and we don't have to divide things up so I'm not too worried.' She looked around the room shrugging her shoulders, 'I could even end up living here,' but seeing Marie's look of disbelief she added swiftly, 'No, seriously I'm going to be alright.'

Bryony went downstairs with Marie and after waving her off, she checked the calendar and confirmed there was nothing needing her immediate attention so she decided to tell Justin she was leaving early. Reaching the reception area, she was surprised to see Justin's wife Ellie leaning on the desk talking to him. As Bryony approached, Ellie smiled and greeted her pleasantly. 'Good afternoon Mrs. Portland, how are you.'

Bryony listened absently to the couple as they talked enthusiastically about their new baby, but her ears pricked up when Ellie said she would be able to return to part-time work earlier than planned. Her mother had offered to look after baby Nathan now that he was feeding well and seemed happy to be left in her care. Of course, Ellie would understand if it wasn't convenient, and Bryony had to try and hide her eagerness when she assured her it would suit very well.

If there was one person, she could have faith in and be happy to work with, it was Ellie. Efficient and enthusiastic, she was a favourite with the visitors who often sought her out to deal with their queries or problems, and she would also receive a warm welcome from the rest of the staff. It was a very satisfactory solution to a tricky situation.

The alcohol she'd drunk with Marie meant she couldn't drive home, and feeling reluctant to walk, she asked Justin to call her a cab. A knowing glance passed between him and his wife before he turned his grinning face back to Bryony.

'Why don't I drive you?' he said, 'and Ellie can hold the fort while I'm gone.'

'Are you sure? Bryony began, but Ellie was already behind the desk. 'I can't wait,' she beamed, and Bryony gave in.

When Justin dropped her off, she saw two cars she didn't recognise parked on the curve of the drive. She let herself in and stood silently in the hall, listening to men's voices in the kitchen, but other than Colin, she couldn't make out who they were or what they were saying. Edging closer she realised they were preparing to leave, and she wanted to confront them before they did. Colin wouldn't be expecting her home so early, and because she hadn't driven the car round to the garage, he hadn't heard her return.

She opened the door and walked in just as they were all gathering the papers on the table in front of them. Colin was flustered, but after a moment of embarrassment the two men quickly composed themselves and folded the large sheets of paper before putting them securely in their briefcases.

'I'm sorry to disturb you,' Bryony said calmly, 'but I wasn't aware there was a meeting going on in my kitchen.'

'It's quite alright,' one of them said, 'we were just leaving anyway. Thanks for your hospitality.'

When Colin returned after seeing them out, she stood with her back to the table and watched him collecting the cups and saucers they'd used. She could stand it no longer. 'Well? Aren't you going to tell me what's going on?'

'There's nothing going on,' he replied, 'at least nothing for you to worry about.'

'So, what is that?' she asked, pointing to the paper he'd left on the table. And don't tell me it's nothing, I can see it's a plan of this house and land.'

He shrugged dismissively, unmoved by her indignation, and that made Bryony wary. 'It's the orchard we're discussing, if you must know. I'm thinking of having it cleared. I knew you'd object but we can't keep paying a useless gardener to maintain it when it produces nothing worthwhile. I'm aware you've got this romantic idea about living in a manor house with orchards and tennis courts, but it isn't realistic anymore, and they're never used.'

'And what will you do with it?'

'I have no idea, that's why they were here, to give me their ideas.'

She turned and opened the folded paper and saw a plan of the orchard with measurements and graphs. 'You must have some thoughts on what we can do with it.'

Colin shuffled his feet nervously, his confidence wavering. 'I favour allotments,' he said timidly, and braced himself for her reply, which didn't disappoint.

'Allotments!' she cried in exasperation, 'what on earth will you do with allotments?'

'Apparently there's a long waiting list for them, and it would bring in some money, which is something you are always telling me I should do.'

She began to walk towards the door, 'I'm going to get changed,' she said, and then stopped and turned to him. 'Does this have anything to do with the separation, are you selling my home from under me?'

'No, I'm not selling your home,' he replied, and she left the room without catching the look of guilt on his face.

Chapter 35

Sharon heaved herself off the sofa. She'd never reached this size before and she was finding it hard to move about without a great deal of effort, even though she still had a few weeks to go. Sometimes she felt as though there were twins in there, but when she'd mentioned it at the hospital, only half in fun, she'd been reassured it was fluid and not another baby making her so big. Sharon secretly gave a huge sigh of relief, the consequences of giving birth to twins in these circumstances was not on the agenda.

Lily's calls were rising in crescendo so she hurried as fast as she could towards the stairs, calling as she went, to try and calm her down. 'They'll be where you left them,' she shouted. 'But they're not,' Lily wailed, 'somebody must have moved them.'

'I can't imagine why anyone would move your ballet shoes,' Sharon muttered under her breath, but she was filled with remorse at the sight of Lily standing in the middle of her bedroom, her bottom lip trembling. Sharon tried to put her arms round her, but Lily wriggled free. 'Mummy I'm going to be late!'

'No, you're not, because Louisa's coming to take you and she's never late. Now let's find these shoes.'

In fairness to Lily, she would never have found the ballet pumps which were hidden on the top shelf of her wardrobe, obviously tidied away by Tom. 'Silly daddy,'

Sharon said, but Lily quickly jumped to his defence. 'Daddy's not silly,' she called happily, as she ran downstairs and straight into Louisa's arms.

'I'll pick her up as usual,' Louisa said, 'so have a rest while you can.' She looked knowingly at the bump and the awkward way Sharon was moving, and she mouthed thank you over Lily's head as she helped her to put her coat on.

'Are you doing anything special for the next hour?' Sharon asked impulsively, and when Louisa shook her head, she asked her to come back after she'd dropped Lily off. 'I might be tired,' she said, 'but I'm desperate for some adult company.'

'Great, I'll see you soon.'

While Louisa was gone, Sharon set up the coffee and sliced some of the cake she'd made the previous day. Tom was quite happy with the current situation and would be more than pleased if she said she was going to stay at home after the baby was born, but she constantly tried to put him right on that score. There was no way she was going to give up her job, especially since Mrs. Portland had eased off on the number of hours she was expecting her to work. As nothing had been discussed between them, she'd initially felt very vulnerable, especially when Justin told her his wife Ellie was returning earlier than planned, but when Mrs. Portland had pointed out the similarities between their situations regarding maternity leave, she relaxed a little.

In the end, she'd been left with no choice and conceded it was time to go when her feet and face started swelling, and heartburn and indigestion were a daily occurrence. If it wasn't for the fact she knew exactly when conception had occurred, she would be convinced they had got the dates wrong.

'Look who I found on the doorstep,' Louisa called, when she returned with Marie in tow. 'I'm sorry,' Marie said, 'I just thought I'd call on my way to the pharmacy to check if you need anything, but I don't want to intrude, so I'll leave you two in peace.'

Sharon looked at Marie and smiled affectionately, aware of her genuine concern as the expected date for the birth drew nearer. 'You've come rather a long way around to get to the pharmacy, and I'm grateful, but no thanks, I don't need anything. But you must stay and have a coffee with us.' When Marie began to protest, Sharon put her hand up, 'No argument, you're staying.' Listening to Louisa humming in the kitchen as she prepared the drinks, Marie and Sharon exchanged glances. Marie's voice trembled. 'She is so happy and excited, and so is Damian. I can't thank you enough for what you are doing.'

'I don't want thanks,' Sharon replied, 'but I must confess I'll be glad when this little one is born.' She put her hands on her tummy and Louisa walked in to see the answering kick from the baby. Louisa placed the tray on the coffee table before spreading her fingers on Sharon's tummy. 'Oh, I can't wait to hold him,' she whispered.

'I'm going.' They all turned towards the door, catching a glimpse of Sam hurrying passed on his way out. Sharon hoped he hadn't seen them all looking so attentively at the bump he was still feeling so embarrassed about. All being well, it had all calmed down at school now, but due to his refusal to discuss it, she had no idea if things had got better or not for him.

Ben naively kept her up to date with the position at his school, and as some kids there still talked about his mother giving their baby away, she wasn't feeling very optimistic.

Marie and Louisa were very sympathetic when Sharon briefly explained the situation to them, but as there was nothing they could do to help, it left them all feeling helpless. 'Poor Sam,' sighed Marie, 'it can't be easy for him.'

'I know, but I don't know what to do, he won't let me get near him and Tom's not much help these days, he's so busy. Talking of which, and to briefly change to another contentious issue, do you have any idea what's happening about the mere?'

Marie shook her head. 'I don't think anyone knows, but I hope it will be decided soon and then maybe we can get back to normal.'

'Or not, whatever the case may be,' Sharon replied, 'I think Tom's gone to see someone about it this morning, but I don't know who or why. He never tells me much, which is really annoying one way, and good in another.'

'I know, I feel the same,' agreed Marie, 'especially as I'm not absolutely dead against it, but I can't tell Stuart and that's really difficult. It's the first time in our marriage that I haven't been open about something important to us both.'

Sharon was intrigued, she had no idea Marie felt this way. 'Do you mean you want it to go ahead?' she asked and was surprised when Marie replied. 'I wouldn't put it as strongly as that, but I won't be devastated if it does.'

'I can't believe it,' Sharon said, 'all this time, I thought we were on opposing sides, and I dreaded it threatening our friendships.'

'It would never have done that,' Marie responded swiftly, but Sharon wasn't convinced. 'I only hope most people will realise that Tom is a very small cog in a very big wheel,' she sighed, and Marie and Louisa nodded in agreement.

'I must be going' Louisa said, looking at her watch, 'or I'll be late for Lily, and that will never do. Is it okay if I take her for lunch again? It's sort of becoming a regular thing, and I realise it might be putting you under pressure when I can't do it anymore.'

Sharon smiled. 'We'll face that when the time comes, don't worry about it.'

Marie accepted Louisa's offer of a lift home. 'I might even join you for a burger,' she said, 'I think Stuart's at some sort of meeting too. I'll be glad when this thing's sorted out, whichever way it goes.'

'Me too,' Sharon said, 'what do you think will happen if this development does go ahead?'

'I've no idea,' Marie replied, 'have you?'

Sharon shook her head. 'No,' she replied truthfully, 'but there's something going on, I'm sure of it. For some reason Tom doesn't seem as uptight about it being turned down, as I'd expect him to be.' She shook her head. 'I'm probably imagining it, but I'll try and enjoy it while it lasts.'

Marie picked up her shopping bag, but before following Louisa she hesitated. 'I was going to say exactly the same thing about Stuart, in fact, the other day when he was reading about it in the local paper, he smiled and said, "there are more ways than one of skinning a rabbit.' They all agreed it was strange that both men, who's opinions were poles apart, were both behaving as if they were confident of winning.

After they left, Sharon couldn't help considering the implications of what had been said. In some ways, if the plans were turned down Tom had more to lose, because a significant contract would mean employment for a lot of people, and security for themselves. But for Stuart, it was impossible to put a price on the land, even though he had nothing to gain financially. If both men were more relaxed about the outcome it could only mean one thing. Someone must have come up with an option which was more acceptable to both sides. It was a fanciful idea, but something to cling on to.

Instead of preparing dinner, Sharon decided to take it easy for the rest of the day and order a curry from the local takeaway. She would just have to have an extra-large dose of the indigestion medicine before eating it, and damn the consequences.

Chapter 36

The mood on the streets was one of elation when the news was posted on the council website. The councillors and Planning Committee, had done everything that was required and the local plan was up to date and in order. People were still left guessing, when the developers stated they wouldn't be taking further action but hinted at the possibility of an alternative site being considered. Gossip was rife, but Stuart, after checking with Marie, grabbed his coat and waltzed her round the room, before going to meet Russell for a celebratory drink. Glad of the peace and quiet, she sat and considered exactly how it had left her feeling.

Although Stuart kept putting off making a decision about giving Damian and Louisa the money for a deposit, they had discussed it several times and she sensed they were edging nearer to agreeing what to do. She knew he would never have agreed to contributing anything towards what he saw as the destruction of his beloved mere, but what other choices were on offer.

She'd surreptitiously been checking out the estate agents, but apart from the odd property situated on the edge of town, she'd seen nothing remotely within their budget. One day, as she was approaching an estate agent's office, she'd veered away after catching sight of Louisa looking at the properties displayed in the window. Maybe, now that all this fuss was over, Stuart would whip up as much enthusiasm for helping his own son to find somewhere to live as he'd lavished on birds and the wildlife inhabiting the mud.

After making herself a drink, she settled down for a quiet read, but the phone started ringing as soon as she opened her book. Expecting it to be Sharon ringing about the news, she was surprised to hear Bryony's tearful voice, asking her to go to meet her at the hotel as soon as possible. She refused to explain what was wrong but was almost begging Marie to do as she asked, which left her with no choice but to agree. She left a short note for Stuart before setting off, on what she suspected would turn out to be another grossly exaggerated mission of mercy.

The hotel was lit up and welcoming when she arrived, and Marie wished Bryony could appreciate what she had, especially as she'd given up the man she loved to achieve it. Even so, Colin was a kind enough man, if a bit boring, but Marie had always believed that married to the right person he could have been a lot more interesting. She couldn't imagine what was upsetting Bryony now, but speculation was useless, as she'd already reached reception.

Jason gave her a knowing look as she approached and told her Mrs. P. was waiting in her room. When she asked if he knew what was wrong, he dropped his head to one side, and indicated half and half by sticking his thumb horizontally out of his fist. As she was walking towards the lift, a group of people were walking into the small meeting room, and she was surprised to see Greg amongst them, talking animatedly to a young woman she recognised as a councillor. Greg waved when he saw Marie, but they both continued their separate ways without stopping to speak. It seemed very much as though his presence here had something to do with Bryony's distress, but if that was so he seemed either unaware or unconcerned about it.

Tapping gently on the door, she went in without waiting for a reply and saw Bryony standing at the window, obviously still very upset. Walking over to join her she glanced out of the window, but there was little to see in the gentle glow radiating from the lights of the hotel. The sun was dropping over the horizon in a blaze of colour and a few vessels were silhouetted on the water. It was a restful scene but obviously it hadn't worked its magic on Bryony, who was coiled like a spring. 'Is it something to do with Greg?' she ventured to ask, and when Bryony made no reply she added, 'I'm just wondering because I saw him downstairs.'

Bryony shook her head and her voice was curiously flat. 'Greg's here in the hotel? I wasn't aware of that, but no, this has nothing to do with Greg. It's my scheming, lying husband.'

Marie froze. 'So, you know then,' she said softly, but Bryony stood, as if in a trance, and Marie braced herself for the inevitable eruption, but the volcano had turned to ice.

'I might have guessed you'd know,' Bryony said, 'but obviously you didn't think to tell me. I suppose I'm the only person in Merebank who didn't know my husband was cheating on me. It's ironic when you think about it, everyone believes I'm aware of everything that goes on around here, but I was totally oblivious to this, and it's right on my own doorstep. I knew something was going on, but he wouldn't tell me what it was. Until today.'

Bryony had been dabbing her eyes with a tissue, but now she was pulling it to shreds and bits were falling on the floor beside the chair. Marie resisted the impulse to bend down and pick them up. 'I'm sorry,' she said, playing for time, 'I just didn't want to hurt you. What exactly has he told you?'

'That there's a plan B for the housing development, and it means selling off our home and our land.'

Marie gasped. 'You can't mean he's selling The Lodge?'

'That's exactly what I mean, despite him promising me he had no intention of doing so.' She sat down and Marie gratefully did the same. Bryony closed her eyes and began to speak slowly and methodically. 'I found them poring over the plans of our land, planners or architects, I can't remember, but when they'd gone, I challenged him, and he promised me he didn't intend to sell anything except the orchard.' She opened her eyes and she looked at Marie. 'Can you guess what he said it was going to be used for?' Marie shook her head. 'Allotments. Can you believe that?'

'To tell you the truth, I'm struggling to make sense of any of this, are you telling me you're selling The Lodge and the surrounding land to the developers? For a housing estate? Surely it wouldn't be big enough?'

Bryony's lip curled. 'It will be if Clive Robinson sells his adjoining land, which seemingly he's agreed to do. It won't be as large as the original plan, but big enough apparently.'

'I can understand why you don't want an estate on your doorstep,' she said, 'but it may not be as bad as you imagine.' Bryony looked at her with derision. 'I can't think of anything worse than knocking my home down to build an estate of cheap houses. How would you like it if it happened to you?'

'When you put it like that, I'd hate it.'

'Exactly. It's even worse because he didn't warn me about it.'

'Well,' Marie said, 'I suppose it had to be kept under wraps, and maybe Plan B only emerged as a possibility when it looked like Plan A wasn't going to happen.'

'Are you saying I wasn't to be trusted?'

'No,' she replied wearily, standing up to put her coat on, 'I'm not saying that, and if you're going to twist everything I say, there's no point in us discussing any further.'

'You don't understand,' Bryony said bitterly, 'it's my home.'

Marie's patience was wearing thin. 'And at the end of it all, you will end up with a lovely home, which is more than can be said for a lot of people. I'm sorry Bryony, but I really must go.'

As she was about to leave, Bryony stopped her. 'When I said Colin had lied to me, you acted as if you already knew about it, and yet you were shocked when I told you about the land. What else did you think I was talking about?'

Marie fumbled with her gloves, deliberately dropping one to give her time to think. 'Mmm, I've completely forgotten. I think it was something to do with... no, it's gone. Must go now, bye.' She'd just begun to move away when Bryony said thoughtfully, 'but you said you were sorry, if I remember rightly.' Marie pretended she hadn't heard and moved as quickly as she could towards the lift where she turned to wave, but Bryony was deep in thought as she watched her go.

The following morning, she awoke refreshed and received Stuart's offer of breakfast at The Sands with enthusiasm. Sensing he was building up to telling her something of importance, she tried to curb her impatience and feign indifference, but he wasn't fooled.

'You can't kid me,' he laughed, 'I know you're itching to know, and I'll put you out of your misery, but first you have to tell me something.' Swiftly checking there was no-one within hearing distance, he leaned over the table and asked, 'Do you still want to help Damian and Louisa with a deposit on a house?' The question was so unexpected she hesitated momentarily, wondering what he was going to say. 'Of course, I do, I've never stopped thinking about it. Why are you asking now?'

'You made me think, when you talked about them managing with a baby in that flat of theirs, especially the problem of a pram with all those stairs, and I've been making a few enquiries. We can access the money for a deposit, within reason, and I agree with you that we should do it. I also had a word with Fred Williams and asked him to keep an eye out for something within their price range, but what I didn't expect was for it to happen so quickly. The Carrington's place is up for sale, they've upped and gone into a rest home together. The family have put it on the market and want a quick sale to pay the fees.'

Marie looked at him in astonishment. 'It could be lovely, but it's in a pretty bad condition, they've done nothing to it for years.'

'Exactly. The price reflects that, which is why it's in their price range. There are enough of us to help Damian with the essentials, but the other things they will have to do as and when they can afford it.' He looked at his watch, 'The thing is, we don't have much time, it's on his books as from today, and Fred thinks it will be snapped up by a developer. He's doing it all fair and square of course, he's already agreed a selling price with the family, and he'll put any offer to them as normal. We'd better be going; we're meeting Damian and Louisa and we don't want to keep them waiting.'

'Where are we meeting them? Marie asked as they walked towards the square.

'In the coffee shop next to Fred's place. I thought we'd better tell them what we're thinking of doing, before going to see the house, if only to give them a chance to refuse if they don't like the idea.'

'I don't think there's much likelihood of that,' she said squeezing his arm, 'I think they are going to be over the moon. You're a dark horse, Stuart Fowler, and I do love you.'

'Likewise,' he replied, smiling.

Chapter 37

Bryony read and re-read the letter from her solicitor and still couldn't make sense of it. If she was understanding it correctly, Colin was rescinding almost all his share, or was it simply his involvement, in the business. The details were unnecessarily cloaked in legal jargon which she couldn't understand, and she couldn't be bothered trying.

The trouble was, she had very little time before getting ready for the afternoon engagement, and to make matters worse Ellie had phoned in to say she was unable to work because the baby had a temperature, and Sharon was unable to stand in because she wasn't feeling well. Despite all this, Justin assured her he had the situation under control, so she went upstairs to the privacy of her room and cast her eyes once more over the document.

The more she tried to understand it, the more ridiculous it seemed. They were turning the simple process of legalising a mutually agreed separation into a very complicated arrangement. She was convinced none of this was Colin's doing, so she decided to have a word with him. He wouldn't be able to understand the letter either, but they could put up a united front and direct the people representing them to cut through the legalities and talk about the bare bones of their agreed requests.

She hadn't seen him all morning, so her first port of call was his room down the corridor. She tapped on his door, and when there was no reply she tapped again and called his name. Putting her ear to the door she thought she heard a muffled sound, but when there was still no response, she turned the knob, and finding it was locked she returned to her room. Somehow, something didn't feel quite right, and after checking with Justin, who confirmed Colin had been unavailable to take an important call, she decided to investigate further and apprehensively returned to his room. If he was in there but unable to call out, it was reasonable to assume he was either very ill or drunk, so she tentatively slipped her skeleton key in the lock, and dreading what she might find, she gently pushed open the door. When she caught a glimpse of his body writhing under a billowing mound of duvet, she began to have an idea of what was wrong.

Not knowing if Ralph or a member of staff may be in earshot, she kept her voice low. 'What on earth's going on?' she hissed. When Colin heaved himself up the bed, it confirmed what she already guessed. He wasn't alone in the bed. Surfacing breathlessly, his face flushed and shocked, he spluttered, 'Bryn, what are you doing here?'

Staring pointedly at the bed, she replied, 'more to the point, what are you doing here?'

Before he had chance to reply, a woman appeared next to him and Bryony gasped in astonishment. 'Well, well,' she exclaimed, 'what a surprise.'

Colin sat up clutching the duvet to his chest. 'I'm sorry Bryn,' he said, 'you weren't meant to find out like this. We were going to tell you soon I promise. We need to talk,' he implored, as she turned to walk away but she spun around to face him, her eyes glinting with anger. 'How right you are,' she spat, 'but I'm saying nothing in front of this trollop. Come to my room when you're ready, but not before you're decent. For God's sake put some clothes on.'

In her room, she leaned against the door, her heart hammering in her chest. She was shaking with shock. Never would she have believed Colin capable of having an affair, but worse than that, he'd done the unthinkable and conducted it in what was virtually their own home. Hearing him approach her room, she moved away and curtly told him to come in.

'I'm sorry, Bryn,' he said again, 'I really didn't want you to find out like this. Shall we sit down and discuss it reasonably? I can't talk to you while you're prowling about like that.'

'How dare you bring her here?' she spat, 'I suppose this means all the staff are aware of what's been going on. As a matter of interest, how long has it been going on?'

He was looking at her helplessly, unable to decide which of her questions to answer first, but then he straightened his back and faced her down. 'It doesn't really matter how long it's been going on,' he replied, 'because it's more than just a fling, I love her, and she loves me. And no, the staff are not aware, because believe it or not, this is the first time I've brought her here. We've been very discreet,' he added quietly.

'It's been very cosy for you hasn't it? No wonder she offered to be my secretary, and you put her in charge of the chains. It's all falling into place now. I suppose this is what the separation is all about, you're leaving me for mousy little Janet Bancroft.'

'No, I'd decided that before we ever got involved, and I'd appreciate it if you didn't speak about her in that way.'

'I'll speak about her in whatever way I choose. So, you don't believe she's a little gold-digger?'

'No, I don't. Even I wouldn't be stupid enough to fall for that again.'

Bryony winced at his jibe. 'Do you trust...?' She waved her arm dismissively, 'that woman?'

'I've told you I love her, so of course I trust her. This isn't the right time to discuss the legalities of the situation, but I just want you to know this will not affect the outcome of your position here. You will still be in charge of running the business, and you will get what is rightfully yours.'

'There is no-one else in the family prepared to run it,' she said bitterly. 'I'm not really interested, but where does Janet Bancroft fit into your plans?'

'We're going to live together eventually, but first I intend to get settled in my new job. Then hopefully we'll buy somewhere in the future.'

Bryony sneered. 'Job! What job could you do? You've never had a proper job in your life!'

'I've already got a position,' he told her, with a slight air of self-satisfaction. 'I'm to be the new steward at the golf club when Neville Smith retires.'

Bryony sank onto the bed in shock. 'You don't know anything about running a golf club.'

'No, but I can learn, anyway it's mainly about running the bar and helping to co-ordinate events, and even you must agree I'm capable of running a successful bar. Have you been too busy to notice how smoothly our own wine bar is run, and how it's become a favourite meeting place for locals as well as visitors? The right wines don't jump onto the shelves, and the barrels don't change themselves Bryn. Anyway, the golf club committee seem to think I'm capable, and that's all that matters.'

Her head was spinning with the duplicity of it all. 'You'd better leave,' she told him bitterly, 'and make my apologies this afternoon, I won't be going.'

'Do you want me to tell them you're not feeling well.'

'Tell them what the hell you like.'

He nodded, and backed towards the door.' 'I'm really sorry it's ended like this, but I hope we can stay friends after it's all sorted out.' Unable to speak, or even look at him, she turned her back to him, and taking his cue, Colin left her and closed the door behind him. After a few minutes she heard the door to his room open and close again, before muffled footsteps passed her room.

When she was sure they'd gone, she went to see Ralph, who as usual, was delighted to see her.

Ralph never shied from facing problems head on, and today was no exception. 'I suppose you've come about the solicitor's letter,' he said gently.

'In a way,' she replied, 'but I just wanted to see you, I felt a bit down and you always make me feel better.'

'That's kind of you, but I suppose we may as well discuss it now you're here. Have you talked with Colin yet?' She told him what had happened, and he smiled despite himself. 'Oh dear, that's typical Colin I suppose, but who would have guessed he'd do something like this.'

'Did you know?' she asked, and he assured her the only thing Colin had confided to him was a brief outline of the divorce settlement. 'I've been such an idiot,' she said, 'I didn't have an inkling, and yet it's been going on right under my nose.'

Ralph shook his head. 'It's surprising how people can cover their traces when they've a mind to, it happens all the time. What you've got to do now is work out the best way for you both to move on. I think the terms that have been set out are very reasonable, so you should be well placed financially.' He hesitated and she lifted her head to look at him. 'I think we both know you won't lose any sleep about the emotional side of the break-up of your marriage,' he said gently.

Her attention was caught by sight of the official car pulling up outside, and she watched Colin stride confidently down the steps with Janet Bancroft following closely behind. His term of office had done him a lot of good, but somehow it had passed her by. A fleeting notion giving Janet Bancroft some credit for it was swiftly dismissed.

'I presume you're not attending due to what's happened,' Ralph said, standing beside her. 'It's unlike you, but these are very exceptional circumstances.'

'I really don't feel well,' she replied, 'I've got a throbbing headache, I think I'll go and take some medication and then lie down for a while.' She leaned on him, resting her head on his shoulder. 'It must be difficult for you too, after all, it's your house and land, to say nothing of the business. Don't you feel sad?'

'Not really, I've seen it coming for a long time. Times are changing and we have to move with them.'

Gently pulling away, she dropped a kiss on Ralph's cheek and stumbled back to her room, where she closed the blinds and lay down on the bed.

She must have dozed off and after what seemed like only moments, the phone rang. At first, she ignored it, but when it stopped and then began again, she lifted the receiver.

'I told you I didn't want to be disturbed,' she said crossly.

'Believe me, you'll want to see this person,' Justin insisted. 'He wants to come to your room. Oh, sorry Mrs. P. he's already on his way.'

Bryony sprang into action. There was only one man who would dare to do that, and she had only seconds to make herself presentable. Making a conquest could be just the fillip her ego needed.

Chapter 38

Marie got up from the chair and walked across to Stuart who had nodded off with the remote control in his hands. She'd seen and heard enough about the forthcoming election for one day, and she was tired and ready for bed. A second before she switched the set off, the newscaster's face turned even more serious as he stopped speaking and listened to a message being relayed to him. In a very sombre tone, he announced some breaking news concerning an explosion during a concert at Cotton Hall in Manchester, resulting in some deaths and many more injured.

She watched as pictures of the disaster filled the screen, but when she turned to rouse Stuart, she was shocked to see him already staring at the television, the colour draining from his face. 'Oh my God,' he gasped, rising slowly from the chair, his eyes riveted to the screen. 'Sam!' His body was rigid, and he was deaf to Marie's entreaties until she took hold of his arm and shook him firmly.

'What do you mean?' she cried, 'Sam's in Benton for the weekend, staying with a friend. You know he is.'

Stuart turned his head and looked at her through stricken eyes. 'No, No, he isn't,' he said, 'that's just it, he isn't. He's gone to that concert.' Covering his face with both hands he began to moan. 'Oh God, what have I done?' Gently she took hold of his trembling hands and moved them away from his face, but what she saw scared her and she pleaded with him to tell her what was wrong. With the chilling commentary in the background, Stuart repeated, 'Sam's at that concert,' and she felt the floor tilting under her feet.

Shaking with dread, she forced herself to ask, 'you said you'd done something, what did you mean. What have you done?'

His voice was shaking. 'He confided in me, but Sharon and Tom don't know.' She stared at him in disbelief, he wasn't making any sense. He was very fond of Sam, but he certainly wasn't close enough to influence him, but more importantly he would never encourage any child to disobey their parents. 'Are you telling me you helped him to lie to Tom and Sharon?'

'No, of course not,' he replied angrily, 'you know I would never do that. Anyway, he didn't exactly lie to them, he simply didn't tell them what he was going to do. But he told me, and I did nothing, which is just as bad.'

'Are you absolutely sure he's gone?'

He nodded his head. 'Yes, he's there alright, he's been talking about it for months. Wait a minute and I'll prove it to you.' Marie watched him pick up his mobile and scroll the screen with an expertise she didn't even know he possessed. 'There,' he said as he handed it to her. An image of Sam with a very pretty girl beamed from the screen and before she could ask who it was, Stuart said simply, 'Sam, and his girlfriend Jodie.' He pointed to the date and time, in the corner of the screen. Scrolling down she saw a short message. 'Hi Stu, here we are at the concert. Having a fun time. Sam.' The full impact of all he was telling her thudded into her head, momentarily immobilising her, but Stuart jumped into action. 'I must ring Tom and Sharon.'

'Be careful what you say,' she warned him, 'it's going to be a terrible shock.'

'There's no easy way to do this,' he replied, 'and I'll get what I deserve.'

Marie sank into a chair and tried to make sense of what Stuart had told her, but within seconds Tom's voice reverberated around the room. The phone was on loudspeaker and she could hear every intake of breath, every word of denial, and could almost feel his body shaking as Stuart broke the awful news to him. At first, he denied the possibility of it being true, reiterating again and again that Tom was in Benton staying with his friend Max, but when Stuart finally cut through his protests, the shock turned to anger and, as he'd expected it was directed towards him. At the sound of Sharon's voice repeating the same questions Tom had thrown at him, he seemed to recover his senses.

'Listen to me,' he said firmly 'there will be time for all these recriminations later, but what you need to be doing is getting yourselves over there. Marie and I will be with you in a few minutes to stay with Ben and Lily.' By the time he'd replaced the phone Marie had grabbed both their coats, and he shrugged his on as he moved towards the door. 'Do you think we need to take our nightwear?' Stuart asked, 'it's going to be a long night.'

'I don't think we'll get much sleep,' she replied, 'but what we do will probably be on the settee or a chair.'

'I suppose you're right. Come on love, let's go.' Although it only took a few minutes to reach them, Tom and Sharon were already waiting by the door, and they ushered them inside. Sharon was struggling to control her tears and Tom looked puzzled and angry.

'I'm sorry I reacted like I did,' he said to Stuart, 'but before we go, I want you to tell us everything you know.' Stuart nodded. 'There isn't much to tell. Sam wanted to go to this concert, but he thought you wouldn't allow it, so he decided to tell you he was staying with a friend as usual. That of course, is true, but he omitted to say where else they were going. That's all there is to it really.'

'Didn't you think to tell us or try to stop him?' Tom asked.

'Yes, why didn't you?' sobbed Sharon.

Stuart shrugged his shoulders, his face anguished. 'Maybe I should have told you, I don't know, but I could never have stopped him, it was already arranged by the time I knew. He's your son not mine, and he's old enough to make his own decisions. Anyway, you're wasting valuable time, you need to be going, to find your son.'

Marie held Sharon tightly and told her in a whisper she would be praying for them all. She wanted to tell her to think of the baby she was carrying and to take no risks, but it might seem she was more concerned about her own future grandchild than she was about Sam, so she said nothing.

Tom and Sharon hurried over the gravel to the car but before they reached it, Stuart called out. They both turned, their faces pale under the security light. 'I just thought I'd better tell you,' he said, 'the friend Sam has gone with, is a girl.'

'A girl?' Tom repeated in astonishment, 'Do you mean girl as in a girlfriend?'

'That's something you'll have to ask when you see him?' Stuart replied, and as Sharon and Tom sped away, he added under his breath, 'if you see him.'

'Don't talk like that,' Marie cried as they went inside and closed the door behind them. She sank onto the sofa. 'I don't understand why Sam confided in you, or how you were able to view a photograph. I wasn't aware you could do anything beyond ringing me or answer my calls. You certainly have a lot of explaining to do.' She was unable to keep the hurt out of her voice and when Stuart sat next to her and tentatively put his arm round her shoulders, she remained stiffly upright.

'I'm sorry love,' he said, 'I know I should have told you. If I had done, probably none of this would have happened.' Marie shook her head, 'I wouldn't be too sure of that, we both know how tricky it can be dealing with teenagers.'

'Yes, but you see, the problem with Sam isn't that simple, it's more a case of his parents being too busy to listen to him. I don't think I'm overstating the case when I say he was desperate to let them know how he was feeling but he didn't think they were interested.'

'So how did you get so involved?' she asked.

'It all started with that time I met him by chance on the beach, I think I told you about that.'

'Yes, I remember, but that was ages ago. What connection is there with this?'

'None really, except we've spent quite a bit of time together bird-watching, and I suppose he gradually started confiding in me. I enjoyed his company, and for some reason he seemed to enjoy mine, but he didn't talk very much, so it's ironic he told me about this.' Pressing the heels of his hands into his eyes, he sighed. 'I wish he hadn't.'

'You mustn't say that,' Marie told him, 'if he hadn't done, Tom and Sharon wouldn't know where he is.'

'That's just it,' he replied, 'they still don't know where he is.'

'They'll find him, and he'll be safe,' she told him with a conviction she didn't feel. Much later, while Marie was in the kitchen making yet another cup of tea, he switched on the television and watched in horror the unfolding details of the confirmed bomb attack. Sensing her presence behind him, he quickly turned it off, but not before she had witnessed some of the horrific scenes being shown. Trying to overcome her own sense of shock, she said gently, 'come and sit down, you're not doing any good looking at that.'

Still shaking, he allowed her to lead him to the sofa, and sank into it with exhaustion. 'If only I'd told them,' he said again, but she sat next to him and took his hand. 'You must stop blaming yourself for this,' she told him, 'you didn't ask Sam to confide in you, he did it because he needed someone to listen to him, and he trusted you. If you'd broken that trust, he would have had no-one to talk to.'

'I suppose you're right.'

'I know I am, and apart from all that, I don't believe it would have made any difference if they had known because they wouldn't have stopped him going anyway.'

'I hadn't thought of that, but I suppose it's quite possible because I think his girlfriend bought the tickets as a birthday present.'

'There you are then. Should I make a fresh cup of tea? These have gone cold.'

'No thanks love, I'm awash with tea. I wouldn't say no to a whisky though. Oh, I wish we knew how Tom and Sharon are getting on?'

'Me too, but they'll be in touch as soon as they know something.' she replied.

'I know, that's what's worrying me.'

Chapter 39

A few seconds later, the door burst open and she was swept into a tight bear hug and kissed firmly on her lips. 'Hugh,' she gasped, 'where have you come from?'

'Vietnam, well London actually.'

She held him at arm's length and looked him up and down. He seemed to be exuding health, and something she couldn't quite discern. 'Why didn't you tell me you were coming?' she demanded.

'We wanted to surprise you; I hope you don't mind.'

'Well, you've certainly done that, but of course I don't mind. You said we, have you brought a friend?'

'Better than that, are you ready for an even bigger surprise?' Enjoying the moment, he grinned at Bryony's expression, a mixture of expectation and irritation. He obviously hadn't lost his weird sense of humour, which during his youth had often been directed at her, and for a while was the bane of her life. 'Okay,' he said at last, I'll put you out of your agony. I've brought my wife.'

Bryony slumped onto the edge of the bed; it was turning into quite a day of unexpected news.

'Hugh, I didn't even know you had a girlfriend, how long have you been married?'

'I'll explain later, but she's downstairs waiting to meet you.'

She shook her head in bewilderment, but she hadn't seen him for so long, she just wanted to keep him to herself for a little while at least. 'Before we go down, let me look at you. I must say you look remarkably well, I expected you to be all skinny and malnourished, and here you are, tanned and fit.'

'Mum, you've seen me regularly when we've been Face-Timing,'

'I know, but I don't trust those things, you could have been enhancing it somehow.'

Hugh guffawed, his eyes scanning the room. 'Is dad around?' he asked, 'then I can fill you in together.'

'No, he's at an official function, but he won't be long. Even so, I'm not waiting until he comes back before you tell me all your news. Why didn't you tell me you were getting married?'

'We wanted it to be low-key.'

'Oh,' Bryony said, 'well you certainly seem to have achieved that. Anyway, you shouldn't have left her downstairs on her own. I hope someone's taking care of her.'

'She isn't on her own,' he replied, 'Amelia and Piers are with her,'

Bryony knew she was staring, and she closed her mouth quickly. 'Amelia and Piers are here, why?' She watched Hugh carefully as he shuffled from foot to foot, reminiscent of the naughty little boy of his childhood. Taking a deep breath, he said, 'They're here because they were the witnesses at our wedding yesterday, in London.'

She was shocked, and hurt, but for now she wouldn't let him see it. Slipping a smile into place, she hugged him close. 'I'm so happy for you,' she whispered, 'now let's go down, I'm longing to meet her. But before we do, tell me her name.'

Hugh's face lit up. 'Lucy,' he said, 'and mum, I know you're going to love her.'

And Bryony did love her, from the moment they met she knew the girl was right for her son, and in no time at all they were drinking champagne to celebrate the marriage of Hugh and Lucy. Hugh explained how they'd wanted a very simple wedding without any fuss but were hoping to have a big party with all their friends and both families, here at the hotel. Bryony was ecstatic, and she didn't allow Hugh's enthusiastic response to Colin's arrival dent her happiness. The sight of Janet Bancroft removing and taking charge of the chains was irritating and conjured up images of earlier, but even that failed to lower her spirits. Let her see what a happy family looked like.

After all the explanations and celebrations, Bryony asked Luke to prepare a special meal for them later that evening. Despite Amelia's protestations that her room upstairs would be adequate, Bryony asked Ellie to show Amelia and Piers to a luxury guest room, and the newly-weds were thrilled when they were taken to the bridal suite.

Ralph, who'd been at the cinema with friends when his grandchildren made their surprise arrival, was pleased to hear the news from Bryony when she popped in to see him later. He listened with interest and gladly agreed to join them for the celebratory meal later that evening. 'You must be delighted to have Amelia home again, it's strange how these things happen sometimes.'

Bryony clasped her hands together and pressed them under her chin in a gesture of delight. 'I am, of course I am, but it's also lovely to have Hugh back. It's been such a long time since I've seen him, and I can't help wondering what he's going to do now he's married?'

Ralph folded his arms and sat back in his chair. 'I suppose we'll find out tonight,' he said, 'I must say I'm looking forward to it immensely.'

Chapter 40

They were at the last set of traffic lights before the motorway and they hadn't spoken since leaving home. Sharon was systematically speed-dialling Sam's number every few seconds, sometimes without even waiting for the automated, indifferent voice telling her Sam was unable to take her call. 'Oh, Sam, please pick up,' she begged, willing him to answer. She'd already left lots of messages on his voicemail telling him he wasn't in trouble and imploring him to get in touch, but still there was no response.

'You'll run out of battery if you keep that up,' Tom said to her. His voice was brusque with emotion and she knew he was suffering just as much as she was. 'I don't care,' she cried, 'what else can I do?' Tom nodded,' I know love,' he said, 'but we might need it later, and if Sam is trying to get us, he'll keep getting the engaged signal.'

She hadn't thought of that, but knowing Tom was right she resisted the impulse to continue and laid the mobile on her belly, before cradling the weight of the baby in her arms to ease the strain on her back. 'This is all my fault,' she said quietly, 'I didn't think about the effects on our children when I promised Louisa and Damian I'd have a baby for them, especially Sam, I've not given him enough attention even though I knew he was unhappy.'

'What do you mean, he's unhappy? I think he's settled down well.

'Tom,' she said, her voice rising, 'you've got no idea how he's been feeling. He was devastated at not being picked for the school football team.'

Tom bridled indignantly. 'I went to school about that and saw his football manager and he didn't see what the problem was.

'Kids don't want their parents fighting their battles for them, especially when it involves visits to school. Awkwardly, she edged her body sideways, but no matter how hard she tried, she couldn't get comfortable in the rigid car seat.

'Tom. Stop it!' she cried. 'I can't bear it. Why are we arguing when we don't know what's happened to Sam? He could be dead, and all we can do is blame each other and talk about football.'

'Don't say that,' Tom shouted back, 'he's not dead!'

'You heard what they said on the television,' she sobbed, 'some dead.'

'And there are many more survivors,' Tom replied firmly, 'so Sam is one of those. I can feel it; I would know if he was dead.' His voice was fading away. 'Anyway, we don't know for sure he was even there,' he said.

Sharon leaned her head back and closed her eyes. They did know Sam was there, Stuart had a picture, but she didn't point that out to Tom, she knew he was clutching at straws. She tried to summon some conviction, a sense of hope, but there was nothing there, she felt empty, drained of emotion and strength, except for an all-consuming sense of fear that Sam could be dead.

The motorway was getting busier as they approached Manchester, and to add to Sharon's discomfort she urgently needed the toilet. When the signs for the services came into view, she asked Tom to pull in, but it was difficult to find a space in the car park. After driving round several times Tom tried to persuade her to get out of the car while he waited for a space, but although she was getting desperate, she refused, terrified of not being able to find him in all the chaos.

The place was busy with people, their frightened faces illuminated by the lights of mobile phones as they desperately searched for news. Understandably, very little information was available, but in the distance the sounds of emergency vehicles shattered the night air into sharp fragments of terror and fear.

'How near are we?' sobbed Sharon, as Tom negotiated his way into a tight parking space. 'The next turn-off is Benton,' he replied, 'so it's not very far now.' Sharon nodded, but she was completely disorientated and couldn't work out the distance to Manchester, although she'd travelled this route many times in the past.

Tom helped her out of the car, and after arranging a meeting place, she joined a long queue for the lady's toilets. Fortunately, her condition elicited a sympathetic response from many of the women who moved to make way for her to go to the front of the queue.

She'd barely reached the toilet when she felt a rush of fluid burst from her body, and for a few seconds she felt relief that she'd made it before the embarrassment of an accident. But something didn't feel right, and when she tentatively touched the warm moistness on her inner thigh she sagged with despair. The baby was coming, and her previous labours had progressed quickly after her waters had broken. Shuddering with shock, she sank onto the toilet and tried to pull herself together, but it was useless. After a while, she became aware of people trying to open the door, so she knew she had to move. She left the cubicle with muttered apologies to the people waiting, before lingering over washing and drying her hands to give herself some time to try and decide what to do.

If she told Tom what was happening, he would take her straight to a hospital, and she wasn't prepared to risk that, so she walked as casually as possible to where he was impatiently waiting with a coffee in each hand.

Sipping the warm drink in the safety of the car, she tried to keep calm and put the problem of the baby out of her mind. Sam was her priority; giving birth would come later. She disguised the early contractions, by passing them off as backache caused by sitting too long in the car. Tom was concentrating on the road, and one thing was certain, nothing on earth, was going to hinder their attempts to find Sam.

Their progress seemed to be getting even slower and the pains in her back were getting stronger. Sharon bit her lip to hold in the cry of pain, when suddenly the silence in the car was shattered by the sound of her mobile phone. A powerful contraction gripped her womb, but the groan of pain was masked by her cry of desperation when she almost dropped the phone, in her haste to answer it.

'It's Sam,' she whispered, as she pressed the accept button, but earlier she'd set the volume to loudspeaker to make sure they heard it, and now the car was filled, not with Sam's voice, but the sirens of emergency vehicles, people screaming, and loud bangs, which reverberated around the confines of the car. 'Hello? Hello?' Sharon cried. 'Hello, can you hear me Sam?' but as suddenly as the phone had rung, it now cut off.

'I'm trying to call him,' she cried, but there was no response, so she switched it off and waited. After a few moments it rang again, and this time there was the faint sound of a voice, but it wasn't Sam, and it sounded like a woman. There was a lot of crackling and the signal kept breaking up, but she could just make out the sound of her own name and something which vaguely sounded like Benton. 'Is Sam there?' she screamed, 'is he alright?'

'No.... I really....no signal.... try...' The connection was broken and couldn't be retrieved.

Neither of them was capable of speaking for a few moments, until, her voice trembling she whispered, 'Do you think she was telling us Sam is alive but injured?'

Tom's voice was grim. 'I don't know love,' he said quietly, 'I think you could take that message either way. I wonder who was speaking, and why have they got Sam's phone?'

'Maybe Sam asked her to ring,' she replied, 'I didn't recognise the voice, although it seemed vaguely familiar. I wonder if it was Max's mum? I didn't know her very well, but it could have been her.'

'Well, that figures,' Tom said, 'he probably went to the concert with Max, and possibly his mum went to pick them up. Why don't you try Max's home number?'

'I have, lots of times' she replied, 'but there's no reply. I've left a message on the answer-machine.'

Tom's voice quivered. 'I suppose they're already there,' he said.

Sharon decided not to remind him of Stuart's last words to them about Sam going to the concert with a girl. 'I think she was trying to tell us they were at Benton General,' she said instead, 'do you think we should go there?'

'Why would they be there when the accident is near Manchester? It doesn't make sense.'

'Maybe there are too many injured people for them to cope with. Oooh no,' she moaned, as she was gripped by an even stronger contraction, and Tom turned to her in alarm. 'Sharon, what's going on?'

'I think the baby's coming,' she replied through gritted teeth.

He didn't query her; she knew her body well enough to be able to read the signs. 'How long have you been having contractions?' he asked cautiously.

'About a couple of hours.'

'Oh, God help us. We're stuck in a traffic jam, with no visible signs of moving and you're about to give birth any moment!'

She told him it might be ages before the baby arrived, but even she wasn't convinced, and they both knew it was very unlikely. Without any words of warning he put his hazard lights on, placed his hand on the horn and swiftly manoeuvred his way onto the hard shoulder. Sharon watched with horror as he drove at speed, all the way to the next intersection.

She began to cry. 'What are you doing? We've got to find Sam, I want to find Sam.' Tom briefly put a reassuring hand on her knee, and pointed out it was an impossible situation they'd found themselves in, but this way he could at least get her to a hospital before resuming his journey to Manchester. The area was familiar to him and they weren't too far from Benton General, so he would make sure Sam wasn't there and then he'd have to leave Sharon, before getting back on the motorway. She was so distressed about the delay this detour was causing them, she begged him to go straight to Manchester, but spurred on by the speeding up and strengthening of her contractions, he ignored her and drove towards Benton.

'We're nearly there now,' he said, looking at her as she gripped the handle and took panting breaths, and a few minutes later they arrived at the hospital. He tried to help her out of the car, but she was doubled up, unable to move. Running to the entrance, he grabbed a wheelchair and was immediately approached by a porter who ran beside him to the car, listening to Tom's explanations as they went. Together they got her into the chair and the porter wheeled her away and told Tom to go to Accident and Emergency, as some of the local people caught up in the tragedy were being treated there.

Sharon was taken to a small ward where she was examined, before being asked to give her personal details and a quick resume of the pregnancy. Several medical staff drifted in and out of the room, and as each one learned the circumstances surrounding her arrival here, there was no mistaking their expressions of concern. Tom was obviously her next of kin but recognising he would probably be out of reach for a while, they asked her for an alternative contact. Without hesitation she gave Louisa's number. 'Please will you ring her now,' she said, 'she's my birthing partner and the mother of the baby.' Sharon closed her eyes and didn't see the looks of consternation on the faces surrounding her, as she briefly explained the situation they were in, but the brief intake of breath followed by a few seconds of silence, told her all she needed to know. Opening her eyes, she tried to reassure them. 'Don't worry, I'm not rambling, I really am a surrogate mother and there's nothing to worry about, everything's in order.'

She was taken to the labour ward and told the midwife and doctor were on their way, but in the meantime, they were going to make a few routine checks. She took very little notice of the wavy lines when she was connected to the machine, and averted her eyes from the screen during the scan, as it all meant nothing to her compared with the fear of losing Sam. The midwife arrived and performed a thorough but gentle examination, but when she pulled off her gloves, she told her it would be quite a while before she would be giving birth. Sharon secretly doubted her, she was convinced the baby would be delivered very soon, and that was fine by her as she wanted to be with Tom when they finally found their son.

She had no idea how much time was passing, but the contractions were getting closer and stronger, bringing with them a need to push, but all she kept hearing were voices telling her she wasn't ready yet.

'Sharon, you'll hurt yourself and the baby if you start too soon, I know the contractions are strong, but for some reason they are not dilating the cervix. We are going to give you an injection to try and get things moving, is that okay with you?' She nodded and whispered urgently. 'Yes. Do anything to speed it up. I need to get out of here.'

Gripping the metal rail above her head, she tried to ride the next wave of pain and told herself it wouldn't be long now, when she suddenly realised something was going wrong. The voice of the gynaecologist had changed from quietly reassuring to urgent and loud when he spoke to her.

'Sharon,' he said, 'Can you tell us when you felt your first contraction?' She shook her head. 'You told us your waters broke during your journey here, have you any idea what time that was, just roughly?' Sharon shook her head, 'Nooo... Sorry. I think it was a few hours ago.'

'Never mind, but I think...' His voice was cut short by a long, shrill scream from the machine and the calm mood in the room suddenly changed. 'Theatre,' he shouted, tell them we're on our way now.' Sharon felt the bed rolling out of the room and sensed the doctor running past. 'We're taking you down to theatre,' the midwife explained, holding her hand as they sped down the corridor, 'the baby is in distress and it's too late for a natural birth, so it will be delivered immediately by Caesarean Section. Do you understand what I'm saying?'

'Of course,' Sharon whispered, 'go ahead.'

She closed her eyes as they wheeled her into the operating theatre and summoned up what little strength she had left. 'Please save my baby,' she prayed, 'and please save Sam, and please, please, don't let it be a choice of one against the other.'

Chapter 41

Bryony basked in the joy of having the whole family together for the first time in years.

She could see some of the other diners looking over whenever the noise level rose, but for once she didn't care, she was buoyed up by the fervour of the evening and more than a few glasses of champagne. Hugh's wedding was the first topic of conversation, and she couldn't resist a slight dig about having been excluded, but a warning look from Amelia soon stopped her. The last thing she needed was another family argument.

The food as usual was delicious, and at the end of the meal she impulsively asked the chef to join them in a toast to the happy couple, and when she caught sight of Justin peering inquisitively around the corner, she invited him too.

Extra champagne was brought out, and Bryony relaxed and enjoyed herself more than she had done for a very long time. 'I can't tell you how happy I am to have my children back home,' she said effusively, but Colin was quick to correct her. 'Don't forget,' he said, 'they're my children too.' Bryony was shocked by the look of affection which passed between Amelia and Colin at his affirmation of his role in her life, but she was determined not to let it spoil her evening.

She touched Hugh's shoulder. 'I will only forgive my son for making me miss his wedding, if he tells me he's going to stay for a long visit. So, tell me, how long are you staying?'

'It's funny you should ask that,' Hugh replied, 'because I was just about to bring it up. The thing is, in a way it's entirely up to you and dad.'

'In what way?' she asked, 'you know you can stay as long as you wish.'

Hugh took hold of Lucy's hand and looked at the faces around the table. Amelia gave him a knowing wink and Piers nodded encouragingly. His eyes hesitated on Colin before stopping to rest on Bryony. 'Well,' he said dramatically, and she held her breath, 'we're thinking of staying. If it's alright with you and dad, and grandpa of course, I'd like to settle down and help run the family business.'

The hush around the table spread to the whole room as Bryony tried to grasp the implications of what he'd said. 'But you haven't got any experience,' she spluttered in amazement, and Hugh burst out laughing.

'Mum, I've got a degree in Business Management and Politics, I've run orphanages, set up schools, you name it I've done it. Oh, I know I've got a lot to learn, but what do you think, can I join the staff here, on the first rung of the ladder obviously? I'm very adaptable, I promise.'

Bryony stared at him incredulously. 'Are you being serious?' she asked, 'because if you aren't it's not funny.'

'I'm very serious, ask the others if you don't believe me.'

Bryony glanced round the table until the smiling expressions told her all she needed to know, and her eyes alighted finally on Hugh's beaming face.

'It's funny,' he told her, 'but I've always believed I was destined to work in the family business, I suppose

I just wanted to follow my dream of working abroad first, and now I've got it out of my system. What do you say mum and dad, shall we give it a go?'

Bryony ignored the inclusion of Colin, as she now knew he was absolving himself of any interest in the business, so she directed her attention instead to Hugh's wife. 'What about you Lucy, are you happy about coming to live in Merebank?'

Slightly embarrassed about the spotlight being turned on her, Lucy blushed but replied firmly. 'Yes, Hugh has talked about it a lot, and I'm looking forward to living here. My family live in Cheshire, so we will be close to them, which is perfect.'

'We want to settle down, so it might as well be here,' Hugh chipped in, before turning back to Bryony, 'but I don't want any preferential treatment.'

'Don't worry, you won't get it from your mother,' Colin said ruefully.

Ralph's face was full of pleasure and his smile was broad when he winked at Bryony. 'We didn't see this coming either,' he said, 'but it's the best news I've had in years.'

Bryony nodded. 'It's unbelievable, and wonderful.'

'Phew. That's a relief,' Hugh exclaimed, 'I wasn't sure how you'd both take it.' He looked from Colin to Bryony. 'You never know, but once I've learned the ropes, you two might be able to take early retirement, and enjoy yourselves travelling around the world together.'

Bryony was on the cusp of correcting him when Ralph caught her eye. 'First things first,' he said to Hugh, 'you've got a long way to go.' He stood up and raised his glass, 'I'd like to welcome Lucy to our family, and Hugh to the family business.'

They all stood around the table; their glasses raised in a toast to the Portland family. Lucy gave Hugh a nudge. 'Haven't you forgotten something?'

'Oh yes,' he grinned, 'we're going to have a baby.'

Bryony didn't notice the champagne spilling onto her dress as she fell back onto her seat.

Chapter 42

Sharon woke to the sound of babies crying and the low, murmuring voices of nurses and mothers. It took a few seconds before she could orientate herself and remember where she was and why. An overwhelming sense of fear took hold of her, and desperate for news, she leaned over to press the call button lying on the bed beside her. Unable to reach it without grimacing with pain, she leaned back and glanced around the room. What was missing? Where was the cot, and more importantly, where was her baby? Panicking, she reached up and pulled the emergency cord as hard as she could. She vaguely remembered the baby being delivered, but she was heavily sedated and everything following the birth was hazy. What had happened after that? She was sure the baby was alive when it was born, but she could clearly remember the panic surrounding her before the birth and she was filled with dread.

A nurse came running into the room but froze when Sharon demanded to know where her baby was. The nurse hesitated, obviously struggling to know what to say, intensifying Sharon's fear. 'Please tell me what's happened to my baby,' she begged, 'and why isn't it here with me?'

The nurse checked the drip attached to Sharon's arm. 'She was taken to the neo-natal ward at first, but nothing's happened to her and she's in the nursery now, to give you time to rest.' She hesitated, unsure if she was saying too much. 'But anyway, I don't think...'

Impatiently, Sharon interrupted. 'So, it's a little girl?' Reading the name tag on the nurse's badge, she gently clasped her hand. 'Tessa, I can't possibly rest until I know how she is. Please tell me, or I might have to go and find out for myself.'

'Oh no, you mustn't,' the nurse replied, 'she's perfect and absolutely adorable. As you know, she was distressed before the birth, but she's fine now.'

'Please bring her to me,' Sharon said gently.

The nurse nodded and started to leave. 'I'm not really allowed to fetch her, but I'll ask someone,' she promised, 'I'll be back soon, but please don't move before I return, or I'll get into trouble.'

A short time later, a doctor came into the room, and standing by her bedside he skimmed the notes in his hand while Sharon waited impatiently. Eventually he looked at her and asked how she was feeling.

'Can we leave out all the niceties, and get to the point?' she protested. 'I'm frantic with worry about my son, and now you're making me scared there's something wrong with my baby. Please tell me if you've heard from my husband, is there any news?'

The doctor shook his head. 'I'm so sorry Sharon, we've only heard from your husband once since he left, and he had nothing to report. I promise, we'll let you know as soon as we hear anything.'

Wearily, she slumped back onto the pillow. She felt so physically and emotionally drained, even the effort of sitting up tired her. 'I would like to have my baby now,' she said, closing her eyes. A few seconds passed while the weight of indecision hung in the air. He was young and had probably never encountered a situation quite like this before, but Sharon was losing her patience, and when he tentatively asked if it would be more advisable to hand the baby directly to its prospective parents, she snapped.

'I appreciate everything you've done for me but give me some credit. I'm aware of the legalities of the situation, and the baby is mine, and I want her with me.'

The doctor nodded. 'I'm sorry Sharon. I must admit, this is a first for me and I and don't quite know how to handle it, but I was only trying to make it easier for you. I'll ask the nurse to bring your baby in.'

Sharon closed her eyes, wearily murmuring, 'thank-you.'

She was going through the motions, refusing to consider the unthinkable situation happening in Manchester. It was impossible that Sam could be caught up in a terrorist attack, they were ordinary people who lived at the seaside. Why would anyone want to kill him? She was waiting for Tom to come and tell her it was all a terrible mistake, but she'd heard nothing from him, and his phone didn't seem to be working.

Tessa came into the room with the baby held close to her body, and Sharon pulled herself up and eagerly held out her hands. The nurse gently laid the baby in the cradle of her arms, and Sharon ran the back of her little finger across her downy cheek. 'Oh, you beautiful little girl,' she whispered. 'Tessa, will you leave us for a while,' she asked, without looking up, and Tessa left the room without a word.

Holding the baby in the crook of her arm, she watched as the tiny mouth started routing around and nuzzling her breast. The hospital robe she was wearing was tied at the back, but the top bow was easily released and after exposing her breast she held the baby close. It took only a few seconds of gently guiding the baby's head, before she latched onto the nipple and began to suckle vigorously. Sharon felt each tug tightening her womb, and a surge of emotion flooded her whole being.

'Mrs. Lester, do you think you should be doing that?' Sister Craven asked a few minutes later as she walked into the room and began to check the monitor and saline drip. 'I'm not being pedantic for the sake of it,' she added with feeling, 'but it makes me feel a little concerned when I see you bonding with the baby. You're doing a wonderful thing for that anxious couple, and I don't want you to make things even more difficult for yourself.'

Sharon looked down at the contented, sleeping baby and tenderly eased her off the breast. A tiny bubble had formed on the perfectly shaped lips, bringing back memories of her own children when they were born. Reluctantly, she handed her to the Sister before tying the woven cord at the back of the nightdress. 'I'm a great believer in the value of the colostrum, even if a baby is going to be bottle fed,' Sharon explained, 'so I only wanted to do what is right for her.'

'She's lovely, isn't she?' Sister said, 'her parents are going to be over the moon when they see her. It's a shame to wake her, but it seems like she's ready for a nappy change. Where would you like the cot, when I've finished?'

'In here please,' Sharon said firmly, 'do you know where my phone is, I want to make a call.'

'It should be in your locker with your handbag. I'll be back in a few minutes to unhook you from this contraption and then you can go into the bathroom and freshen yourself up, ready for any visitors.' Sharon nodded and found her watch and mobile in the drawer of the locker beside her bed. In the main compartment, someone had placed a plastic bag with small items of toiletries together with numerous free samples and vouchers.

She sensed she was being shielded from hearing any updates about the atrocity and she'd deliberately not turned the television on, but she was desperate to find out if Sam was safe and it was possible Sister Craven might know something, however seemingly insignificant. Her heart sank when she found her phone was out of charge, so she had no option but to ask the person who was busily attending her physical comforts. 'Sister, please will you try and find out what is happening. I know now why my husband hasn't contacted me, but he must have spoken to someone.'

The Sister's face clouded over, but she was quick to try to reassure Sharon they would keep her informed of developments of any kind. She reiterated they hadn't heard from Tom since his communication soon after he'd left the hospital, but from the reports coming out of Manchester, they knew the roads were chaotic and more importantly, some of the mobile servers were out of action. 'That's probably why you haven't heard from him,' she added kindly.

'My phone needs charging and I need to contact my friend,' Sharon said, 'Louisa Fowler. Do you know if she's aware the baby's been born?'

'She is, you gave us her details when you were in labour and asked us to get in touch. She didn't make it in time to be with you for the birth, but they came straight away, and they've been waiting ever since. I believe they are quite anxious. Do you want me to send them in when you're ready?' Sharon nodded nervously. 'Yes please,' she replied. After assisting Sharon to the small en-suite bathroom, she left promising to find a suitable charger, and any available news about the attack. Sharon leaned on the washbasin to steady herself. She freshened herself up, and turned to face the room, but it began to tilt around her. Holding the door frame tightly, she prepared herself to do the hardest thing she'd ever done in her life.

With the baby returned to her arms, and visibly shaking, she waited for their arrival. They tapped on the door before entering, and with hands gripped tightly together they tentatively approached her bed. Their faces were etched with concern, and keeping their eyes away from the baby in her arms, they asked if she'd had any news about Sam. Sharon shook her head, and Louisa began to speak, her voice trembling. 'Sharon, we'll understand if you've...' Silence filled the room and Sharon looked at them and clasped the baby to her breast.

'She is a gorgeous baby,' she said, 'and you are so lucky to have her.' She held her out, and their shoulders sagged with relief. Louisa, her face filled with apprehension and overwhelming love, gazed at her child, before looking at Damian who was unashamedly crying. He tentatively took the baby from Louisa. Fighting back her own tears, Sharon asked them if they'd chosen a name, and it was Damian who dragged his eyes away from the sleeping child and told her proudly. 'She's to be called Pearl.'

'Oh, that's lovely,' Sharon exclaimed, 'and so appropriate.'

'What's more,' Louisa said, without taking her eyes away, 'she's perfect, just like a pearl.'

While the new parents gazed at their new baby, Sharon explained she'd already breastfed Pearl, and she was going to express some milk for one further feed. Following that they would be on their own. 'I don't know if you've made any decisions about which formula to use, but I'm sure they will give you all the help you need here,' she said.

Louisa nodded and told her they'd already had a short discussion with one of the midwives. 'We didn't want to do anything, until...' Her voice petered out, but Sharon didn't need to hear, it was obvious they'd been on a knife edge for hours.'

'Well,' she said brightly, 'you are going to have to make lots of decisions now she's born.'

A nurse entered the room and began to check Sharon's temperature and blood pressure. 'I'll be back in a few minutes,' she told them, 'to take the baby back to the nursery.' She didn't miss Damian's spontaneously possessive move to hold the baby tighter, and she laughed. 'Don't worry,' she told him, 'you'll be coming too, both of you in fact. You haven't got very long to learn how to change a nappy and feed a baby. It's going to be a baptism by fire, as I suspect you are just about to be faced with the first soiled nappy, and that's always a challenge.'

Damian groaned, but Sharon thought she'd never seen him look happier. After they left, she lay back and let her mind drift. When she became aware of people entering and leaving the room, she kept her eyes shut, feigning sleep, unwilling to engage in meaningless chatter and small talk. She had no idea if she was staying here, or if she was going to be discharged and although she didn't care, the thought of going home without Sam was unthinkable.

A shadow fell across her face, as someone moved very close to the bed and gently and unmistakably laid a hand on hers. She kept her eyes closed as he bent down and kissed her softly on the lips and all the suppressed tension burst out of her and she wept, great sobbing, tears. 'I'm sorry,' she whimpered at last, but he was unable to hear because he was holding her so tightly her face was pressing on his chest, and she could hardly breath. 'I love you,' he said, again and again, until at last, the shaking subsided and she pulled away and closed her eyes. She couldn't bear to see what might be written on Tom's face. 'Sam,' she whispered, where's Sam?'

'He's not far away,' Tom replied, and her heart missed a beat when she heard the unmistakable sound of Sam's voice.

'I'm here,' he said, 'a bit battered and bruised, but I'm here.' He limped towards the bed, leaning heavily on a crutch. 'Hi, mum,' he said timidly, 'how are you?'

Her eyes snapped open and she stared at him with disbelief. 'Oh, never mind about me,' she cried, 'come here let me hold you. I want to make sure you're really here.'

Ruefully, he rested his arm on the crutch and gauged the distance between himself and the bed. Grimacing slightly, he said, 'I don't know if I can bend down that far.' Sharon rested her elbows on the bed to pull herself into a sitting position and stretch her arms towards him. 'I thought we were going to die mum,' he whispered, 'I was so scared, really scared.' Holding him as close as possible she murmured, 'I understand, and I'm so sorry, but you're here now, safe and sound.' His body shuddered, 'but what about all those others?' he asked, as he squeezed her gently and slowly pulled away.

'We'll talk about that later,' she promised, 'but just for now can I concentrate on your safe return to us?'

'Okay,' he agreed, easing himself from her embrace. Sharon told them about the arrival of Pearl and Sam informed her he had his own surprise in store. 'Is this about your girlfriend?' she asked.

'How did you know?' Sam exclaimed.

Sharon smiled. 'Mums have a way of knowing these things, now when am I to meet her?'

'Now, if you like, she's waiting next door.'

'Well, what are you waiting for,' Sharon asked, 'go and bring her in.'

While Sam was out of the room, Sharon asked Tom if he knew who'd tried to phone them on Sam's phone, and she was shocked when he told her it was Serena. She'd been waiting for Chantelle in the foyer, but Chantelle was still in the body of the building when the explosion occurred. Serena recognised Sam as he was being carried away, and when she saw his phone drop on the floor, she managed to reach over and pick it up, but by then he was nowhere in sight. She was slightly injured, and unable to follow them, but having heard Benton Hospital mentioned, she'd guessed he might be taken there. She tried several times to ring them and having finally made contact, the weak signal was lost completely.

'We must thank her,' Sharon said, 'I haven't spoken to her since the day she saw me at the hospital and spread the word about the baby. How is she, and Chantelle?'

'Serena's okay, but Chantelle's had surgery for internal injuries, I think she is quite poorly but out of danger.'

'Poor Serena,' Sharon replied, 'she must be worried sick. We must thank her for what she did.' Tom pulled two chairs up to the side of the bed. 'I already have,' he said, 'but I'm sure she'd like to see you when you're feeling stronger.'

'Why didn't they tell me Sam was here? I kept asking if there was any news of him.'

'He wasn't here. I found him in a Manchester hospital, just as he was going down to theatre, but I couldn't get hold of you, and then when I did manage to contact this place, you were in theatre giving birth.'

'Well, he's here now,' she murmured.

Sam entered the room, with his good arm around the girl at his side. He was obviously very shaken and in a state of shock, but he managed to smile as he said proudly. 'Mum. This is Jodie.'

Jodie was beautiful despite the bruises shadowing her face, and she approached the bed unaided and held out her hand to Sharon, who grasped it between her own. 'It's lovely to meet you,' Sharon said, 'and I'm so pleased you're not badly hurt.'

'That's mainly because of Sam,' Jodie replied, turning to look at him. 'When he saw something falling on us, he pushed me away and then threw himself on top of me. It caught my shoulder, but Sam took the full force.'

Sam squirmed with embarrassment. 'It was nothing,' he insisted, but Jodie was insistent. Sharon listened to the exchange between the two young people with admiration tinged with regret. It was obvious Sam had matured into a young man while they weren't looking, and they would never be able to recapture that time, but they'd been given a second chance, and she was determined to take it. Jodie was dishevelled, her hair and clothes dusty, but her dark eyes were glowing whenever she looked at Sam. It was obvious she was going to play a big part in their lives in the future, and Sharon felt a deep swell of happiness.

When Louisa and Damian returned for a very brief visit with Pearl, everyone's attention went to the newborn baby, but after they left, the room fell silent. Jodie was the first to speak but her voice shook with emotion. 'They're so happy,' she said.

'Yes,' Sharon said, 'and it's so nice to have something positive to celebrate, after all the sadness.'

'Oh, I've just remembered something,' Sam said. 'Dad, will you help me send a text to Stuart. Turning to Sharon he started to explain that Stuart had known he was going to the concert, but she quickly reassured him that they were already aware of it. 'As it happens, it was Stuart who told us you were there.'

'I've already spoken to him, Tom said, I told him that you were safe and that he's a grandad.'

Sam smiled. 'What did he say?'

'He was over the moon about both pieces of news.'

'And Marie?'

Tom laughed out loud. 'Well you know Marie, she didn't know whether to laugh or cry, so she did both at the same time.'

In view of the doctor's decision to keep Sharon in overnight, Tom was taking Sam to stay with his grandma, where he would be in danger of being killed by kindness. As Jodie lived close by, they would be able to see each other, which obviously was part of the reason for their perpetual smiles. Although she was tired, Sharon dreaded being alone after everything that had happened, so she was relieved when Tom explained that in view of the unusual circumstances, he'd been told he could come back and stay the night with her.

Tom took Jodie back to her parents, and Sam lingered, trying to find the words he wanted to say. Sharon waited patiently, longing to take him in her arms to comfort him, but she knew it wasn't the right time.

'I'm sorry mum,' he said. 'What do mean? Sharon asked, 'you've got nothing to be sorry for.' 'Yes, I have,' he replied, 'it's an amazing thing you've done for Louisa and Damian, and I'm sorry I was such a berk at the beginning.'

'It wasn't your fault,' she said gently, 'I'm afraid dad and I didn't handle it very well, but none of us had experienced anything like it before. Thanks anyway, that means a lot to me.'

He shuffled slowly towards the bed and with difficulty bent down to kiss her. 'Bye mum, see you soon. I'm just going to stay with Jodie while dad has a word with you, before he takes me to grandma's house.'

When Tom returned, he sat on the bed and filled her in with all the details of his search after he'd left Sharon at the hospital. Then he listened while she told him about the emergency birth, and her emotions when she first saw the new-born baby. When he asked her if she'd been tempted to keep the baby, especially while Sam was still missing, she told him truthfully how she'd felt when she'd fed her, but added, 'No, she's totally Louisa's and Damian's, she was always their baby. But I know one thing, I'm never going through that again.'

Tom sighed with relief. 'Thank the Lord, for that. Can I have it in writing?'

'With pleasure,' she replied, and then a thought struck her. 'Has anyone told Mrs. Portland?' she asked, 'she'll be furious if everyone knows before she does.'

Tom's frown furrowed his brow. 'You're not thinking of going back there.'

'And why wouldn't I?'

'Why not indeed? How stupid of me to ask.' He was still grinning, when a doctor they hadn't seen before, entered the room and asked if he could have a word with them about Sam. He'd talked briefly with their son, soon after his physical injuries had been dealt with, and although he gave the impression he was coping perfectly well, it was imperative for him to be assessed, as there was no way of knowing how seriously Sam would be affected mentally.

Sharon gasped. 'How stupid of me. I was so pleased to have him back, and he was so perky, I didn't give any thought to his mental state.'

'Me neither,' Tom added.

'Don't be too hard on yourselves,' the doctor said kindly, 'that's a natural reaction, just as Sam's is. He's young and resilient, and at first adrenalin keeps you going, but the seriousness of the attack will have a profound effect on him, and he will probably need professional help for quite a considerable time. He has lived through a terrorist attack and seen things no young lad should see, and that isn't going to go away for a long time. He'll need a lot of support,' he said, 'but I'm convinced he will get it.'

After he left the room, they discussed the basic problems they would have to deal with after Sharon was discharged from hospital, and Sam came home from his grandma's. Tom would obviously have some time off work to look after them both, and to ensure they didn't die from malnutrition, he would ask Marie to help him out. It didn't take long for Tom to take Sam and leave him safe in his grandmother's care, but Sharon was exhausted and already settling down for the night when Tom returned. Half asleep, she slid down the bed and although a simple truckle bed had been brought in for him, Tom lay half on and half off her bed, with his arm fixed firmly around her.

A baby started crying and Sharon murmured, 'That's Pearl.' As other babies joined in the chorus, Tom asked, 'How on earth can you possibly know that? Struggling to keep awake, Sharon replied. 'I just do.'

Tom lifted her hair and gently kissed the nape of her neck, sending a shudder of pleasure down her weary body.

The cries of newly born infants mingling with the placatory noises of the parent's responses, awakened a long-forgotten instinct in Tom's memory. He shuddered. 'Damian and Louisa are very lucky,' he murmured, 'but I'm so glad it isn't us.'

'So am I,' Sharon replied, with feeling.